Does Torture Work?

Does Torture Work?

JOHN W. SCHIEMANN

OXFORD
UNIVERSITY PRESS

OXFORD
UNIVERSITY PRESS

Oxford University Press is a department of the University of Oxford. It furthers
the University's objective of excellence in research, scholarship, and education
by publishing worldwide. Oxford is a registered trade mark of Oxford University
Press in the UK and certain other countries.

Published in the United States of America by Oxford University Press
198 Madison Avenue, New York, NY 10016, United States of America.

Library of Congress Cataloging-in-Publication Data
Schiemann, John W.
    Does torture work? / JohnW. Schiemann.
        p. cm.
    Includes bibliographical references and index.
    ISBN 978-0-19-026236-5 (hardback : alk. paper)
    1. Torture. 2. Questioning. 3. Military interrogation. 4. Terrorism—Prevention.
5. Crime prevention. I. Title.
    HV8593.S345 2016
    364.6'7—dc23
                                                         2015016041

To Carol

If we are against torture, we are committed actually to arguing with our fellow citizens, not treating those who defend torture as moral monsters.

—MICHAEL IGNATIEFF, *"Moral Prohibition at a Price," in Torture*

The ... Force of Numbers ... can be successfully applied, even to those things, which one would imagine are subject to no Rules. [W]hen a Mathematical Reasoning can be had, it's as great a folly to make use of any other, as to grope for a thing in the dark, when you have a Candle standing by you.

—JOHN ARBUTHNOT, *Of the Laws of Chance*

The utility of moral and political philosophy is to be estimated, not so much by the commodities we have by knowing these sciences, as by the calamities we receive by not knowing them.

—THOMAS HOBBES, *Elements of Philosophy*

CONTENTS

LIST OF FIGURES

LIST OF TABLES

Does interrogational torture work? What do we mean by "work"? How good does the information have to be for torture to "work"? How often must it provide good information to be considered effective? What is the price of this degree of effectiveness? How frequently must torture be used to achieve it? How harsh must the torture be? Will innocent detainees be tortured or only guilty ones?

My goal in this book is to answer these questions. Doing so is vital.

The Bush administration employed interrogational torture because it assumed that it works. Many Americans think it works and can be justified in some circumstances. And if there were another terrorist attack on the United States, such calls would only increase. But if these people are wrong, then we should not torture. We fail to get the information we need, and this is bad in a war against terrorists. Moreover, it means we are engaging in pure sadism. Being tough and pragmatic in defense of the country is American; being sadistic is not very patriotic. Even most people who favor using torture would agree not to use it if they thought it did not work. What is more, we actually make the United States even worse off by spoon-feeding recruitment propaganda to Al Qaeda and other terrorist groups. Bad information and more terrorists mean that more Americans die. On 9/11 I saw the smoke from the World Trade Center from the building where I teach in New Jersey; I understand the impulse to revenge. Revenge may be sweet, but is it worth more innocent lives?

It may be that we would reject interrogational torture even if it did work, as un-American or on other moral grounds. In other words, demonstrating that interrogational torture is effective may not be a sufficient condition to justify its use, but it is surely a necessary condition: If it does not work, then it cannot be justified as an interrogation technique.

Although the questions I raise are old if unsettled ones, the approach I take to answer them is unorthodox. I analyze interrogational torture using a mathematical modeling technique called game theory, though this book contains almost none of the math.[1] Game theory is a type of applied mathematics used to figure out what people (should) do in strategic situations, when what choice you want to make depends on what your opponent does (and vice versa) and what you get in the end depends on everyone's choices—not just yours (true for your opponent too). Detainees and interrogators are in exactly this sort of game, and this makes game theory an applicable, useful, and powerful way of examining it. Another nice thing about game theory is that it sometimes generates some surprising and counterintuitive results. This book is one of those times. I am going to challenge not just conventional wisdom, but also your own intuitions and even basic instincts about torture and interrogations.

There are many decent and reasonable people who do not like the idea of torture but think it is necessary to protect America and Americans from terrorism. If this describes you, then I hope I can convince you that it is worth examining through reason and logic the assumption that torture works. If you are someone who already opposes torture, I hope I am able to convince you why it is necessary not to treat proponents as "moral monsters" but instead to examine the effectiveness claims of torture proponents. Either way, I hope you will agree that this is a question important enough to take seriously and pursue seriously. Torture is no game.

John W. Schiemann

ACKNOWLEDGMENTS

The *idea* for this book began with an observation in a paper by Roger Koppl. That paper prompted me to write a journal article published in March 2012 (Schiemann 2012*a*). In the course of writing that article, I benefited greatly not only from conversations with Roger, but also discussions with Ken Benoit, Bruce Peabody, and Tobias Åkerlund. Ken kindly invited me to Trinity College, Dublin to present a draft of the paper. Andrew Healy, Roger Koppl, Darius Rejali, David Smailes, Georg Vanberg, Ken Benoit, Rene Lindstädt, Bruce Peabody, Matthew Alexander, and several anonymous reviewers for *Political Research Quarterly* offered many useful suggestions which found their way into not just the article, but also into the book. Marek Slaby generously provided help with some of the formal mathematical work in the paper, for which I'm also grateful. In addition to Tobias, Pierce O'Reilly, Dinah Y. Olaniyan, Michael Carr, Devon Douglas Bowers, and Kyle Morgan also provided excellent research assistance.

The idea for this *book* began, as many good ideas tend to do, over good Kentucky bourbon. My wife Carol Rounds, her brother Steve Rounds, and I have a tradition of discussing a book over bourbon when he is in town. While I was still working on the paper, Carol suggested taking my work on torture to a wider audience. This book is a result of their encouragement and support; so if, after reading through to the end, you decide that "it could have been a pamphlet," you can blame them.

I incurred additional debts while writing the book. Tori Rosen, Ivana Širović, and Jason Aplon's reading of initial drafts of the early chapters helped me write better for a non-academic audience, as did students in several classes. Abagail Eckert graciously double-checked the references, for which I am grateful. My friend, departmental colleague, and office neighbor Bruce Peabody provided his habitual perspicacious commentary on selections from the manuscript, as did Steve Rounds. Marek Slaby again helped me clean up the mathematical notation. Three anonymous reviewers for Oxford University Press offered helpful suggestions, especially on the need to strike the right tone. The reader will decide whether I succeeded or not in that regard. With respect to OUP, I am also grateful to my editor, Angela Chnapko, for her enthusiastic support of the project from my very first contact with her and her careful reading and suggestions for the full manuscript. I am additionally indebted to the LaTeX community for posting code online I could freely steal. Chip Carey kindly invited me to participate in a Symposium on Torture in the Americas at Georgia State University in March 2015. The discussions I had there were very helpful. As always, my terrific colleagues in the Department of Social Sciences and History provided the (usually dark) humor and perspective necessary while writing a book. I am grateful to Peter Woolley for his invitation to speak at the Politics on the PublicMind lecture series as well as to Geoff Weinman for financial support from Becton College over the course of the project.

I would like to thank separately Scott Gartner, Scott Gates, Carol Rounds, and my old friend and colleague Ken Benoit, all of whom read the entire manuscript and improved it with their comments. Livio Di Lonardo painstakingly worked through all the formal material and offered very useful suggestions to clarify the argument in many places. I am grateful for his close reading. Carol and Ken read with such incredible care and detail that I am tempted to blame them for any remaining errors. (But I won't.)

Finally, I am grateful to the love of my life, Carol, and our wonderful daughter Em for providing not only encouragement, but also much-needed balance during this project. I promise I'll give the ps, qs, and boxes a rest for a while.

John W. Schiemann

Interrogating Torture

I also have belonged to those groups of men who believe they can produce the truth with white-hot iron. Well, let me tell you, the white heat of truth comes from another flame.

—UMBERTO ECO, *The Name of the Rose*

Shortly after 3:00 am in the early morning darkness of March 28, 2002, on Canal Road in Faisalabad, Pakistan, Abu Zubaydah heard the front door being kicked in. Grabbing some fake passports and cash, he ran to the roof, sprinted to the edge, and jumped to the roof of the neighboring house one story down. Four Pakistani police officers were waiting. As one of Zubaydah's compatriots struggled with a policeman's AK-47, the gun went off. The single bullet hit Zubaydah in the thigh, shattering coins in his pocket, ricocheting off his femur, and sending shrapnel into his groin and stomach.[1]

As he lay bleeding in the back of a police pickup truck, he was nearly mistaken for a low-level terrorist and summarily shot by a Pakistani officer. FBI and CIA agents, however, recognized him as the target of the raid and he was taken in the back of the pickup to a local hospital. His condition worsening, Zubaydah was flown by military helicopter to a Pakistani military hospital in Lahore. The CIA officer accompanying him tied him to the bed with a sheet and stayed with him as he drifted in and out of consciousness. Within a few days he was loaded into a rickety old ambulance and driven to the Lahore airport.

A white, nondescript Gulfstream jet, probably with the tail number N379P, was waiting on the tarmac for him. The FBI and CIA loaded Zubaydah on the plane and secured him, and the plane took off. Although he was unaware of it, Zubaydah then went on a U.S. taxpayer-funded world tour over the next several days. The CIA changed pilots and stopped off on different continents in order to disguise the final destination: a secret prison near Udon Thani, an hour by car northeast of Bangkok. He was met at the "black site" by a CIA doctor, anesthe-siologist, and medic who had prepared a field hospital for him. Two FBI agents, Ali Soufan and Stephen Gaudin, both experts on Al Qaeda, were also waiting.

Soufan and Gaudin got to work right away, questioning Zubaydah when the medical team was not cleaning his multiple wounds. They even helped care for him, holding ice to his lips and cleaning him up after he soiled himself. Their combined efforts were not enough, however, and Zubaydah began to develop sepsis. The CIA station chief hurriedly cooked up a plan to disguise Zubaydah as a soldier and they rushed him to a hospital. Only a tracheotomy and hand-pumping air into his lungs during the ride to the hospital kept him alive. The surgery saved his life and when he awoke, Soufan and Gaudin immedi-ately began questioning him, using an Arabic letter chart to communicate since Zubaydah had a breathing tube in his mouth and could not speak. On April 8 the breathing tube was removed and Zubaydah continued to cooperate and pro-vide information to the FBI agents. On April 10, 2002, he identified a picture of Khalid Sheikh Mohammed (hereafter KSM) as "Mukhtar," the mastermind behind 9/11.

While Zubaydah lay in the hospital, talking to Soufan and Gaudin, a new CIA team sent from CIA headquarters in Langley, Virginia had renovated the black site to include a special cell, with hidden cameras and microphones to record Zubaydah's every move. The team from the CIA's Counterterrorism Cen-ter (CTC) included the CIA's chief operational psychologist, an interrogator, a polygrapher, analysts, as well as support and security staff.

It also included James Elmer Mitchell, a military psychologist who had never even observed an interrogation, let alone conducted one. Mitchell spoke none of the relevant languages, had no background knowledge of, or experience in, the Middle East, and knew nothing about Al Qaeda or terrorism. What he did have was experience with the military's SERE program and, reportedly, a thousand-plus-dollar-a-day contract with the CIA. SERE stands for Survival, Eva-sion, Resistance, Escape, a program designed to train service members how to resist torture by actually undergoing limited versions of it under tightly con-trolled conditions. Mitchell's contract with the CIA was to reverse-engineer these methods to get Al Qaeda detainees to provide intelligence. Mitchell's presence, in other words, signaled that Zubaydah would face a very different approach to interrogation upon his return.

On April 15, 2002, a doctor sedated Zubaydah and a CIA team drove him back to the black site. He awoke four hours later, manacled to his bed, in an all-white room, brightly lit with four halogen bulbs. His guards were covered in black from their balaclavas and goggle-covered heads to their boot-encased toes and they communicated with each other using only hand signals. His hands were cuffed and his legs manacled to the bed or chair, with intermittent loud music played in his cell. The new interrogation plan conceived by Mitchell originally called for isolating Zubaydah, but since his medical care precluded this, the team opted the next day for interrogating him around the clock, with short breaks for sleep.

For the remainder of April the CIA and FBI questioned Zubaydah, who provided information on Al Qaeda plans, capabilities, leadership, decision-making, training, and tactics, as well as information on terrorists in Pakistan. On April 20 he provided information which eventually led to the capture of Al Qaeda operative Jose Padilla, the so-called dirty bomber. He also provided information on plots to blow up apartment buildings and the Brooklyn Bridge, as well as other plots.

Despite this cooperation, CIA analysts on the ground at the black site and back at headquarters in Langley remained convinced that Zubaydah was holding back information on pending attacks on the United States and operatives residing in the United States. As a result, in early May the CIA accepted Mitchell's proposal to start employing coercive measures, including sensory deprivation. Once again Zubaydah was stripped naked, manacled to a chair, and subjected to loud music. This time, white noise was added to the coercion playlist and he was deprived of sleep for 48 hours. At this point a CIA medical officer decided that the methods had crossed the line of what constituted torture and, afraid for his ability to practice medicine in the future, returned to the United States. Soufan himself did the same in May when he discovered a large box in the interrogation area and learned that Zubaydah would be confined in it. Special Agent Gaudin reported through a different chain of command in the FBI and remained for several more weeks, participating in the CIA-directed interrogations until early June 2002, when he too was ordered back home by the FBI. From that point on, the CIA had full control. During May and the first half of June, Zubaydah continued to provide information, but not on pending threats or terrorist cells in the United States. Since both local CIA analysts and their bosses back in Langley were convinced that Zubaydah had this information, they switched tactics.

On June 18, 2002, Zubaydah was put into his cell. He remained there, in isolation for 47 days, until August 4. Not one question was put to him.[2]

In the meantime, the CIA began seeking written approval from the Department of Justice to employ more coercive techniques. They got it in the August 1, 2002, Department of Justice Office of Legal Counsel memo to the CIA (Bybee 2002). The memo identified ten "Enhanced Interrogation Techniques" (EITs) that CIA interrogators could use on Zubaydah: attention grasp, walling (pushing or slamming a detainee against a flexible wall with the neck wrapped to prevent whiplash), facial hold, facial slap, cramped confinement, wall standing (leaning against a wall supported only by the fingers for lengthy periods), stress positions, sleep deprivation, confinement in a box, possibly with a feared insect, and waterboarding (Bybee 2002, pp. 2–4). With the approvals in hand, the CIA was ready to go back to work on Zubaydah.

Ten minutes before noon on August 4, 2002, the black-clad "ninjas" entered Zubaydah's cell. In total silence, without asking a single question, they shackled and hooded him and removed his only article of clothing, a towel wrapped around his waist. Wrapping a towel around his neck, they swung him around and slammed him into the concrete wall. They removed his hood and grabbed his face, making him watch while a large box was brought into the room and placed on the floor to resemble a coffin. Interrogators told him the only way he would ever leave the secret prison was in that box.

Interrogators demanded he provide "detailed and verifiable information on terrorist operations planned against the United States, including the names, phone numbers, email addresses, weapon caches, and safe houses of anyone involved." Zubaydah's denials of knowing any of that information were met with slaps and grabs to the face. Over the next six hours he was shut up in the large box, pulled out, walled, forced into a smaller confinement box less than two and one-half feet square, and put in stress positions. Around half past 6:00 pm he was tied to a gurney and waterboarded for the first time. Over the next two and a half hours, he was waterboarded multiple times, repeatedly coughing, vomiting, and involuntarily spasming against his restraints. At one point, he fell unconscious, "bubbles rising through his open, full mouth," requiring medical intervention to revive him. At 8:52 pm interrogators stopped waterboarding.

"Aggressive interrogations," however, did not. For the next 20 days straight, 24 hours a day, Zubaydah was walled, grabbed, slapped, and forced into stress positions. Altogether he spent over half of that entire period (266 hours or 11 days, 2 hours) in the large (coffin size) confinement box and over a day (29 hours) in the smaller box. He was waterboarded two to four times a day, with multiple applications each time. When he was left by himself, he was put into a stress position, left on the waterboard with his face covered, or confined in one of the boxes. He was kept nude, dirty, sleep deprived, hungry, and subjected to loud music or white noise. His previous wounds began to reopen under the strain, but CIA headquarters stipulated that interrogations "took precedence over preventive medical procedures."[3]

Zubaydah continued to provide general information on Al Qaeda before, during, and after the use of the EITs. He did not, however, ever provide information on terrorist cells or operational plans for attacks against the United States.

Bush administration officials as well as many (but not all) in the CIA have claimed that the techniques saved lives because of the information they generated about future attacks. Did they? Did—does—interrogational torture work?

Quaestio in early Roman law meant only "questioning" or "interrogating" witnesses. As torture worked its way into Roman jurisprudence from the second and third centuries C.E., the term "became synonymous with torture" so that the same word in Medieval Latin had come to mean "torture," as did the Old French *question* (Lea and Peters 1973, pp. x–xi).[4] Water torture, for example, became known as *question d'eau.*

Quaestio quaestionum—interrogating (interrogational) torture—is the purpose of this book. The Zubaydah case illustrates some of the questions which must be raised and answered in any appraisal of an interrogation program using coercive techniques. Do the EITs of the CIA and the aggressive counter-resistance techniques of the military rise to the level of torture (Haynes II 2002, p. 1)? Who, exactly, is the detainee? How much does the detainee know (if anything)? What is the value of what he knows? How do you know whether an interrogation technique is working? How does an interrogator know when to stop, when a detainee has told all he knows? Is there a slippery slope problem with interrogational torture or can it be strictly controlled? Will innocents be tortured? Will they falsely confirm information to avoid torture? How reliable is coercive interrogation generally? Does it work most of the time, some of the time, or only rarely? How much bad information is generated?

KANTIANS, KHANIANS, AND PRAGMATISTS

Chapter 2 assesses whether the EITs amounted to torture and what we know about the effectiveness of interrogational torture. For many, of course, the question of torture's effectiveness is irrelevant: Torture is unjustified whether or not it is effective. Call this rights-focused group *Kantians* after the famous German philosopher Immanuel Kant. For others, the degree of torture's effectiveness is just as irrelevant, but for a different reason: The 9/11 attacks provided the United States all the justification it needs to torture suspected terrorists. Call this group *Khanians*, after Genghis Khan, who is said to have tortured someone who had wronged him by "by pouring molten silver into his ears and eyes."[5] For this group, vengeance, not intelligence, is the goal.

There is also, however, a third group of Americans for whom torture is justified only because, and insofar as, it is effective, and who would oppose it otherwise (call this group *Pragmatists*). In a 2011 survey, I found that while fewer than one in six Americans consider himself or herself a *Kantian* and the same is true for *Khanians*, more than four in ten consider themselves *Pragmatists*. This group, nearly two-thirds of all those who think that harsh interrogation methods can sometimes be justified, says that the techniques would not be justified if they were not effective.[6] A December 2012 Huffington Post/YouGov poll found that a little more than a third of Americans are "not sure" whether information gained from torture is reliable, only one point below the percentage that thinks it is unreliable (a further 29% thought that information from torture was reliable).[7] Two years later, after the release of the Senate Intelligence Committee report, Huffington Post/YouGov found that the "not sure" group had jumped to 37%, with the "reliable" vs. "unreliable" camps evenly divided at 31% and 32%, respectively.[8] So more than one in three Americans are not sure whether interrogational torture works, and four in ten say it is justified only if it does work.

Thus, determining whether interrogational torture works—and at what human cost—is essential. It may be that interrogational torture cannot be justified under any circumstances, but if it is to be justified at all, it must be effective. First, if it does not work, then the only possible public justification for its use—it is the only method we have left when detainees refuse to talk—disappears and any further use is pure sadism. Second, and just as importantly, if it does not work, then this means that interrogators are not getting the information necessary to save lives. Even its proponents would argue against it under these conditions. As Bagaric and Clarke admit in their pragmatic defense of torture, this is a "knock-down argument" for "if this objection were valid [they] would change [their] minds and not countenance torture in any circumstances" (Bagaric and Clarke 2007, p. 53).

A NEW APPROACH: GAME THEORY

I examine whether or not there is such a knock-down argument in this book. *Kantians* will find me rhetorically complicit in torture for even considering the question of effectiveness.[9] *Khanians* want to torture out of revenge and will not be persuaded by reason and logic about effectiveness. *Pragmatists*—perhaps you fall into this group—may very well, however, be open to reasoned and logical arguments evaluating the supposed effectiveness of interrogational torture. Moreover, given the absence of sufficiently reliable and systematic evidence to convince *Pragmatists*, reason and logic are the only alternatives we have left.

The preeminent vehicles for making reasoned and logical arguments are formal logic and mathematics.[10] A branch of mathematics called game theory is particularly applicable to the problem of interrogational torture. If you've ever had to merge lanes in traffic, then you already know a little about game theory because you've actually played it. Although everyone might be happier taking turns to merge, everyone is afraid that others might jump ahead and that they will be stuck in traffic longer. As a result, everyone crowds up, honks, and yells, and the traffic slows down even more. Everyone is behaving rationally, in their own self-interest, and the result is everyone stressed out and late for dinner.

The film *A Beautiful Mind*, about the mathematician and game theorist John Nash, provides another, if dated and sexist, example. There is a scene in the movie where Nash and four other (straight male) mathematicians are at a bar and five women walk in, one of whom is a blonde. The men start arguing about who should go for the blonde, but Nash, in a game theory epiphany, tells them that if they all hit on the blonde they will "block each other" and make the other women angry for being made to feel second fiddle. As a result, none of them "succeeds." Consequently, Nash argues, it makes more sense for them all to court the brunettes and ignore the blonde. The brunettes will respond favorably and everyone is happy (except the surprised blonde).[11] Thus, game theory is a way to describe and think about situations in which two or more people have choices to make, and which action they end up taking affects both: (1) what action everyone else wants to take as well as (2) what each person gets in the end, after everyone has chosen.

Cop shows provide a more familiar example. In the third episode of the first season of the popular crime show *Law and Order SVU*, Detectives Benson and Stabler are questioning a suspect, a woman named Deborah, in the murder of one fashion model and the brutal assault on another. They catch her in a lie and Detective Stabler says to her: "Why don't you talk to us while we can still help you?" She responds with "I've enjoyed about as much of your help as I can take." Stabler and Benson then walk out of the interrogation room and ask Detectives Munch and Cassidy whether they got anything on the other suspect, Carlo Parisi, whom Munch and Cassidy had interrogated. When Benson learns that neither team had gotten their suspects to admit to anything, the following exchange takes place (with some tweaks to the script)[12]:

BENSON: Munch, do us a favor.

MUNCH: What?

BENSON: Get Carlo to sit in this chair and tell him his options. We've got enough on him with the statutory rape charge to send him upstate for 5 years. If he tells us what happened, we'll do what we can to get that reduced to a lesser charge so he's out in a year. On the other hand, if Deborah rolls on him, and he stays mum, we'll get him on the murder one charge and he's going away for at least 15. If they both cooperate, we'll have more evidence against them but still help them out and they'll each get 11 years.

STABLER: We'll sit Deborah by Carlo so they see and hear everything and then give her the same choice. She's already admitted to scoring crank at Till's party, so we've got 5 years on her too, even without anything from Carlo.

MUNCH: Ah, cute. The Prisoner's Dilemma.

CASSIDY: What's that?

MUNCH: See, no matter what the other one does, they each spend less time in prison if they talk. They both know this, so they both talk. And we put them both away for 11 years each, even though if they could just both bite their tongues and wait it out, they'd be out in 5. But they never do!

CASSIDY: Damn, I love this job. I'll get Carlo.

Carlo and Deborah are playing a Prisoners' Dilemma. If Carlo keeps quiet, Deborah has two options. She gets 5 years if she does not talk and 1 year if she does. So she is better off talking in that case. If Carlo talks, Deborah again has two choices. She gets 15 years if she stays quiet and 11 years if she talks too. So she is better off in this case talking as well. In other words, Deborah is always better off if she talks (assuming, as we are, that she wants to spend as little time in the slammer as possible). So she will choose to rat out Carlo. And since it is exactly the same situation from Carlo's perspective, he will do the same thing and the result is that each spends 11 years behind bars—6 years longer than if they had both managed to "keep their big mouths shut."

I have summarized the situation in Table 1.1. Deborah's choices are the rows and Carlo's are the columns.

A row–column combination is an outcome, a combination of Deborah's choice and Carlo's choice. Each outcome, that is, each row–column combination, has a pair of payoffs—in this case a jail sentence, one for Deborah (on the left) and one for Carlo (the sentence on the right). Take, for example, the combination of choices where Deborah stays silent (the top row) and Carlo rats her out (the right-hand column). Deborah gets 15 years and Carlo gets 1 year, as just described above.

I have bolded the "Rat Out"–"Rat Out" outcome because that is the *equilibrium* of this game.[13] Equilibria are where game theory's rubber hits the road. They are the outcomes of the game; they tell you what will happen. The idea is as straightforward as it is important. An equilibrium is just a stable combination of actions; neither player wants to make a different choice given what the other player has chosen. To help fix this idea, go back to the bar scene in *A Beautiful*

Table 1.1. LAW AND ORDER SVU PRISONERS' DILEMMA

		Carlo	
		Stay Silent	*Rat Out Deborah*
Deborah	*Stay Silent*	5 years, 5 years	15 years, 1 year
	Rat Out Carlo	1 year, 15 years	**11 years, 11 years**

Mind for a moment. Is it an equilibrium for all the mathematicians to go after the brunettes (assuming that there is an additional brunette and that the men all prefer the blonde, as in the movie)?

Imagine that you are John Nash. If your friends are playing this strategy—they are hitting on the brunettes—do you have incentive to switch your strategy— from the remaining brunette to the blonde? Yes, you do. You will not be blocked by your friends, so it makes sense to go for it. You would switch your strategy and go for the blonde. But of course, the exact same reasoning is true for your friends, so they would switch too. Consequently, Nash's proposal in the movie is not an equilibrium at all.[14]

Return now to the bolded equilibrium of the *Law and Order SVU* game. Deborah, for example, would not "go back in time" after Carlo has chosen "rat out" and switch her move to "stay silent" even if she could, because that would move her up to the outcome where she gets 15 years instead of 11. The same is true for Carlo, so neither has an incentive to switch her or his strategy. In contrast, the outcome in which Carlo "stays silent" and Deborah "rats [him] out" is not an equilibrium because Carlo *does* have an incentive to switch his strategy (because he would get 11 years instead of 15 years). Munch was right about it being "cute" (at least for the detectives). Seemingly weirdly, individual rational behavior results in an outcome in which the players are worse off than if they had somehow managed to stay silent.

These are just a few examples, but they should give you the flavor of the game theoretic approach. You have people (players) who have choices to make, with those choices (strategies) leading to various outcomes, each with its own set of rewards or penalties (payoffs). Importantly, the choices that one player makes— that is, the strategy that he or she chooses—affects both (a) the strategy that the other player wants to take and (b) the payoffs to both of the players. Their interaction is strategic. The same is true of interrogational torture, and that makes game theory applicable, useful, and powerful.

Interrogational torture is not a game in the sense of being fun, but it *is* a game in this strategic sense. The interrogator is trying to figure out what the detainee knows. If the detainee is innocent, he is trying to find a way to convince the interrogator of that fact. If the detainee does have information, he is trying to find a way to avoid giving it up. So game theory is actually pretty well suited to model the kind of interaction that takes place between a detainee and an interrogator. Game theory allows us to model the incentives and the strategies of the detainee and the interrogator and see what would happen.

But it is more than merely applicable. What makes game theory useful are the outcomes that are derived from the game modeled on interrogational torture: the equilibria. These outcomes are basically combinations of detainee and interrogator actions, just like the "rat out"–"rat out" equilibrium in the Prisoners' Dilemma. So in interrogational torture, one outcome or equilibrium might be "talk," "don't torture" while another might be "don't talk," "torture."

We will do the same thing for interrogational torture. We will compare the predictions, the equilibria, emerging from our game theoretic model of interrogational torture to what torture proponents say happens when interrogational torture is used in real life. In the usual course of social science research using game theory, the model generates predictions which are then tested empirically, using data from the real world to assess how useful the model is in explaining the phenomenon of interest. In contrast, we will use the predictions from game theory as *substitutes* for the data we do not (and never will) have and will compare them to the claims—the predictions—made by torture proponents about its effectiveness (Laver 1997, p. 4).

In other words, we can use the equilibria in place of the data we will never have to identify the conditions (if any) under which a detainee provides clear and valuable information. Modeling interrogational torture also permits us to assess the frequency of torture by identifying how often torture—including torture of an innocent detainee—occurs in equilibrium. Finally, it is possible to use some of the formal mathematical results from the model to derive some implications about the likely severity of torture when it is used. In other words, the outcomes of a game theoretic analysis will help us answer the important questions I raised at the outset.

Game theory, however, offers even more. It is not only applicable and useful, it is also powerful. As a type of deductive reasoning, game theory relies on systematic, logical reasoning to derive outcomes (equilibria) from a set of clearly stated assumptions. You cannot be wishy-washy using game theory. You cannot hide behind vague and unstated assumptions and you cannot waffle in your reasoning from those assumptions to your conclusions. All of this makes a game theoretic argument, like other forms of deductive arguments, valid.

When the assumptions are also true, when they correspond pretty closely to the real world, and when you validly derive outcomes from those assumptions and those outcomes also correspond to what happens in the real world, then you have something powerful: a valid and true argument. That gives us some confidence that we are actually getting at the real-world phenomenon that we are trying to model with game theory. Finally, the formal mathematical properties of game theoretic models often provide unexpected and counterintuitive insights and relationships which might otherwise go unnoticed.

RATIONALITY, TORTURE, AND PAIN

Before saying a little more about exactly how we will do this, it may be help-ful first to address two understandable objections to applying game theory to interrogational torture, one ethical and one about the relationship between pain and our ability to make choices. The ethical objection is that it is dehumanizing to reduce the pain of torture to a bunch of numbers. How can you reduce the excruciating pain and fear of waterboarding, for example, to a negative payoff? Is it not monstrous to try and do so?

This understandable instinct is, however, rooted in a common but signifi-cant misunderstanding conflating *reduction* and *representation*. A game theoretic model does not reduce anything. Reduction entails a complete explanation of the complex whole of one thing in terms of something (or several somethings) simpler or more elemental constituting it. We could, in principle anyway, re-duce cooking to chemistry by explaining the transformation of starch, sugar, and yeast into a French pastry. We could go further and explain chemistry in terms of physics.

Fine, but game theoretic models (or other models for that matter) do not reduce anything. The re*present*; they do not re*duce*. Models, like other represen-tations of things in the world, simplify, but do not reduce, reality to re-present it in a way that is more intelligible, meaningful, or revelatory for particular purposes (Clarke and Primo 2012, pp. 4–9, *passim*).

Consider some different models, or representations, of torture. Vann Nath, a former prisoner of the Khmer Rouge in the infamous Tuol Sleng prison in Cambodia, painted scenes of torture in the prison, including waterboarding.[15] Or how about a musical representation or reflection on torture? The Palestinian composer Suhail Khoury was inspired by his torture in an Israeli prison to write "Shabeh," an instrumental piece performed by the group Karloma on the CD *Jerusalem after Midnight*.[16] Finally, Thomas Kennedy offers a fictional literary representation in his moving story of Chilean torture victim Nardo and his strug-gle to love again in the novel *In the Company of Angels*. At one point, Nardo speaks in the third person of the tortures he suffered, of having his hands bound be-hind his back and "his head plunged into a tank of water afloat with excrement" (Kennedy 2010, p. 164).

Each of these is a re-presentation of torture; the first and third are versions of water torture. It would be inaccurate, if not downright insulting, to charge these artists with "reducing" torture to splashes of color, bundles of air vibra-tions, and blotches of ink. Each re-presents the reality of torture in a different way for different purposes, but does not reduce torture to the medium of that re-presentation. Nor, because they simplify, do they capture everything about torture (Laver 1997, p. 1). The same will be true of a game theoretic model. Our model will not "reduce" pain to numbers, nor will we claim that the model captures every aspect of, or perspective on, interrogational torture.

The second objection also stems from the fact that pain is front and center in torture. The idea here is that the pain and domination in torture are so overwhelming that they rule out any reasonable conception of choice, preference, calculation, or strategy—in short the ability of the individual to make choices, as is required by game theory (Howes 2012). Wisnewski and Emerick (2009), for example, present a critique of pro-torture arguments rooted in the assumption that torture strips its victims of their human agency—that is, their ability to make choices. In doing so, they rely heavily on the philosophers Elaine Scarry and David Sussman.

Scarry, who presents perhaps the most extreme "anti-agency" or anti-choice position, asserts that "torture systematically prevents the prisoner from being the agent of anything" (Scarry 1985, p. 47). The pain caused by torture is "world-destroying" because it results in the "obliteration of the contents of consciousness. Pain annihilates not only the objects of complex thought and emotion but also the objects of the most elemental acts of perception" (Scarry 1985, pp. 29, 54). In other words, the pain from torture is so transformative that people can no longer make choices and can no longer act rationally. Indeed, Scarry goes so far as to claim that the physical pain of torture destroys language itself (Scarry 1985, pp. 4, 6, 19, 49, 54, and *passim*).

If this were true, and not empirically absurd, there would be no interrogational torture whatsoever: Interrogation presupposes that the person being interrogated can use language. If the actions of actual torture victims are not enough to belie such claims, studies of torture victims demonstrate that many of them not only maintain their agency, but actually *enhance* it (Rejali 2007, p. 442). Scarry can maintain this position only because she repeatedly rejects the possibility that the motivation for torture could be information, so that "what masquerades as the motive for torture is a fiction" (Scarry 1985, p. 28, also pp. 12, 20, 29, 57, 329–330).

While it is clear that torture is also used for punishment, for intimidation, and to compel confessions, it is just as clear that torture has been employed for information in the past and present. Scarry herself, of course, admits this reality. "But for every instance in which someone with critical information is interrogated, there are hundreds interrogated who could know nothing of remote importance to . . . the regime" (Scarry 1985, p. 28, also p. 29). This is a claim about the rarity of prisoners with information, not the nonexistence of interrogational torture. This sort of "uncritical indignation" does no favors for the anti-torture argument (Peters 1973, p. xxii).

In short, a desire for information actually *does* and *did* motivate much state torture, is *perceived* by the public and by (some) ethical theorists as motivating torturers, and is the *only possible public defense* of torture by proponents. Each is sufficient to scrutinize claims of torture's effectiveness; jointly they constitute a compelling case.

Sussman (2005, pp. 14–15) would also seem to argue against the ability to apply game theory to torture:

> [T]orture is not only a violation of the value of rational agency, but a violation that is accomplished through the very annihilation of such agency itself, if only temporarily or incompletely.

The caveat "incompletely" is key here, however. Sussman admits as much when he says that "the victim is presented with a dilemma about submission or resistance." This suggests that some room for choice, for action, does indeed remain.

The crucial point is that interrogational torture *presupposes* (rational) agency on the part of the victim. If an interrogator walks into an interrogation room to find the prisoner a babbling madman (and believes the babbling is not an act), it makes no sense to torture him. Sussman himself makes this case quite persuasively. After drawing a nice distinction between coercion, which requires the coercee to possess rational agency in order to respond to the incentives created by the coercion, and brainwashing, the goal of which is to replace the agency of the victim with the agency of the brainwasher, he positions torture somewhere between the two. "Any particular act of torture will tend to shade off in one direction or another: [T]he more effectively the torture undermines the victim's rational capacities, the *less effectively it can also be coercing him by appeal to his incentive structure* (and vice versa)" (my emphasis) (Sussman 2005, pp. 10–11).

In other words, the philosophical position that torturers totally dominate their victims adopts the same caricature of interrogational torture presented by its strongest proponents. According to this view, torturers know how to inflict pain so effectively that all room for agency, calculation, strategizing, and choice is removed. The torturer controls the environment so completely, breaks the victim down so thoroughly, that he does exactly what the torturer desires. The will of the torturer becomes the will of the tortured.

This is exactly what the designers of the Bush interrogational torture program believed: They would "break" detainees who thought they could hold out and make them willing to talk. There are, unfortunately, plenty of first-person accounts demonstrating that such a model—whether in the guise of the television program 24, in the mind of Dick Cheney or SERE psychologists, or in a work of political philosophy such as Scarry or Wisnewski—is a fantasy.

Take the case of the man

> who, after repeated tortures and revocations [of his confession under each torture session], when asked by the judge why he retracted his confession so often, replied that he would rather be tortured a thousand times in the arms than once in the neck, for he could easily find a doctor to set his arm but never one to set his neck (Lea and Peters 1973, p. 123).

It is clear from passages such as this, from torture victims' *own* accounts, rather than the reflections of philosophers, that they value things—avoiding pain, protecting information, convincing the interrogator that they are innocent—and order them in particular ways. The fact that torturers also want something from their victims—information or even a confession—indicates that they have goals too. Many victims, by their own accounts, think of themselves as having at least two actions, confessing or not confessing, providing information or not. The same is true of interrogators in their selection of whether or not to torture. Finally, both sides understand, even if imperfectly and under uncertainty, how those actions lead to outcomes.

OVERVIEW OF THE ARGUMENT

Heading off the potential ethical and philosophical objections clears the way for applying game theory to the question of interrogational torture's effectiveness. Since, as the next chapter will show, we cannot answer the question empirically— that is, with data from the real world—then not only *can* we apply it, but we *ought* to do so. How will this work?

Our starting point is to build a model of interrogational torture based on the vision of its proponents, of the pragmatists who say it is necessary in some circumstances. This vision is a pragmatic, normative model of how interrogational torture *should* work, or was supposed to work, according to its proponents. CIA and other government documents are full of safeguards and checks and procedures designed to limit and control torture. The CIA may have exceeded them, but these need to be incorporated into our analytical model just as much as does the reality of what goes on in an interrogation booth. The analytical model can be neither a strawman used to argue against interrogational torture, nor a quixotism used to argue for it.

In addition to identifying the constraints on the game theoretic model, the pragmatic model has another objective: identifying the criteria against which the pragmatic model will be assessed as effective or not effective. As an example of this idea, take the recently created Consumer Financial Protection

Bureau (CFPB). Ignoring the partisan bickering for the moment, note that this is a government program designed to achieve certain goals, including "write and enforce rules for banks and other firms, aiming to protect consumers from deceptive and abusive loans and other financial products and services" and "monitor and report on markets for consumer financial goods and services ... and how consumers interact with them."[17] The goals suggest the criteria by which it should be measured, the "benchmarks" it should achieve, to use government and corporate management-speak. Data can then be gathered and compared against these benchmarks. For example, according to the CFPB website, "interest rate hikes on existing accounts have been dramatically curtailed," late fees and overlimit fees have been reduced, and credit card costs are clearer.[18] These data suggest that the CFPB may be making some progress toward its goals. If it did not meet these benchmarks, then the CFPB would be considered less successful. Now, you may be a Republican opposed to this agency on principle and thus may disagree with the very goals of the program. But if the program fails to achieve even its own goals, that is a real problem even for those Democrats in favor of it.

Our pragmatic model of interrogational torture will work in the same way. It will identify some of the criteria by which pragmatic *pro*ponents of interrogational torture—not *op*ponents of interrogational torture—would judge its success. Once we have done that in Chapter 3—that is, once we have identified both the constraints on the way interrogational torture would be practiced in our model as well as identified some of the criteria of success against which to compare the outcomes of the model (the equilibria)—we can build a game theoretic model of interrogational torture in Chapters 4 and 5.

Having constructed a model that respects the proponents' view, we then solve it in Chapter 6, just as we solved the Prisoners' Dilemma when we found the unique Nash equilibrium. Solving the game means finding the equilibria. These equilibria have important general properties we explore in Chapter 7 before examining each equilibrium and its particular properties in Chapters 8 to 11. Each of those chapters also narrates a case study of interrogations and torture from the real world to illustrate the equilibrium under discussion.

The equilibria and these general properties are our substitutes for the missing empirical data to compare against the benchmarks, and this is the task we take up in Chapter 12. Chapter 13 goes beyond describing *what* happens when torture is used for information to explain just *why* what happens happens as well as reflects on the use of formal models in political philosophy. Finally, a Postscript compares the predictions of the pragmatic model as well as those of the game theoretic model to the findings of the investigation of the CIA detention and interrogation program by the Senate Select Committee on Intelligence, released after the previous chapters were largely complete.

*   *   *

This sketches the argument that I will make in the rest of this book. To provide a bit more detail, here is a road map through that argument, chapter by chapter. Each chapter ends with this format, providing a short summary of each step reached in the argument to that point as well as identifying the next step.

The argument proceeds by answering the following questions:

1. Are the EITs torture? What do we know about the effectiveness of interrogational torture? (Chapter 2)
2. How closely does the Bush program approximate the ideal model of interrogational torture? What are the limits on torture in the pragmatic model? What benchmarks define the success of the pragmatic model? (Chapter 3)
3. What are the outcomes of the Bush Interrogational Torture (BIT) model? (Chapter 4)
4. What does a more realistic model of interrogational torture (RIT)—but one still faithful to the pragmatic model's core principles—look like? (Chapter 5)
5. How do we solve the RIT model? (Chapter 6)
6. What are the equilibria and outcomes of the RIT model and what can we say generally about them? (Chapter 7)
7. What does each of the outcomes look like? What are its properties? What is an example of the outcome in the real world of interrogational torture? (Chapters 8 to 11)
8. How do the RIT model outcomes compare to the pragmatic model's benchmarks in Chapter 3? (Chapter 12)

*   *   *

The first step in the argument, then, is to examine whether the EITs used by the CIA and similar techniques used by the U.S. military amount to torture and what we know about the effectiveness of interrogational torture in eliciting valuable information.

Dangerous Torment

It is torture when an investigation is conducted with torment and force. . . . Torture is a weak and dangerous thing that may fail the truth.

—ULPIAN, *Justinian's Digest*

Marina Gonzàlez stood before the Toledan inquisitors Fernando de Mazuecos and Ferndando Rodríguez del Barco on April 29, 1494, and rejected their accusations of heresy. With this refusal, she was taken immediately to the torture chamber, stripped of her skirts, and bound tightly to the rack with cords, including her head. "They put a hood in front of her face, and with a jar that held three pints, more or less, they started to pour water down her nose and throat." She refused to confess after the first pint so they poured the remaining two pints before removing the hood and cord from her head. She again refused to confess, was tied down again, and endured another three pints from the jar before the inquisitors ordered her brought down from the rack (Homza 2006, p. 45).

Juan de Salas stood before the inquisitor Moriz in Vallalodid on June 21, 1527, and once again denied he had blasphemed the evangelists. As a result, he was taken directly to the torture chamber, accompanied by the executioner Pedro Porras and the notary Henry Paz in addition to Moriz. Bound tightly to the *escalera*, a kind of grooved table that raises the legs above the head, a "fine wet cloth was put over his face, and about a pint of water was poured into his mouth and nostrils . . . nevertheless, Salas still persisted *in denying the accusation*" (emphasis in original). After several more rounds of questioning, denials, and water-pouring, Salas was taken down from the *escalera* (Llorente and Lovett 1967, pp. 121–122).

John Clarke passed the "weeping and lamenting" Samuel Colson on his way into the examining room in the Dutch fort at Amboyna on February 16, 1622.

Clarke was pulled two feet off the ground up onto a large door, his limbs outstretched and bound tightly with cords. A cloth was tied around his neck and folded up in a cone toward the top of his head. "That done, they poured water softly upon his head until the cloth was full, up to the mouth and nostrils, and somewhat higher; so that he could not draw breath, but he must withall suck-in the water: which being still continued to be poured in softly, forced all his inward parts, came out of his nose, ears, and eyes, and often as it were stifling and choking him, at length took away his breath and brought him to a swoon or fainting. Then they took him quickly down and made him vomit up the water." When he had recovered, his Dutch captors repeated the procedure three more times. Clarke's continued resistance, his refusal to confess to a plot to take over the castle for the English, led the examiners to believe that he was possessed by the devil for withstanding so much. After adding burning his skin to the water torture and "leading" him along with the necessary details, he confessed and he was carried out by four men to the castle dungeon (East India Company 1665, pp. 10–12).

Jean Bourdil walked past a doctor and a priest and into the torture chamber of Toulouse on May 27, 1726. Surrounded by hooks, pulleys, ropes, weights, and other means of stretching human joints, he took an oath to tell the truth to his interrogators. A little while later, after those hooks, pulleys, ropes, and weights had failed to elicit his confession to the charge of killing two soldiers— just as they had two days prior—he was subjected to the *question d'eau* five times.

> The *question d'eau* consisted of fastening the wrists of the accused to an iron ring bolted into the wall at waist height, and the feet, to another ring embedded in the floor, thus extending the prisoner's body to its full length at a slant. Trestles of varying heights were then wedged under the prisoner's back, forcing a further extension of the body. Finally, his face covered by a linen napkin, water was forced down his throat through a cow's horn, as much as sixteen liters at a time (Silverman 2001, p. 46).

During each session, Bourdil was asked to tell the truth, to confess to his guilt in the crime, or his complicity in the crime, or his knowledge of those who were guilty. After the fifth session the linen rag was removed from his mouth, and he was unstrapped from the bench and likely set down by a fire and ministered to by the doctor before being returned to his cell.

In New Castle, Alabama, on January 6, 1881, F.H. Gafford, an employee of a coal company, gave testimony to the Joint Special Committee of the state legislature conducting an inquiry into the treatment of convicts in Alabama. Mr. Gafford's company "rented" convicts from the state as part of its convict leasing program and was asked about the punishments employed for "wilful neglect of work." In order to secure compliance, Mr. Gafford testified that the company generally employed the "strap" but that on three occasions in the three years of his employ, they had "punished with water." "In water punishment the man is strapped to his back and the water is poured in his face on the upper lip, and effectually stops his breathing as long as there is a constant stream. It is a very dangerous punishment" (Alabama State Legislature 1881, p. 7).

Ramon Navarro, a Filipino lawyer, had failed to provide the information sought by his Japanese interrogator after a morning of interrogation.[1] It was World War II, and the Japanese occupiers of the Philippines were seeking information on guerilla activities. At around 2:00 pm, the interrogator, Major Chinsaku Yuki, ordered Navarro to remove all of his clothes and lie down on his back on a bench. Navarro complied with both orders. Yuki then tied Navarro's feet, hands, and neck to the bench. Once Navarro was secured to the bench, Yuki put a cloth on Navarro's face and began pouring water from a nearby faucet on Navarro's face. The stream of water continued until Navarro lost consciousness. The process was then repeated four or five times over the next two hours. At that point, Navarro told his interrogator a lie in an attempt to stop the "treatment." When Yuki discovered the lie, he repeated the procedure on Navarro another two or three times.

Captain Chase Nielsen, a B-25 navigator, had provided nothing but his name, rank, and serial number to his Japanese interrogator on the afternoon of April 24, 1942. After failing to elicit more information on what would later be called the Doolittle Raid, the interrogator had four soldiers pin his arms and legs to the floor. Another soldier wrapped his face with a wet towel and poured water on the towel.

> They poured water on this towel until I was almost unconscious from strangulation, then they would let up until I'd get my breath, then they'd start all over again. I felt more or less like I was drowning, just gasping between life and death ... (Nelson 2003, p. 245).

Nielsen was rescued at the end of the war, but returned to Shanghai to testify against his captors at a war crimes trial.

Thomas D. Harrison, a U.S. Air Force pilot, bailed out of his disabled jet on May 21, 1951, near Sinuiju, North Korea, and was captured. He refused to provide his captors any information, even after being starved for nine days.

One day in November he was beaten with clubs and sticks before being subjected to the "water treatment" (Hansen 1953, p. 17):

> They would bend my head back, put a towel over my face and pour water over the towel. I could not breathe. This went on hour after hour, day after day. It was freezing cold. When I would pass out, they would shake me and begin again. They would leave me tied to the chair with the water freezing on and around me (Hansen 1953, p. 17).

Henri Alleg refused to divulge to his French paratrooper interrogators where he had been hiding, despite a beating and two sessions of electrical torture shortly following his arrest on Wednesday, June 12, 1957, in Algiers. Still strapped by his wrists and ankles to a black plank, one of his interrogators asked him if he "knew how to swim" and the paratroopers picked up the plank and carried Alleg into the kitchen of the apartment in the unfinished building that served as the interrogation center the Algiers suburb of El-Biar (Alleg, Calder, and Sartre 2006, p. 48). They rested the plank on the edge of the sink and two paratroopers held up the other end. One of the troopers near the sink attached a rubber tube to the tap and then wrapped a rag around Alleg's head. His mouth wedged open with a small piece of wood, they told him to move his fingers when he wanted to talk. Then they

> turned on the tap. The rag was soaked rapidly. Water flowed everywhere: in my mouth, in my nose, all over my face. But for a while I could still breathe in some small gulps of air. I tried, by contracting my throat, to take in as little water as possible and to resist suffocation by keeping air in my lungs for as long as I could. But I couldn't hold on for more than a few moments. I had the impression of drowning; and a terrible agony, that of death itself, took possession of me. In spite of myself, all the muscles of my body struggled uselessly to save myself from suffocation. In spite of myself, the fingers of my two hands shook uncontrollably. "That's it! He's going to talk," said a voice (Alleg, Calder, and Sartre 2006, p. 49).

When Alleg again fell silent after he had caught his breath, the torturers yelled, "He's playing games with us! Put his head under again!"

> This time I clenched my fists, forcing the nails into my palm. I had decided I was not going to move my fingers again. It was better to die of asphyxiation right away. I feared to undergo again that terrible moment where I felt myself losing consciousness, while at the same time fighting with all my

power not to die. I did not move my hands, but three times I knew again this insupportable agony. In extremis, they let me get my breath back while I threw up the water. The last time I lost consciousness (Alleg, Calder, and Sartre 2006, pp. 49–50).

Nguyen Cong arrived at LZ English on the southeastern coast of Vietnam in the fall of 1968. Suspected of belonging to the Viet Cong, he was interrogated on the morning of August 21 by Staff Sgt. David Carmon, of the 172nd Military Intelligence detachment. Carmon later admitted to using the "water rag" in his interrogations: "I held the suspect down, placed a cloth over his face and then poured water over the cloth, thus forcing water into his mouth. The suspect, after becoming choked on the water, confessed that he was a VC and stated he was a propaganda man" (Nelson and Turse 2006). In the Cong case, Carmon "poured water on his face from a five gallon can" (Criminal Investigation Division 1971, August 23, p. 10). Carmon and other interrogators also slapped, kicked, and beat Cong (Nelson 2008, pp. 62–63). Carmon later said that "our intentions were never to hurt anyone, we simply wanted the information . . . . This is the reason that we primarily used water. Water poured over a cloth gave a sensation of drowning that generally scared the PW into talking" (Nelson 2008, p. 65). A little before 11:00 am and still under interrogation, Cong went into convulsions and died from a ruptured spleen, as a result of either external trauma or malaria.

Kevin Coffman was arrested in Coldspring, Texas, in the fall of 1979 for drug possession and put in the old San Jacinto County jail.[2] Having been sentenced to six months in the jail for a misdemeanor offense, he was made a "trusty" after a couple of weeks.[3] One morning after about two months in jail, he was taken along with another inmate, Craig Punch, to the new county jail still under construction. Each prisoner was placed in his own cell; and Deputy Sheriff Floyd Baker handcuffed Coffman to a brace in the wall, securing him to the chair he was sitting in. Coffman was left alone for a time before deputies Baker, Carl Lee, and John Glover entered his cell.

Deputy Baker folded a towel along its longer axis twice, wrapped it tightly around Coffman's face, and pulled his head back. Deputy Glover "took a bucket of water and slowly poured it over the towel, asking [Coffman] questions every once in a while" (Coffman 1983, p. 211, lines 1–6). Coffman was being questioned over a theft of money from the property room (as a trusty he had access to it). The deputies divided their labor neatly, with Glover pouring the water, Lee refilling the bucket, and both Glover and Baker asking questions. Coffman struggled so much that even with the handcuffs the deputies had difficulty holding him down, so they tied his feet together with belts and secured his feet to his hands with handcuffs. When asked at trial about why he was struggling, Coffman said he was frightened. He was "afraid of drowning; it was hard to breathe. . . . I was just trying to fight that bucket of water" (Coffman 1983, p. 212, lines 10, 12). "It seemed like it lasted forever, but I guess maybe two hours" (Coffman 1983, p. 213, lines 8–9). Coffman testified that he knew nothing about the money, but told two lies to stop the torture, and eventually the deputies stopped.

About one year later, on a late September evening in 1980, James Hicks was transferred from the Montgomery County jail to the new San Jacinto County jail.[4] Accused of taking San Jacincto County Sheriff James Parker's tractor, Hicks denied knowing anything about it. Parker responded that Hicks would be "begging to tell them where the tractor was" and Hicks was taken to a small holding cell in the back of the jail. After half an hour, Hicks was made to change into white coveralls and then, after about another half hour, he was taken by Deputy Baker to a detox cell. The cell was about ten feet by eight feet with a "little concrete ledge built on the back part of the cell" six or eight inches off the floor, which sloped to a drain in the middle (Hicks 1983, p. 23, lines 21–22). The only piece of furniture in the room was a wooden armchair.

Baker kept asking him where "our" tractor was. Other deputies and a trusty came in and out. At one point, Hicks was blindfolded. His hands were handcuffed behind his back and he was sat in the chair. Deputy Baker gave leg irons to a trusty and instructed him to shackle Hicks's legs to the legs of the chair. Hicks stood up and kicked the trusty. A struggle ensued with deputies Baker and Lee struggling to shackle Hicks to the chair. Lee would hit Hicks with a blackjack everytime Hicks kicked him, at least six times, so that his eyes began to swell nearly shut very quickly.

Once Hicks was subdued and shackled to the chair, the deputies tied a rope around his midsection and Deputy Baker covered Hicks's nose and mouth with a towel. They set the chair backside down on the floor with the legs resting on the concrete ledge and Hicks's head down on the floor, sloping toward the drain. "Then they poured water over my face through the towel and drowned me. . . . I was drowning. . . . I thought I was going to drown" (Hicks 1983, p. 29, lines 20–24; p. 30, line 5). This went on for "probably" five to ten minutes, though "it seemed like a lot longer" (Hicks 1983, p. 30, lines 1–3).

After "stomping" on Hicks's stomach, the deputies set the chair back up, removed the blindfold, and began questioning him again about the location of the tractor. Eventually, Hicks gave them a location, though he knew there was no tractor there. When asked why he told the deputies that, Hicks said, "I didn't want them to do it again. I would have took them anywhere, just about" (Hicks 1983, p. 33, lines 4–5).

According to one of the now infamous "torture memos" from the Justice Department's Office of Legal Counsel (OLC), in waterboarding

the individual is bound securely to an inclined bench, which is approximately four feet by seven feet. The individual's feet are generally elevated. A cloth is placed over the forehead and eyes. Water is then applied to the cloth in a controlled manner. As this is done, the cloth is lowered until it covers both the nose and mouth. Once the cloth is saturated and completely covers the mouth and nose, air now is slightly restricted for 20 to 40 seconds due to the presence of the cloth. This causes an increase in carbon dioxide level in the individual's blood. This increase in the carbon dioxide level stimulates increased effort to breathe. This effort plus the cloth produces the perception of "suffocation and incipient panic," i.e., the perception of drowning. The individual does not breathe any water into his lungs. During those 20 to 40 seconds, water is continuously applied from a height of twelve to twenty-four inches. After this period, the cloth is lifted, and the individual is allowed to breathe unimpeded for three or four full breaths. The sensation of drowning is immediately relieved by the removal of the cloth. The procedure may then be repeated. The water is usually applied from a canteen cup or small watering can with a spout. You have orally informed us that this procedure triggers an automatic physiological sensation of drowning that the individual cannot control even though he may be aware that he is in fact not drowning (Bybee 2002, p. 3–4).

KSM was led by a guard from his cell into another room in March 2003, in a secret prison in Stare Kiejkuty, Poland, one of the CIA's "black sites." The room, its essential contents—a tilted gurney or bench with arm and leg restraints, a couple of cloths, and a pitcher of water—and its purpose were all well known to Mohammed. Over the course of that month, he had spent a lot of time in this room, though he probably couldn't say exactly how much. What happened now was more or less what had happened over 180 times since the beginning of March.

He was strapped to the "special bed," with his head on the downward side of the incline (International Committee of the Red Cross 2007, p. 10). With his head held immobile by one of his captors, one of the cloths was placed over his face, covering his nose and mouth. With a doctor and a psychologist looking on, water was poured onto the cloth. KSM ingested enough water to "distend" his abdomen, and water gushed out when his stomach was pressed. To prevent him from ingesting the water, interrogators cupped their hands around his mouth in order to maintain a continuous "pool" of water. At one point, contractors

Jessen and Mitchell seized an opportunity to pour water into his mouth when he attempted to speak (United States Senate 2014*a*, pp. 112, 114).

Now, suppose I tell you I am writing a history of the Inquisition and its trials and I write the following sentence about what happened to Marina Gonzàlez in 1494 and to Juan de Salas in 1527: "Upon the refusal of Gonzàlez and Salas to provide any information, the inquisitors employed enhanced interrogation techniques." Or what if I'm writing about imperial competition and I write the following sentence about the Amboyna case of 1622: "At a time of increasing tensions with the British and the possibility of a plot to seize the strongest of the Dutch fortifications, the commander ordered enhanced interrogation techniques be used upon John Clarke." Or suppose I'm writing about police interrogation methods in the United States and I use the following to describe what happened in San Jacinto County in 1983: "In a departure from usual police practice, Sheriff Parker used enhanced interrogation techniques."

Do these descriptions ring hollow to you? Do they sound anachronistic? Do they sound euphemistic? Now suppose it is the year 3157. You are writing a history of interrogations and torture and cover the same cases we just considered above. Would you use the word "torture" to describe the Gonzàlez, Salas, Bourdil, the Alabama prisoner, Navarro, Nielsen, Harrison, Alleg, Nguyen, Hicks, and Coffman cases, but use the phrase "enhanced interrogation techniques" to describe the KSM case? Would you claim that pouring water over a cloth into someone's mouth is torture in 1494, 1527, 1622, 1726, 1881, 1942, 1958, 1969, and 1983, but not in 2003? Probably not. But this is what the Bush administration's Justice Department attempted to claim.

The U.S. Department of Justice has not always held this view. Here's the phrase used repeatedly by the U.S. district attorney in the trial of the San Jacinto County sheriff and his deputies in 1983: "water torture" (Coffman 1983, p. 213; Hicks 1983, p. 5). Even the lawyers for the defendants used the term "water torture" to describe the events (Coffman 1983, pp. 225, 226, 230).

The only difference between the techniques used on James Hicks and KSM is two decades. A cloth covers the mouth, water is poured over the cloth to produce a drowning sensation—the act is the same. If the act itself does not change, then it is the same thing, whether we use a euphemism or whether or not the laws written around it have changed. Waterboarding is torture. It was torture when it was used by the Inquisition in 1494 and it was torture when it was used by the CIA in 2003. It meets the everyday "interocular trauma" test.[5]

What about the other enhanced techniques, individually and in combination? Do they constitute torture? How effective is torture in eliciting information and intelligence? The next section takes up the first two questions before turning to the effectiveness question.

ARE "ENHANCED INTERROGATION TECHNIQUES" TORTURE?

When most of us think of the word *torture*, the first thing that comes to mind are images of medieval dungeons with racks and red-hot pokers or perhaps the more modern electrocution. These techniques, however, can cause permanent physical injury or at least permanent physical scars, signs that the body had been tortured at one time. Such evidence is inconvenient in democratic regimes which are more subject to public monitoring and which make explicit claims to protecting human rights. As a result, democracies invented what Darius Rejali in his masterful study has called "clean" or "stealthy" methods of torture (Rejali 2007, p. 8). Such methods are designed to accomplish exactly the same goals as the previous methods (confessions, information, intimidation), but leave no marks.

There may be a further advantage of such techniques for democratic regimes if the methods are ever revealed to the public, as they were under the Bush administration: They do not seem "as bad" as those earlier "medieval" methods, making them more palatable for at least some people. But to say that sleep deprivation or stress positions are not "as bad" as the rack or electrocution or splinters under the fingernails or even waterboarding is both trivially true and beside the point. The fact that Andy is a bigger jerk than Billy does not at all mean that Billy is not a jerk. This is, though, a common "defense" of torturers (Conroy 2000, p. 112).

The Bush interrogation program was full of such so-called torture lite techniques (Bowden 2003, p. 53). The military employed the following measures: yelling, light deprivation, stress of a female interrogator, long (20 hours) interrogations, removal of comfort items (includes religious items), forced grooming, stress positions, isolation, hooding, nudity, and inducing fears—for example, with dogs (Phifer 2002, pp. 1–3). The CIA, however, went much further.

One of the Justice Department memos by Jay Bybee to the CIA approved the following methods: attention grasp, walling, facial hold, insult (facial) slap, cramped confinement (perhaps with insects), stress positions (including wall standing), and sleep deprivation (Bybee 2002, pp. 1–4). A later internal CIA memo defined "standard techniques" as 'isolation, reduced caloric intake, use of loud music and white noise, and diapering (Central Intelligence Agency 2003c, p. 1). The same memo added "abdominal slap" to the roster of "enhanced techniques" (Central Intelligence Agency 2003c, p. 2). A CIA Office of Medical Services memo from December 2004 listed shaving, stripping (nudity), hooding, and isolation as the least intensive of the techniques, with continuous light or darkness, uncomfortably cool environment, and shackling in various positions further up the scale (Central Intelligence Agency 2004b, p. 9).

The secret prison or "black site" in Bucharest, Romania, apparently even had cells specially constructed on "springs to keep the floor shifting and the prisoners constantly destabilized."[6] Then, of course, there were the standard conditions of confinement (white noise/loud sounds and constant light) and "conditioning techniques" (nudity, dietary manipulation, and sleep deprivation) (Central Intelligence Agency 2004a, pp. 5–6). Finally, the procedures during the capture and transport (rendition) of the detainee to the black site, to which many if not all the detainees in the program were subjected, included cutting clothes from the body, stripping, nude photographs, shackling, sensory deprivation in the form of blindfolds, hoods, and earmuffs/headphones, a rectal exam, and, in some cases, forcible sodomy in the form of sedation by suppository (Carle 2011; Marty 2006, p. 24).

In fact, the Bush administration wasn't even original in the name they gave the program. The Nazis beat them to it. The Gestapo euphemism for its interrogational torture program was *verschärfte Vernehmung*—which translates as "sharpened" or "enhanced" interrogations (Sullivan 2007). Some of the techniques called for under *verschärfte Vernehmung* are identical to the EIT program, including food manipulation (reduced food), darkness, and sleep deprivation. Like the CIA, the Nazis also imposed limits on who "qualified" to receive the treatment and which techniques required the presence of a doctor.

As difficult as any of these techniques were when used in isolation, their combined use was more powerful than the sum of their individual parts. Indeed, the Office of Legal Counsel (OLC) in the Department of Justice had become concerned by the end of 2004 about the effects of the techniques used in combination. The OLC requested more information from the CIA, and the latter responded with a December 2004 memo. This memo, along with CIA cables and emails, eyewitness testimony, and other governmental and non-governmental investigations, provides a comprehensive, detailed, and chilling picture of what rendition and torture "lite" looked like.

In fact, it is possible to narrate what the memo called a "prototypical" rendition and interrogation based on this memo, described on the cover as a "generic description of the process," as well as other declassified CIA documents, eyewitness testimony, journalist reports, and government and non-governmental investigations (Central Intelligence Agency 2003c; Central Intelligence Agency 2004a; Central Intelligence Agency 2004b; Marty 2006; International Committee of the Red Cross 2007; United States Senate 2014a; Carle 2011). In the following story, I have made up the names and some small details for narrative purposes, but the description hews closely to CIA guidelines and descriptions.

"A PROTOTYPICAL INTERROGATION"

Khalid al Zushiri was just exiting the jetway into the airport terminal when the two police officers standing by a door asked him his name. When he confirmed it, they opened the door and politely asked him to step in. Nervous and unsure what was going on, he complied and was greeted by four large men dressed from hooded heads to booted toes in black. All he could see were their eyes through little holes in their masks. He noticed one pair was blue just before a blindfold was tied around his head from behind. The ninjas surround him immediately, one patting him down, one handcuffing his wrists, and another shackling his feet together. The cuffs and foot manacles were then chained together.

Scarcely before he knew what was happening and could struggle or even utter a word of protest, he could feel his clothes being cut from his body and hear the pieces being searched and tossed into a bag. By the time his shirt had been cut clear off his body and put into a bag, he recovered enough from his initial shock to protest and resist but he was told, in a menacing and low tone, to stay quiet. Many pairs of hands held him fast. The ninjas pulled his shoulders back so that he stood up straighter and then let him go, stepping away from his body. For a moment no one seemed to move. Then, even through his blindfold, he detected a flash of light. Suddenly the blindfold was removed and, right before the flash went off again, he saw one of the ninjas pointing a camera at him. He was quickly turned in the opposite direction, there was another flash, and the blindfold covered his eyes once again.

If he was surprised by how quickly they had removed his clothes, leaving him standing stark naked and shackled in a roomful of strangers, he was even more shocked by what came next. Latex-covered fingers began to explore his body, starting at the top and working their way down. They rustled through his hair, then over his ears, and his lips, opening and probing in his mouth. The hands then hoisted him onto a table, at first face down, and then turned on his side. They pulled his knees up to his chest. When he felt the latex gloves start to spread his buttocks, he struggled and squirmed, but he couldn't move an inch. He gasped and contracted involuntarily as the latex-covered finger probed his anus. Its removal came as a relief, but only for a moment, for the finger returned, this time inserting something in his rectum and leaving it there.

The hands stood him back up on the floor and removed the handcuffs and foot manacles before pulling something over his legs. It felt small like underwear, rather than pants, but of a strange material. As it was secured around his waist, he realized it was an adult diaper. They then began to dress him; and by the time they were putting his arms in the sleeves, he realized it was a one-piece jumpsuit.

Any hope this would all now stop once he was dressed ended when he was put back in the cuffs and manacles. None of the men had said a word, not to him and not to each other. Someone then placed earphones or earmuffs on his head, adjusting them so that they stayed snug over his ears. Now it was so silent that his own breathing sounded loud. A long and loose hood dropped over his head, resting on his shoulders.

The hands then half-carried, half-walked him across the room to a van parked right next to the door. He could tell it was a van because they laid him down roughly on the floor and the ninjas all got in with him. The van drove for only a minute or two before stopping. The door opened and the hands dragged him out. They again half-carried, half-walked him to some steps. He noticed that he had started to feel a little woozy and had trouble moving his feet properly for the steps. The hands didn't seem to notice, though, and he was propelled upward for a couple of seconds. One of the hands pushed his head down and he stepped onto a new surface. As they pulled and pushed him along, he banged into the sides and realized they were plush armrests. He was on an airplane, a luxury one. Panic again started to rise in his throat, but it competed with sleepiness now and didn't get very far. He was set down on the floor, and his cuffs and manacles were chained to the seat legs on the floor of the plane. Someone pulled his hood back for a moment and then they let him go. There was movement back and forth around him for a minute or two before the floor started rumbling and vibrating as the plane start to taxi. The last thing he felt before he drifted into unconsciousness was the floor pressing on him as the plane ascended steeply into the air.

Barely 20 minutes had passed since he stepped into the room.

He had vague memories of take-offs and landings, people bustling around him, and someone lifting his hood every once and awhile, but he didn't fully come to until he found himself bouncing around in the back of small van. He asked where they were taking him, why they had kidnapped him. When no one answered, he raised his voice, but was told to keep quiet. The door to the vehicle opened and he felt very cold air before being hustled inside a building. They dragged him along, turning once or twice, before standing him up against a wall. He heard a door close behind him.

Someone removed the hood but he remained blindfolded. Again he tried to protest and again he was told to keep quiet. As several large, strong men held him tight, including his head, another began cutting the hair off his head, adjusting the blindfold when necessary. When they had cut everything off close to his scalp, they switched to an electric razor and shaved him bald before shaving off his sparse beard. Then they removed his manacles, blindfold, diaper, and jumpsuit, and took several photographs of him front and back.

After he had been put back in the diaper and manacled sitting down in a chair, a new masked man came into the room. He told Khalid he was going to give him a physical examination and started asking Khalid questions about his health while he probed and prodded. Did he have any allergies? Any history of heart problems? Khalid lurched back and forth between trying to answer these questions and begging the "doctor" to find out why he had been kidnapped as well as asking, What is going on? The doctor said only that Khalid "should start cooperating" and that the sooner he cooperated, the better off he'd be, while listening to his heartbeat with a stethoscope.

Following the medical questions, the doctor began asking him other questions, including whether anyone in his family had a mental illness. Despite his terror, Khalid was indignant enough to retort that the only crazy people he knew were standing around in masks. Immediately upon uttering these words, one of the men holding him slapped him hard across the face. Khalid was quiet except for answering the doctor after that. When the doctor was finished, they put the blindfold and hood back on him, stood him up, and led him along a short hallway to another room. The manacles made it difficult to keep up with the guards. Inside the room they adjusted his chains in order to shackle him to a chair. The room was cold and he requested clothes. They ignored him. When they removed the hood and blindfold, he blinked and squinted, for the room was all white and very brightly lit. The only other object in the room beside the chair was a bucket and a horizontal bar over his head near the ceiling. One of the masked ninjas told him they'd be back soon to question him and that Khalid would be given one chance to cooperate with them. Suddenly, as he shut the door, screaming-type rock music began blasting from a speaker near the ceiling.

True to their word, they came back sometime later; exactly how long he couldn't say. They removed his diaper and walked him naked, hooded, and manacled, back down the hallway to the first room, where he was again chained to the chair. When they removed the hood, there was an American sitting on a chair across from him, the two chairs centered in the small room. The American showed him some pictures of young men and asked Khalid to identify them. When Khalid said that he couldn't, that he didn't know any of them, the American put the pictures down and, saying this was Khalid's "last chance," asked for the email address of a Walid bin al-Shibawi. Sweating heavily, Khalid claimed he'd never heard of al-Shibawi and had no idea what his email address was. He tried to continue, protesting his innocence, protesting that they had the wrong man, but his words were cut short by a slap to his stomach from one of the masked guards. The American told Khalid that they would do what it took to get information from him, no one knew where he was, and that things were about to get a lot harder for him. Then he rose from his chair and left the room without another word. The ninjas unchained him from the chair, refastened his manacles, put his hood on, and returned him to his cell.

This time his handcuffs were chained to the bar near the ceiling, with the chain adjusted so his arms were fully extended up toward the ceiling. If he slumped, his wrists pulled painfully against the cuffs. His foot manacles were chained to the floor. The screaming music now alternated with a loud hissing sound, like steam escaping from a radiator. Sometimes it sounded more like crackling. He was still nude, save for the diaper, and the room was cold. To his surprise, when they removed the hood and blindfold, it was still pitch dark. They had turned the lights off. At least, he thought, he had some measure of privacy now and might even be able eventually to sleep, despite the painful pressure on his arms. A splash of cold water in his face disabused him of that illusion. Every time he would start to fall asleep, one of the guards would slap him or spray water in his face.

They came for him about a day later, though he couldn't tell whether it was day or night. After he was led into another room, he felt a towel go around his neck and panicked for a moment, thinking they meant to strangle him. But the towel was held tight only against the back of his neck, not his throat, and the hood was removed.

A new American stood in front of him now, holding the ends of the towel. He explained to Khalid that he was alone with them and no one knew where he was. His future depended completely on whether and how he cooperated with them. If he cooperated, his situation would improve immediately. If it didn't, then it would get worse—a lot worse. Khalid again tried to protest that they had the wrong man, but was slapped hard by the American before he could finish his sentence.

Begging and protesting only earned him more slaps, in the face and on the stomach. Then suddenly the man holding the towel spun him around once and slammed Khalid into the wall. The towel prevented his head from bearing the full force of the blow. Khalid was surprised at the sound it made, and he realized after several more throws against the wall that it was made of plywood and covered the masonry wall behind it. He still didn't tell them what they wanted to hear, and the slaps and throws against the wall continued. Other times they would make him stand leaning against a wall, holding himself up by his fingertips or using only his forehead, with his hands cuffed behind his back and his legs spread wide apart. When he dropped his arms or tried to reposition himself, the guards slapped him and put him back against the wall until he finally collapsed.

This cycle of hanging from a chain in his cell, sometimes in the dark, sometimes under bright lights, followed by the wall slamming, slapping, and standing against the wall, went on for days, perhaps weeks. He lost track of time. They fed him only a nutrition drink and he was always naked, cold, hungry, and filthy, for he hadn't bathed in weeks. He was forced to clean himself when the diaper was removed using only a bucket of water and his hand.

One day, when the hood was pulled off in the interrogation room, he noticed what looked like a simple coffin on the floor. As his eyes widened, the interrogator told him the only way he'd be leaving the prison was in that box. Following another round of fruitless questioning, the guards forced him into the box and closed the lid. Khalid now noticed the holes in the box for breathing, but he couldn't look out of them. The guards had draped a cloth over them and it quickly became very hot and stuffy. He screamed and pushed against the box but couldn't get out. Buffeted by the constant loud music, he lost track of time, eventually soiling himself.

At some point, the box opened and he was roughly dragged out and held firmly by the guards in front of the interrogator. More questions. More responses deemed unacceptable. More slaps and walling. Then they turned him around and he saw a much smaller box, less than three feet on a side. His struggles went nowhere as they dragged him to the little box. The ninjas stuffed Khalid into the small box, his knees jammed tightly against his chest in a fetal position, and locked the lid. It was dark, hot, and stuffy and once more the harsh music blared. This lasted for several hours before he was pulled out and questioned again.

He could no longer keep track of the sequence; but various combinations of standing for hours, hanging from the handcuffs, being splashed with water, slapping, wall-slamming, and being stuffed in the boxes went on for days. A few days after his first experience with the boxes, they once more brought him to the interrogation room. When they removed his hood, he saw something new: a portable bed like you see in a hospital, but with leather straps on the sides. On a table next to the gurney was a small towel and a dozen bottles of spring water. He wasn't sure what it all meant and at first he didn't even struggle as they led him to the gurney. As they began to tie him to it, though, he tried to protest and wiggle out, to no avail. The bed was tilted with his head on the down side. One of the interrogators gripped Khalid's head so that he couldn't twist it to the side. He looked up and saw the other interrogator's face as a cloth was placed over his mouth and nose. He screamed as the interrogator began soaking the cloth with water.

This is torture "lite."

It would be pedantic in the extreme to document here how these methods have their origins in traditional tortures and have traditionally and legally been considered torture. Others have already established this very well (Rejali 2007, McCoy 2006, Otterman 2007, Conroy 2000, Wallach 2006, Department of Justice 2009, pp. 251–254, 260–261; Ohlin 2010, Parry 2010, Scharf 2010, Haas 2009, Schwarz and Huq 2013, pp. 65–82). Even our own military considered them torture less than a decade before 9/11. A U.S. Army Field Manual classified several of these techniques ("infliction of pain through . . . bondage," "forcing an individual to stand, sit, or kneel in abnormal positions for prolonged periods of time," "any form of beating") as "physical torture" and others ("food" and "sleep deprivation") as "mental torture" and expressly forbid their use, arguing that "the use of force is a poor technique, as it yields unreliable results, may damage subsequent collection efforts, and can induce the source to say whatever he thinks the interrogator wants to hear" (Department of the Army 1992, pp. 1–8).

Americans are certainly skeptical of claims that the techniques do not constitute torture. Following the release of the Senate Intelligence Committee's report on the CIA interrogation program in December 2014, Huffington Post/YouGov asked Americans whether it is acceptable or unacceptable for the United States to use some of the CIA's interrogation methods. Americans responded as shown in Table 2.1.[7] Rectal feeding, by which pureed food is forced up a detainee's anus, received the least support, followed by the confinement box, threatening a detainee or his family, waterboarding, nudity, and walling. Only sleep deprivation was deemed acceptable by an absolute majority, with slapping and punching considered acceptable by a plurality.

A CBS poll at the same time asked whether respondents consider four techniques to be torture or not.[8] Seven in ten viewed threatening family members (73%), sleep deprivation (70%), and waterboarding (69%) to be torture. Another 57% considered ice water baths to be torture. In short, like waterboarding, the other EITs pass the interocular trauma test.

"Enhanced interrogation techniques" is a euphemism for interrogational torture.

The "tough" statements of Bush administration and CIA officials about going to the "dark side" and the "gloves coming off" suggest that what they have really objected to was the possibility of legal proceedings, not the fact of torture itself. Given their political and personal responsibility to prevent another attack after

Table 2.1. DECEMBER 2014 HUFFINGTON POST/YOUGOV SURVEY
ON TORTURE TECHNIQUES

Technique	Acceptable	Unacceptable	Not Sure
Slapping/punching	44	35	21
Walling	40	41	19
Nudity	37	44	19
Sleep deprivation	55	30	16
Waterboarding	35	45	20
Threatening detainee's family	30	55	15
Threatening detainee with violence	31	51	18
Confinement box for days	28	52	20
Rectal feeding	11	73	16

9/11, an attack they thought imminent, one can sympathize with their dilemma. (Try to imagine for a moment that it was *your* job to keep America safe while the smoke still rose from lower Manhattan.) Like many of their predecessors (including many Democrats by the way), they believed (and no doubt still believe) that interrogational torture works. If everyone—including Bush administration officials—know that the EIT program was torture, it is all the more important that the program was effective in gathering otherwise unobtainable information that saved innocent lives.

Still, it does not follow from the fact that interrogational torture's effectiveness is in the political interest of its proponents that interrogational torture was *not* effective. We take up the question of effectiveness next.

A FRAGILE AND DANGEROUS THING

Gasping for breath, Ammar has just been waterboarded but has yet to give up any information on the Saudi group to Daniel, a CIA interrogator. Daniel tells him, "It's cool that you're strong. I respect it, I do. But in the end everybody breaks, bro. It's biology" (Boal 2011, p. 6). After some humiliation, time in a confinement box, deception, and the temptation of good solid food, Ammar does indeed "break" and give up some names which will eventually help lead to the location of bin Laden. This may be a scene from the Hollywood movie *Zero Dark Thirty*, but it captures the widely held assumption that everyone breaks under torture. Just contemplating a routine trip to the dentist makes the claim that torture works seem reasonable.

Does it? Does torture work? The Roman jurist Ulpian said that torture "is a weak and dangerous thing that may fail the truth."[9]

This commonplace idea that torture eventually works on everyone, the gut feeling that there is only so much any human can withstand, is an instance of what we might call the dangerous seduction of intuition. It is seductive because it seems so self-evidently obvious. It is dangerous because it can nevertheless be wrong. After all, Senator John McCain gave up no useful information to his North Vietnamese captors; he just provided the names of the Green Bay Packers offensive line as fellow members of his squadron and the names of cities that had already been bombed as supposed future targets (Salter and McCain 1999, p. 194).

Not that it is surprising that we are seduced by it. There are plenty of other examples of such successful seductions. It seems pretty reasonable (and did to humans for thousands and thousands of years before Galileo and Copernicus) that the sun revolves around the earth. It does not. It seems reasonable that the earth is flat, but it is a sphere. It seems obvious that the various features of humans and other animals must have been designed, yet logical reasoning and overwhelming empirical evidence demonstrates that evolution by natural selection and random mutation accounts for what we see. It seems reasonable that measuring something cannot change the nature of the thing you are measuring, yet quantum mechanics tells us that this is not true at the subatomic level. These examples point to the fact that intuition can sometimes lead us astray. Interrogational torture is another one of those instances, as the Gonzàlez, Salas, Bourdil, and other cases underscore.

These cases (and there are others) challenge our intuition that torture *always* works. Still, one case (or even a few cases) cannot tell us very much about how it works in general. This is an empirical question and really requires an empirical answer—that is, an answer based on actual evidence or data. Empirical evidence comes in two forms: observational data we would get from the real world of interrogations and experimental data we would get from the artificial world of running an experiment.

In the latter, we would start with the "null" or baseline hypothesis that torture is not effective in eliciting information. We would then see whether we could, through lots of experiments, amass evidence showing that torture did generate information. If we have enough, that would give us enough confidence to reject the "ineffective" hypothesis. Those experiments would involve randomly assigning people to groups with different information levels and types and degrees of torture.

Now, if you felt like you were reading a page from Nazi doctor Joseph Mengele's diary when you read this description of an experiment, then you understand the obvious ethical problem ruling out an experimental approach to the problem. So experimental data are out. What about observational data? It comes in two forms: the Full Monty or dribs and drabs. Each has its problems.

In the Full Monty version, an analyst would sit down in front of a CIA computer and open up a database of all CIA interrogations. This file would include everything the CIA knows about the detainees, including their background, the information they provided, whether or not they were tortured and, if so, which techniques, and so on. Each row represents the interrogation of a detainee; and all the other information, such as the amount of information they provided or the severity of the torture employed, is given in the columns.

Ethical considerations forbid this type of research as well, as the CIA itself recognized in its response to the Senate Intelligence Committee report. Explaining why no assessment of effectiveness was ever completed, it noted, among other factors, that "Federal policy on the protection of human subjects" would have "encumbered" a "systematic study over time of the effectiveness of the techniques" (Central Intelligence Agency 2014, p. 48). In other words, it would be unethical for the CIA (or anyone else) to figure out whether what the CIA did was effective or not!

But let's press on. The nice thing about the Full Monty version is that everything that can be known is right there. If you've ever seen a spreadsheet, it's easy to imagine what that data file might look like.

The first column would be filled with the names of the detainees, with the succeeding columns containing the data on the variables for each detainee. So the CIA might have some scale for each of the variables in the columns after the detainee's name, let's say 0 to 100, with 0 representing no information or information of no value and 100 representing lots of information or extremely high-quality information. Similarly, the CIA might have some scale for the severity of the torture employed, from no torture, 0, to the maximum, perhaps 100.[10] There might be a variable for other interrogation methods used by the FBI and military interrogators.

One might think that the analyst could then just perform some pretty simple statistical tests to compare using torture against other methods and to look for the effects of torture on information. Do the numbers in the information columns tend to go up as the numbers in the torture columns go up (supporting the pro-torture position)? Or do they go down (supporting the anti-torture position)? Or is there no real tendency at all (again supporting the anti-torture position)?[11] If there is a tendency to go up, how strong does this tendency have to be to say torture works? We would have to decide this (ahead of time!), but this would seem to be the right way to go about answering the question.

Not so fast. The not-so-nice thing about even the Full Monty version is that everything that *can* be known is not everything that *needs* to be known. Leaving secrecy considerations aside, any such database would suffer from methodological, empirical, and epistemological problems.

Methodologically, the relationship between torture and information is not as straightforward as it might seem. The type and severity of torture employed by the interrogator was not independent of the information acquired and believed to be possessed by the detainee. In fact, the more likely a detainee was to have information, the more likely he was to get tortured. In other words, torture is endogenous to information, biasing any attempts to infer the effectiveness of torture.[12]

The empirical problem concerns the ratio of the complexity of the cases to the number of cases. The individual interrogation cases (one detainee, one set of interrogations) are likely to be very different from each other, if not unique. They will differ along many dimensions: each detainee's position in the enemy organization, what they know, how fresh that information is, their level of training, their cultural background, their idiosyncratic strength of will and pain thresholds, the circumstances of their arrest, the techniques employed and how they were employed (timing, sequence, severity, number of repetitions), the quantity of information divulged, if any (however you would measure that), and the quality of any information divulged (ditto). Each one of these factors would be an additional column in the spreadsheet.

All this, by the way, assumes no cases of mistaken identity, something we know does happen (more on this later). Against this complexity is the number of interrogations in which some coercive methods were used. Although there have been thousands of interrogations in Iraq, Afghanistan, Guantanamo Bay, and various black sites, it would appear that the number of interrogations employing torture is small (in absolute as well as relative terms) even if we include the renditioning and conditioning techniques (as we should). This presents a real problem for teasing out whether torture works: Lots of variables and few cases will create the problem of indeterminacy. You just cannot draw any conclusions from the data.

Here's a more prosaic example of this problem: home brewing. When you brew beer at home, as I do, a thousand things can screw up your beer or at least make it come out differently than you thought (and hoped): different combinations of malt extract and hops; bad extract or stale hops; bad yeast pack; sluggish initial yeast production; contamination of the wort during cooling; sanitization problems with the fermenters, spoons, bottles, kegs, etc.; poor temperature control; and lots more. So if you end up with skunky beer, it can be pretty hard to figure out what happened and make the appropriate changes. This is especially true if you only brew a couple times a year, as I do.

The same is true with interrogations. There just are not enough cases of coercive interrogations (one would hope, since the claim was to use them in only extreme cases) to draw firm conclusions about whether they worked or not. In truth, the only way to avoid the indeterminacy problem is to torture more. Since the complicating factors are not going to change, the only way to counteract their effect is to increase the number of cases in which torture is used, so that there are more cases (row entries) with each particular combination of factors (values in the columns). This takes us back into Mengele territory. Moreover, it bears emphasizing that this would only make doing the analysis *possible*; whether or not that analysis would actually end up showing that interrogational torture works would still be up for grabs.

The problem is, however, even worse than this. Even if this problem were somehow circumvented, there would still be a fundamental epistemological problem—and always will be. Those cool fMRI pictures of the brain from notwithstanding, we can never know what is in another person's head. This is just as true for the CIA. Indeed, this fact is what make interrogation necessary in the first place. But it results in two problems, one if we observe information and one if we do not.

Suppose we observe that a detainee has provided useful information. The analyst is sitting at that computer in CIA headquarters and sees that in case 16, a detainee revealed the location of a safe house, but nothing else after repeated waterboarding. Assume for simplicity that quality is not a problem; it was truly valuable information (the house was still active and previously unknown to us). How would we know whether to put this down as a case of "a little information," "some information," or "full information," let alone a particular number between 0 and 100? The fact is, we cannot know. It may be that this was all the detainee knew, but it may also be the case that it was a small fraction of what he knew.[13]

Now suppose we observe that a different detainee has failed to provide useful information. The analyst has moved on down to case number 17 in the CIA data file. In this case, the detainee refused to provide anything of value even after waterboarding. What can we infer from this? The detainee might be hiding information, but it might be the case that he truly does not know anything of value; our lack of access to a detainee's mind means that the detainee can never prove what he does not know. This is just as true of the completely innocent as it is of the detainee who has provided everything of value he knows, but is asked to provide more. Thus, the two problems of observing information and observing no information are actually equivalent. If we expect the detainee to provide some information X, and he provides some other information Y, where Y can be anything from false information to "I don't know," then we can never know whether the absence of X is due to deception or ignorance.

The upshot is that these data cannot tell us whether torture works as claimed because we will never know whether the detainee knew more than was revealed, and this will be true of any CIA dataset, past, present, and future. There will never be a column in that CIA file called "Total information known by the detainee." These fundamental and irresolvable ethical, methodological, empirical, and epistemological problems mean that even the Full Monty would not solve the problem.

So, with the Full Monty not an option either, we are left with what evidence of torture's effectiveness has emerged in dribs and drabs over the centuries of the practice, from the Ancient Greeks to more recent torture by France, the United States, the United Kingdom, and Israel. It does not add up to anything very clear. A review of cases from the early history of juridical and ecclesiastical interrogational torture (Pennington 2008, Lea and Peters 1973, Peters 1999, Langbein

2006) to the use of "stealthy" torture in the modern world, including democracies (Pfiffner 2014, Rejali 2007), provides plenty of examples of false confessions and fabricated information, obstinate resistance to torture, and far fewer cases of torture producing information. Nevertheless, the "data" emerging in dribs and drabs from the bleak history of interrogational torture are "too fragmentary, dirty, and wrapped in national mythology, accusation, and rumor to allow for precise, validated causal claims" (Rejali 2007, pp. 7, 566). In other words, the information we have available about torture's effectiveness in generating information falls far short of the normal social scientific standard required to draw firm conclusions one way or another.

Not even the Senate Intelligence Committee's comprehensive (over 6,700 pages and over 38,000 footnotes relying on CIA cables, emails, interviews, and other documents) report—discussed in the Postscript—of the CIA program has been able to convince defenders of the program (United States Senate 2014a). The Republican minority on the committee released its own report; and former members of the Bush administration, including President Bush himself, came forward to vigorously defend the program (United States Senate 2014b). The CIA too defended itself in a response originally written back in June 2013, but released with the committee's summary and findings in December 2014 (Central Intelligence Agency 2014).

Public opinion mirrors this disagreement and ambivalence, as captured in four surveys taken shortly after the release of the report.[14] The question wording differs slightly across the four polls, asking whether the CIA methods resulted in "mostly reliable" information, "produced valuable information," "provided intelligence," and the like. I put the poll results together in Table 2.2 (collapsing "often" and "sometimes" into Reliable and "rarely" and "never" into Unreliable for the CBS News survey). There is as little consensus among the broader public as there is among politicians. A little more than half think that the methods generate reliable information in the first three surveys, with the other half saying that they are unreliable or are not sure. The Huffington Post/YouGov survey finds a plurality not sure, but essentially a three-way tie. Certainly the evidence available has failed to convince torture proponents. Bagaric and Clarke, in their defense of interrogational torture, dismiss the evidence as "a distracting

Table 2.2. SUMMARY OF SURVEYS ON INFORMATION FROM TORTURE

Survey	Reliable	Unreliable	Not Sure/No Answer
ABC/Washington Post	53	31	16
CBS News	57	32	11
Pew Research Center	56	28	16
Huffington Post/YouGov	32	31	37

and superficial numbers game" in which torture proponents and opponents hurl competing anecdotes at one another (Bagaric and Clarke 2007, p. 58).

*   *   *

The argument thus far has shown that

1. EITs are torture and the effectiveness of interrogational torture is an open question. (Chapter 2)

The next step in the argument is to examine how closely the Bush program approximates the ideal model of interrogational torture and identify the benchmarks defining success of the pragmatic model.

Benchmarking Interrogational Torture

The goal of interrogation is...the collection of intelligence in a predictable, reliable, and sustainable manner.
—CIA MEMO ON THE INTERROGATION PROGRAM, DECEMBER 2004

CIA DETENTION AND INTERROGATION PROGRAM

Mission
The Detention and Interrogation Program leads, executes, and enables end-to-end integration of terrorist capture, detention, and interrogation operations worldwide, leveraging synergistically its core competencies and SERE best practices in order to move the needle on national security.

Vision
Delivering impactful, efficient, effective, and agile terrorist capture, detention, and interrogation operations to take the United States to the next level in the war on terror.

Core Values
Innovation
Agility
Secrecy

Supporting Values
Dedication
Respect for the law

This is Swiftian and, admittedly, a *little* over the top on the business-managementese, but my threefold purpose in this chapter is serious.[1] First, one of the main purposes of this book is to assess the effectiveness of interrogational torture as a government *program*, as public policy (Pfiffner 2010). There is a tendency to think about the effectiveness of interrogational torture in imagined one-off scenarios, usually the ticking time bomb case. Given this perspective, it is good enough if it works even rarely. Perhaps this is acceptable in philosophical discussions of whether torture can ever be justified and, if so, under what circumstances. But we would not want to evaluate a government program this way. It is certainly not how a conservative skeptical of government power and intrusion would want to evaluate a government program.

Imagine, for example, defending the Consumer Financial Protection Bureau based on one successful case. Once torture becomes part of a detention and interrogation program, it will apply to many cases and it should be assessed like any other government program. So while the mission and vision statements above are fictitious, there really were goals and procedures and guidelines, and these must be examined to understand and evaluate the Bush interrogational torture regime as a government program.

Second, examining the program's design and planned implementation will help inform building the game theoretic models in the next two chapters. Declassified CIA documents make clear, and even the most strident critics of the program should acknowledge, that the CIA sought to create training programs, guidelines, and other procedures to control and monitor the program in order to keep it within the law, as interpreted by the Justice Department memos. Indeed, one of those declassified documents, the May 2004 CIA Office of Inspector General (OIG) report, was the end result of the program's *own* request that an incident in which interrogation rules were violated be investigated by the OIG.

In other words, it is important to recognize and take account of these limits and controls so that we do not construct a strawman model of interrogational torture, a ridiculous model that is then easy to pick apart. We might do this, for example, by assuming all interrogators are sadistic and use as much torture as often as possible. Or we might assume that detainees never have any information to provide, or always lie if they do have information. We must avoid mischaracterizing the program for two reasons. First and foremost, we want to remain intellectually honest and create an accurate model. Second, it is also necessary to prevent torture proponents from dismissing the model out of hand as an unfair representation of both their views and the actual program.

Finally, reviewing the purpose and goals of the program is necessary to identify—returning now to management jargon—the "benchmarks" for the program's success. These are indicators of interrogational torture's success in the eyes of the *pro*-ponents, not *op*-ponents. These goals, or predictions, of what the program was supposed to do are the standards against which we will compare the results of the analytical models in the chapters that follow.

For those viscerally opposed to torture, this chapter will read more than a little creepily.[2] Moreover, my presentation may seem to sanitize the use of torture in the Bush administration by focusing mostly on the CIA, ignoring torture at Abu Ghraib for example, and by giving the CIA the benefit of the doubt on the limits and controls in the program. And it is true that I cede much to proponents. I do so for a very important reason: to let them make the best possible case. If even this case fails to work as proponents claim, interrogational torture has failed.[3]

THE IDEAL MODEL

The Bush interrogational torture program is a real-world application or implementation of what we might call the ideal or normative model of interrogational torture. Such a model is an abstract, theoretical, and idealized sketch of how interrogational torture *should* work. These ideal models generally appear as part of an argument justifying the practice and, as part of that justification, aim to show how torture would be limited in scope, monitored and supervised, and the like. Thus, it may be helpful to begin by examining some of these more general arguments for interrogational torture, not in order to engage their arguments justifying the practice, but rather as a way of identifying some of the normative principles and ideas associated with limiting and controlling torture for interrogations.

It will also be helpful for another, more important reason. With the normative model in hand, we can see how close the Bush program comes to the idealized model. The "distance" between them may allow us to not only assess the Bush pragmatic implementation in light of the abstract ideal, but also examine the ideal model using the Bush application as a test case.

In other words, if that distance between ideal theory and Bush application is not too great, then the Bush program is a close approximation of that ideal model. This may please the architects of the CIA program. More importantly for our purposes, such a close approximation means that a test of the Bush model over the remainder of the book is also a test of the larger, more general claims of the ideal model. If the test supports the Bush model, it simultaneously supports the idealized model; if the test undermines the Bush model, the general idealized model also suffers. A close approximation between the two thus allows us to assess not just the Bush interrogational torture program, but also interrogational torture generally.

Proposals from Philosophy and Law

Philosophers love thought experiments, and thinking about the conditions under which torture might be justified is a popular one. The founder of utilitarianism, Jeremy Bentham, for example, responded to Beccaria's critique of torture in the late 1770s by considering what we now call the "ticking time bomb" scenario.[4] Bagaric and Clarke (2007) advance the modern-day version of the Benthamite argument.[5] As part of their defense of torture, they outline the necessary conditions for torture as well as limits on it (Bagaric and Clarke 2007, pp. 35–38). In their view, torture is acceptable:

1. only when the "right to life is imperiled"; as the number of lives threatened goes up, so too does the permissibility of torture,
2. only when used as a last resort, when no other options are available,
3. only when the threat is immediate,
4. only if the minimum degree of pain necessary to elicit information is applied, and
5. only when the probability is high that the person being tortured possesses the necessary knowledge.

Bagaric and Clarke put these variables into a formula. If the combined values exceed the threshold defined by the formula, torture is warranted. Once above the threshold, higher values permit more severe forms of torture. Still, the person being tortured must never be killed and even methods which would result in long-term injury are to be avoided, so there are practical limits on what can be done. These limits should be kept secret by the way, so that detainees don't have "an incentive to hold out" (Bagaric and Clarke 2007, p. 36).[6]

Utilitarian philosophers are often joined by legal scholars thinking about torture; and, in fact, it is in their writings that we see some of the most detailed proposals for rules and limitations guiding its implementation. Parry (2004, p. 159), for example, similarly argues that unless there is "firm suspicion" that the person to be tortured "has specific knowledge about specific imminent attacks, coercive interrogation should not be an option." A high probability of the requisite knowledge is not enough, however. The threat must be "extreme" as well: "[C]oercion must be a last resort, not a routine practice, even with people as little deserving of our sympathy and as likely to have specific knowledge as the leaders of al-Qaeda" (Parry 2004, p. 159).

Civil rights lawyer and law professor Alan Dershowitz is probably the most prominent advocate of institutionalizing the torture that he says will occur whether we want it or not.[7] He is (in)famous for proposing a "torture warrant" which would provide for some sort of review and check on the police or security services (Dershowitz 2002, pp. 158ff). A warrant would promote "accountability, record-keeping, standards, and limitations" (Dershowitz 2003, p. 277). It would also, "if properly enforced," "probably reduce the frequency, severity, and duration of torture" (Dershowitz 2003, p. 281). The result would be "judicially monitored physical measures designed to cause excruciating pain without leaving any lasting damage" (Dershowitz 2002, p. 159). How can we generate this "excruciating pain"? After contrasting our acceptance of lethal injection with our resistance to torture, and remarking that "[i]n our modern age death is underrated, while pain is overrated," he suggests a "sterilized needle ... shoved under the fingernails" (Dershowitz 2002, pp. 149, 148).

Richard Posner, a respected judge and legal scholar in the utilitarian tradition, argues that "[t]orture must be allowed" in an "extreme case" such as when tens or hundreds of thousands of lives are at risk (Posner 2004, p. 293). Whereas Dershowitz is comfortable with torture's efficacy, Posner admits it may be problematic. As a result, "the less certain is the need for or the expected efficacy of torture, the more lives have to be at risk to justify it under the balancing, or cost–benefit, or sliding-scale approach" (Posner 2004, p. 293).[8] Posner is skeptical of Dershowitz's torture warrant, however, saying that it wouldn't serve as much of a check anyway and inevitably officials would attempt to push the "outer bounds of the rules" (Posner 2004, p. 293).[9]

Another Posner legal scholar, writing with Adrian Vermeule, presents a much more elaborate framework in which "a warrant requirement [is] only one piece of a much larger regulatory structure" (Posner and Vermeule 2006, p. 699). They argue that coercive interrogation "should be made legal, albeit subject to numerous legal protections" (Posner and Vermeule 2006, p. 674). Their legal regime borrows from existing rules on "the regulation of the use of deadly force" by police and "emphasizes three elements: (1) rules that state what is permitted and what is not permitted, (2) immunity for officials who obey the rules and punishment for those who violate the rules, and (3) ex ante regulations such as warrants" (Posner and Vermeule 2006, pp. 700, 675). Important elements of their plan include (Posner and Vermeule 2006, pp. 701–703):

- Bagaric and Clarke-like thresholds for using torture requiring "reasonable certainty that an individual possesses information that could prevent an imminent crime that will kill at least n people, where n

is some number that reflects the balance of gains and losses from coercive interrogation."

- Limits or restrictions on what techniques may be employed. "[E]xcessive" methods causing "too much harm relative to the benefits" would be prohibited, whereas "moderate" methods such as "sleep deprivation, disorientation" and other methods used by the CIA on Al Qaeda are "a good starting point."
- Limits or restrictions on the quantity or intensity of torture, "to the minimal amount of coercion that is necessary."
- Limits or restrictions on who can be tortured via rules that would "limit the use of coercive interrogation to members of terrorist groups known to use violent methods against U.S. civilians." If this is deemed too narrow, it might be expanded to include kidnappers for example.
- Warrants issued by a "magistrate or judge" "only when coercive interrogation will likely yield information that will prevent a crime that will kill *n* people."
- "Immunities and punishments:" Violation of the rules regulating interrogational torture should be sanctioned.
- "Training and expertise:" An interrogational torture program requires training to minimize errors, as is the case with deadly force and firearms training.
- Oversight of "instances of coercive interrogation . . . by special commissions of experts or self-appointed public watchdogs."

Following Dershowitz, Posner and Vermeule advocate "legality and openness," via "explicit rules" which "can be easily evaluated" and amended if there are problems (Posner and Vermeule 2006, p. 703). In short, their

strategy involves a complex regulatory regime of rules-with-exceptions, involving a prohibition on official infliction of serious harms, permission to inflict such harms in tightly cabined circumstances, an immunity regime that requires officials to follow the rules in good faith but protects them if they do so, and review procedures to reduce error and enhance transparency. In this baseline regime, the circumstances in which serious harms may be inflicted are specified ex ante, rather than being remitted solely to the discretionary mercy of juries, judges, and the executive after the fact (Posner and Vermeule 2006, p. 707).

Conservative attorney and commentator Andrew McCarthy agrees that "[t]he task, then, is to create controlled, highly regulated, and responsibly accountable conditions" for torture, which would be "permitted only under circumstances of immediate peril" and conducted "under stricture and with scrupulous judicial monitoring" (McCarthy 2006, pp. 108, 110, 109). These regulations and conditions include Dershowitz's torture warrants, "issued only on a showing of reasonable grounds for believing that a catastrophe was impending, that the person to be subjected to torture had information about this event" (McCarthy 2006, pp. 108–109).

Another conservative commentator, Charles Krauthammer, also references the ticking time bomb scenario and argues that "[g]iven the gravity of the decision, if we indeed cross the Rubicon—as we must—we need rules" (Krauthammer 2004, p. 312). Despite recognizing that there will be no reciprocity from Al Qaeda, Krauthammer advocates a complete ban on torture in the military for "reasons of military discipline and military honor" (Krauthammer 2004, p. 313). Krauthammer would permit torture outside the military (presumably for the CIA) in two circumstances: the ticking bomb scenario and the case of a "slower-fuse high-level terrorist" (Krauthammer 2004, p. 313). Torture in each case would be governed by a different set of rules.

In the case of the ticking time bomb, "[n]othing rationally related to getting accurate information is ruled out" (presumably even extreme pain). In the slow-fuse case, the "level of inhumanity of the measures used . . . would be proportional to the need and value of the information. Interrogators would be constrained to use the least inhumane treatment necessary relative to the magnitude and imminence of the evil being prevented and the importance of the knowledge being obtained" (Krauthammer 2004, p. 313).[10]

Only "highly specialized agents who are experts and experienced in interrogation, and who are known not to abuse it," may torture. They would be required to obtain written permission from either cabinet-level political authorities or a "quasi-judicial body modeled on the FISA court system" (Krauthammer 2004, p. 313). If even that would take too long for a bomb ticking down, then the authorities would still need to secure "ex post facto authorization within, say, 24 hours of their interrogation" to ensure review of their actions (Krauthammer 2004, p. 314). The purpose of the review process is to ensure that torture is used for information gathering only; as much as we might think he deserves it, not even KSM should be tortured out of revenge (Krauthammer 2004, p. 314).

Krauthammer draws a distinction in terms of torture's effectiveness between whether it works occasionally and whether it is reliable more generally, and he follows utilitarian philosophers such as Bagaric and Clarke in stating that it is sufficient if it works just sometimes (Krauthammer 2004, p. 314). He goes on to cite approvingly the view that "the toughness of interrogation techniques should be calibrated to the importance and urgency of the information likely to be obtained" and doing so "would permit some very aggressive techniques" on a "small percentage of detainees who seem especially likely to have potentially life-saving information" (Krauthammer 2004, p. 315).

Normative Principles

We could continue, examining the proposals of other authors, but even this brief survey reveals general agreement on some basic principles of an interrogational torture program:

1. **Restricted conditions under which torture is authorized:**
   (a) Innocent lives must be in danger; this danger must be reasonably short term, if not actually immediate.
   (b) Torture is to be employed as a last resort, when no other options are available.
   (c) There must be a high probability that the person to be tortured has the required (specific) information necessary to save the innocent lives.
2. **Restrictions and controls on how torture is employed:**
   (a) The particular torture techniques employed as well as the severity and duration of their use should be the minimum necessary to elicit the required information.
   (b) The techniques and the nature of their application would also be scaled to the particular circumstances, in particular the gravity of the threat.
   (c) The permitted techniques, as well as their limits and controls, would be stipulated ahead of time, perhaps with explicit prohibition of specific techniques.
   (d) Torture should be conducted only by specially trained officers, perhaps in special units.
3. **Oversight:**
   (a) Requests for torture authorization should be vetted in advance in the form of a warrant by higher authorities, whether (1) a judicial body such as a special court, or (2) very high-ranking officials in the executive branch; in the event that torture was employed without a warrant issued, authorities must obtain the authorization within a short period following the torture.
   (b) Officers employing torture acting in good faith receive immunity from prosecution, but any violations of rules and procedures are punishable offenses.

(c) The torture program should be subject to some sort of independent oversight body, perhaps composed of experts if the torture must remain secret.

How close did the design of the Bush interrogational torture program come to this ideal?

THE PRAGMATIC MODEL

Remarkably close.

Although many details remain classified, enough material has been publicly released to get a good picture of the program's design. While no real-world government program ever matches perfectly a theoretical ideal, the design of the Bush interrogational torture program not only incorporates almost all of the ten points above, but actually goes beyond them in some ways. Keep in mind that at this point we are examining the Bush interrogational torture program as it was *supposed* to work, as envisioned by its architects and proponents. In doing so, we draw on the documents and other evidence for the policies guiding the program. Most of those architects and proponents claim that is how it *actually* worked, in reality, as well, but assessing that claim is not (yet) our purpose. Consequently we do not examine here evidence of how it worked in practice, but will return to this question in the Postscript.

1. **Restricted conditions under which torture is authorized:**
   (a) Innocent lives must be in danger; and this danger must be reasonably short term, if not actually immediate.
   (b) Torture is to be employed as a last resort, when no other options are available.
   (c) There must be a high probability that the person to be tortured has the required (specific) information necessary to save the innocent lives.

An August 1, 2002, memo from the Office of Legal Counsel (OLC) in the Justice Department to the CIA in response to their request for authorization to torture Abu Zubaydah begins by saying that the CIA "is certain" he has information on attacks in the United States and Saudi Arabia he won't divulge, so other methods have been exhausted. Moreover, the level of "chatter" is at pre-9/11 levels (Bybee 2002, p. 1).

The CIA issued formal guidelines for the detention and interrogational torture program at the end of January 2003. The Interrogation Guidelines memo stipulated that approval for EITs required signing off by the Counterterrorism

Center (CTC) Director as well as the Chief of the CTC Legal Group, and only if, among other conditions, the "specific detainee has information about risks to citizens of the United States or other nations" and "use of EIT(s) is appropriate in order to obtain the information" (Central Intelligence Agency 2003c, p. 3). A December 30, 2004, memo to the OLC lawyers in the Justice Department providing background on the program does make it clear that while torture was used as a last resort, detainees were not given much time during the first interview to demonstrate their willingness to cooperate "in a relatively benign environment." The "standard on participation is set very high." The detainee had to supply "information on actionable threats and location information on High Value Targets at large." If the detainee provided only "lower level information," CIA interrogators discontinued the neutral approach and moved to more aggressive techniques (Central Intelligence Agency 2004a, p. 3). Still, torture was not used right away.

The military adopted the same strategy. An October 11, 2002, memo, later approved by Secretary of Defense Donald Rumsfeld on December 2, 2002, authorized three categories of "aggressive counter-resistance techniques" in escalating fashion. First, however, interrogators would attempt the "direct approach" using rewards such as cigarettes and cookies (Phifer 2002, p. 1). Only if the detainee were determined to be "uncooperative" would the first category of techniques be applied. The proposed Category III techniques would be applied only to "exceptionally resistant detainees," likely under 3% of the total (Phifer 2002, p. 2). Another memo on techniques approved by Rumsfeld, dated April 16, 2003, also contained an appendix (B) of General Safeguards (Department of Defense 2003, pp. 5–6). Use of the techniques was permissible only if "there is a good basis to believe detainee possesses critical intelligence" (Department of Defense 2003, p. 5).

Thus, in the case of both the CIA and the military, torture was only supposed to be approved under quite limited conditions.

2. **Restrictions and controls on how torture is employed:**
   (a) The particular torture techniques employed, as well as the severity and duration of their use, should be the minimum necessary to elicit the required information.
   (b) The techniques and the nature of their application would also be scaled to the particular circumstances, in particular the gravity of the threat.
   (c) The permitted techniques, as well as their limits and controls, would be stipulated ahead of time, perhaps with explicit prohibition of specific techniques.
   (d) Torture should be conducted only by specially trained officers, perhaps in special units.

As a result of scandals associated with Latin American death squads, by 9/11 the CIA had largely gotten out of the business of running detention and inter- rogations directly, though not renditions (Central Intelligence Agency 2004c, pp. 9–10).[11] As a result, there were no formal guidelines on confinement or in- terrogation methods until the end of January 2003. Up to that point, guidance to CIA officers in the field consisted of "informal briefings and electronic com- munications" and "orally on a case-by-case basis" (Central Intelligence Agency 2004c, pp. 25, 29). The CTC did pilot a "two-week Interrogator Training Course designed to train, qualify, and certify individuals as Agency interrogators" in November 2002 (Central Intelligence Agency 2004c, p. 31). Former SERE in- structors participated in designing the course, which consisted of classroom instruction the first week and " 'hands-on' training in EITs" in the second week (Central Intelligence Agency 2004c, pp. 31–32). Later, in June 2003, the CIA launched a similar course for the "debriefers," the substantive experts" who question detainees after interrogators have employed torture to make them "compliant" (Central Intelligence Agency 2004c, p. 33).

According to the internal CIA investigation in 2004, these "ad hoc" instruc- tions and the failure "to provide adequate staffing, guidance, and support for those involved with the detention and interrogation of detainees," including "comprehensive written guidelines for detention and interrogation activities," were partially responsible for some of the abuses that took place (Central In- telligence Agency 2004c, pp. 102–103). Still, it's the OIG's job to find problems. Moreover, even the OIG noted that guidance "improved considerably during the life of the program" (Central Intelligence Agency 2004c, 6).

Restraints and limits were visible even before formal guidelines were issued, however, in the original torture memo of August 1, 2002, describing the 10 EITs. That OLC memo is replete with limits and controls designed to prevent un- authorized harm and limit the effects to only those intended. In the "walling" technique, for example, detainees are shoved against a wall, but the wall is a spe- cially constructed false one that provides some cushion and the detainee's head is protected by a collar to prevent whiplash (Bybee 2002, p. 2). The memo notes that the confinement space torture would last no more than 18 hours for the large box and two hours for the small box, and sleep deprivation would last no more than 11 days (Bybee 2002, p. 3). Waterboarding is also described as limited to 20 to 40 seconds per application, after which the detainee would be allowed to take three or four breaths and the entire procedure would not last for more than 20 minutes total (Bybee 2002, p. 4).

In addition, a medical expert would be in attendance monitoring the de- tainee's mental and physical condition and had the authority to end the interro- gation to prevent severe mental or physical harm (Bybee 2002, p. 4). Moreover, the memo states that not all the techniques would necessarily be used and most would not be repeated, and that they would be used in an "escalating fashion" (Bybee 2002, p. 2). The CIA also recognized that the psychological effects of the various techniques also depended on the individual and thus stipulated that candidates for torture would first be given a psychological assessment, as had been done for Abu Zubaydah (Bybee 2002, p. 7).[12] Elsewhere the memo discusses other safeguards; for example, if interrogators put an insect in the confinement box, they must tell the detainee that it is harmless so as not to lead him to believe that it could sting and cause pain or even death (Bybee 2002, p. 13). All of this was reaffirmed by a new set of OLC memos issued in December 2004 and in May 2005, even though the August 1, 2002, memo was withdrawn and waterboarding was no longer being used by the CIA.[13]

The first formal guidelines were signed by CIA Director Tenet on January 28, 2003. A memo regulating "Confinement Conditions" instructed that "[d]ue provision must be taken to protect the health and safety of all CIA Detainees including basic levels of medical care" (Central Intelligence Agency 2003b, p. 1). An Interrogations Guidelines memo issued the same day set out the formal procedures for the CIA torture program (Central Intelligence Agency 2003c). The memo distinguished between two types of "Permissible Interrogation Techniques": "Standard" and "Enhanced" (Central Intelligence Agency 2003c, p. 1).

The standard techniques, which were defined as "techniques that *do not* incorporate physical or substantial psychological pressure," included isolation, sleep deprivation, food manipulation (reduction), deprivation of reading material, use of loud music or white noise, and the use of diapers (emphasis in original) (Central Intelligence Agency 2003c, p. 1).[14] The description of the standard techniques included limits on their duration or intensity. Sleep deprivation was not to exceed 72 hours; caloric intake could be reduced, but must remain sufficient to keep the detainee healthy; loud music and white noise must be kept below the level which would damage hearing; and the use of diapers could not exceed 72 hours. The enhanced techniques, which "*do* incorporate physical or psychological pressure beyond Standard Techniques," included the techniques we've seen previously: attention grasp, walling, facial hold, facial/insult slap, abdominal slap, cramped confinement, wall standing, stress positions, extended sleep deprivation, extended use of diapers, use of harmless insects, and waterboarding (emphasis in original) (Central Intelligence Agency 2003c, p. 2).[15]

The actual employment of these techniques was strictly regulated according to the guidelines. First, only pre-screened (medical, psychological, security) and trained interrogators authorized to use EITs were permitted to do so, only on that specific detainee, and only after they had signed an acknowledgment form indicating that they had read the guidelines, understood them, and promised to follow them (Central Intelligence Agency 2003c, p. 3). Second, medical and psychological experts must participate in the torture sessions to monitor the detainee's physical and mental health. These officers had the authority to suspend interrogations if they believed "significant and prolonged physical or mental injury, pain, or suffering is likely to result" (Central Intelligence Agency 2003c, p. 2).[16] Finally, the guidelines required detailed record keeping on "the nature and duration of each technique, identities of those present, and a citation to the required Headquarters approval cable" initially authorizing the torture. All this information was to be documented in cable traffic between the black sites and headquarters (Central Intelligence Agency 2003c, p. 3).

The CIA's Office of Medical Services (OMS) was also late with its own formal guidelines for doctors and other medical officers, not issuing the first set until April 2003, then again in September 2003 as "Draft" guidelines (Central Intelligence Agency 2004c, p. 104). There is also a set of OMS guidelines dated December 2004 (Central Intelligence Agency 2004b).[17] The OMS guidelines bear on the Bush pragmatic model in three ways:

1. as stipulating general or procedural limits on the severity and duration of particular techniques and their combined use,
2. as providing for monitoring detainee health generally and during individual torture sessions, and
3. as providing for chronic and, if necessary, acute care.

CIA medical staff helped design the techniques, including their limits; provided initial, baseline, medical assessment of the detainees, including signing off on whether they could be tortured; monitored the detainees' condition during the torture; and provided routine chronic care throughout their detention.

CIA medical staff provided assistance with the design of the techniques. So, for example, the OMS:

1. helped set temperatures for "uncomfortably cool environments,"
2. provided a formula for "estimating daily fluid and nutritional requirements" designed to "enhance compliance with interrogators" while still maintaining detainee health,
3. set water temperatures for different exposure duration times in water dousing,
4. set decibel levels for different exposure duration times,
5. specified the exact positioning of arms and duration times for vertical shackling,
6. stipulated the length of sleep deprivation, and
7. set the duration limits for confinement in the two boxes (Central Intelligence Agency 2004b, pp. 10–17).

Appendix A of the 2004 guidelines provided, in summary chart form for each technique, the medical limitations, the "rationale" for the limitation, and the relevant medical reference (e.g., OSHA and WHO guidelines) (Central Intelligence Agency 2004b, pp. 28–30).

Medical attention began immediately upon arrival at the black site. "New detainees are to have a thorough initial medical assessment upon arrival at the first Agency detention facility, with a complete documented history and physical addressing in depth any chronic or previous medical problem. This assessment should especially attend to cardio-vascular, pulmonary, neurological and musculoskeletal findings." [redacted] "Vital signs and weight should be recorded, and blood work drawn." [redacted] (Central Intelligence Agency 2004b, p. 6).[18]

If, following this initial assessment, a detainee refused to cooperate and enhanced measures had been approved by headquarters, the latter were "conditional on on-site medical and psychological personnel confirming from direct detainee examination that [the methods were] not expected to produce 'severe physical or mental pain or suffering'" (Central Intelligence Agency 2004b, p. 9). The 2003 version of the guidelines called for "subsequent medical rechecks . . . on a regular basis" (Central Intelligence Agency 2004c, p. 150). Medical officers were required to monitor detainee health during the application of enhanced techniques and had the authority to stop them if there were problems (Central Intelligence Agency 2004b, p. 9).[19] A footnote stated that a physician was required to monitor waterboarding, while either a physician or a physician's assistant (PA) was qualified to monitor the application of the other techniques (Central Intelligence Agency 2004b, p. 9, footnote 3). Finally, regular medical care of the detainees included administering medications for chronic medical problems, monitoring fluid and nutritional intake, monitoring "urine output" if necessary, and treating acute problems (Central Intelligence Agency 2004b, pp. 9–10).

Other memos and documents set out similar restrictions and controls on the techniques. For "water dousing," the detainee must be placed on a towel or sheet, not naked on the bare cement floor, and the air temperature must exceed 65 degrees unless the detainee is to be dried immediately to prevent hypothermia (Central Intelligence Agency 2004c, p. 76). A "Waterboarding Memo" from August 2004 clarified the procedure and guidelines for the OLC (Central Intelligence Agency 2004d). Approvals for waterboarding (for a specific detainee) lasted for 30 days and specified the following limits and definitions (Central Intelligence Agency 2004d, pp. 1–2):

1. Not more than 20 days during a 30-day period.
2. No more than four waterboard sessions per day.

3. A session was the total of time strapped to the waterboard, with multiple applications of water possible during a single session and no predefined limits on the length of a session.

4. An application was the time period during which water was actually poured on the cloth held on the detainee's face and was not to exceed 40 seconds. The vast majority of applications were shorter than this. Individual sessions lasting 10 seconds or more were limited to no more than 10 applications in any one waterboarding session.

A CIA background paper of December 30, 2004, prepared for the OLC echoed the OMS guidelines (and explicitly cited them in places) in terms of limits and constraints on the techniques (Central Intelligence Agency 2004a, pp. 4–8, 15–16). It instructed, for example, that the facial hold technique be applied so that it "is not painful." The effectiveness of the techniques was assessed as the interrogation proceeded, and the ones deemed most successful will be emphasized while those "with little assessed effectiveness will be minimized" (Central Intelligence Agency 2004a, p. 15). Finally, "[a]ll CIA interrogations are conducted on the basis of the 'least coercive measure' principle. Interrogators employ interrogation techniques in an escalating manner consistent with HVD's [High Value Detainees'] responses and actions" (Central Intelligence Agency 2004a, p. 18).

A clear example of the care taken by the CIA to keep the detainees healthy for torture is captured by an April 2005 memo on altering the shackling method for sleep deprivation. Interrogators and on-site medical officers had noticed that vertical shackling had created the "potential for unacceptable edema [swelling] in the lower limbs of detainees" subjected to standing sleep deprivation. Consequently, the interrogators shifted the detainees to horizontal sleep deprivation so they could continue sleep deprivation without edema problems.

The detainee was placed horizontal on the floor on a thick towel or blanket to protect against body heat loss on the cold floor. The detainees' hands were manacled together, arms outstretched, either beyond the head or to the side of body and anchored to the floor so that they could not "be bent or used for balance or comfort." Ditto for the ankles and legs. The length of shackles to the anchoring point was carefully calibrated to be "sufficiently uncomfortable to detainees to deprive them of unbroken sleep" but without straining or stretching the limbs or joints and allowing the legs to recover from the vertical position. Once the medical officer determines that the detainee has recovered from edema, he is moved back to sitting or standing shackling for continued sleep deprivation (Central Intelligence Agency 2005, p. 1).

The same memo discussed guidelines for using waterboarding, sleep deprivation, and dietary manipulation together. The guidelines permitted dietary manipulation and sleep deprivation in conjunction with waterboarding. Indeed, they stipulated a liquid-only diet in preparation for waterboarding "in order to avoid aspiration of regurgitated food" (Central Intelligence Agency 2005, p. 4). Limits on sleep deprivation would be "strictly" monitored when used in conjunction with waterboarding, and other techniques such as slaps and water dousing would not be applied while the detainee was strapped to the waterboard, though it was possible they might be used on the same day as the waterboarding (Central Intelligence Agency 2005, p. 2).

Documents on U.S. military interrogations also reflect these restrictions, limits, and controls on how torture is employed. The October 11, 2002, memo approved by Secretary Rumsfeld mentioned earlier, authorized three categories of "aggressive counter-resistance techniques" in escalating fashion. Category I consisted of yelling and various forms of deception clearly not rising to torture. Category II techniques included: stress positions, limited to four hours; lengthy, but limited, interrogation sessions; and hooding, but with guidelines to ensure unobstructed breathing.[20] Category III techniques were the most aggressive and included threats of death to the detainee or his family members, waterboarding, exposure to cold weather or water "(with appropriate medical monitoring)," as well as "grabbing, poking in the chest, with the finger, and light pushing" (Phifer 2002, pp. 2–3). These could only be applied, however, by specially trained interrogators (Phifer 2002, p. 2). In the end, the memo approved only the last of the Category III techniques involving mild physical contact.

The other memo on techniques approved by Rumsfeld containing the appendix (B) of General Safeguards stipulated the following limits (Department of Defense 2003, pp. 5–6):

- Only at strategic interrogation facilities.
- There is a good basis to believe detainee possesses critical intelligence.
- The detainee is medically and operationally suitable for techniques (in combination).
- Interrogators are specifically trained in techniques.
- Development of a specific interrogation plan which includes "reasonable safeguards, limits on duration, intervals between applications, termination criteria and the presence or availability of qualified medical personnel."
- Appropriate supervision.

The overarching goal was "to get the most information from a detainee with the least intrusive method, always applied in a humane and lawful manner with sufficient oversight by trained investigators or interrogators" (Department of Defense 2003, p. 5).

In short, both the military and CIA interrogational torture programs included explicit limits, controls, and restrictions on how torture was to be applied.

3. Oversight:
   (a) Requests for torture authorization should be vetted in advance in the form of a warrant by higher authorities, whether (1) a judicial body such as a special court or (2) very high-ranking officials in the executive branch; in the event that torture was employed without a warrant issued, authorities must obtain the authorization within a short period following the torture.
   (b) Officers employing torture acting in good faith receive immunity from prosecution, but any violations of rules and procedures are punishable offenses.
   (c) The torture program should be subject to some sort of independent oversight body, perhaps composed of experts if the torture must remain secret.

The Bush administration never established a procedure for torture warrants within the executive branch, let alone a system under the judicial branch analogous to the FISA courts that (nominally) provide oversight over government surveillance within the United States. Nevertheless, both the CIA and the military did require high-level approval within the executive branch before the application of most torture techniques.

Although even standard techniques should be approved in advance whenever possible, the use of Enhanced Techniques (torture) had to follow a more rigorous set of guidelines for approval and application (Central Intelligence Agency 2003c, p. 3). First, in addition to the conditions above that the detainee have critical information and a determination that EITs are necessary to get it, torture would only be approved if and when "medical and psychological personnel" had determined that the techniques would not result in "severe physical or mental pain or suffering" (the standard in the August 1, 2002, torture memo) (Central Intelligence Agency 2003c, pp. 2, 3). Second, both the Director of the CTC (Counterterrorism Center) and the Chief of the CTC Legal Group had to approve each specific technique used against each specific detainee. If interrogators felt that it was necessary to go "beyond the 30-day approval period" for the initial application of enhanced techniques, they were required to "submit a new interrogation plan to HQS [headquarters] for evaluation and approval" (Central Intelligence Agency 2004a, p. 17). Thus, while the "conditioning" and standard techniques" required a lower level of preapproval, despite the fact these techniques also amounted to torture, there was a requirement to secure higher-level permission to apply specific enhanced torture methods against a specific detainee, even if this approval did not need to go beyond the Director of the CTC.

In the case of the military, the approval required for torture went a little higher up. The request for Category III techniques by Guantanamo interrogators in October 2002 included the provision that they could be applied "only by submitting a request" up through the chain of command all the way to the Commander of USSOUTHCOM (Phifer 2002, p. 2). Eventually, only "mild physical contact" within the Category III techniques was ever approved: Death threats, waterboarding, and water dousing were ultimately rejected. The fact that and the way in which those techniques were rejected provide further evidence of the limits and controls on torture. Interrogators did not always get what they asked for. Similarly, the April 2003 Rumsfeld memo with the General Safeguards appendix required "appropriate specified senior approval for use [of torture] with any specific detainee (after considering the forgoing and receiving legal advice)" (Department of Defense 2003, p. 6).

In terms of immunity and punishment for abuses, the case is more mixed. Certainly the OLC lawyers who authorized torture (primarily John Yoo and Jay Bybee), CIA officials from CTC Director Rodriguez to field agents at the black sites, and military officers in the upper chain of command down to Guantanamo interrogators have all received *de facto* if not *de jure* immunity, as have all top Bush administration officials.[21] The Justice Department's Office of Professional Responsibility did find that Yoo and Bybee committed "professional misconduct" and recommended disciplinary proceedings, but this recommendation was countermanded by Associate Deputy Attorney General David Margolis and the matter was dropped (Lichtbau and Shane 2010).[22]

Although Obama administration Attorney General Eric Holder announced an investigation into the treatment of over 100 CIA detainees shortly after taking office, only two cases were referred for full criminal investigation. Manadel al-Jamadi died at Abu Ghraib prison in 2003 and Gul Rahman died in 2002 at the CIA prison outside Kabul known as the Salt Pit (Lichtbau and Schmitt 2011). These investigations also concluded with no charges filed (Shane 2012).

The prosecution of prison guards at Abu Ghraib is well known; the prosecution of guards at the Bagram (Afghanistan) detention facility is less well known. In both cases, however, the abuses were considered the result of "bad apples," not official interrogation policy, and no high-ranking officers were prosecuted.

Finally, neither the CIA nor the military torture programs can be said to have satisfied the final condition of independent oversight. Congressional leaders were briefed on the CIA program, but were held to secrecy and were unable to intervene in any meaningful way.

This last point about oversight notwithstanding, it nevertheless remains re-
markable just how closely both the CIA and military interrogational torture
programs hewed to the ideal model. A report from the Department of Defense
working group that drew up the list of techniques eventually approved by Secretary of Defense Rumsfeld in the April 16, 2003, memo captures nicely in one
brief paragraph this close correspondence. I have inserted the normative ideals at
the appropriate points:

> The following list includes additional techniques that are considered effec-
> tive by interrogators [*effectiveness*], some of which have been requested by
> USCENTCOM and USSOUTHCOM. They are more aggressive [*torture*]
> counter-resistance techniques that may be appropriate for detainees who
> are extremely resistant to the above techniques [*last resort*] and who the in-
> terrogators strongly believe have vital information [*life-saving information*].
> All of the following techniques indicate the need for technique-specialized
> training and written procedures to insure the safety of all persons, along
> with appropriate, specified levels of approval and notification for each
> technique [*training, limits, controls, and oversight*] (Danner 2004, p. 191).[23]

PRAGMATIC PREDICTIONS, NORMATIVE BENCHMARKS

The Bush interrogational torture program, then, provides a useful test case for
the ideal, normative model advocated by philosophers and law professors. The
Bush program adheres very closely to the normative ideal, making a test of that
program simultaneously a test of the general normative model. My use of a test
case here is analogous to test cases in law, rather than empirical testing of a scientific theory. One cannot test a scientific theory (which makes claims about the
empirical world) with a single datum. A single case from the real world which is a
very close approximation to a normative scheme, however, *does* provide a test of
that scheme.

This testing will take the form of comparing the outcomes of the game theoretic models with the predictions of the idealized model. The ideal model just
sketched suggests how interrogational torture *should* work, how we *expect* it to
work. "Should" and "expect" mean two things here.

When a father tells his child, "I expect you to behave today," it entails both a
prediction of the behavior the father expects to observe as well as the standard of
right behavior against whatever behavior is actually observed will be compared.
The same is true here with interrogational torture.

On the one hand, the ideal model tells us what is *supposed* to happen, what we
can expect to see when torture is used. This is closer to the idea of an empirical

prediction, of what *will* happen. On the other hand, it has a normative component; it tells us what we *want* to happen, what we want out of the program, and
thus how we should judge or evaluate it.

The two ideas are joined in the corporatese "benchmark." A benchmark of the
ideal model, "valuable information" let's say, states both what we think we *will*
find as well as what we *should* find—that is, a normative standard against which
we compare and measure what we *do* find. If we do, in fact, find lots of valuable
information from torture, then the benchmark of success is met; if we do not,
the benchmark is not met and there are problems with the program. What are
the benchmarks for an interrogational torture program like that under the Bush
administration?

We can begin by thinking about the brutal means–end logic of interrogational
torture. The end is (good, reliable) information; the means are torture.

Consider information first. The purpose of interrogational torture is to generate valuable intelligence that cannot be collected otherwise. The epigraph to this
chapter, taken from a CIA background paper and repeated here, captures this
nicely: "[t]he goal of interrogation is to create a state of learned helplessness and
dependence conducive to the collection of intelligence in a predictable, reliable,
and sustainable manner" (Central Intelligence Agency 2004*a*, 1). Each of these
three terms—predictable, reliable, and sustainable—is crucial.

Take "sustainable" first. The idea here is that the interrogation program should
produce intelligence over (some period of) time. That is—*even in the eyes of the
CIA itself*—it is a sustained program and should be evaluated as such, rather
than in the one-off manner implied by the ticking time bomb defense. This is,
of course, much closer to the way we evaluate other government programs and
hold them accountable.

Now consider "reliable." An interrogational torture program should be "reliable" in two ways. First, the information itself generated by torture should be
reliable. The CIA can rely on it because it is good (useful, "actionable," etc.) and
not bad (false, misleading, contradictory, etc.) information.

The second meaning of reliable is really the same as the last CIA criterion, "predictable." The idea here is that interrogational torture should produce
this good information in a reliable way. You use torture, you get the valuable
information, at least almost all the time.

This requires two assumptions. First, it assumes that (nearly) all detainees
have valuable information to give up. Second, it assumes that (nearly) all of these
detainees actually do give up (nearly) all that information under the threat of
(more) torture. They do not hide information and refuse to answer, nor do they
provide (much) false information.

In other words, if interrogational torture is a reliable method, then you can
predict getting good information rather than bad or no information at all. There

should be a lot more good information than bad information. Put another way, the ratio of the outcomes with good information to all the outcomes that can happen should be very high.[24]

Consequently, we can identify two aspects or components of a benchmark associated with getting good information, connected to the two meanings of "expect," one more empirical or predictive and one normative:

BENCHMARK 1

INFORMATION RELIABILITY

1. *Prediction:* Most detainees have information and give up (nearly) all of it so that the ratio of clear and valuable information to all information will be high.
2. *Normative Standard:* Interrogational torture is successful if and only if detainees give up (nearly) all their information so that the ratio of clear and valuable information to all information is high (Information).

Now consider the "means" part of the means–end logic of interrogational torture. On this instrumentally rational view, torture forces detainees to give up information they would not otherwise divulge. Historically, the logic or calculus here is brutal: Pain is increased until the information is revealed. The CIA program, with its emphasis on the distinction between interrogations (torture) and debriefing (interrogations or questioning) and a philosophy (mythology) rooted in learned helplessness, dependency, and other concepts from 1950s psychological research, was self-consciously "scientific" and attempted to distance itself from that historical calculus. As we have seen in Chapter 2, however, the gradual escalation of techniques in both theory and practice reveals that this inescapable and brutal logic of torture tends to persist.

Nevertheless, the review of the limits, controls, oversight, restrictions, and the like on the Bush torture program above does demonstrate that there was an attempt to impose limits both on what tortures could be employed and on the duration of those that were authorized. In other words, there were upper limits on that basic, brutal calculus. The fact that the CIA itself investigated some instances when those limits were violated demonstrates that it considered those limits important criteria for assessing the program. Moreover, apologists repeatedly defend the program with reference to these limits and the restraint showed by the CIA and the military.

This suggests two further benchmarks with respect to the "means" part of the "means–end" logic, one referring to the *frequency* with which torture is employed and one referring to the intensity or *severity* of any particular application. Once again there are two aspects of each, one empirical or predictive and one normative or evaluative:

BENCHMARK 2

TORTURE FREQUENCY

1. *Prediction:* Torture will be employed infrequently, just on a few particularly resistant detainees who refuse to provide information, so that
   (a) the total frequency of torture is low,
   (b) Cooperative detainees are not tortured after they have provided all their information,
   (c) Innocent detainees are not tortured for telling the truth.
2. *Normative Standard:* Interrogational torture is successful if and only if torture is not employed too frequently:
   (a) the total frequency of torture is low (Total Frequency),
   (b) Cooperative detainees are not tortured after they have provided all their information (Cooperatives),
   (c) Innocent detainees are not tortured for telling the truth (Innocents).

And:

BENCHMARK 3

TORTURE SEVERITY

1. *Prediction:* When torture is employed, its severity will approximate the minimum degree necessary to compel valuable information.
2. *Normative Standard:* The program succeeds only if torture is not employed too severely—well beyond the minimum degree necessary to compel valuable information (Severity).

Putting the predictive benchmarks together provides the ideal outcome sketched by apologists of the Bush program, in its predictive and normative variants:

BENCHMARK 4

TORTURE JUSTIFICATION OUTCOME

1. _Prediction:_ A minimum degree (severity) and amount (frequency) of torture is used against only the most resistant detainees with valuable information, who give up all, or nearly all, that valuable information. Neither cooperative detainees who have provided all their information nor innocent detainees are tortured.
2. _Normative Standard:_ Torture in interrogations is justified if and only if torture
   (a) is not used against cooperating detainees who have provided all their information (Cooperatives),
   (b) is not used against innocent detainees (Innocents),
   (c) does not exceed the minimum frequency (Total Frequency) and severity (Severity) "necessary" and
   (d) (the threat of) torture generates all, or nearly all, the valuable information possessed by knowledgeable detainees (Information).

Note that each of these is a _necessary_ condition; violating any one of the four conditions is sufficient for the failure of the program according to the proponents' benchmark.

We will draw on these predictions and evaluative standards as we build, solve, and then analyze the games modeling interrogational torture. The limits, controls, and restrictions discussed above will inform the building of those models to ensure that we do not construct a strawman model which is an unfair and unrealistic representation of the Bush torture program. A more immediate problem is a quixotic model, to which we now turn.

*   *   *

The argument thus far has shown that:

1. EITs are torture and the effectiveness of interrogational torture is an open question. (Chapter 2)

2. The Bush program approximates closely the ideal model of interrogational torture and includes limits on torture; the Bush and ideal models provide benchmarks for comparison with the game theory models to come. (Chapter 3)

The next step in the argument is to investigate what outcomes are in fact generated by the Bush model.

A Quixotic Model
of Interrogational Torture

For this is righteous warfare, and it is God's good service to sweep so
evil a breed from off the face of the earth. ... I engage them in fierce and
unequal combat.

—CERVANTES, *Don Quixote*, VIII

Having seen how the Bush model of interrogational torture *should* work, in both
the predictive and normative senses of "should," we now turn to examining how
the Bush model *would* work.[1] To begin this process, we will build a game that
explicitly reconstructs the implicit model behind the Bush interrogational torture program we just saw in Chapter 3. This is the Bush Interrogational Torture
model, or BIT for short.[2]

BUILDING BIT

Take a moment and recall the game in Chapter 1 from the *Law and Order SVU*
episode. In that Prisoners' Dilemma game there were two players, the criminals
Deborah and Carlo, who were faced with the choice of whether to keep quiet or
rat each other out. Each was better off ratting out the other than staying silent (no
matter what their partner-in-crime did), and so that is exactly what happened.
They spilled their guts and spent more time in prison than if both had kept their
mouths shut.

In an interrogational torture game between an interrogator and a detainee, the
choices are somewhat different, the outcomes will be different, and the equilibria

will be different, but the basic logic sketched before is the same. Consider each part of the game: players, actions, payoffs, and what they know when they make their moves.

Players

The first part is the set of players. There were two players in the *Law and Order SVU* game: the two suspects Deborah and Carlo. Although Detectives Stabler and Benson (and Munch and Cassidy) were in the story, their role was really limited to just setting up the Prisoners' Dilemma game between Deborah and Carlo. The detectives weren't actually players *in* the game. The only moves available (keep quiet or rat out) were those for the suspects.

How many players are there in BIT and who are they? Just as the key dynamic in the *Law and Order SVU* episode was the game played between the suspects, in BIT we are interested in what happens between a detainee and an interrogator. The detainees were questioned in isolation and they have to make choices on their own, not with any other detainee, so clearly the detainee is a player.

In contrast, we might think that there is more than one interrogator, since there certainly were in reality. The question, however, is whether this makes a difference for the basic interaction of interest to us. It does not. The different interrogators worked as a team, they replaced each other, and they did essentially the same thing: asked questions, subjected the detainees to EITs, and asked more questions. It is irrelevant for our purposes whether someone was a "debriefer" or an "interrogator." From the detainee's perspective, they were on the same side: against him. Thus, in BIT we also have two players: an Interrogator and a Detainee. To keep them clear while easing exposition in the rest of the book, I'll assume the Interrogator is female and the Detainee is male.[3]

Actions

In the simplest version of an interrogational torture game, the Interrogator might have two choices: "torture" or not "torture," where "not torture" means using alternative interrogation techniques such as deception, trickery, rapport-building, and the like. We could complicate this by, say, making each one of the EITs a different move. The interrogator might then have the moves "not torture," "sleep deprivation," "stress positions," and so on. Of course, we could go further and give the interrogator multiple moves within "sleep deprivation," such as 48 hours, 72 hours, and so forth. As you can see, things can get complicated very quickly. Different tortures will probably work differently on different detainees, for example.

Thankfully, we don't need to get this complicated because adding that complexity doesn't get us any further anyway. At some point, some form of torture is supposed to compel the detainee to talk. That's the basic logic of torture. We preserve that basic logic and still keep things manageable by just giving the interrogator the choice between two possible moves: "torture" or not "torture."

Moreover, this remains consistent with the basic structure and procedures of the Bush program discussed in Chapters 2 and 3. Although, as Chapter 2 demonstrated, the rendition process itself and the "conditioning" measures at the black sites were torture in and of themselves, not all detainees were subjected to EITs because they provided information. If a detainee refused, however, he faced the prospect of escalating EITs until he cooperated. For Abu Zubaydah this meant a gradual increase in the severity of EITs from nudity, noise, temperature manipulation, and sleep deprivation through confinement boxes and waterboarding. The detainees understood that the EITs were "not going to stop, ever, unless they cooperated" (Thiessen 2010, p. 116).

Thus, if CIA interrogators decided that the detainee had not revealed the necessary information, then they tortured; and once torture was initiated, they continued until the detainee was deemed compliant (demonstrated by providing information). Then they stopped. At some point, in other words, the basic choice confronting the interrogator is whether or not to torture (more).

Similarly, the Detainee might have two choices, "reveal information" and "not reveal information." Here too we might make things more complicated to reflect the reality that what information is revealed (quality) and how much (quantity) is a pretty important part of interrogational torture. True enough.

Note, though, that what counts as sufficient quality or quantity is the subjective assessment of the interrogator (or, as was apparently the case in reality, CIA headquarters on the seventh floor in Langley). The basic idea was this: If the detainee provided information of sufficient quality and quantity—however defined by the interrogator—then he was not tortured (again). If he did not, he was tortured.

So we can think of "reveal information" as "disclosing sufficient previously unknown information which is of value to the Interrogator." "Not reveal information" has four interpretations:

1. not enough good (enough) information
2. truthful, accurate, but nonvaluable information
3. false and misleading information
4. no information whatsoever

"Not enough good (enough) information" means that the Detainee provided previously unknown and valuable information, but it is of very low quality or quantity so as to count practically as "not reveal information." "Truthful, accurate, but nonvaluable information" means that the Detainee provides information to the Interrogator but that information is out of date or information the Interrogator already knew or information that for other reasons provides no added value to the Interrogator. "False and misleading information" means information that actually leads the Interrogator astray, diverting attention and resources away from plots, people, locations, etc., of value. This is doubly dangerous for the Interrogator: The real danger (plots and other activities) continue unabated, and human and technical resources are wasted on wild goose chases. Finally, "no information whatsoever" means that the Detainee stays silent, providing neither valuable nor false information.

In short, once again the simple binary case is sufficient to capture the basic dynamic of interrogational torture: "information" and "no information," keeping in mind the latter's four very different interpretations.

Outcomes and Payoffs

This would generate, just as in the Prisoners' Dilemma, four outcomes based on the two possible choices for each of the two players:

1. "information" and "torture,"
2. "no information" and "torture,"
3. "information" and "no torture,"
4. "no information" and "no torture."

The two players will, of course, value those four outcomes very differently. If you're the Interrogator for example, and you prefer to use torture only as a last resort as did the CIA, then the best outcome of the four for you would be "information" and "no torture": You got the information and didn't have to use torture. The worst might be to use torture and still not get information. Now suppose you're the Detainee with valuable information you're trying to hide. "No information" and "no torture" would be the best for you, while "information" and "torture" you might consider the worst, because you both suffered torture and also gave up information.

These subjective evaluations of the outcomes are the payoffs to each player. We can represent them in multiple ways: in words, in a ranking (best, second best, etc.), or numerically, which includes algebraically, with variables, like the x and y you remember from high school math class. In the *Law and Order SVU* episode, the payoffs represented actual years in jail, with the assumptions that being in jail is unpleasant and more years in jail is less pleasant than fewer years

Table 4.1. *LAW AND ORDER SVU* PRISONERS' DILEMMA, ORDINAL PAYOFFS

		Carlo	
		Stay Silent	*Rat Out Deborah*
	Stay Silent	3, 3	1, 4
Deborah			
	Rat Out Carlo	4, 1	**2, 2**

in jail. That allowed us to figure out the (single) outcome, or equilibrium, of that game.

We could, however, have used any set of numbers just so long as they were true to the way Deborah and Carlo ordered their outcomes (i.e., most preferred to least preferred). Table 4.1 provides another representation of the exact same game, this time with numerical payoffs corresponding to how each of them ranked the four possible outcomes, with higher numbers more preferred to lower numbers so that four is best and one is worst.

Compare this to the game in Chapter 1 and see for yourself that this version is equivalent to the one above. From Deborah's perspective, for example, the four she gets for ratting out beats the three she gets for staying silent if Carlo stays silent. The two she gets for ratting out beats the one she gets for staying silent if Carlo rats her out. So, either way, she's better off ratting Carlo out (making it her *dominant strategy*).

Since the game is exactly the same from Carlo's perspective (this is a symmetrical game), the same logic applies to him and so the equilibrium is the same as the game with the payoffs in years (bolded once again). Assigning numerical values like this can help make the solving of the game just a bit faster than comparing words, but the process is exactly the same. Before thinking about the payoffs to the players in BIT, we must first consider a part of BIT which is different from the *Law and Order SVU* Prisoners' Dilemma.

Timing and Information

In contrast to the classic prisoners' dilemma where the players move at the same time, in ignorance of the other's choice, BIT is a *sequential move* game: One player moves before the other does, and both players know this (and know the other player knows it).[4]

So who moves first, the Interrogator or the Detainee? The Detainee, because it is always the threat of (more) torture that is supposed to compel compliance with the Interrogator's wishes (Schelling 1966, pp. 70–71). Once the Detainee knows the torture is over, he has no incentive to reveal any more information.

As we saw in previous chapters, according to those close to the Bush interrogation program, high-value detainees were "interrogated" (tortured) to make them compliant and were then "debriefed." Note that even if this is true, it makes no difference in terms of the fundamental strategic problem facing both an interrogator and a knowledgeable detainee. Torture makes you compliant. Why does it make you compliant? You don't want to be tortured anymore. You resisted enough that they employed "enhanced techniques" on you. You resisted those for a while until you gave in and became compliant. So it is always the threat of more torture in front of you that makes you cooperative now. This is the inescapable logic of interrogational torture whenever and wherever it is practiced. Consequently, in our game the Detainee moves first, either providing information or not revealing information, and then the Interrogator observes this move (hears, sees, evaluates this information or the lack thereof) and decides whether to torture or not.

Timing is central to our game in a way it is not for the Prisoners' Dilemma because the Interrogator's preferred action depends on what the Detainee has already done. If the Detainee has provided (enough) information (of sufficient quality), the Interrogator does not want to torture. If, however, the Detainee has not provided that information, then the Interrogator does want to torture him. The Detainee, of course, knows this all too well, and anticipation of the Interrogator's move will influence his own, first move. Thus, it is the information available at the time each actor moves that makes the sequencing important.

What information did each player have, according to the Bush model? The Detainee knew that there was one other player besides himself, the Interrogator. Indeed, a central element of the EIT "dependency" idea was that the Detainee should come to think of the Interrogator as the only other relevant person for the Detainee. Second, the Detainee would know, or quickly learn, that the Interrogator had the option to torture; he would know her two possible actions. Finally, he would know her basic payoffs. For example, he would know that she preferred not to use torture to get information, but was willing to do so if necessary. As far as the Interrogator in the Bush model is concerned, in addition to knowing which move the Detainee had made, she would also, for example, know that the Detainee preferred to keep information secret and that the Detainee preferred not to be tortured.

As with so many other things, all this can be made a little clearer with a picture. Sequential games are best represented by something similar to the familiar decision tree. Figure 4.1 represents the BIT game with the players in boldface, their actions in italics, and their payoffs for each outcome at the end of the branches of the tree.

Starting from the left, the first choice node is the Detainee's, who can reveal "information" (moving up the top branch) or provide "no information"

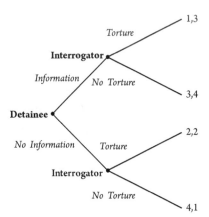

Figure 4.1 Bush Interrogation Game
with a Cooperative Detainee

(moving down the bottom branch). After each of these two moves, the Interrogator chooses either "torture" (up) or "no torture" (down). The numbers next
to the tip of each branch are the payoffs to the players, with the payoff to the
Detainee on the left and the payoff to the Interrogator on the right.

I have used numbers to represent how they order the four outcomes in the
same way as in the Prisoners' Dilemma above, from four (the best) to one
(the worst). The numbers are arbitrary; the important point is that they prefer
some outcomes more than others and we capture that with these simple payoffs.
(We'll change the payoffs a little later to make it more realistic.) With one exception, discussed in just a moment, these orderings (rankings) should be relatively
uncontroversial.

Take a look at the Interrogator first. The Interrogator receives her highest payoff (4) when she gets the information she seeks and does not have to use torture.
This is consistent with the fact that the CIA used torture as a last resort only on
detainees that it perceived had more information but who refused to divulge it.
They preferred not to use torture if at all possible and gave detainees a chance to
cooperate before initiating EITs.

The Interrogator's mission is to extract information; she receives her lowest
payoffs from the two outcomes in which she does not get it, in the lower two
branches of the tree. Her lowest payoff (1) occurs when she fails to use torture
despite not having received any information. Her job, her mission after all, is to
get the information, and torture is one of her means to do so. If she fails to employ
it, she has failed at her job. If she does not receive information and so tortures, she
at least has done her job and so receives a higher payoff of 2. Although she does
not prefer to torture after having been provided (sufficient) information, this is
less of a problem for her than not receiving the information at all, and so provides
her with a higher payoff (3) than the two outcomes with no information.

The Detainee, naturally, ranks the four outcomes very differently. His highest payoff of 4 occurs when he provides no information and is not tortured. His lowest payoff (1), the worst outcome, comes when he provides information and is tortured anyway.

It is the ordering of the next two outcomes which may be controversial. Assuming no ties, there are two possibilities. In the first, he would rather give up information and not be tortured than hold the information and be tortured. Call this type of Detainee *Cooperative*. The payoffs in Figure 4.1 reflect this preference: "information" and "no torture" provides a payoff of 3, whereas "no information" and "torture" provides a payoff of 2.

In the second possibility, this preference is reversed. The Detainee would rather hold the information or give false information and be tortured than give up information and not be tortured. (Just reverse the Detainee's payoffs of 2 and 3 in Figure 4.1.) Call this type of Detainee *Resistant*.[5]

As we will soon see, much depends on which type of Detainee we choose. For now we will assume that the Detainee is the Cooperative type because that is what the Bush program assumed: All detainees would eventually become compliant as a result of the EITs. Once we have worked through the model in this way, we will return to the question of Cooperative vs. Resistant Detainees.

SOLVING BIT

We now have a stripped-down, very simple model of interrogational torture representing—and faithful to—the assumptions of the Bush program. The next step is to "solve" the game—find the outcome (or outcomes) that would result from each player attempting to maximize his or her payoffs–that is, get the highest number. To do this, we need two new ideas: how to reason backward and getting rid of implausible Nash equilibria.

Backward Reasoning and Incredible Threats

In Sergio Leone's classic Western, *For a Few Dollars More*, the Clint Eastwood character asks another gunman, "Do you mind tellin' me how you got here?" The response from Colonel Mortimer is: "I just reasoned it out. I figured you'd tell Indio to do just exactly the opposite of what we agreed and he's suspicious enough to figure out somethin' else. Since El Paso was out of the question, well, here I am."

Now imagine that it is late April in New Jersey and is warm. Some of my students wake up at 10:30 am (an early start for them), notice it's a gorgeous day, and think to themselves, "Hmmm ... we could go play Ultimate Frisbee on the library lawn or we could go to Schiemann's 11:20 game theory class. He's covering subgame perfect equilibrium today. If we play Ultimate, we'll have a lot of fun and probably see Jordan, who is really hot. If we go to class, we won't see Jordan or have fun playing frisbee, but we know subgame perfect equilibrium will be on the final exam and we'll be better prepared." ... "Hmmm ... Wait! Ken is a total nerd and always goes to class. We can get the notes from him. Game on!"

Just as with Colonel Mortimer, in this (unfortunately not terribly contrived) example, my students looked ahead at the downstream consequences of each choice, evaluated them, and reasoned back to make the best (if not necessarily the smartest) choice given their preferences. "Backward reasoning" doesn't sound very smart, so the game theory jargon for this idea is *backward induction*. We'll use it to solve our models.

The second idea involves *noncredible threats*. A noncredible threat is a threat that the threatener has no incentive to carry out if it ever comes time to actually do so. The problem for us is that you can have an outcome in a game which is a Nash equilibrium, but which relies on this sort of noncredible threat. That doesn't sound very plausible or rational, and we want to find a way to get rid of that implausible kind of equilibrium.

In order to do this, we first need to be a little more precise about how exactly an equilibrium is defined. In Chapter 1 we defined it as a stable combination of actions or strategies by the players. And it is. But a player's strategy is a complete set of instructions of what to do, what choice to make at every possible point where she could make a choice. In the Prisoners' Dilemma, both players choose once and simultaneously, so each player's instructions have just one move (e.g., "rat out"). The same is true of the Detainee in BIT; the Detainee has one move, and he moves first, so the instructions contain just one element: "information" or "no information."

In the case of the Interrogator, things are a little different. The Interrogator has to have a contingency plan. She has to decide what she would do if the Detainee reveals information and what she will do if he does not. There are two points at which she could choose because the Detainee moves first and has two choices. The Interrogator's instructions must be complete, with no ambiguity, a road map for whatever comes her way, even if she knows that only one choice will ever materialize. To adapt an example from a very good introductory text on game theory, think of this set of strategies, this complete plan of action, as instructions to another Interrogator. If this second Interrogator replaced the first Interrogator, she would know exactly what to do for every possible move of the Detainee and so make exactly the same choices the first Interrogator would have (Dixit, Skeath, and Reiley 2009, p. 27).

Here is a sample set of such instructions, with the first element the Interrogator's response if the Detainee provides information and the second element the Interrogator's response if the Detainee chooses "no information":

("no torture","torture"),

corresponding to "don't torture after 'information' and do torture after 'no information'."

Another set of instructions might be

("torture","torture")

corresponding to "torture after 'information' and torture after 'no information'" too.

The set of strategies that make up an equilibrium, called a *strategy profile*, contains this full set of instructions for each player in the game. Writing the equilibrium for BIT will thus look a little different from the Prisoners' Dilemma, which had just two elements, one for each player. In BIT, the Detainee's strategy will still consist of one move, but the Interrogator's strategy for the game, her instructions, will contain two moves, one for each possible move by the Detainee. Here is a strategy profile in BIT (not necessarily an equilibrium though):

{"no information", ("torture","torture")}

corresponding to the following: The Detainee plays "no information" and the Interrogator plans to torture whatever move the Detainee makes, after both "information" and "no information."

The reason why all this is important goes back to those noncredible threats. It can happen that a player's strategy might contain a choice for a contingency that is not actually reached in a particular Nash equilibrium, but would require making a move that is not in his interest at that point if he *were* to have to choose there.

As an example, take a look at the {"no information", ("torture", "torture")} strategy profile once again. According to this profile, the Detainee would stay silent, refusing to reveal information, and, since the Interrogator is torturing after "no information" in this profile, she tortures. Along this path of play, the Interrogator is never confronted with the choice of what to do after the Detainee plays "information" because the Detainee plays "no information." But, the complete set of instructions requires the Interrogator to consider this possibility and have a response, and the response in this strategy, in this set of instructions, is "torture."

Would the Interrogator *really* want to choose "torture" after the Detainee has chosen "information"? (Remember, we're assuming that "information" means full, complete, good-quality information sufficient to please the Interrogator.)

No.

In the CIA program, torture was used as a last resort only if a detainee refused to talk. Once the detainee "became compliant" and talked, there was no need and no desire to torture. This is captured by the lower payoff of three if she tortures and four if she does not. Choosing "torture" is not in her interest, so threatening or promising to do so is not credible. She would not do it if she actually had to choose at that point. The second Interrogator who got those instructions would be confused, wondering what the heck is going on.

Even though this strategy combination or profile doesn't make sense in that way, it could still be a Nash equilibrium. To see this, we need to solve for the equilibria in the game, which we are now prepared to do.

Looking for Equilibria

Go to the upper branch at the top right of Figure 4.1. The Detainee has provided information and the Interrogator must choose between "torture" and "no torture." If she chooses "torture," she receives a payoff of 3 and if she chooses "no torture," she receives a payoff of 4. Since larger numbers represent better outcomes, 4 is better than 3 and she chooses "no torture." (Yes, it really is this easy.) So the Detainee knows that if he chooses "information," the Interrogator will choose "not torture," and he (the Detainee) will get a payoff of 3. To keep track, write this "3" next to "information."

Both the Detainee and the Interrogator must now consider what would happen if the Detainee chooses "no information" (that is, he chooses to stay silent or reveal nonvaluable, or false information) in the lower branch of the tree. Once again, the Interrogator can "torture," this time receiving a payoff of 2, or "not torture" and receive a payoff of 1. Two beats 1, so she tortures. The payoff to the Detainee for this outcome is 2.[6] Thus, the Detainee knows that if he does not reveal information, he will get a payoff of 2. Write this "2" next to "no information." His choice, then, is between "information," paying 3, and "no information," paying 2. Three beats 2, and he chooses "information."

So, the Detainee chooses "information" and the Interrogator chooses "no torture" for payoffs of 3 and 4, respectively. We are not quite done, however. We still need to double check that this outcome is a Nash equilibrium—a stable combination of actions in which neither player has an incentive to switch his or her choice of action given the other player's actions. We did this for the *Law and Order SVU* game and confirmed that neither Deborah nor Carlo would unilaterally change his or her move—that is, switch their strategies given what his or her erstwhile partner was doing. How about here?

Consider the Interrogator first. Would she want to switch from "no torture" to "torture" after the Detainee has provided information? As we just said above, no. She gets four for "not torture" and three for "torture," so she would not switch her strategy. In game theory lingo, the Interrogator has no incentive to *deviate*.

How about the Detainee? Would the Detainee want to deviate, given the Interrogator's strategy? The Detainee knows that if he could go back in time and choose "no information," he can expect to get tortured (because the Interrogator gets a payoff of two for torturing and one for not torturing when the Detainee fails to provide information). Getting tortured for holding on to information (a payoff of one) is worse than providing information and avoiding torture (a payoff of two). So the Detainee will not deviate either and {"information", ("no torture","torture")} is a Nash equilibrium in this game. Call this equilibrium the *Valuable Information, No Torture Equilibrium*. (Notice that we wrote both of the Interrogator's moves—including the one that is not chosen in this equilibrium: "torture" after "no information.")

Is this the only Nash equilibrium in BIT?

To find out, let's take a look at a different strategy profile: {"no information", ("torture","torture")}, according to which the Detainee does not reveal information and the Interrogator tortures no matter what (i.e., after both information and no information). As Figure 4.1 shows, this results in payoffs of two each to the Detainee and the Interrogator.

Does either have an incentive to deviate, given what the other player is doing?

Take the Interrogator first. If she switches to "no torture," her payoff would be one, which is less than two, so she would not deviate.

How about the Detainee? Given the Interrogator's strategy of ("torture","torture"), if he switches to "information," he gets tortured anyway and receives a payoff of one, which is less than the two he is getting, so he would not deviate either. This is, in other words, a Nash equilibrium.

But it's weird. It depends on the Interrogator doing something manifestly against her interests, taking an action she knows she would not want to do, if she was actually faced with the move "information" by the Detainee. The Interrogator's instructions, her strategy, tells her to play "torture" after receiving "information," even though this makes her worse off than playing "no torture." Why should the Detainee give any credence to the Interrogator's strategy? It just is not credible.

Is there a way to avoid this problem?

There is. And we already found it. When we used backward induction to find the first equilibrium, we assumed that the Interrogator's move at both of her decision points, or nodes, was optimal, the best she could do at that point. That's why she chose "no torture" after "information" but "torture" after "no information."

In contrast, the strategy profile constituting the second Nash equilibrium requires the Interrogator to play "torture" after "information," even though this makes her worse off than if she played "no torture." This can happen because "information" lies off the equilibrium path of play. We assumed that the Detainee was playing "no information," so the Interrogator's decision node after "information" is never reached.

The difference between the two equilibria is this: The Interrogator's instructions for the first equilibrium are better. If she follows them, she maximizes her payoffs no matter where she is. If she is in the upper branch, after "information," and she plays her corresponding strategy, "no torture," she maximizes her payoff at that node. If she is at the bottom node, after "no information," and she plays according to her instructions, she plays "torture" and again maximizes her payoffs. So she does the best that she can do in each subpart of the game. The same cannot be said for the second set of instructions, which would require her to play "torture" after "information" and receive three instead of four.

A strategy which results in a Nash equilibrium not only in the larger game, but also in every subgame, is a more compelling candidate for a rational strategy. An equilibrium which results from a strategy profile of this kind is therefore a more compelling type of equilibrium. This "refinement" of Nash equilibrium is called a *subgame perfect (Nash) equilibrium*, or SPE for short.

The "subgame" part comes from what we just said about the strategy profile constituting a Nash equilibrium in every part of the game in which the players could theoretically move, even ones that are not reached on the path of play.[7] The "perfect" is tied to the players' knowledge of the history of the game: who has moved and when. Together they capture the idea that the strategy profile is a Nash equilibrium for the entire possible history of the game. No player has an incentive to deviate from his or her strategy in the profile no matter what decision node is reached. If an unexpected, off-equilibrium path move were to occur, they would still do best by following the strategy. As is standard for sequential games like BIT, we will solve for SPE like the *Valuable Information, No Torture Equilibrium* and thus rule out Nash equilibria based on noncredible threats or promises.[8]

Now both the Detainee and the Interrogator know what they *would* do in every possible circumstance of the game. This tells them what they *should* do and tells us what they *will* do (because we assume that they are rational). In other words, we can make a prediction based on the SPE, the *Valuable Information, No Torture Equilibrium*, and compare it to the ideal outcome of the pragmatic model and the claims of the Bush administration. We have, in other words, a prediction from our *analytical* model which we can compare to the benchmark predictions of the *normative*, ideal, model in Chapter 3.

What is this prediction?

The Detainee reveals information and the Interrogator does not torture.

INTERPRETING BIT

Notice anything odd here?

Torture never occurs in equilibrium. The threat of torture compels the Detainee to divulge (enough quality) information to please the Interrogator, who therefore does not torture. This makes sense, in a way, since it is always the threat of future torture which elicits information now. Threats work when they don't actually have to be carried out. After all, your threat of no ice cream unless your child eats her broccoli is intended not to deprive her of ice cream but to get her to eat broccoli. If she refuses to eat the broccoli, your threat has failed. But the BIT result does not make sense insofar as the model predicts *zero* torture. None at all.

It also fails to match up with what actually happened in the EIT program. Not all detainees were subjected to the enhanced torture techniques, not even all "high-value detainees." For some, just the "dislocation" of rendition or the threat of EITs was enough. But of course some detainees didn't provide enough information and/or good enough information and *were* tortured, and some were tortured *a lot*. So this is not the outcome predicted in Chapter 3.

So something is clearly wrong here. Recall the point I made earlier that the ordering of some of the Detainee's payoffs might be controversial but we went ahead and assumed for this game that the Detainee was *Cooperative* in the way we defined it purely in terms of his preferences: The outcome "information" and "no torture" was preferred to the outcome "no information" and "torture." What if we were to assume that the Detainee was *Resistant* in that those preferences were reversed so that the Resistant Detainee would rather stay silent and endure torture than avoid it at the cost of revealing information?

Although the so-called simple folklore of pain has given rise to the commonplace assumption that "everyone talks, it's just a question of when," Chapter 2 demonstrated that the reality is far different (Bagaric and Clarke 2007, pp. 58–59). There are many who do not break under torture, at least not in time to provide anything valuable to their interrogators. Rumney, for example, points to court records of torture interrogations in France from the sixteenth to the mid-eighteenth centuries showing a failure to extract confessions ranged from a low of 67% to a high of 95% (Rumney 2006, p. 491). Rejali documents cases from around the world in which detainees endured horrific torture and did not break. In the resistance to the Nazis across Europe, for example, "hardcore members did not normally break" (Rejali 2007, p. 496, also Chapter 21 *passim*). The CIA's own interrogation manual from the 1980s asserts that "materialization of fear is likely to come as a relief. The subject finds out that he can hold out and his resistance is strengthened." "In fact, most people underestimate their capacity to withstand pain" (Central Intelligence Agency 1983, pp. K-2, K-8).

One of the more famous cases comes from Vietnam, that of Navy Commander and later Rear Admiral Jeremiah Denton. Shot down over Vietnam in 1965, he spent seven years and seven months in captivity. Four of those years were in solitary confinement, "including two years in a cell the size of a refrigerator."[9] Despite this and other brutalities, he managed to blink the word "torture" using Morse code during an interview the North Vietnamese hoped to use for propaganda purposes. This was the first confirmation of torture of U.S. servicemen in North Vietnamese prisons. Denton never provided the North Vietnamese with any information. The history of interrogational torture is littered with similar stories (e.g., Lea and Peters 1973, pp. 68, 75, 91, 123, 128, 130, 131, 159).

So a Resistant Detainee is possible. Would that change anything?

As a matter of fact, this is easily checked. Figure 4.2 reproduces Figure 4.1 but with the payoffs changed to reflect the fact that the Detainee is Resistant, preferring to be tortured rather than give up information. Follow the same logic as before and identify the outcome.

What did you find?

You should have found a new SPE: {"no information", ("no torture","torture")} with payoffs of three and two to the Detainee and Interrogator,

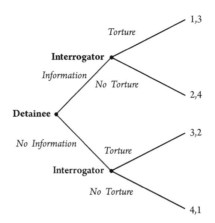

Figure 4.2 Bush Interrogation Game
with a Resistant Detainee

respectively. Note that the Interrogator's strategy is the same in this version as in the first: no torture if information is provided, torture if it is not. What has changed is the Detainee's strategy. This time, like Jeremiah Denton and many before and after him, the Detainee prefers to suffer torture (payoff of three) rather than give up information and avoid torture (a payoff of two) and thus chooses the bottom branch, after which the Interrogator tortures.

Anything odd about *this* result?

This time it is information which does not occur in equilibrium. We get torture, but no information. We might call this the Denton equilibrium. Whatever we call it, this outcome matches up neither with the claims of Bush program proponents nor with the pragmatic model in Chapter 3. In contrast to the predictions in there, in which torture is used infrequently but compels information, we get frequent torture—indeed, we get torture *all the time*—but no valuable information whatsoever. This is also implausible, and so this setup will not work either.

A QUIXOTIC MODEL OF INTERROGATIONAL TORTURE

What's wrong?

To figure this out, begin by returning to our finding in the first version of the Bush model, namely that the Detainee always provided sufficient information (in terms of both quantity and quality) and was *never* tortured. This is consistent with the Bush assumptions: The high-value detainees had information, torture was so effective that it would draw that information out of them, and the interrogators would know they had given enough not to torture them. Does this sound realistic to you?

Imagine you are an interrogator. You have a file on the detainee you are about to interrogate so you know something about him, maybe even quite a bit. But not everything, or he wouldn't be at a black site chained to the ceiling, clothed in a diaper and a hood, and subjected to deafening tones of the Red Hot Chili Peppers. And the detainee knows this.[10]

In particular, you don't know two sets of things.

First, there are some things you don't know about the information (you think) he has. You don't know how much information of interest to you he possesses. You don't know the quality of the information he has. You might have some idea, but you won't know for sure. That's why you're interrogating him. And if he does provide you with some information, you won't know for sure whether he has more.

Second, you don't know how much pain he can take. Since you accept the brutal logic of torture, you assume that some techniques generate more pain than others and that more pain is worse than less pain for a given Detainee, but you also know that people differ in terms of what they can take. In other words, what you do not know is how far you'll have to go to get this particular detainee to talk. In fact, this is what happened in the second version of the model. The detainee refused to provide any information whatsoever and was tortured all the time. The "scientific" assumptions of the Bush program assumed that this was impossible. We know, however, that this was not the case historically in general terms and not always the case in the CIA program in particular. Plenty of people have resisted far worse. As the Interrogator you know this too, and when you confront the detainee you won't know whether the detainee is the first or second type.

Actually, there is a third possibility: that the detainee knows nothing whatsoever. This again was assumed away by the Bush administration, but we know from the history of torture that innocents get swept up by mistake in any torture program. There is, in any case, at least *some* chance that this could happen; the probability is not absolutely zero. So in addition to the *Cooperative* and *Resistant* Detainees, both of whom possess information, there is the possibility of an *Innocent* Detainee as well.

Now put yourself in the shoes of the detainee. In both versions of the BIT model, the detainee knows that if he provides information, he will not be tortured. How certain of this would you be if you had been kidnapped, hooded, cuffed, earmuffed, forcibly sodomized and tranquilized, stripped naked and put in a diaper, hung from the ceiling by manacles, doused with cold water, and subjected to white noise and cold temperatures for days on end? Why might you have doubts about an interrogator's promise?

A couple of reasons. First, it is difficult for the interrogator to make this promise credible, since she has complete power over you. Even after you provide information, you're still being held captive who knows where. What if the interrogator wants some revenge for 9/11? What if she's a little sadistic? What's to stop her now that she has the information she needs? She's already emphasized many times to you that no one knows where you are and that you are completely dependent upon her. What is she going to do with you anyway? Remember that we are talking about detainee perceptions, not reality. It does not have to be the case that any CIA interrogators actually *were* sadistic—indeed, I am assuming that they were far from it—only that the detainee *believes* that there is a chance of this.

Second, even if this is not a problem, the detainee might have doubts that the interrogator will believe he has told her all he knows. After all, he knows both that she does not know everything and that she knows he will try to hide as much as he can. So the detainee knows that the interrogator will be skeptical—that is, will not necessarily believe him when he says he has divulged all he knows, even if he has done exactly that.

There is an additional element of uncertainty about information on the part of the interrogator. Precisely because the interrogator is trying to find out information, she may be uncertain as to the value of information which is provided to her. For example, Gestapo torturers "in many cases had no clear idea of what information they wanted and just tortured haphazard [sic]" (Rejali 2007, p. 116). This possibility must also be taken into account.

So there is quite of bit of uncertainty here that is assumed away in the Bush program and thus in the BIT models representing that program. In game theory jargon, the BIT models are games of complete and perfect information. Information is *complete* insofar as both the Detainee and the Interrogator know the other players in the game (each other), all the actions each one can take, and what each player receives for each outcome (the payoffs). As alluded to above, information is *perfect* insofar as the players know the "history" of the game; they know what moves the players previous to them have made.

Of course, all models must simplify and make assumptions, but the assumption of complete and perfect information is too unrealistic, too *idealistic*, to capture what really goes on in interrogational torture. In Cervantes' magnificent novel, the "breed"—the "them" with whom Don Quixote engaged in "fierce and unequal combat" in the epigraph to this chapter—were actually windmills and not giants. The Bush description of the interrogational torture program was an imaginary ideal, a giant, rather than the reality of a windmill.

We tilt at imaginary giants when we follow that description and model interrogational torture along the lines of BIT. And just as poor Don Quixote was unseated by the windmill, we were unseated by the outcomes of the BIT models.

Still, unlike Don Quixote, who persisted in his delusion, the BIT models help us face reality, telling us what needs to be added to the full model, to which we now turn.

*   *   *

The argument thus far has shown that:

1. EITs are torture and the effectiveness of interrogational torture is an open question. (Chapter 2)
2. The Bush program approximates closely the ideal model of interrogational torture and includes limits on torture; the Bush and ideal

models provide benchmarks for comparison with the game theory models to come. (Chapter 3)

3. The Bush model generates strange, quixotic outcomes. (Chapter 4)

The next step in the argument is to model the Bush interrogational torture program more realistically.

A Realistic Model
of Interrogational Torture

I regard it in fact as the great advantage of the mathematical technique
that it allows us to describe, by means of algebraic equations, the general
character of a pattern even where we are ignorant of the numerical values
which will determine its particular manifestation.

—FRIEDRICH VON HAYEK

Part of the purpose of Chapter 3 was to identify the constraints and limits on torture in the Bush program so as to avoid creating an easily criticized strawman
model of interrogational torture. The BIT model in Chapter 4 hewed closely
to the Bush ideal, but instead ended up producing an overly idealized, quixotic
model distant from reality both in the way torture worked and in the outcomes it
generated. Thus, building a realistic, but still fair, model requires navigating carefully between two types of caricature, between the Scylla of a strawman and the
Charybdis of the quixotic.

As if this were not difficult enough, there is another set of extremes to avoid:
analytical oversimplicity and realistic overcomplexity. The game theoretic model
of interrogational torture must simplify—all models must do so—but it should
not ignore essential features of the real world. That is, we must cut away some
(well, a lot actually) of the extraneous detail in order to get at the fundamental
dynamic that drives outcomes, but keep those details, those features of the real
world of interrogational torture that are the factors actually doing the driving.
Not just fenders, hubcaps, AC, and side view mirrors, but even doors, roof, and
trunk must go. But the engine, wheels, transmission, steering column, and other
necessary features must stay.

Some of these necessary features were missing from the idealized BIT models in the previous chapter, and to locate them we return to the basic elements of the BIT models: players, actions, information, and payoffs.

PLAYERS AND ACTIONS

The BIT game rightly portrayed the essence of interrogational torture as a game between a Detainee and an Interrogator. It got the *number* of players right. What it failed to capture, however, was the nature, or *type*, of each player. We saw that it made a big difference in terms of the interpretive link to the real world as well as the outcome of the game whether the Detainee was Cooperative, and so preferred to give up information to avoid torture, or was Resistant, and preferred to suffer torture rather than give up information. Although both the Cooperative and Resistant types exist in reality, and the interrogator never knows for sure which type she faces in an interrogation room, the BIT models forced us to choose one or the other. Once we chose, then all Detainees were of that type for sure, and that is what generated the bizarre outcomes. Neither the setup (knowing for sure a Detainee's type) nor the outcome (information and no torture in the first model) corresponded to the real world—even according to torture proponents.

Recall from the end of the last chapter that we should consider the same possibility for the Interrogator. Might the Detainee be similarly uncertain about the nature of the interrogator across from him? Imagine that you have valuable information, have been captured, and are being threatened with torture. Among the many horrible things running through your mind might be a doubt whether you'll be tortured even if you *do* provide information.

A scene from another classic Western, *The Good, the Bad, and the Ugly*, brilliantly illustrates this idea as well as the strategic effects when both players know this. If you are not familiar with the film, the character Angel Eyes has just had another character, Tuco, tortured for the location of some gold. Tuco provides the name of the cemetery but not the grave in which it is buried, since he doesn't know. He tells Angel Eyes, however, that Blondie knows the grave. After sending Tuco away, Angel Eyes has Blondie brought in and the following exchange ensues:

BLONDIE: (after scuffing his boot on the floor stained with Tuco's blood)
   "You're not going to give me the same treatment?"
ANGEL EYES: "Would you talk?"
BLONDIE: "No, probably not."
ANGEL EYES: "That's what I thought. Not that you are any tougher than Tuco . . . but you're smart enough to know that talking won't save you."

Angel Eyes is not a nice man (he's the "Bad" in the movie's title) and will execute and perhaps torture Blondie once Angel Eyes has the location of the grave. Blondie knows this and so does not talk.

In other words, is the Interrogator simply *Pragmatic*, and willing to torture only as a last resort to extract information from a noncooperative and knowledgeable Detainee? Or is the interrogator *Sadistic*, an Interrogator who tortures even after information has been obtained?[1] It is necessary to assume the (possible) existence of a Sadistic Interrogator in our real-life model not because it conforms to the pragmatic, normative model but because it (sometimes) conforms to reality.

More importantly, the Detainee will naturally be uncertain about whether an interrogator will refrain from torturing even if full information is provided. Interrogators who are nonsadistic in the psychological sense may also torture due to an organizational culture in which interrogators feel a need to prove their dedication by a willingness to "do what it takes" or by an incentive structure that rewards interrogators for the quantity rather than the quality of the information provided (or both).[2] It is simply not plausible to assume that a detainee would have no doubt that if he were to reveal information, even all of it, he would not be tortured anyway. This uncertainty will influence the behavior of the Detainee, so, in order to examine the effects of interrogational torture by a Pragmatic Interrogator, this perception must be taken into account, even if we are ultimately only interested in the behavior of a Pragmatic Interrogator, who only tortures as a last resort.

Together then, we have uncertainty about both player types. Each player will know his or her own type, of course, but neither will be certain of his or her opponents' type, just as you wouldn't be if you were an interrogator or a detainee. The Interrogator is uncertain whether the Detainee is knowledgeable and Cooperative, is knowledgeable and Resistant, or possesses no information (Innocent). The Detainee will be uncertain about whether the Interrogator is Pragmatic or Sadistic.

Game theory takes these uncertainties into account by adding a third player to the game, Nature, as in Figure 5.1.[3] Just as Mother Nature "decides" on whether or not it will rain, so Game Theory Nature decides on whether the Detainee will be one of the three types and the Interrogator will be one of the two types. And just as we assign probabilities to Mother Nature's choices, we will assign probabilities to Game Theory Nature's moves.

Nature thus has three choices at her first move, with each selecting one of the Detainee types along one of three branches. In the top branch the Detainee is the Cooperative type, in the middle branch the Detainee is the Resistant type, and in the bottom branch the Detainee is the Innocent type. Similarly, to capture the Detainee's uncertainty about which type of Interrogator sits across from

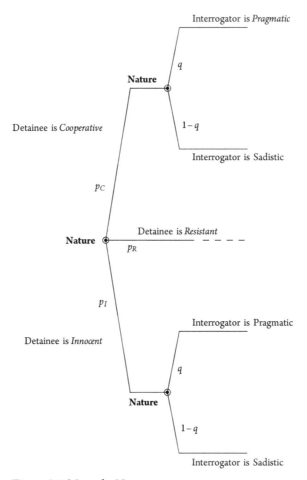

Figure 5.1 Moves by Nature

him, Nature moves again, selecting the Interrogator's type as either Pragmatic or Sadistic. Figure 5.1 captures these two moves.

Note three features about Figure 5.1. First, because all succeeding moves from Nature's choice of the Resistant Detainee are identical to the Cooperative Detainee branch of the tree, in order to save space Figure 5.1 represents them with the single line from the Resistant Detainee continuing as a dashed line.

Second, notice the letters p and q along the paths of Nature's moves. These are the probabilities that the Detainee is of that particular type. Neither we nor the players would know these probabilities, so there are no numbers attached; we let them take on any value between zero and one by labeling them with letters. (The convention in game theory is to use p and q for probabilities, but you could choose any letter or symbol you wanted.) Since probabilities always add up to one, if the probability that the Interrogator is the Pragmatic type is q, then the probability that she is of the only other possible type, Sadistic, must be $1-q$. Since there are three types of Detainees, we distinguish them by their subscripts, the little letters attached to the p, with p_C corresponding to the Cooperative Detainee type, p_R to the Resistant Detainee type, and p_I to the Innocent Detainee type. Of course p_C, p_R, and p_I together add up to one.

Finally, Nature moves prior to the two "main" players, the Detainee and the Interrogator, after which the Detainee and the Interrogator move. So you can think of the BIT game from the last chapter starting at the end of each of the lines on the right side of Figure 5.1. Figure 5.2 captures this by expanding the drawing in Figure 5.1 with the BIT games at the end of each combination of Nature's moves.

Pause here for a moment. The game tree may look more complicated than it actually is. Remember that since each player is uncertain of the other, we have six possible combinations: two Interrogator types for each of three Detainee types. Each branch, or path, through the tree represents one of these combinations. The topmost path, for example, represents the case when a Cooperative Detainee faces a Pragmatic Interrogator.

The basic set of moves between the "main" players from this point forward, however, is the same as in the BIT model. (In order to keep the figure as neat as possible, the "no" in "no information" and "no torture" is represented with the symbol $\sim$.) Since neither player will know for sure which branch of the tree he or she is on when he or she moves, we need to put the moves of the BIT game at every combination. Imagine, for example, that you are a Pragmatic Interrogator and you have just observed the Detainee's move of "no information."

Is this because the Detainee is Cooperative, but thinks you will not torture, perhaps because he thinks *you* think he is Innocent? Is it because the Detainee is Resistant and never reveals information, whether or not you torture? Or is it because the Detainee is Innocent and cannot even answer your questions?

In other words, the Interrogator will not know in which branch of the tree she sits as she prepares to make her choice. Because, however, the Detainee's moves are identical—in this particular case, "no information"—and her own moves are identical, the game looks exactly the same in each of these three branches. Both facts—the uncertainty and the sameness of the choice—are represented by the dashed vertical lines connecting the Pragmatic Interrogator's decision node after the Detainee has chosen "no information." (Remember that while there are three nodes, one for each type of Detainee, only two are shown, one for the Cooperative Detainee and one for the Innocent Detainee, to keep the figure manageable.)

Similarly, a Cooperative Detainee, for example, will wonder whether he is in the upper branch playing against a Pragmatic Interrogator or the lower branch

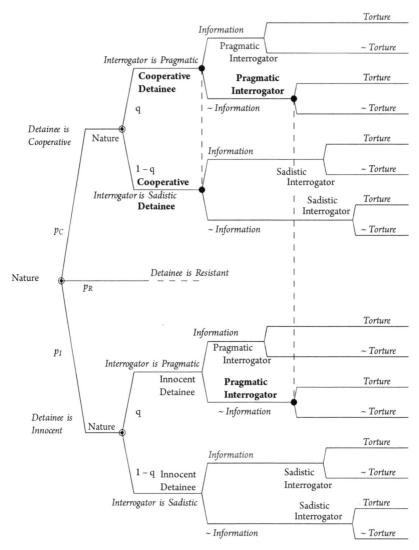

Figure 5.2 Representing Uncertainty

playing against a Sadistic Interrogator. This uncertainty is also represented in Figure 5.2 with dashed lines connecting the points where he must make his choice and is unsure which type of Interrogator he faces. Figure 5.2 shows just these two dashed lines as examples; the full game will have one for each combination, six altogether.[4]

After these moves by Nature setting up different possible states of the world (for example, a Resistant Detainee facing a Pragmatic Interrogator), the game proceeds just like the BIT model. The Detainee chooses to either reveal information ("Information") or not reveal information ("~Information"). Following the Detainee's choice, the Interrogator either tortures or does not torture. Keep in mind that at the point the Detainee and the Interrogator make their moves, neither knows which state of the world, which branch of the tree, he or she is making that choice from, captured by the dashed lines connecting their decision points (nodes).

QUESTIONING TYPE

One important aspect of interrogations in the real world that the BIT model did not consider was the nature of the questions asked by the Interrogator, namely whether they were *leading* or *objective*. Under objective questioning, the Interrogator does not tell the Detainee what she wants to hear. Under leading questioning, the Interrogator *does* let the Detainee know what would please her. While leading questioning clearly provides no new information, it is clear from the history of torture that it inevitably emerges when Interrogators torture.

We saw this in the case of John Clarke, who confessed in the Dutch Amboyna case only when his Interrogators fed him the particulars (East India Company 1665, pp. 10–12). It is for precisely this reason that medieval European civil and Inquisitorial torture had rules prohibiting asking leading questions during torture sessions, though these were likely more honored in the breach than in the observance (Peters 1999, p. 68; Lea and Peters 1973, p. 111; also Langbein 1978, p. 7).[5] Indeed, even the CIA's own 1983 Kubark manual noted the "pitfalls produced by asking questions that suggest their own answers" in the annotated bibliography at the end of the document (Central Intelligence Agency 1983, p. 110). Nevertheless, the CIA's and later the military's reliance on SERE methods originally used by the KGB to extract forced (and false) confessions makes it even more likely that such questioning was used (Mayer 2008, pp. 158, 164).

There are thus two versions of the model: objective and leading questioning. Although the leading questioning variant does not provide new information, but instead can only confirm what the interrogator wants to hear, to the extent it is employed, it needs to be examined to identify what can happen when interrogators employ both torture and leading questioning. The goal is to model what happens in an interrogation room in which torture is permitted; and since leading questioning happens frequently, it must be modeled.

In the leading questioning version, then, each of the three types of Detainee can choose either "information" or "~information" (staying silent or providing information which is not valuable). Under objective questioning, when the Interrogator does not reveal what she wants to hear, the Innocent Detainee has only one move, "~information." (Thus, the moves in the bottom half of Figure 5.2 portray the leading questioning version of the game, when the Innocent Detainee has the "information" option as well as "∼information.")

INFORMATION UNCERTAINTY

Before turning to how the players evaluate the outcomes of their choices (payoffs), it is first important to note two significant features of the move "information" by the Detainee in the model. The first is uncertainty about whether the Detainee has revealed all he knows. The second is the clarity of the information's value to the Interrogator.

Information Hiding

At some point an interrogator must decide whether or not the detainee is still withholding information, whether the detainee had up to that point revealed a little or a lot. In addition to the information already provided, this decision will also be based on factors external to the detainee's behavior, such as his or her hypothesized role in the organization or what other detainees have said about him.

In other words, under both objective and leading questioning, the Interrogator may believe that a Cooperative Detainee who chooses "information" may actually have more information, that the Detainee is still hiding something. If so, then the Interrogator would want to torture to compel full disclosure. This uncertainty is captured by the "information completeness" parameter f, which is just a number between zero and one, the probability that the Detainee has revealed all he knows. In other words, it's the probability of full information disclosure. Multiplied by the payoffs, it weights the outcome to take into account the fact that getting that payoff is uncertain. Everything else being equal, an uncertain payoff is less valuable than the identical payoff for certain because there is a chance we may not get it.

Here is a very simple example of how it works. Suppose you come to my casino and I offer you the chance to play a very simple game. I flip a fair coin. If it lands on heads, you win $10; if it lands on tails, you win $1. How much would you pay to play my game?

If you are perfectly risk neutral, not more than $5.50.[6]

Here's why.

You have to discount the value of each outcome by the likelihood that it actually occurs. Since my coin is fair, the chances of getting heads and thus $10 on any particular toss is 50% or .5. So you discount the $10 by the .5—that is, you multiply them together and you get $5. You also have a .5 chance of getting tails, netting $1, so you need to discount the value of that outcome in exactly the same way, by multiplying them, for $.50. Now you put both outcomes back together, by adding these products, and you have $5.50. This is the weighted average of the two outcomes.[7]

In other words, the *expected* value of this bet is $5.50. This is what you can expect to get in the long run, on average, if you played this game over and over again. Sometimes you'd win $10, sometimes you'd win $1, and over a long haul, you could expect to net $5.50.

Let's apply the same reasoning to our game.

To keep the arithmetic simple, let's say the maximum value of information the Detainee might have is 100. If the Interrogator believes he has provided all of it, she gets 100. But if he has not provided all of it, she gets something less. It might be only a little less, so that she gets 90. Or it might be a lot less, so she gets just 10. (Of course it might be any number less than 100; these are just easy examples.)

Now these amounts, these information values, are independent of the *likelihood* that he has provided everything, just as the coin toss was independent of the dollar amounts won for heads and tails. I could have raised the stakes to $20 for heads and $2 for tails, but that would not change the probabilities of getting heads or tails. A Detainee with valuable information may have provided a lot or only a little of the information he possesses. The same goes for a Detainee who possesses only a little valuable information.

Consider the two extreme cases when the Interrogator is absolutely certain. In the first case she is certain that the Detainee has provided all the information he has. In the second case she is just as certain that he did not, and is still hiding valuable information.

In case one, the Interrogator is convinced that this information is all the information he has. The Detainee has provided the maximum of 100. She is 100% certain that this is the maximum, so $f = 1$. Since one times whatever value the information given is the same as that value, in this case she gets 100. And since the probability that the Detainee has provided full information is 1, the probability that he is witholding anything is zero (i.e., $1 - f = 0$). Zero times anything is zero, so the value of this possible outcome, whether it is 90 or 10, is zero. Adding them together, just as we did for the coin toss example, provides a payoff of 100. (Obviously in this case the Pragmatic Interrogator has received everything she wanted and so does not want to torture.)

Now suppose that she is absolutely certain the other way: that the Detainee is hiding information. There is some amount of information which he has not divulged, so she ends up with 90 or 10. She's not on the fence about whether he is hiding information; she is 100% sure that he's holding something back, worth, say, 10 or 90. If f is the probability of proving full information, then being positive that he is holding back means $f = 0$. Zero times anything is zero, so weighting the value of the full information outcome paying 100 makes it 0. Since the probability of full information disclosure is zero, then the probability of getting only partial information is 1 (it's certain). This means multiplying 1 times whatever the value of the partial information is, which in our running example is 90 or 10. Obviously adding them together is just the same as this outcome, 90 or 10. The expected payoff, then, is 90 or 10, and the Interrogator would want to compare that value to what she would get if she decided to torture in order to see which is better for her.

We'll return to those payoffs in a moment. For now, imagine an intermediate (and more realistic) case. The Interrogator is just not sure. She suspects that the Detainee is hiding information, but she is not certain. Maybe she thinks that it could go either way; it's 50–50, reminiscent of the coin toss example. Of course, it could be 80–20, 25–75, or something else, but let's stick with 50–50.

Applying the same weighting procedure as before, this time with $f = .5$, we multiply .5 times the value of getting full information (100), which gives us 50, and .5 times the value of getting partial information (since $1 - .5 = .5$). If the value of partial information is 90, then this product is 45; if the partial information is worth 10 to the Interrogator, then this product is 5. So the expected value this time is $50 + 45 = 95$ (assuming partial information $= 90$) or $50 + 5 = 55$ (assuming that partial information is worth 10).

In short, the value of the move "information" to the Interrogator will be determined not just by the intrinsic value of the information actually provided but by the probability that the information provided was the maximum there is. At some point, f will be low enough that she will prefer to torture rather than be satisfied with a partial disclosure.

Note, though, that in the model, the decision to torture after a Detainee has revealed that information can be interpreted in two ways in terms of what it represents in the real world. On the one hand, it can be interpreted as the case in which a Detainee really *is* hiding more information and gets tortured. This would be "justifiable" torture on the pragmatic view. On the other hand, it can also be interpreted as the case in which the Detainee has revealed everything he knows but is tortured anyway because the Interrogator does not believe him. This would be unjustified torture, again, even for proponents. This outcome in the game, in other words, will be just as opaque and open to interpretation in the model as in the real world. This setup captures the fundamental problem of interrogation: The Interrogator can never be sure of what the Detainee actually knows. If he provides information, is it all of it or only a portion? If he fails to provide information or provides misleading information, is it because he is attempting to hide it or because he really does not have it? Of course, the Detainee is well aware of this fundamental uncertainty on the part of the Interrogator so f is common knowledge.

Information Clarity

The second feature of the move "information" by the Detainee is the clarity of the information provided. Under leading questioning, of course, this is irrelevant, since the Interrogator knows exactly what she wants to hear. Under objective questioning, however, the Interrogator may not always recognize "information" as valuable even when it is given. In fact, the less the Interrogator knows about the Detainee, the more this is likely to happen. In short, the Interrogator may recognize it as useful information, but might also perceive it as false or otherwise not valuable information. Thus, the "information clarity" parameter u represents the Interrogator's uncertainty about whether the Interrogator understands that the information is valuable. Since u weights the Interrogator's payoffs in exactly the same way as f, we need not go through that again.

There is a difference from f though, insofar as the Detainee will be unaware that the Interrogator has this uncertainty. A Detainee choosing "information" assumes that it will be recognized as valuable and plays accordingly. In game theoretic terms, u is the *private information* of the Interrogator; the Detainee is not aware of u.

This is an unorthodox assumption in game theory. I adopt it in this more realistic model because this happens in the real world of interrogation. While it seems likely that a Detainee will know that the Interrogator will suspect him of hiding information (i.e., that f exists) and that he cannot prove what he does not know, he is likely to believe that the Interrogator will recognize valuable information if he in facts provides it to her. Either it will be immediately seen as valuable or it can be verified later.

Indeed, *there is no point to torture or to conduct any other form of interrogation unless the interrogator can recognize at least some information as valuable.* What is an unorthodox assumption from the perspective of game theory is a natural and necessary assumption from the perspective of the real world of interrogation. In principle, both types of information uncertainty could be applied to the Sadistic Interrogator as well, but since (as we will see shortly) the Sadistic Interrogator tortures no matter what move the Detainee makes, this is irrelevant.

PAYOFFS

In the Prisoners' Dilemma in Chapter 1, in the BIT models of the last chapter, and in the expected payoff examples above, the payoffs to the players were actual numbers: years in jail (the first example), numbers representing the preferred order of the outcomes to the players, with 4 better than 3, 3 better than

2 and so forth (the BIT models), or numbers representing cardinal (as opposed to ordinal) values. Cardinal values such as the 100 for complete information and the 10 for partial information show not just the ranking of the outcomes (one over the other), but *how much* one is preferred over the other, the *intensity* of that preference.

But what goes into arriving at this ordering or these values? Rather than just a number showing the relative preference for this outcome compared to the other possible outcomes, it would be nice to show what it is about this outcome that makes it more or less attractive. We can do this by substituting these numbers with (combinations of) variables (i.e., letters) which can take on a range of values and which are more closely tied to the actions leading to the outcomes. This is the x and y from high school algebra.

Detainee Payoffs

Take, for example, the outcome when a Detainee has provided intelligence information and has not been tortured afterward. Two things have happened to the Detainee. First, he has provided information. Since this is a knowledgeable Detainee, this is not good for him, a loss of some sort. We can represent this intuitively by representing this value as the quantity v, the value of the information he divulged. Giving it up means losing it, or $-v$. Second, the Detainee has *not* been tortured, and this means no additional loss. So in total, the Detainee gets $-v$ in this outcome. We'll apply this same idea of representing costs with negative signs to the other variables as well.

Now consider the outcome in which a Detainee has refused to provide information and has been tortured afterward. In this case, the Detainee keeps the information, so there is no $-v$, but he suffers torture. We can represent (not reduce!) this loss with $-k$ (we need the symbols "t" and "c" elsewhere, so we'll use "k" for the phonetic mnemonic **k**ost of torture to the Detainee). So in total, the detainee gets $-k$ in this outcome.

How about the other two possibilities? If the Detainee provides no information but is not tortured, then he suffers no losses at all and receives a payoff of zero. If he provides information and gets tortured afterward anyway, then he pays both "costs," for a payoff of $-v - k$. Now go back to the Cooperative vs. the Resistant Detainee types in the previous chapter. This variables approach to payoffs gives us a neat and clear way to distinguish the two.

The Cooperative and Resistant Detainees are identical insofar as they most prefer not to reveal information and not get tortured, ending up with the best they can do, 0. They also both least prefer to reveal information and still get tortured anyway, which results in the worst payoff of $-v - k$. Where they differ and, indeed, what distinguishes them is the value of information relative to the costs of being tortured.

Both have information v they do not want to give up. But whereas the Cooperative type of Detainee prefers to give up information rather than be tortured, the Resistant Detainee is willing to suffer torture rather than give up information. As discussed in Chapter 4, Jeremiah Denton's torture at the hands of the North Vietnamese provides a clear example of this.

The costs $-v$ and $-k$ are the same, but the difference between the two Detainee types is captured nicely by the way they order these payoffs. For the Cooperative Detainee we have $-v > -k$, so that $-v$ is a better payoff than, is preferred to, $-k$. For the Resistant Detainee $-k > -v$, so that suffering the costs of torture is preferred to the costs of giving up information.[8] If $-v > -k$, then $v < k$. Similarly, if $-k > -v$, then $v > k$.[9]

This makes sense; for the Cooperative Detainee, the value of the information is less than the pain of torture, whereas for the Resistant Detainee, the information is more valuable than magnitude of the torture. Thus, the full preference ordering for the Cooperative Detainee is $0 > -v > -k > -v - k$, while for the Resistant Detainee it is $0 > -k > -v > -v - k$. These orderings follow the numbers in the BIT models in the last chapter and capture neatly and compactly the differences between the two Detainee types.

What about the payoffs to the Innocent type of Detainee who has no v to give up? While it is theoretically possible for the Innocent Detainee to behave either like the Cooperative or the Resistant Detainee, depending on his aversion to lying and falsely confessing, we will assume that the Innocent Detainee mirrors the preference ordering of the Cooperative Detainee. Whereas the Innocent Detainee would prefer not to lie, to falsely confirm something he knows nothing about, he is willing to do so if the alternative is telling the truth (i.e., "no information" because he has none) and getting tortured. In other words, replacing the v of the Cooperative and Resistant Detainees with l for lying, the preference ordering is exactly the same: $-l > -k$, for a full ordering of $0 > -l > -k > -l - k$.

Variables have a third advantage beyond linking payoffs to actions and permitting the easy characterization of different player types. By not tying the results of the model to a particular set of values, the results will be more general. In the expected value example above, we specified two versions of partial information, one worth 90 and one worth 10 to the Interrogator, with expected payoffs of 95 and 55 respectively. It should be clear that they might lead to radically different outcomes—for example, torture in one case but not in the other. The model could (rightly) be criticized for assuming a particular set of values, and we wouldn't know whether the results held true for a different set of values. Using variables makes the model more flexible, helping us understand, as Hayek says in the epigraph, "the general character of a pattern even where we are ignorant of the numerical values which will determine its particular manifestation."[10] In other words, we don't need to know particular values of partial information, 10 or 50 or 90 or whatever, to examine the general effects of partial information. This makes the model more powerful because it provides more analytical leverage.

There is a fourth advantage. Using variables will also allow us later on to see what happens to the different equilibrium outcomes of the model as the values of different variables change. What, for example, happens to Cooperative Detainee truth telling as the value of the information goes up? What happens to outcomes in which there is no torture when the costs of torture to the Interrogator go down? By letting those values vary, rather than fixing them to particular numbers, we can (and will in Chapter 7) answer these and other similarly important questions.

Interrogator Payoffs

To assign variables to the Interrogator's payoffs, we will use the first BIT model as our point of departure. In what follows we assume that the game is between a Cooperative Detainee and a Pragmatic Interrogator. The Interrogator seeks information from the Detainee; if he supplies it, she receives a benefit. Call this V for the value of the information. Recall that in the BIT model the Interrogator preferred not to torture if the Detainee had provided information. This was consistent with the real constraints and limits on torture we discovered in Chapter 3, in which torture is employed as a last resort.

A preference on the part of the Interrogator not to use torture if she can get the information otherwise suggests that using torture is somehow costly for the Interrogator as well. Even if she is willing to use it, torture does not come "free." She pays a price every time she uses torture, even when she deems it necessary. Call this cost of using torture $-c$. The cost $-c$ might represent psychological, reputation, morale, or other costs to Interrogators (and the government employing them).[11]

Moreover, since the Pragmatic Interrogator uses torture only to extract information from knowledgeable Detainees, she bears an additional cost $-a$ for "unnecessary" torture—that is, torture of an Innocent Detainee who does not reveal information (i.e., tells the truth) or of any Detainee who reveals full information. Adding the additional variable or parameter $-a$ complicates the model a little but is necessary to be consistent with the ideal and pragmatic models of interrogational torture in Chapter 3, in which a Pragmatic Interrogator prefers to torture only when absolutely necessary and does not want to torture "unnecessarily" (again, from the proponents' point of view). Thus, if the Interrogator receives information and does not torture afterward, she receives V; if she does torture afterward, she receives $V - c - a$.

If the Detainee fails to provide information and the Interrogator tortures, she pays the permanent cost of torture $-c$ but receives no information, leaving her with just $-c$. If she fails to torture after the Detainee has refused to provide information she "pays a price" $-r$. This captures an element central to the rationale for using torture: establishing the credibility of the threat to use torture if the Detainee does not provide valuable information. That is, it captures the idea that, once torture becomes an interrogation tactic, interrogators suffer reputation costs if Detainees fail to provide useful information but the Interrogator still does not torture. An Al Qaeda training manual captured in Afghanistan provides support for this belief. According to an Interrogator who read the manual, it viewed "America's aversion to torture ... as a symbol of American weakness" (Mackey and Miller 2004, p. 180).

Putting the cost payoffs together, then, we have $-c > -r > -a$. Alternatively, we have $0 < c < r < a$. Note that this means we are building in a strong aversion to torturing innocents by making the additional cost a larger than the reputation costs r. Given this aversion assumption favoring the proponents' argument, it will be interesting to see whether and how often innocents are tortured in the full model. Figure 5.3 presents the BIT model with these payoffs in variable form.

Even though this game replicates the same problems plaguing the original BIT, let's take a closer look at it for a moment because it does provide a good and easy illustration of how to solve a game using variables for payoffs.

We solve this game just as we did before. It is clear that if the Detainee provides information (along the top branch), then the Pragmatic Interrogator

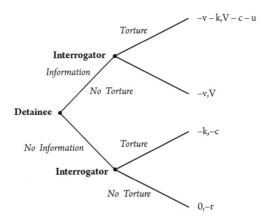

Figure 5.3 Bush Interrogation Game with Variables for Payoffs

will not torture because $V > V - c - a$. She gets the benefits with no costs. So she does not torture.

What about the bottom branch, when the detainee has not provided any information? Her choice is to torture and receive a payoff of $-c$ or not to torture and receive a payoff of $-r$. We know that torture is a last resort for the Pragmatic Interrogator, but this is precisely that time. In the post-9/11 world, the "gloves are off" and the costs of letting a suspected terrorist hide valuable information $(-r)$ are higher (that is to say, worse) than the costs of torture $(-c)$. In other words, the Interrogator suffers losses in either case, but the losses from using torture are not as large as the losses from the reputation costs, or $-c > -r$ and the Pragmatic Interrogator will choose torture. More generally, once torture is admitted as an interrogation technique, it must be the case that using torture is preferred to not using torture for some level of non-information disclosure.

Note that these orderings are the same as in the BIT model and make sense in the same way they did in that model with numerical payoffs. The Pragmatic Interrogator prefers to get information without torture, but is willing to "do what it takes" (i.e., torture) to compel the Detainee to give up information, rather than let a suspected terrorist get away.

Finally, there are the payoffs to the Sadistic type of Interrogator. The Sadistic Interrogator receives the same value from information V as the Pragmatic Interrogator, but naturally enough considers the use of torture to be a benefit rather than a cost. Thus, there is no c or a, but instead the variable s, which represents the sadistic benefit the Sadistic Interrogator receives from torturing regardless of whether or not the detainee has provided information.

A REALISTIC INTERROGATIONAL TORTURE GAME (RIT)

We have made important and necessary changes to BIT while staying faithful to core features of the pragmatic model. We have retained the pragmatic model's conception of torture as a last resort in the form of the Pragmatic Interrogator type who prefers not to torture if full information is provided and who suffers costs from using torture and even an additional cost from torturing innocents or those who have already provided full information. We have also assumed that there are indeed detainees who have intelligence information and are willing to give it up only under (the threat of) torture, as assumed by the Bush administration and advocates of interrogational torture more generally. Table 5.1 summarizes the variables and their symbols.

Other changes we have made add the realism necessary for us to know that we are dealing with windmills and not giants. In the first set of changes, we added the very real uncertainty that interrogators will have about how much the detainee

Table 5.1. KEY TO SYMBOLS FOR PAYOFFS

Element of Model	Symbol	Meaning
	v	**V**alue of information to Cooperative and Resistant Detainees
Detainee	l	**L**ying cost to Innocent Detainee
	k	Torture **k**ost to Detainee
	V	**V**alue of information to Interrogator
	c	**C**ost of using torture to Interrogator
	a	**A**dditional cost of using "unnecessary" torture to Interrogator
Interrogator	h	Value of **h**idden information to Interrogator
	r	**R**eputation losses to Interrogator for not torturing upon receiving no information
	s	**S**adism benefit to the Sadistic Interrogator for using torture
	f	Probability the Detainee has provided **f**ull information
Uncertainty	u	Probability the Interrogator **u**nderstands information is valuable

knows and indeed whether he knows anything at all. We also added detainee uncertainty about whether the interrogator is sadistic and will torture him no matter how much information he gives up. We include this possibility *not* because we think CIA interrogators actually *were* sadistic—indeed we'll assume they were pragmatic in what follows—but because it is very likely that detainees might worry they were sadistic. Any person subjected to torture in interrogations would wonder about this. In the second set of changes, we added the uncertainty that real-life interrogators actually have about the value of information and how much had been disclosed. Thirdly, we replaced numerical payoffs with the more general variable payoffs linked more intuitively to the actual actions the players take. Finally, distinguishing between objective and leading questioning results in two versions of the model.

Putting all this together generates the Realistic Interrogational Torture (RIT) game in Figure 5.4. Admittedly, it looks a bit messy and complicated, but it is really only the accumulation of all the individual changes we have made. Before we walk through the game, it is important to note that Figure 5.4 actually presents an amalgam of two versions of the game, with the payoffs for objective questioning in the upper branch (Cooperative Detainee) and the moves for the leading question variant of the model in the lower branch (Innocent Detainee).

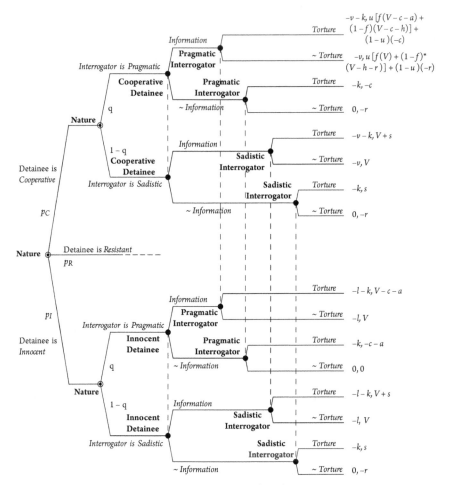

Figure 5.4 Realistic Interrogational Torture Game (RIT)

In the objective questioning version, the Innocent Detainee does not have the move "information" as he does in the Figure 5.4. In the leading questioning version of the game, when the Interrogator tells the Detainee exactly what she wants to hear, uncertainty about the value of the information (u) makes no sense and would disappear from the payoffs to the Interrogator. The branches for the Resistant Detainee type are again omitted to keep the diagram manageable, but recall that they are identical to the Cooperative Detainee. The Resistant Detainee just has the different preference ordering.

The RIT game begins with Nature making two moves, first selecting one of the three Detainee types, Cooperative, Resistant, or Innocent, with the associated probabilities p, before then selecting one of the two Interrogator types, Pragmatic or Sadistic, with the associated probabilities q and $1 - q$. The uncertainty of both players about their opponent is captured by the dotted lines connecting their choice nodes and the fact that the game from those nodes are identical to each other.

At this point, then, there are six BIT-like games, one for each combination of Detainee type (3) and Interrogator type (2).[12] The games differ somewhat, however, in their payoffs, since the different player types feel differently about the actions and the outcomes. Start at the top-right branch of the tree, when Nature has chosen the Cooperative type of Detainee and the Pragmatic type of Interrogator. The Cooperative Detainee has chosen to reveal information and the Interrogator has chosen to torture.

What does each player get from this outcome? The payoffs are listed in this order: *Detainee, Interrogator* and separated by a comma. So, just as we described above, the Detainee gets $-v-k$ because he has revealed information and also been tortured. The payoffs to the Interrogator are, to use a technical term, goopier, but then her job is more complicated in real life too.

First take a look at her payoffs from the inside out. You may have heard the expression "surrounded by uncertainty." In the case of the Pragmatic Interrogator's payoffs, this is *literally* true. At the core, or center, of her payoffs are the same payoffs from the BIT models, $V - c - a$. Now, though, they are surrounded by uncertainty: the probabilities f and u on one side and their complements, $1 - f$ and $1 - u$, on the other side. The fundamental idea is that the basic payoffs from the BIT model are now weighted by this uncertainty, just as in the simple examples above.

To see this, now look at her payoffs from the outside and work your way in.

The first thing to consider is whether or not the Interrogator has **understood** that the information is valuable. If she has not understood that the information is valuable (alternatively: she has understood the information to be not valuable), then she gets just $-c$, the costs of torture with no benefit of the information. Just as above, this outcome is weighted by the likelihood it occurs $(1 - u)$.[13] If, on the other hand, she *does* understand the information to be valuable, then this outcome (everything in the brackets) is weighted (multiplied) by its likelihood, u.

The next thing to consider is whether the Interrogator believes that it is all the information the Detainee possesses—that is, that there has been **full** information disclosure. Just as with the clarity variable u, the probability of full information f weights that possibility, in which the Interrogator receives the **value** of the information minus the permanent torture **cost** $-c$ and the **a**dditional cost of "unnecessary" torture $-a$, while the likelihood of the other possibility, less than full information $(1 - f)$, weights what she receives then, the value of whatever information is received minus the permanent costs of torture $-c$ and the costs of hidden information $-h$.

Before we move down to the next branch and combination of moves, a word is in order here about interpreting "information" and "no information" in RIT versus BIT. In the BIT game of the last chapter, we interpreted "no information" to mean "not enough good (enough) information" along with the other three interpretations. We've made things a bit more realistic in RIT by bringing in $-h$. This means that *any* valuable information provided by the Detainee counts as "information," unlike in BIT, where we excluded nominal but valuable information.

This is an improvement in another way as well: It provides greater benefit of the doubt to proponents. Now, even the smallest amount of information counts as valuable information. The Interrogator may still decide it's not enough and torture, of course, but in RIT no valuable information is "lost" by counting it as "no information." As a reminder, this leaves the following three interpretations of the move "no information" by the Detainee:

1. truthful, accurate, but nonvaluable information
2. false and misleading information
3. no information whatsoever

In the next branch down, everything is the same except that the Interrogator has chosen not to torture. In this outcome, the Detainee stills pays the cost $-v$ for giving up information but does not suffer the loss of $-k$ as well. Notice that the Interrogator's payoffs are very similar to the first branch. There is still some uncertainty about the value of the information and whether or not the Detainee has revealed all he knows. There is also the penalty or cost of $-h$ if it turns out the detainee has hidden information.

The differences are related—not surprisingly—to not using torture along this path of play. On the one hand, there are no costs $-c$ or $-a$ since the Interrogator did not use torture. On the other hand, if it should turn out that the Detainee failed to provide full information or the Interrogator failed to understand the information as valuable but did not torture, the Interrogator pays the reputation costs $-r$.

The payoffs to the remaining outcomes are much simpler. In the next two branches down, the Pragmatic Interrogator confronts a Cooperative Detainee, but the Detainee has not provided information to the Interrogator. In branch three (counting from the top down), the Interrogator tortures; in branch four she does not. If she tortures, the Detainee suffers the cost $-k$ but keeps the information and thus pays no cost for that. The Interrogator pays the permanent cost of torture $-c$ but receives no benefit V. This time, though, she does not pay the additional cost –*a* because torture after "no information" is considered "necessary" torture on the pragmatic view. If the Interrogator fails to torture, then the Detainee suffers no losses (the best the Detainee can do). The Interrogator, however, pays the reputation costs –*r* for failing to torture after receiving no information.

In the next set of four branches a Cooperative Detainee faces a Sadistic Interrogator. The payoffs to the Detainee are exactly the same; the payoffs to the Interrogator, however, differ. A Sadistic Interrogator still receives the benefit *V* from valuable information if the Detainee reveals it, but pays no costs from using torture. On the contrary, because this Interrogator type is **S**adistic, she receives an additional *benefit s* whenever she uses torture.

The middle branch of the tree, in which the Detainee is the Resistant type, looks exactly like the upper branch just described. The lower branch of the tree, in which an Innocent Detainee squares off against both a Pragmatic and a Sadistic Interrogator, is much simpler. Here is why.

First, recall that if an Innocent Detainee has the option to provide information, then we must be in the leading question variant of the model. If I am an Interrogator asking leading questions, and the Detainee is answering them, then there is no uncertainty about the clarity of the information. Consequently, there is no *u* variable weighting the payoffs. Now it is true that *V* is not new information but instead confirmation of preexisting belief, but this is what an Interrogator asking leading questions values, so we keep the same payoff. The rest of the payoffs to both types of Interrogators are exactly the same as with the other detainees. As for the Innocent Detainee's payoffs, he suffers the same costs from torture as the other types of detainees, –*k*, but since he has no information, his costs of providing "information" to the Interrogator are the costs of being forced to lie to avoid torture: –*l*.

With these more realistic moves and payoffs, we now have a more realistic model of interrogational torture that steers a middle path between the two sets of extremes identified at the outset of the chapter. It balances reality with fidelity to the pragmatic model on the one hand and incorporates what is necessary while abstracting away what is nonessential on the other. In order to see what happens in this model, we need to solve it, to which we now turn.

*   *   *

The argument thus far has shown that:

1. EITs are torture, and the effectiveness of interrogational torture is an open question. (Chapter 2)
2. The Bush program approximates closely the ideal model of interrogational torture and includes limits on torture; the Bush and ideal

models provide benchmarks for comparison with the game theory models to come. (Chapter 3)

3. The Bush model generates strange, quixotic outcomes. (Chapter 4)

4. The Bush interrogational torture program is more realistically modeled as objective and leading question variants of an incomplete information game, with three types of detainees, two types of interrogators, and uncertainty about the amount and value of information provided. (Chapter 5)

The next step in the argument is to solve this more realistic model.

A Brutal Logic

An equilibrium is not always an optimum; it might not even be good.
This may be the most important discovery of game theory.
　　—IVAR EKELAND, *The Best of All Possible Worlds: Mathematics and Destiny*

If interrogational torture is to work the way its proponents claim, then it must
follow a brutal cost–benefit, pain–information logic. Now that we have a more
realistic model, but one still faithful to the pragmatic model in Chapter 3, it
is time to trace out this brutal logic, solving for the RIT model's equilibria.
In following this logic, systematically and relentlessly, we will use bloodless
and sterile language to reconstruct a bloody and dirty work. This, however,
is the logic of the pragmatic model and it must be faced squarely by those
advancing it. The equilibria we find tell us what can happen, and under what conditions, when torture along the lines of the pragmatic model is admitted into an
interrogation room.

　　In one sense, this chapter and the next constitute the core of the argument.
The deductive argument about what happens when interrogators torture is actually located in the nitty-gritty mathematical derivation of the equilibria and
the investigation of their properties. As you've already seen, the math is really
just an accounting device to keep track of the logic, but we will all but eliminate
it here. For those interested, the derivation of all the equilibria can be found in
Appendix A.

　　We will solve RIT the same way we solved the BIT model, with one additional step. The Interrogator will use the move made by the Detainee ("no
information," for example) to see if that gives her a better idea of what type of
Detainee she is facing. Updating your beliefs in this way requires a new tool,
Bayesian belief updating. Once we have this tool in hand, we'll check for two
equilibria of the RIT game. Having walked through an example of how to solve

for equilibria, we leave the derivation of the other equilibria for Appendix A and turn to their properties in Chapter 7.

UPDATING YOUR BELIEFS

Suppose you've returned to my casino and I offer you the opportunity to play a new game. I'll give you $10 if you can guess the suit (club, diamond, heart, or spade) of a card I'll draw randomly from a regular 52-card deck. If you guess wrong, you give me $2 (in other words you lose $2). Let's say that I charge you $3 to play this game.

Would you pay the $3 to play this game?

In order to figure this out, you will want to consider the likelihoods of winning the $10 and losing the $2. At this point, before I've drawn the card, what are the chances you'll pick the right suit and win the $10? One in four, or 25%, because the total of 52 cards are divided equally among the four suits (13 cards each). Of course this also means that your chances of guessing wrong and picking one of the other three suits are three in four, or 75%. Not great odds, admittedly.

Still, you can use this information to calculate the expected value of this bet in exactly the same way we did in the last chapter. Just as before, the expected value is just the weighted average of the two outcomes, where the weights come from the probabilities or chances that each outcome occurs. For this game it is .25($10) + .75(−$2) = $1. If you were to play this game over and over again, your average per game winnings would be $1.

Assuming you're still risk neutral, as in the last chapter, this isn't a profitable game for you (though, like a real casino, it would be for me). You would pay $3 and expect, on average, to win $1.

Now suppose that, as in real life, I'm not very handy with cards, and as I draw the card in front of you, you notice that it is red. It flashed too fast for you to tell the particular card or even the particular suit, but you did notice that it was definitely red and not black.[1]

So there we are: I've drawn the card, you haven't paid yet, and I ask you whether you want to put down the $3 and play. What would you do? Would you reason as before and decline my offer? Or would you change your mind? (We'll keep assuming you're risk neutral through the rest of this example.)

If you stick to your guns, that means that you would ignore the new information, the fact that you know the card is red and not black. Does that sound reasonable? Is it *rational* to continue to insist that there is, say, only a 25% chance the card I'm holding is a diamond? Or that there is still a 25% chance that the card is a spade?

No. It's not rational or reasonable. Given that the card is red, you know it *cannot* be either a club or a spade (which are both black) and that it *must* be either a diamond or a heart. You don't know which of the two, but you do know it has to be one of them. There is no good reason for you to stick to your old beliefs; you should revise or update them given this new information.

So what are your updated beliefs? Well, you know now you're going to guess either "diamond" or "heart" because it has to be one of these two and there is an equal chance of either one. With no other information, you have a 50/50 chance of picking the right one. Still not great, but your chances have improved significantly from the .25/.75 chances before I drew the card.

How does this affect your expected value calculation? Substitute in the .5 and .5 for the .25 and .75 from before, so that you have $.5(\$10) + .5(-\$2) = \$4$. This changes things pretty dramatically. You can now expect to win \$4 on average, not \$1. With the \$3 price tag on this game, you can expect to come out ahead by \$1 and it now makes sense to take the bet and put down your \$3. If I keep drawing cards like this, it won't be long before I'm out of the casino business.

The point of all this is that it is irrational to ignore relevant new information when deciding on a course of action. Of course, the key here is relevant; had I drawn the card more expertly so that you only saw the back of it, you would have no new information, and your estimates should stay as they were before. But if there is truly new relevant information, as in my card draw, then you would be irrational to ignore it.

We will assume that the Interrogator is as reasonable as you are and apply the same principle to the RIT model. The Detainee moves first and that move may tell the Interrogator something about his type. Under objective questioning, for example, the move "information" tells the Interrogator that she is facing a Cooperative Detainee because Innocent Detainees cannot provide the information and Resistant Detainees will not provide any information. Knowing the Detainee's type is important to the Interrogator because the action she wants to take in response depends upon which type the Detainee is as well as upon the action the Detainee has taken (and her other beliefs about whether all the information has been divulged, etc.).

Bayes' Rule is the mathematical formula for updating beliefs in this way, and we will use it to calculate expected payoffs and solve for perfect Bayesian equilibria (PBE), an extension of subgame perfect equilibria (SPE) from the previous chapter.[2] The only difference is that players update their beliefs using Bayes' Rule whenever possible and use those beliefs to calculate their expected utilities.

We will give the pragmatic interrogation model the full benefit of the doubt and assume the Interrogator updates her beliefs rationally (that is, according to Bayes' Rule) whenever possible, uses those beliefs to estimate which type of Detainee she is facing, and then calculates her expected payoffs in our game.[3]

FINDING EQUILIBRIA

The three general steps for solving for PBE in RIT are as follows:

1. Posit a set of possible strategies (moves) by each of the three Detainee types.
2. Figure out each Interrogator type's optimal response to both possible moves of the Detainee, given the assumed Detainee strategies and updating beliefs according to Bayes' Rule where possible.
3. Go back and check to see if any of the Detainee types would want to change his strategy given the Interrogator's anticipated responses.

If the answer to 3. is yes and one or more of the Detainee types *would* want to switch his strategy, then the strategy profile (the Detainee candidate strategies and the Interrogator responses) is *not* an equilibrium. If the answer is no, and all the Detainee types would stick to the candidate strategies, then we *have* found an equilibrium. Let's see how each step works in practice.

Step #1: Candidate Strategies

The first step is to trot out a candidate equilibrium by simply imagining a move by each player and/or player type. For example, in the RIT game, we might imagine the set of strategies (no information, no information, information). Another would be (no information, no information, no information). In the first example, the Cooperative and Resistant types of Detainee both provide no information, while the Innocent Detainee falsely confesses information (under leading questioning, obviously). In the second example, all three Detainee types fail to provide useful information. We will always assume this order in listing the strategies for the Detainee types: (Cooperative, Resistant, Innocent).

Why begin by assuming a set of strategies and why do we have to have one for each of the Detainee types? After all, there is only one actual Detainee sitting across from an Interrogator.

Remember that acting rationally is acting systematically, considering all the possibilities, and game theory reflects that idea by having the players consider all the possible combinations of their moves. Just as a football coach tries to have a defensive alignment for any offensive setup, the Interrogator wants to have a plan of what to do for any possible move by the Detainee. And because there are different types of Detainee, this means the possible moves of each Detainee type. Each possible combination could be an equilibrium and we need to check them all.

The Interrogator must think something like the following. "I don't know which type of Detainee I'm facing or what he will do, but one possibility is (no information, no information, information). Another possibility I must consider is (no information, no information, no information)."

Still, the situation is not *that* bad; not *every* combination is possible and some can be ruled out. The first candidate, for example, (no information, no information, information), can only happen under leading questioning, since the Innocent Detainee cannot even make this move under objective questioning. The Interrogator can also rule out any set of strategies that has the Resistant Detainee playing "information" since the Resistant Detainee's dominant strategy is "no information." As it turns out, this eliminates four sets of strategies the Interrogator must consider. Abbreviating the move "information" with *info*, here is one eliminated combination, for example: (*info, info, info*).[4]

A rational Interrogator will systematically examine what she wants to do for any possible strategy combinations that remain and, since we are modeling her behavior, we will do the same. Considering both objective and leading questioning and using the same notation as above, this gives us the following list of *pure strategies*, keeping in mind that "no info" can mean false and misleading information or nonvaluable information in addition to no information at all[5]:

1. **Objective Questioning**
    (a) (*info, no info, no info*)
    (b) (*no info, no info, no info*)
2. **Leading Questioning**
    (a) (*info, no info, info*)
    (b) (*info, no info, no info*)
    (c) (*no info, no info, info*)
    (d) (*no info, no info, no info*)

Step #2: The Interrogator's Response

Once the Pragmatic Interrogator has the list of strategy combinations she must consider, she then figures out what her best response is to each, taken one at a time.[6] She does this in three steps:

1. First, she updates her beliefs about the likelihood of each Detainee type using the Detainee's candidate moves as her data for updating her beliefs according to Bayes' Rule.

2. Second, she uses these updated beliefs to calculate the expected utility of each of her moves.
3. Third, she chooses the move with the higher expected utility after "information" and the move with the higher expected utility after "no information," giving her a complete plan of action for every Detainee move.

Take, for example, the first set of strategies under objective questioning: (*info, no info, no info*). Assuming the Detainee types are playing these strategies, what are her updated beliefs about the likelihood she is facing a Cooperative Detainee after observing the move "information"?

You don't even need to get out a pencil and paper for this one: In this candidate set of strategies, only the Cooperative Detainee plays "information," so the probability is 1. In my casino example, this is equivalent to my drawing the card so slowly that you actually could see it was a diamond, not just that it was red. This means that after she sees "information," she knows she is playing against a Cooperative Detainee, and this simplifies things a bit for her (not completely, because there will still be uncertainty about the clarity and completeness of the information). In calculating her expected utility for which action is better, "torture" or "not torture," she needs only to consider her payoffs in the upper part of the tree, after the "Detainee is Cooperative" node.[7]

What if she observes "no information"? Here things are not as clear. "No information" is consistent with the candidate strategies of both the Resistant and the Innocent Detainee. She can rule out the Cooperative Detainee type, but she doesn't know which of the other two sits across from her.[8] In the casino example, the color red ruled out spades and clubs, but still left the possibility that it could be either a diamond or a heart. This remaining uncertainty is important because while she prefers to torture a Resistant Detainee, she does not want to torture an Innocent Detainee. This time when she calculates her expected utility for which action is better after "no information," either "torture" or "not torture," she needs to weight the payoffs by the likelihood that she is playing them against a Resistant Detainee versus an Innocent Detainee.

The weights come from Bayes' Rule. We'll calculate them in a moment, but before we do, consider the other possible set of strategies under objective questioning: (*no info, no info, no info*). In this case, all three Detainee types play "no information." What does the move "no information" tell us about the Detainee's type?

Nothing at all. In my casino example, this is equivalent to my drawing the card expertly so that you only see the back of the card and no new information is provided. When this happens, you stick to your original estimate that the card is a diamond (.25). Our Interrogator will do the same. Since there is no new information, there is no reason to change her beliefs, and she sticks with her initial or *prior* beliefs (p_C, p_R, and p_I).[9]

Return now to the first candidate set of strategies, (*info, no info, no info*).

The Interrogator needs to figure out her optimal (best) response after both "information" and "no information" so she has a complete plan of action regardless of which action ends up being played. So she needs to calculate and compare her expected utilities of "torture" and "not torture" after "information" and after "no information."

AFTER "INFORMATION"

Take "information" first. Since only the Cooperative Detainee plays "information" in this candidate set of strategies, by Bayes' Rule (common sense!), she knows (probability = 1) she is in the topmost branch of the tree after the nodes "Detainee is Cooperative" and "Interrogator is Pragmatic" (she knows her own type). Accordingly, she knows she will receive the payoffs from that node. All she needs to do is simplify the payoffs to "torture" and "not torture" and choose the one giving her a higher payoff.

The calculation proceeds just as in the previous chapter, we just have more variables. Working through that algebra, the expected utility of "torture" is $uV - uh + ufh + ufr - r$. The expected utility of "no torture" is $uV - uh - ufa + ufh - c$. The Interrogator will prefer to torture when the expected value of "torture" is greater than the expected value of "no torture"—that is, when the first quantity is greater than the second quantity: $uV - uh + ufh + ufr - r > uV - uh - ufa + ufh - c$.

You're to be forgiven if at this point you're wondering how far all this has gotten you if you're left with this soup of letters, an uncomfortable flashback to high school, glazed eyes, and increasingly clammy hands. You'd also be right if you're thinking that which action provides the higher payoff depends on the values of the variables.

To see the next step, consider your quandary about whether or not to take an umbrella with you in the morning. When you stand in the morning darkness of your hallway deciding whether or not to take your umbrella, you don't know what state of the world you'll be in at 5:00 pm: whether it will be raining or not. There is an imaginary dotted line connecting your morning choice nodes for these two states of the world: it ends up raining and it doesn't end up raining. Your morning choice is the same in both cases: take, don't take your umbrella. You just don't know at which node you stand when you make that choice.

Your decision will depend on two factors: how likely it is to rain and how you feel about some of the possible consequences of your choices. You'll want to think about how bad it would be if it rained and you didn't have your umbrella or how annoying it would be to tote around an umbrella in the sunshine. Your decision is easy if the chances of rain are really high or really low or you're wearing some new and fragile item of clothing or just had your hair done. Otherwise, for the intermediate cases, you'll have some threshold, maybe only unconscious, for taking the umbrella versus not taking it.

The situation is actually very similar for the Interrogator. Think about what she wants to know. She is trying to decide whether or not to torture because although she's received information, she doesn't know for sure whether she's received all the Detainee knows. So let's solve the above inequality for f, the probability that the Detainee has revealed all of his information. This will tell us at what value of f she switches from "no torture" to "torture," just like you might switch from "no umbrella" to "take an umbrella" when the forecast says 65% chance of rain. A little bit of algebra gives us $f < \frac{r-c}{u(r+a)} \equiv \hat{f}$, where $\hat{f}$ is just a label for this particular value of f, read "hat f," and $\equiv$ just means "is defined as."

This says that the Interrogator will torture when her confidence (belief f) that the Detainee has revealed all he knows drops below the *threshold* $\hat{f}$. To help fix this idea, take a look at Figure 6.1. The horizontal axis is the probability f the detainee has revealed all of his information. Since it's a probability, it ranges from 0 on the left (no chance he provided all the information) to 1 on the right (he's provided everything he knows for sure). If f is equal to or above $\hat{f}$, then she does not torture; she is confident enough that the Detainee has revealed all the information he has. If, however, $\hat{f}$ moved to $\hat{f}'$, then f is below the threshold and she tortures.

Note that this is a real constraint; given that $0 < c < r < a$, there are values of $\hat{f}$ between 0 and 1, which is required for a belief. It also makes intuitive sense; at some point the Interrogator, whether she is a CIA operative at a black site or a medieval European magistrate, believes that the Detainee has revealed everything he knows and "switches" from "torture" to "not torture." This "switching" point is the threshold $\hat{f}$. So even though our game is "one-shot," with each player

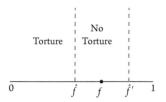

Figure 6.1 Threshold Example

moving one time, the setup captures this intuitive ideal central to the (brutal) logic of torture anywhere and everywhere it has been practiced.

This *information hiding threshold* means that the Interrogator's response actually depends on her belief f. We cannot simply write down "play 'torture' after 'information' " as a response any more than we could write "play 'no torture' after 'information'." The strategies depend on her beliefs and we need to put those down too. So her response after "information" is actually "torture" for $f < \hat{f}$ and "not torture" for $f \geq \hat{f}$.

AFTER "NO INFORMATION"

Now that she has her optimal response after "information," the Interrogator must figure out what to do after "no information." (Remember, she needs a complete plan of action.) What will she do? Remember that in the candidate set of strategies for this possible equilibrium (*info, no info, no info*), both the Resistant and Innocent Detainees play "no information" and the Cooperative Detainee never does. Because the Interrogator wants to take different actions depending on whether she believes the Detainee is Resistant or Innocent, she wants to know the chances of each possibility. Bayes' Rule will tell her those chances.

Rather than trot out an unfamiliar and strange-looking formula, return to the card-drawing example to see the intuition. Once you observed the card was red, you knew it was either a diamond or a heart and couldn't be a club or a spade. In the same way, for this candidate set of strategies, if the Interrogator observes the move "no information," she knows it was made by either the Resistant or Innocent Detainee and couldn't have been made by the Cooperative Detainee, because he plays "information."

Since the diamond and heart were the only possibilities and were equally likely, the updated probability the card was a diamond given it was red was just the ratio of the probability of a diamond to the sum of the probability of a diamond and the probability of a heart, or $\frac{1}{2}$. Our case is similar, so that the updated probability the Detainee is Resistant (p_R) given no information is the ratio of the probability the Detainee is Resistant (p_R) to the sum of the probability the Detainee is Resistant (p_R) and the probability the Detainee is Innocent (p_I). We don't know, however, how likely each is, so we have to stick with the variables to keep it general, or $\frac{p_R}{p_R + p_I}$. The exact same reasoning leads to $\frac{p_I}{p_R + p_I}$ for the updated probability the Detainee is Innocent given no information.

With those updated beliefs in hand, the Interrogator can use them to calculate the expected utilities of her two possible responses to "no information:" "torture" and "no torture." In the (fair) coin toss example in Chapter 5, the outcomes were weighted .5 and .5. In our case here, we don't know the numbers; we instead have the probabilities defined by the variables p_R and p_I, but we'll use them and multiply through in the usual way.

Here's an overview of what we need to do. The Interrogator must calculate the expected utility of "torture" and compare that to the calculated expected utility of "no torture" to see which she prefers. The expected utility of "torture" after "no information" is the payoffs to torturing a Resistant Detainee, weighted by the (updated) probability the Detainee is Resistant, plus the payoffs to torturing an Innocent Detainee, weighted by the (updated) probability the Detainee is Innocent. Ditto for the expected utility of "no torture." When we do all that, we get $-c - \frac{p_I}{p_R + p_I}(a) > \frac{p_R}{p_R + p_I}(-r)$.

As was the case after observing "information," we are left with a soup of letters (parameters actually) that may appear at first not to tell us very much. Once again though, if we go back to what it is the Interrogator wants to know, the way forward is more clear. The Interrogator is faced with "no information" and she knows the Detainee failing to provide that information is doing so either out of intransigence (he is Resistant) or ignorance (he is Innocent). She wants to torture a Resistant Detainee but not an Innocent Detainee. Given a high enough probability the Detainee is Resistant, she is willing to torture. We can find that threshold where she switches from "torture" to "no torture" by solving for p_I, the probability the Detainee is Innocent, given "no information."

More algebra, then, results in $p_I < \frac{r-c}{c+a}p_R \equiv p^*$. This is the *Innocent Detainee recognition threshold*. For values of p_I below this threshold, the Interrogator tortures; values equal to or above the threshold mean that there is enough of a chance the Detainee is Innocent to keep the Interrogator from torturing. Just as with "information," the Interrogator's optimal response depends on her beliefs; she does not have a simple "torture" or "not torture" strategy. Instead, her response after "no information" is "torture" for $p_I < p^*$ and "not torture" for $p_I \geq p^*$.

The multiple uncertainties (about Detainee type, amount of information divulged) have made things more complicated compared to our earlier games. Instead of simply (no torture, torture), representing "play 'torture' after 'information' and 'no torture' after 'no information'," we have two responses after "information" and two responses after "no information," each dependent upon a threshold.

In keeping with the systematic nature of game theory, this means there are four possibilities to consider in terms of whether the beliefs are over or under the two thresholds $\hat{f}$ and p^*: over, over; over, under; under, over; and under, under.

You may not be happy to hear this, but it's actually a little worse. Notice the u in the information hiding threshold $\hat{f}$: $\hat{f} = \frac{r-c}{u(r+a)}$. Remember that the u stands for the probability the Interrogator **understands** that the information is valuable. If u were zero, it would mean the Interrogator thinks the information is worthless (equivalent to no information); if $u = 1$, it means the Interrogator fully understands the value of the information.[10]

Remember, too, that when we set up the game in Chapter 5, we said that while Interrogators sometimes do not fully understand the value of information ($0 < u \leq 1$), the Detainee always assumes that the Interrogator *does* fully understand the value of the information (i.e., $u = 1$). Torture for information makes no sense if the Interrogator cannot understand the value of the information provided. As a result, the Detainee always *assumes* $u = 1$ for the Interrogator.

But what if $u \neq 1$? We need to take into account these misperceptions in the next step, when we check to see if the three Detainee types are willing to stick to the candidate strategies set out for them now that we know the Interrogator's responses.

Step #3: Detainee Deviation Check

Take another look at the information hiding threshold $\hat{f}$ and u's position in the denominator. If the Detainee assumes that $u = 1$, then that means he *thinks* the Interrogator's information hiding threshold is $f^* \equiv \frac{r-c}{r+a}$. If $u = 1$ for the Interrogator, then the two thresholds are identical ($\hat{f} = f^*$). If, however, $0 < u < 1$ for the Interrogator, then $f^* < \hat{f}$ because once u starts dropping below 1, it reduces the value of the denominator, making the value of $\hat{f}$ larger. In other words, the Interrogator's threshold is always greater than or equal to the Detainee's version of the threshold, never less.[11]

This difference complicates the four cases we identified above. We had identified two cases for the threshold $\hat{f}$: f could be over or under the threshold. Now, however, we must take into account the Detainee's version of the threshold. Since the latter can be no larger than the former, this does limit the possibilities, however. In fact, there are three: f is less than both thresholds, between f^* and $\hat{f}$, or greater than both.

Since each case is possible for each of the two possibilities for the innocent detainee recognition threshold ($p_I < p^*$ and $p_I \geq p^*$), we have six cases to consider. Wait! Don't run! We won't do all of these. Let's just work through two of them to complete what we've started and illustrate how to find equilibria in the game.

CASE 1: $f < f^* \leq \hat{f}$ AND $p < p^*$
In this case, the Interrogator's belief f that the Detainee has provided full information falls below both her own threshold $\hat{f}$ as well as the Detainee's version of her threshold f^*. In other words, the Interrogator believes the Detainee is hiding sufficient information to warrant "torture," and the Detainee thinks the

Interrogator believes this as well. There is no misunderstanding or misperception in this case. The $p < p^*$ means that the Interrogator also believes that, after observing "no information," the Detainee is sufficiently likely to be Resistant that she plays "torture." In sum, for this combination of beliefs, the Interrogator plays (*torture, torture*)—that is, "torture" after "information" and "torture" after "no information."

You might think we are done. We posited a set of strategies by the Detainee (each Detainee type) and found the Interrogator's optimal response. The key here is "posit." We just identified a candidate set of strategies; we don't yet know if the Detainee types would actually stick to them now that we (they) know the Interrogator's response. In order to be a (perfect Bayesian) Nash equilibrium, the strategies have to be best responses to each other, and we don't know that yet. We need to check whether (*information, no information, no information*) is the best response to (*torture, torture*); we need to see whether any of the Detainee types has an incentive to deviate from the strategy proposed for him. So let's check.

We know that the Resistant Detainee never reveals information ("no information" is his dominant strategy), so he will not deviate. We also know that, since this is the objective questioning variant of the model, "no information" is the only move the Innocent Detainee even has, so he will deviate either. The only real question is whether the Cooperative Detainee has an incentive to deviate. Does he?

Since $f < f^*$, the Cooperative Detainee knows that the Interrogator "tortures" after "information." He also knows that the Interrogator "tortures" after "no information." If he is going to get tortured anyway (and pay $-k$), he doesn't want to give up information too (and pay $-v - k$). Put another way, he doesn't want to give up information and then be tortured anyway; the whole reason to give up information is to avoid torture. In short, he has an incentive to switch his strategy to "no information." He would, in other words, deviate, and so this set of strategies and beliefs does not constitute a PBE.

Congratulations, you have failed to find your first perfect Bayesian equilibrium. Or, rather, you successfully determined that a set of strategies and beliefs fails to generate a stable outcome. That's useful, actually.

One down, many to go for me, but we'll do just one more together.

CASE 2: $f^* < f < \hat{f}$ AND $p < p^*$

This case is identical to the first case in terms of the Interrogator's beliefs (and so actions) after observing "no information": The Interrogator believes that the Detainee is unlikely to be Innocent, likely instead to be Resistant, so the Interrogator plays "torture." The difference is f; it has "moved" so that it is "between" the Detainee's version of the Interrogator's threshold f^* and the Interrogator's actual threshold $\hat{f}$. This means that the Interrogator again believes the Detainee has provided insufficient information to warrant not torturing him. Just as in the first case, she is sufficiently confident he is holding information back ($f < \hat{f}$) to warrant torture. So, given these two beliefs, the Interrogator plays (*torture, torture*), that is, "torture" after "information" and "torture" after "no information," just as in the first case.

This time, however, the Detainee believes that the Interrogator believes the Detainee *has* revealed enough information not to be tortured ($f > f^*$). This time there is misunderstanding, misperception. Consequently, the Detainee *believes* the Interrogator plays "no torture" after "information" and "torture" after "information."

Once again we need to check whether (*information, no information, no information*) is the best response to (*torture, torture*), keeping in mind that the Cooperative Detainee anticipates (*no torture, torture*). For the exact same reasons as in the first case, neither the Resistant nor the Innocent Detainees will (can) deviate from their strategies. The question is again whether the Cooperative type has an incentive to switch his strategy, as we found he did in the first case.

Since he believes that $f^* < f$, and thus expects "no torture" after "information," he (we) must check to see whether "information" is an optimal response. Here is where the likelihood of a Sadistic Interrogator comes into play. As we saw in the first case, a Cooperative Detainee is willing to give up information to avoid torture, but does not want to give up information and be tortured anyway. That is exactly what will happen if the Interrogator is Sadistic. The Detainee has to try and figure out, to estimate the likelihood, that the Interrogator is Pragmatic (and so does not torture if sufficient information is provided) or Sadistic (and so tortures regardless of what the Detainee does).

Thus, the Cooperative Detainee has his own expected utility calculation to do, weighting the differing payoffs to each action ("information" and "no information") by the two possible states of the world (Pragmatic vs. Sadistic Interrogator). Since the Interrogator is Pragmatic with probability q and Sadistic with probability $1 - q$, the expected utility calculation of "information" comes out to $qt - v - t$. The expected utility of "no information" is just $-t$. Thus, the Cooperative Detainee prefers "information" (the strategy called for in our candidate equilibrium) to "no information" for $qt - v - t > t$.

Since the Cooperative Detainee's (and our) task is to find the threshold at which he believes with sufficient confidence the Interrogator is Pragmatic so as to provide "information," we solve for exactly that, q, which gives us $q = \frac{v}{k} \equiv \hat{q}$. This is the Cooperative Detainee's *information revelation threshold*. If the Cooperative Detainee believes that the probability the Interrogator is Pragmatic is above this threshold $\hat{q}$, then he has no incentive to deviate from "information" and will play the candidate strategy. We have our first perfect Bayesian equilibrium.

In this *valuable information, surprise torture equilibrium*, the Cooperative Detainee gives up information thinking the Interrogator will believe it's all he has and so he won't be tortured. But the Interrogator thinks he has more and so tortures him. In this equilibrium an Innocent Detainee is also tortured because the Interrogator believes he is simply Resistant.

When all the thresholds are calculated, there are 15 more cases to work through (17 in all) under both objective and leading questioning, but you now know the principles and steps behind solving for equilibria.[12] The rest is just tedious (but important!) slogging through the algebra, which you can find in Appendix A.

*   *   *

The argument thus far has shown that:

1. EITs are torture and the effectiveness of interrogational torture is an open question. (Chapter 2)
2. The Bush program approximates closely the ideal model of interrogational torture and includes limits on torture; the Bush and ideal models provide benchmarks for comparison with the game theory models to come. (Chapter 3)
3. The Bush model generates strange, quixotic outcomes. (Chapter 4)
4. The Bush interrogational torture program is more realistically modeled as objective and leading question variants of an incomplete information game, with three types of detainees, two types of interrogators, and uncertainty about the amount and value of information provided. (Chapter 5)
5. By positing a set of Detainee strategies, calculating the Interrogator's expected utility using Bayes' Rule to identify her best response, and checking for incentives to deviate by any of the Detainee types, it is possible to derive a perfect Bayesian equilibrium in which a Detainee is tortured after providing information. (Chapter 6)

The next step in the argument is to describe and examine the properties of this and the other equilibria from the RIT model.

A Matter of Calculation

The result of torture, then, is a matter of calculation . . . .
—CESARE BECCARIA, "OF TORTURE," §16, *Of Crimes and Punishments*, 1764

The calculation steps described in the Chapter 6, albeit different from what Beccaria had in mind, generate nine perfect Bayesian equilibria when applied to all the possible pure strategies of the Detainee. This chapter discusses general features of these equilibria, focusing on the belief thresholds that partly define them to aid the discussion of the individual equilibria in the chapters that follow. In order to better do this, I introduce a way of visualizing the equilibria which we will employ throughout the rest of the book.

I also explore properties of the thresholds by examining the mathematical and empirical properties of both the parameters constituting the thresholds and the thresholds themselves. Some of these properties will turn out to have important implications for the equilibria and the comparison with the benchmarks and thus for the argument of the book. These I will set apart and identify as observations, propositions, and implications.

Since my usage of these three terms differs a bit from the norm, let me first define each. By *observation* I mean a mathematical statement that follows directly and obviously from some other mathematical statement emerging from the model such as the equation for a threshold. By *proposition* I mean a true mathematical statement which follows not quite as directly or obviously from a mathematical statement or statements derived from the model. In addition, these propositions will sometimes rely on empirical assumptions about parameters in the model.[1] In Appendix C, I prove all the observations and propositions in this and the following chapters, proceeding in the same order as in the main text. Finally, by *implication* I mean a broader claim or assertion about interrogational torture which is implied or entailed by an observation or proposition.

It is important to acknowledge up front that, to the extent we make any empirical assumptions, we are stepping away from the rigor of the model and entering a world which is more arbitrary. The assumptions we will make, however, are both reasonable and entirely consistent with torture practices and programs past and present. Moreover, given our larger goal of saying something about torture as it is actually practiced in the world, it is worthwhile doing so. I will signpost very clearly any propositions resting on empirical assumptions and summarize these assumptions at the end of the chapter.

THE EQUILIBRIA

The RIT model's equilibria are summarized by their moves in Table 7.1. Two equilibria occur under leading questioning only (*ambiguous information, selective torture* and *false confirmation, selective torture*) and one occurs under objective questioning only (*valuable information, surprise torture*). The remaining three equilibria occur under both objective and leading questioning (*valuable information, selective torture; no information, torture; no information, no torture*), so there are really six substantively equivalent equilibria.

As we saw in the equilibrium we found together in the Chapter 6, however, equilibria are defined not just by the actions or moves of the players but also by their beliefs. If, for example, the Detainee's belief q that the Interrogator is Pragmatic and not Sadistic falls below the threshold $\hat{q}$, the *valuable information, surprise torture* equilibrium we found in Chapter 6 collapses (i.e., does not exist). Not surprisingly, it turns out that three important beliefs—whether the Interrogator is Pragmatic (q), whether the Detainee has revealed all his information (f), and whether the Detainee is Innocent after the move "no information" (p)—also define the other equilibria as thresholds. Since these beliefs form a crucial part of the definition, they must be included.

The formal structure for doing this in words is: (actions, beliefs) or, more thoroughly,

Table 7.1. RIT GAME PURE STRATEGY EQUILIBRIA

Objective Questioning	Leading Questioning
Valuable information, Surprise torture	Ambiguous information, Selective torture
	False confirmation, Selective torture
Valuable information, Selective torture	
No information, Torture	
No information, No torture	

(move by Cooperative Detainee type, move by Resistant Detainee type, move by Innocent Detainee type),(move by Pragmatic Interrogator after "information," move by Pragmatic Interrogator after "no information")(move by Sadistic Interrogator after "information," move by Sadistic Interrogator after "no information"), relevant beliefs q and/or f of the Detainee, relevant beliefs of the Pragmatic Interrogator (e.g., $\hat{f}, p^*$), including posterior beliefs and beliefs off the equilibrium path of play.

Using our equilibrium from Chapter 6 as an example and employing symbols to reduce the clutter gives $\{i, \bar{i}, \bar{i}\}; (t, t), (t, t): q \geq \hat{q}, f^* < f < \hat{f}; (\mu_i, \mu_{\bar{i}})\}$ for $\mu_{i,C} = 1$, $\mu_{\bar{i},I} = p < p^*$, where i is "reveal information," $\bar{i}$ is "not reveal information," t is "torture," $\mu_{i,C}$ (spoken as "mew sub i, C") is the Interrogator's posterior belief, i.e. the belief updated using Bayes' Rule after the Detainee's move i that the Detainee is type C, and $\mu_{\bar{i},I}$ ("mew sub bar i, I") is the Interrogator's posterior (updated) beliefs using Bayes' Rule after the Detainee's move $\bar{i}$ that the Detainee is Innocent.

If the statement in natural language has the advantage of familiarity but the disadvantage of wordiness, the symbolism has the advantage of being compact but the disadvantage of esoteric abstraction. Neither is terribly helpful, especially if we want to think of all nine equilibria and how they compare to each other and to the benchmarks.

A picture may not be worth a thousand words, but it will be well worth some unfamiliar math symbols and Greek letters. Recall the diagram of the information hiding threshold in Chapter 6 (Figure 6.1). There we had the Interrogator's belief (f) about whether the Detainee had revealed all his information. This belief was arrayed on a line ranging from 0 to 1. The threshold $\hat{f}$ is somewhere on that line. A value of f below the threshold means that the Interrogator is not confident enough that the Detainee has revealed all he knows and thus tortures. For values of f above the threshold, she is confident enough and thus chooses not to torture.

A high threshold $\hat{f}$ means that the space occupied by "no torture" above the threshold is smaller whereas the space occupied by "torture" under the threshold is larger. In other words, a wider range of beliefs supports the Interrogator's use of torture. In this sense, all else being equal, torture is more likely. A low threshold for choosing "not torture," conversely, means that torture is less likely. The range of beliefs supporting the Interrogator's use of torture has shrunk, represented by the shrinking space in that region.

If we add to the belief f the other two key beliefs, q and p, and give each of them an axis as well, we create a three-dimensional space—a cube—inhabited by the equilibria, as in Figure 7.1. The various thresholds from the derivations

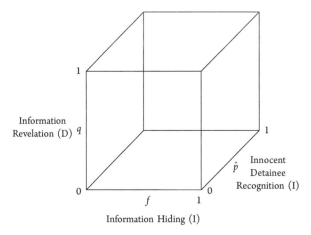

Figure 7.1 Equilibria Parameter Space

of the equilibria will lie along these axes, slicing up the interior space. Each equilibrium will thus take up a portion of this space, defined by whether it exists above or below the various thresholds. This provides a handy way to visually represent the equilibria, see how they change as a function of those thresholds, and, in Chapter 12, compare the RIT outcomes to the normative predictions in Chapter 3.

The vertical axis, q, represents the Cooperative and Innocent Detainees' belief that the Interrogator is Pragmatic rather than Sadistic. The closer to the top (to one), the higher the likelihood the Interrogator is Pragmatic and not Sadistic in the estimation of the Detainee. This belief is important because it partly determines whether a Cooperative Detainee and an Innocent Detainee under leading questioning want to choose "information" or not.

Similarly, the diagonal axis p represents the Pragmatic Interrogator's belief that the Detainee is Innocent upon observing "no information." The closer to one on the p axis, the higher the likelihood the Detainee is Innocent and knows nothing in the estimation of the Pragmatic Interrogator. The horizontal axis f represents the Pragmatic Interrogator's belief that, upon observing "information," the Detainee has revealed all he knows. The closer to one on the f axis, the more likely it is that the Detainee has told the Interrogator all he knows (or that which he is willing to confirm if Innocent under leading questioning). These beliefs are also important because they determine whether or not the Pragmatic Interrogator prefers to torture (because the Interrogator wants to torture after "information" if she thinks the Detainee is hiding more information and does *not* want to torture after "no information" if the Detainee is Innocent since the Pragmatic Interrogator does not want to torture Innocent Detainees).

THINKING ABOUT BELIEVING

Since the equilibria depend on values of q, f, and p being above (below) the different thresholds, it will be important to consider for each equilibrium how the changes in the thresholds affect the equilibrium. The thresholds themselves are defined by the various costs and benefits in the model, captured by different variables or parameters (e.g., the ratio of v to k for the threshold $\hat{q}$). Thus, we must approach the thresholds in two stages and on two tracks in each stage, one formal and mathematical, one contingent and empirical.

First we focus on the variables, examining both (a) what happens to the thresholds as different parameters in the model change (formal mathematical) and (b) the likely values of those parameters in the real world (empirical). Second, we explore some of the properties of the thresholds. Some of these properties will (a) be mathematically derived, formal properties, while others will (b) be contingent, empirical characteristics based on the likely values of the parameters.

Plus ça Change . . . Not

However widely the French proverb may apply in life, it does not apply to our thresholds; they will indeed change as their constituent parameters change. To see these effects, we can do some "comparative statics," which requires some basic derivative calculus to identify what happens to one quantity as another quantity increases or decreases. (We won't actually do any of that calculus here.) The idea is to see what happens to a threshold (say $\hat{f}$) as one of the variables in the formula defining it (say c) increases (decreases).

Take the Cooperative Detainee's information revelation threshold $\hat{q} = \frac{v}{k}$ as an example. It is the ratio of the value of the information v to the costs of torture k (both from the perspective of the Detainee). The first thing to note is that this is a real constraint. Recall that the Cooperative Detainee prefers to give up information rather than be tortured; this is what defines a Cooperative Detainee. This preference is represented by the ordering $-v > -k$. Multiply both sides by -1 to get rid of the negatives and it reverses the direction of the inequality but preserves the relationship, $v < k$. Because both v and k are positive and v is less than k, the threshold $\hat{q}$ must lie between zero and one and thus is a real probability.

Now think about what happens to this fraction as v increases but k stays the same.

It gets bigger and would eventually approach 1 as v approaches k.

What happens as k increases? The fraction—threshold—approaches zero as k grows large relative to v.

For such a simple fraction we don't need calculus to tell us that the threshold $\hat{q}$ increases as v increases but decreases as k increases. Once we start adding in other variables, however, as is the case for the other thresholds, these effects will not be as obvious (at least to me). Calculus helps us figure out what happens to them as the other factors change. The results of performing these calculations on the other thresholds and their variables in Appendix B are summarized in Table 7.2.

Notice how the parameters r, c, and a figure in the remaining five thresholds. The probability of full information revelation u and the probabilities for each of the three Detainee types p_C, p_R, and p_I are parameters of subsets of these five. To see the effects of each variable or parameter, I organize the discussion by parameter, explaining the effect of each on the relevant threshold(s).

REPUTATION COSTS, r

As reputation costs (r) go up, so do both the information hiding ($\hat{f}, f^*,$ and $\tilde{f}$) and innocent detainee recognition thresholds (p^* and $\hat{p}$).[2] This makes sense; it is natural that these costs would affect the Interrogator's decision about whether or not to torture. Recall that the information hiding threshold $\hat{f}$ is the point at which the Interrogator switches from "torture" to "no torture." Moving from left to right along the bottom axis of Figure 7.1, then, a high threshold means a threshold closer to the right side, leaving most of the space occupied by torture.

Now take a look at the p axis, the diagonal line. Moving from the front toward the back from 0 to 1, the thresholds p^* and $\hat{p}$ are the points at which the Interrogator switches from "torture" to "no torture" after observing "no information." A high threshold is one toward the back, leaving the space in front occupied by torture. The higher the perceived costs of failing to torture a knowledgeable Detainee who refuses to provide information, the more likely is the Interrogator to employ torture.

Table 7.2. EFFECTS OF MODEL VARIABLES ON THRESHOLDS

As these parameter values go up...		Reputation Costs (r)	Torture Costs (c)	Additional Torture Costs (a)	Information Clarity (u)	Probability of Detainee D_i (p_i)
...the thresholds	$\hat{f}$	Increase	Decrease	Decrease	Decrease	n/a
	f^*	Increase	Decrease	Decrease	n/a	n/a
	$\tilde{f}$	Increase	Decrease	Decrease	n/a	p_C: Increase
						p_I: Decrease
	p^*	Increase	Decrease	Decrease	n/a	p_R: Increase
	$\hat{p}$	Increase	Decrease	Decrease	n/a	n/a

Note that this is true independent of the value of the suspected information possessed by the Detainee. Even if the information value is low, this threshold could still be high if the reputation costs are high because reputation costs are independent of whatever information a Detainee possesses.

Empirically, these costs are likely to be high for any state that tortures. If torture is to work as a threat, it must be credible. To make it credible, the state must torture if it does not receive valuable information. Failure to do so makes it less likely for future detainees to provide valuable information (or for the same detainee if we assumed multiple rounds of the game). This is why, for example, the Interrogator will torture a Resistant Detainee on whom she knows it has no effect. Interrogators who rely on torture must actually use it if they fail to get the desired information.

TORTURE COSTS, c AND a

Consistent with intuition, the higher the costs to torturing, whether the general costs c or the extra cost a to "unnecessary" torture, both the information hiding ($\hat{f}$ and f^*) and innocent detainee recognition thresholds (p^* and $\hat{p}$) go down, reducing the space supporting torture. Conversely, when these costs drop, when the state is less concerned about either cost of torture, both thresholds go up and torture is more likely.

These costs differ, of course, across states and in the same state over time. In the case of the United States, these costs were probably lowest shortly after 9/11, when Vice President Cheney spoke ominously about going to the "dark side" and CIA counterterrorism chief Cofer Black said the "gloves were off." They may have increased over time, especially once the program started to be revealed and the United States began to suffer a different kind of (international) reputation cost. Nevertheless, these costs cannot be too high for any state that practices torture.

Note, though, that saying the costs are "low" here does not mean they are the same and close to zero. Since $0 < c < r < a$, it is always the case that the costs of torturing an innocent are higher than the reputation costs. So although it would appear that after 9/11, these costs may have lowered, they still exceed the reputation costs (which as we said were high).

This is appropriate, since our model is not a strawman and we are building in incentives *against* torture in order to let proponents make the best case that they can. It does mean, however, that we need to think of "low" differently for c than for a. It may very well be the case that c approaches zero; the costs of 'necessary' torture just were not very high. A low(er) cost for torturing innocents a, however, means that it approaches r so that they are not much more than the reputation costs. It will be helpful to keep these relationships in mind when we turn to the likely empirical values of the thresholds.

INFORMATION CLARITY, u

The final parameter for the Interrogator's information hiding threshold is the clarity parameter u. As it increases, the value of the information is clearer to the Interrogator and the threshold is lowered, decreasing the space supporting torture. This also makes sense; the clearer the value of the information, the less likely the Interrogator is to misinterpret it as not valuable and use torture, thinking the Detainee is lying. Conversely, the more the Interrogator believes the information divulged by the Detainee is not valuable, the more likely the Interrogator is to employ torture. As u falls from 1 toward 0, the threshold grows, increasing the space supporting torture.

It is difficult to say in general whether u is likely to be low or high. No doubt it varies greatly depending not just on the specific information provided by the detainee, but also on the other information available to interrogators. Information from a detainee given one set of background information might make sense and be understood as valuable. The same information in the context of different background information, however, may make little sense and be perceived as lying or misdirection. It seems, then, prudent and conservative not to hazard a guess about the likely empirical value of u.

DETAINEE PROBABILITIES, p

Detainee probabilities—the likelihood that the Detainee is one of the three types—are parameters in two of the thresholds. The probability the Detainee is Cooperative (p_C) and the probability the Detainee is Innocent (p_I) are parameters in the leading questioning version of the information hiding threshold $\tilde{f}$. The probability the Detainee is Resistant (p_R) is a parameter in the innocent detainee recognition threshold p^*.

Whereas an increase in p_C increases $\tilde{f}$, an increase in p_I lowers it. This too matches intuition. As the Interrogator believes that it is more likely the Detainee is Cooperative (and thus has information he would reveal or confirm), the space for torture increases. In contrast, as the Interrogator becomes convinced that the Detainee is in fact Innocent, the threshold drops, replacing that space supporting "torture" with space supporting "no torture."

Here I think we can say something generally and with confidence, even if it is an empirical claim. It seems highly unlikely that an interrogator will think that the shivering, naked, hooded, shackled, sleep- and food-deprived detainee sitting across from her in the basement of a top-secret mini-prison is innocent. Imagine the two alternatives. Imagine you're a professional CIA case officer dedicated to keep America safe and you've been specially selected and trained as an interrogator/debriefer. Your analyst(s) at the black site as well as back in Langley are providing you with information specific to that detainee, information spelling out all sorts of connections and evidence saying he's a bad guy. Every day you read urgent cables from headquarters reiterating the importance of the information the detainee possesses and the need to elicit it pronto. How likely is it that you'll think "no information" means "he's innocent" or even "he's a bad guy, but he doesn't know that information"? Not very.

How about the probability he's resistant and just cannot be broken? This is perhaps more likely than being innocent. After all, you know there are some tough terrorists out there, and that is far more plausible than a completely innocent man ending up in diapers, chains, and a hood in a secret CIA prison in an old equestrian academy on the outskirts of Vilnius, Lithuania. So p_R is likely higher than p_I.

Even so, interrogational torture generally and the CIA program in particular rest on the assumption, to quote the Hollywood film *Zero Dark Thirty*, "everybody breaks, bro" (Boal 2011, p. 6). This suggests that p_R should be low; resistance is ultimately futile and (almost) all detainees are effectively cooperative (i.e., p_C). After all, you've been trained in the techniques and told that they are scientifically engineered to induce "learned helplessness"—that is, to make a detainee completely dependent upon the interrogator so that he will comply with any request for information. You've even heard rumors whispered around the proverbial water-cooler back in Langley about officers who "broke" even the most resistant detainees (Carle 2011, p. 15). And, don't forget, your job is to break the detainee sitting across from you. Your bosses, your colleagues, the American people are counting on you to break him.

How likely are you to think, "sorry, this is just one of those guys who can't be broken"? Instead, even if others have been unsuccessful, you're going to be the one to break him. Finally, note that the CIA's own program *assumed* that all detainees could be broken. The agency did not have provisions for what to do with someone who never became compliant. Moreover, multiple apologists for the program have all maintained the same claim: Everyone broke eventually, just some faster than others (Bush 2011, Cheney and Cheney 2012, Rodriguez Jr and Harlow 2012, Tenet and Harlow 2007, Thiessen 2010).

In short, while it is an empirical claim and not a logical deduction, it seems very probable that interrogators will believe the Cooperative Detainee is the most likely type, followed by the far less likely Resistant type, and then, finally, the even less likely Innocent type (i.e., $p_C \gg p_R > p_I$), where the $\gg$ symbol means "much greater than." This is a reasonable assumption. If so, if p_C is high and p_I low, then, all things being equal, the space supported by torture along this dimension is likely greater.

The final parameter is the probability that the Detainee is Resistant, p_R. As this probability increases, p^* also increases and moves toward the back of the p axis. The space supporting torture increases. The more the Interrogator believes that the Detainee is the Resistant type and not the Innocent type, the more likely she is to torture. Note that this is true even though the Resistant types never divulge information—and the Interrogator knows this. The Interrogator must torture after no information in order to maintain the credibility of that threat even though she knows it will not work on this particular individual. As the probability the Detainee is Resistant decreases, the threshold also decreases, shrinking the space supporting torture because an Innocent Detainee is more likely.

Locating the Thresholds

With the knowledge of what happens to the thresholds as the parameters change as well as what the likely empirical values of (some of) those parameters are, we can apply a parallel strategy to the thresholds themselves. For each threshold, we first explore some of its formal mathematical properties. This will, in some cases at least, constrain the values the threshold can take. Second, we will use the empirically likely values of their constituent parameters, summarized in Table 7.3, to try and narrow the likely range of the thresholds a bit further. If we were to discover that a particular threshold is high (low), for mathematical and/or for empirical reasons, then we'll have a better idea of the conditions necessary for that equilibrium to hold. This, in turn, gives us a sense of how likely—or rare—the equilibrium might be in the real world.

Innocent Detainee Recognition Thresholds, p^*, $\hat{p}$

There are two Innocent Detainee recognition thresholds, one we encountered in the equilibrium we discovered together (p^*) in the last chapter and one after "no information," covering both the "no information, torture" and "no information, no torture" equilibria, each under both objective and leading questioning $(\hat{p})$. Begin with the latter: $\hat{p} = \frac{r-c}{r+a}$.

Think about this fraction a bit, recalling that $0 < c < r < a$. Note that r is both in the numerator and the denominator; absent the other variables, the threshold

Table 7.3. Likely Empirical Values of Model Parameters

Parameter	Value
Reputation costs (r)	High
Torture costs (c)	Low
Additional torture costs (a)	Low
Information hiding (f)	High
Information clarity (u)	—
Probability Detainee is Innocent (p_I)	Very low
Probability Detainee is Cooperative (p_C)	High
Probability Detainee is Resistant (p_R)	Low

would be 1. What makes it less than one and thus a fraction is that r is reduced by c in the numerator but is increased by a in the denominator. Actually, we can be a little more precise. Since $a > r$, the denominator is at least doubled by adding a to r; even if a is just a bit greater than r, then the denominator is going to be $2r$ plus some change. If the numerator is less than r and the denominator is greater than $2r$, then the threshold $\hat{p}$ is less than one-half. We have, then, our first observation:

Observation 7.1 ($\hat{\mathbf{p}} < \frac{1}{2}$). The Interrogator's Innocent Detainee recognition threshold $\hat{p}$ is less than one-half.

As we will see in a moment, Observation 7.1 will help us think about the other innocent detainee recognition threshold. It also, however, will help us think about two of the equilibria in the chapters to come. We now know that the threshold for $\hat{p}$ will have to fall somewhere between zero and one-half. It is also important to point out that, given the assumptions of the model, this *must* be true. This statement does not rely on any contingent empirical assertions or claims or assumptions which may or may not turn out to be true or with which someone might not agree.

So we have narrowed down $\hat{p}$ to between zero and somewhere below one-half. Can we say anything else? Can we narrow it any further? We can if we are willing to use the empirically likely values of the parameters. If we substitute in from Table 7.3 the likely empirical values of the parameters relevant for $\hat{p}$, we get something like $\hat{p} = \frac{\text{High} - \text{Low}}{\text{Double high}}$.

Not terribly math-y, 'tis true, but still illuminating. Recalling that the cost of torturing innocents a approaches r (but cannot drop lower than r), we can think of just doubling the denominator. If the cost of torturing innocents were very high, far exceeding r, then this denominator would get larger and the threshold would drop toward zero. But because those costs are actually quite low, the denominator is likely closer to $2r$. Since the permanent costs to torture c are very low, not much above zero, the numerator approaches r. Together then, these considerations suggest the following proposition:

Proposition 7.1 ($\hat{\mathbf{p}} \lessapprox \frac{1}{2}$). As c approaches zero and a approaches r, the Interrogator's Innocent Detainee recognition threshold $\hat{p}$ approaches one-half from below.

Now consider the other Innocent Detainee recognition threshold: $p^* = \frac{r-c}{c+a}p_R$. The numerator is the same as in $\hat{p}$, but the denominator is smaller (because $c < r$). Thus, absent p_R, p^* would be greater than $\hat{p}$. Since p_R is a probability and is thus between zero and one, values of it below one reduce the numerator. The question is, how much?

Math alone will not help us here. With one very reasonable empirical assumption, however, it can. We said above that the Interrogator is likely to believe that any Detainee chained to a chair in her interrogation room is Cooperative—that is, a Detainee who both possesses information and will give it up under (the threat of [more]) torture. If that is the case, if the Interrogator believes that the Cooperative type is more likely than the other two, then we can state the following proposition:

Proposition 7.2 ($\mathbf{p}^* < \frac{1}{2}$). If the Pragmatic Interrogator believes it more likely that the Detainee she faces is Cooperative than both of the other two types, then the Innocent Detainee recognition threshold p^* is less than one-half; the closer p_R is to zero, the closer p^* is to zero.

The proof is in Appendix C, but the upshot is that a little bit of algebra shows that the greatest probability the Interrogator could assign to the Detainee being Innocent after observing "no information" is something a little under $1/2$. The lower the prior probability p_R, the closer p^* is to 0. The more the Interrogator believes everyone breaks—as is likely—the lower is p^*. Both Innocent Detainee recognition thresholds are thus below one-half, with $\hat{p}$ close to one-half and p^* closer to zero. These constraints will become important when we compare the model results against the benchmarks in Chapter 12.

INFORMATION HIDING THRESHOLDS, $\hat{f}, f^*, \tilde{f}$

There are three versions of the Interrogator's information hiding thresholds, $\hat{f}, f^*,$ and $\tilde{f}$. These are the version under objective questioning, the Detainee's version of the Interrogator's version under objective questioning, and the version under leading questioning, respectively. We take each in turn.

As we saw in Chapter 6, the Interrogator's version under objective questioning is $\frac{r-c}{u(r+a)} = \hat{f}$. Note that, without the u, this threshold is equivalent to $\hat{p}$ and thus less than one-half. Since, however, u varies from just above zero to one, and this has a dramatic effect on $\hat{f}$, causing it to range from just above zero all the way to one (and beyond), we cannot constrain $\hat{f}$ on purely mathematical grounds. Given the wide variability of u in the real world of torture (sometimes it will be high and sometimes it will be low), it is difficult to narrow u on empirical grounds as well.

If, however, we continue to assume c approaching zero and a approaching r, we can place $\hat{f}$ at one-half or greater, giving us the following proposition:

Proposition 7.3 ($\hat{\mathbf{f}} \geq \frac{1}{2}$). As c approaches zero and a approaches r, the Interrogator's information hiding threshold $\hat{f}$ is greater than or equal to one-half.

Now take a look at the Detainee's version of the Interrogator's information hiding threshold: $f^* = \frac{r-c}{r+a}$. The Detainee's version is in fact equivalent to $\hat{p}$ since it does not have the u parameter. As a result, we can make the same observation we did with $\hat{p}$, giving us an observation constraining another threshold:

Observation 7.2 ($\mathbf{f^*} \lesssim \frac{1}{2}$). The Detainee's version of the Interrogator's infor-mation hiding threshold f^* approaches one-half from below.

Thus, the Detainee thinks that the Interrogator's information threshold is somewhere between zero and one-half, but can't exceed one-half. Moreover, we can narrow this remaining range a bit more exactly as we did with $\hat{p}$ above since the equations are identical. That is, given a very small c and an a just above r, f^* is likely to be close to one-half.

Now compare the two versions, $\hat{f}$ and f^*. Suppose u is 1. Then the two thresholds—the Interrogator's actual threshold $\hat{f}$ and what the Detainee thinks it is f^*—are equal. This is the *only* value of u for which the thresholds are the same, for which there is no misunderstanding between them. As u drops from 1, it makes the denominator in $\hat{f}$ smaller, which makes the fraction larger. We can make, then, the following observation:

Observation 7.3 ($\mathbf{f^*} \leq \hat{\mathbf{f}}$). The Interrogator's and the Detainee's beliefs will "agree" on the information hiding threshold only in the special case when the Interrogator understands perfectly the information's value; in all other cases the Detainee's version is less than the Interrogator's.[3]

Finally, consider the Interrogator's version of the information hiding thresh-old under leading questioning: $\tilde{f} = \frac{p_C(r-c) + p_I(-a-c)}{p_C(r+a)}$. This version is, again techni-cally speaking, a bit goopier than the others. Even so, some algebra establishes that, if the prior probability of a Cooperative Detainee is more likely than that of an Innocent Detainee ($p_C > p_I$) as we argued above, $\tilde{f}$ is also less than one-half.

The details are in Appendix C, but the basic idea is this: Suppose $\tilde{f}$ is not less than one-half—that is, that it is equal to or greater than one-half. If so, then if you doubled the fraction, it would be equal to or greater than one. When you do that, you find that it contradicts the assumption that $a > r$ and so it cannot be true. Thus, $\tilde{f} < \frac{1}{2}$.[4]

If we continue to assume a very low prior probability that the Detainee is Innocent (i.e., p_I approaching zero but not getting there), a torture cost c very low (also approaching zero), and a very low "unnecessary" torture cost a (a approaching but always greater than r), we can constrain $\tilde{f}$ a bit further. The left-hand term in the numerator will approach $p_C r$ while the right-hand term in the numerator will approach $-p_I r$. A very low p_I will reduce $-r$, making the numerator close to $p_C r$. With the denominator approaching $p_C 2r$, $\tilde{f}$ approaches one-half. In short:

Proposition 7.4 $\left(\tilde{\mathbf{f}} \lessapprox \frac{1}{2}\right)$. As both p_I and c approach zero and as a approaches r, the Interrogator's information hiding threshold $\tilde{f}$ approaches one-half from below.

By comparing $\tilde{f}$ to f^*, we can say even more. If we assume that there is some chance that a Detainee could be Innocent, even the smallest probability as long as it's positive, then yet more algebra shows that $\tilde{f} < f^*$. The assumption that the Detainee could be Innocent rather than Cooperative or Resistant motivated altering the BIT model and building the RIT model with this type included, so this should not be problematic and provides us with the following proposition:

Proposition 7.5 $\left(\tilde{\mathbf{f}} < \mathbf{f}^* \leq \hat{\mathbf{f}}\right)$. If there is a positive probability that the Detainee is Innocent, the Interrogator's information hiding threshold $\tilde{f}$ under leading questioning is less than the Detainee's version under objective questioning: for $p_I > 0$, $\tilde{f} < f^* \leq \hat{f}$.

It follows that $\tilde{f} < \hat{f}$. In other words, the Interrogator's information hiding threshold is less under leading questioning than under objective questioning. This makes sense. If one is asking leading questions, there is no uncertainty about the value of the information (that's why there is no u in the payoffs under leading questioning). And if the detainee is talking, then it is more likely that you'll get the information you want (since you're providing him with the answers to your questions). In contrast, under objective questioning, getting the answers you want may take longer and will be less likely. It also follows that a lower information hiding threshold under leading questioning also means that there should be less torture than under objective questioning, where the higher threshold shrinks the region supporting "no torture."

This relationship between questioning type, information, and torture has an important implication:

Implication 7.1 (**Torture–Information Trade-off 1**). There is a trade-off between information and torture across questioning types. All else being equal, leading questioning results in less torture and poorer information; objective questioning results in more torture and better information.

From Proposition 7.5, $\tilde{f} < \hat{f}$. Since the former is the Interrogator's threshold for torture under leading questioning and the latter her threshold under objective questioning, it follows that, all else being equal, the region supporting torture is smaller under leading questioning, which generates ambiguous information and false confirmation, than is the region under objective questioning, which can generate better information. While objective questioning (potentially) provides better information, it is necessarily accompanied by more torture than leading questioning, which, however, provides—at best—ambiguous information.

Before leaving f as a threshold, we should note that f is a parameter as well. If you recall the discussion in Chapter 5 and the RIT game tree diagram (Figure 5.4), you'll remember that f is the Interrogator's belief (the probability) that the Detainee has revealed all his information (or said as much as he is willing under leading questioning). As we worked through what became the valuable information, surprise torture equilibrium in the Chapter 6, we solved for f at one point because that helped us think about what the Interrogator needed to assess.

We could have, however, solved for u—the probability the Interrogator understands the information as valuable. Had we done so, we would have ended up with $\hat{u} = \frac{r-c}{f(r+a)}$. Compare this to $\hat{f} = \frac{r-c}{u(r+a)}$, and you can see that they are equivalent, just with f and u switched. While we found it difficult to posit any empirical likelihoods about u, the same is not true for f. As suggested in the section on information hiding in Chapter 5 and elsewhere, it is an interrogator's entire job to be suspicious about whether detainees have told them all they know. They know that a cooperative detainee has an incentive to give away as little as possible. The entire logic of torture in interrogations, then, suggests that f is likely to be low.

We also know a low f to be true not just logically, but empirically as well. The history of torture offers more than enough empirical support to suggest that the interrogator's prior belief f is likely to be low.[5] Since f behaves mathematically just like u and we saw above that as u decreases, the threshold $\hat{f}$ increases, this means that the threshold $\hat{u}$ would behave the same way for low values of f. If we were to relabel the parameter space in Figure 7.1, replacing f on the bottom axis with u, then we would see the threshold $\hat{u}$ closer to the right, with a wide range supporting torture to its left. Obviously, as it moves past one-half, where the Detainee threshold reaches its maximum, space opens up for the valuable information, surprise torture equilibrium.

INFORMATION REVELATION THRESHOLDS, $\hat{q}$, q^*

The last two thresholds $\hat{q}$ and q^* are those of the Cooperative and the Innocent Detainees, respectively, $\hat{q} = \frac{v}{k}$ and $q^* = \frac{l}{k}$. Since they have the same functional form and are subject to the same constraint (both are positive and fractions), they behave identically. In such a simple case there is nothing more to be said mathematically beyond the fact that these thresholds increase as v (l) increases and decrease as k increases. Unfortunately, it is not clear we can say much empirically.

One might think that a knowledgeable but potentially cooperative detainee would have a higher threshold. If they're professionals, they'll be suspicious of interrogators and unlikely to believe their promises not to torture. This is all the more true of modern terrorists in the Middle East, who are very well aware of the horrific tortures they would face in the prisons of Damascus and Cairo. Moreover, they actually may have trained to resist this torture. Clearly the CIA thought that modern Islamic terrorists are a new breed of hardened terrorists trained and committed to resisting interrogations.

And yet, some prisoners clearly do end up believing their interrogators and provide (some) information. Moreover, this threshold depends on the value of the information. Recalling that $\hat{q}$ increases as v gets larger and decreases as k gets larger, it follows that less valuable information is more likely to be divulged (the threshold is lower for low v), whereas more valuable information is less likely to be given up (the threshold is higher). Of course, the threshold's position also depends on the value of k, which varies across even cooperative detainees even for the same torture technique. In short, the empirical ground is too shaky to constrain the Cooperative Detainee's threshold $\hat{q}$.

Before turning to the Innocent Detainee's threshold, note something significant about what we just said about the value of information v and its effect on the information obtained through torture. A Cooperative Detainee is more likely to give up less valuable information than valuable information. This may seem trivially true and obvious but it is important to realize that it emerges logically from the model. We get this result—along with all the other results—from one consistent logical framework. Many authors from classical antiquity forward have spoken about the various things that can happen under torture, but they do not start with *one* logical framework and generate *all* of those outcomes. This relationship suggests the following implication:

Implication 7.2 (**Torture–Information Trade-off 2**). *There is a trade-off between information and torture irrespective of questioning type. All things being equal, interrogators are more likely to get less valuable information than highly valuable information from torture.*

Of course this is true of interrogations generally. The point is that torture does not do any better.

As far as Innocent Detainees are concerned, one might think the threshold would be very low. How and why would an innocent, non-terrorist resist and try to hold out under torture rather than tell the interrogator what she wants to hear? He might be more likely to believe the interrogator's promises too, not having been in such a situation before. And yet, the sad and grim history of torture is replete with stories of innocents who resisted tendering false confessions despite the lure of being lowered from the rack. In short, there is too much variability here as well to constrain the location of this threshold.

Table 7.4 summarizes the likely values of those thresholds about which we can say something theoretically, empirically, or both. The squiggly lines under the inequality signs mean "approaches," and those with the line through it mean "not approaches." So, for example, $\gtrsim \frac{1}{2}$ means "greater than but approaching one-half" while $\underset{\not\approx}{<} \frac{1}{2}$ means "less than and not approaching one-half."

Given both the density of this chapter and the importance of these values in the rest of the argument, it will be useful to summarize the empirical assumptions we have made along the way which support some of these values:

1. The Interrogator's torture costs c are very low, approaching zero.
2. The Interrogator's additional costs to "unnecessary" torture a are also very low, approaching their minimum just above r.
3. The probability of an Innocent Detainee is positive (i.e., some amount, even tiny, above zero), but the Cooperative Detainee is the most probable type, followed (far behind) by the Resistant and then Innocent types $(p_C \gg p_R > p_I)$.

Once again, given the history of torture, these appear to be very reasonable assumptions, but it's important to put them up front and be clear about them.

Figure 7.2 locates these thresholds in the equilibrium parameter space "cube." All the equilibria emerging from the model will inhabit some portion of this space, their boundaries defined by different combinations of the thresholds. The placement of the thresholds and thus the size of the equilibria corresponds to their likely values, as just summarized. I have arbitrarily placed the Cooperative Detainee's threshold $\hat{q}$ a little north of halfway for the moment, but we will relax this assumption later and nothing rests on this placement.

The parameter space will be helpful to us in three ways. First, it aids in understanding the equilibria. Instead of a collection of inequalities—"less than this, more than that, less than this"—we have readily identifiable regions standing in relation to one another. Second, since we now know what determines the values of the thresholds, what causes them to move up or down, we can use this visualization to identify the factors supporting, and not supporting, each

Table 7.4. LIKELY VALUES OF MAJOR THRESHOLDS

Threshold:	$p*$	$\hat{p}$	$\hat{f}$	f^*	$\tilde{f}$	$\hat{q}$	q^*
Likely Value:	$\underset{\not\approx}{<} \frac{1}{2}$	$\lesssim \frac{1}{2}$	$\gtrsim \frac{1}{2}$	$\lesssim \frac{1}{2}$	$\lesssim \frac{1}{2}$	—	—

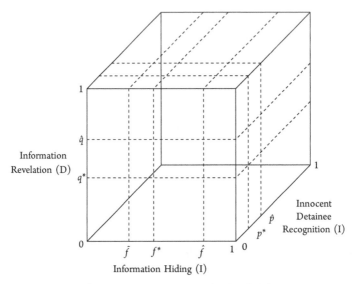

Figure 7.2 Equilibria Parameter Space with Thresholds

equilibrium, helping us interpret each of the narrative case studies. Finally and perhaps most importantly, by locating the equilibria within the entire parameter space, we can assess not just their positions relative to each other, but also the proportion occupied by each equilibrium relative to the parameter space as a whole. In other words we will have a ready way to identify the region(s) predicting both torture and elicitation of information. This will be helpful in evaluating the proponent model's predictions and normative benchmarks about the reliability of information as well as about the frequency and severity of torture in interrogational torture programs.

The important point for the moment is that we draw on both the values in Table 7.4 and the threshold locations in Figure 7.2 as we proceed through each of the equilibria in the next four chapters. For each of the equilibria, then, we will explore how changes in the thresholds affect the nature of the equilibrium, providing us a better understanding of how they connect to the real world. We will also connect them to the real world by illustrating each equilibrium with a case study of torture corresponding to that equilibrium. We begin with surprise torture and the case of an English doctor in Pinochet's Chile: Sheila Cassidy.

*   *   *

The argument thus far has shown that:

1. EITs are torture and the effectiveness of interrogational torture is an open question. (Chapter 2)

2. The Bush program approximates closely the ideal model of interrogational torture and includes limits on torture; the Bush and ideal models provide benchmarks for comparison with the game theory models to come. (Chapter 3)

3. The Bush model generates strange, quixotic outcomes. (Chapter 4)

4. The Bush interrogational torture program is more realistically modeled as objective and leading question variants of an incomplete information game, with three types of detainees, two types of interrogators, and uncertainty about the amount and value of information provided. (Chapter 5)

5. By positing a set of Detainee strategies, calculating the Interrogator's expected utility using Bayes' Rule to identify her best response, and checking for incentives to deviate by any of the Detainee types, it is possible to derive a perfect Bayesian equilibrium in which a Detainee is tortured after providing information. (Chapter 6)

6. The RIT model generates nine perfect Bayesian equilibria, the formal and empirical characteristics of which generate important observations, propositions, and implications, including:

    (a) The Interrogator's thresholds for believing that a Detainee is Innocent after "no information" are less than one-half, with $\hat{p}$ close to one-half and p^* closer to zero.

    (b) The Interrogator's information hiding threshold under objective questioning $\hat{f}$ is greater than or equal to one-half, whereas her information hiding threshold under leading questioning $\tilde{f}$ as well as the Detainee's version f^* of $\hat{f}$ are a little less than one-half.

    (c) Objective questioning (potentially) provides better information, but is necessarily accompanied by more torture, than leading questioning, which, however, provides less valuable information.

    (d) All things being equal, Interrogators are more likely to get less valuable information than highly valuable information.

    (Chapter 7)

The next step in the argument is to describe and interpret each of the RIT outcomes, starting with the *valuable information, surprise torture equilibrium.*

Surprise Torture

Their disbelief was very hard to bear.

—SHEILA CASSIDY, *Audacity to Believe*

We begin with the equilibrium we found together in Chapter 6, the *valuable information, surprise torture equilibrium*. This equilibrium occurs only under objective questioning. In this and the next four chapters, we proceed as follows:

1. Describe the equilibrium and some of its features.
2. Identify the substantive outcome(s) (that is, the real-world counterparts) associated with the equilibrium.
3. Narrate an empirical case corresponding to the outcome.
4. Then return to the model features and reflect on the case in light of the model components.

EQUILIBRIUM FEATURES

In this equilibrium, the Cooperative, Resistant, and Innocent Detainee types play ("information," "no information," "no information"), respectively; the Pragmatic and Sadistic Interrogators play ("torture," "torture"), respectively.[1] The Cooperative Detainee's belief q about the likelihood that the Interrogator is Pragmatic is greater than his threshold $\hat{q}$; that is, he is confident enough that he faces a Pragmatic Interrogator who will not torture him if he reveals information. He also believes that the Interrogator believes he has revealed all his information ($f^* < f$). The (Pragmatic) Interrogator, however, believes he has *not* revealed all of his information $f < \hat{f}$ (hence $f^* < f < \hat{f}$) and is also confident that a Detainee

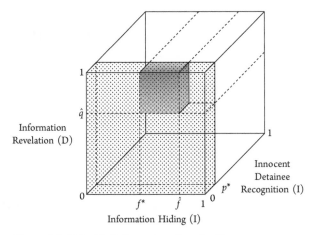

Figure 8.1 Valuable Information, Surprise Torture Equilibrium

who does not reveal information is Resistant and not Innocent $(p < p^*)$ and thus tortures after "no information."

Figure 8.1 locates the surprise torture equilibrium in the parameter space, with the move "information" of the Cooperative Detainee represented by the dark-gray box. The region covered by dots is the space taken up by torture, either the surprise torture of the Cooperative Detainee or the torture of the Innocent and Resistant Detainees who reveal no information, or both. As Figure 8.1 makes clear, this equilibrium depends on the four thresholds $\hat{q}, f^*, \hat{f}$, and p^*.

Information Revelation Threshold, $\hat{q}$

As $\hat{q}$ increases (that is, the point at which the Cooperative Detainee is willing to divulge information), the information region shrinks. Conversely, as $\hat{q}$ decreases, the region increases and we see more surprise torture. All things being equal, in other words, the more the Cooperative Detainee is willing to talk (i.e., the lower the threshold $\hat{q}$), the more surprise torture we should see:

Implication 8.1 (**Torture's Logic and Surprise Torture**). *The more willing cooperative detainees are to provide information, the more likely surprise torture is.*

This is perverse. The more a torture program works according to its own logic by driving down detainees' thresholds for talking, the greater the volume of space supporting torture of those detainees. Moreover, since "no information" is met with "torture" in this equilibrium, a change in the threshold $\hat{q}$ alone does not change the total amount of torture in this equilibrium. This is illustrated by the fact that the shading covers the entire space in front of p^* in Figure 8.1. As the dark-gray surprise torture region increases when $\hat{q}$ decreases, all that changes is that more of the region covered by torture includes the torture of a Cooperative Detainee who has provided at least some information.

Information Hiding Thresholds, $\hat{f}$ and f^*

The relative size of this equilibrium also depends upon f^* and $\hat{f}$. As the Detainee's version of the Interrogator's full information threshold f^* increases (moves to the right), it squeezes the equilibrium, making it smaller, whereas increases in the Interrogator's version $\hat{f}$ make it larger. As the former threshold goes up, as the Cooperative Detainee thinks the Interrogator thinks he has not divulged everything and will torture him, the region in which he decides not to provide information increases. There will be less surprise torture of a Cooperative Detainee because he does not trust the Interrogator enough not to torture him to reveal the supposedly hidden information.[2]

The equilibrium space gets larger as $\hat{f}$ increases and f^* stays the same because the Interrogator's threshold, or bar, for not torturing has gotten higher. There is more surprise torture because there is more space occupied by a misunderstanding of the Interrogator's belief that the Detainee has revealed all the information he has. Obviously as f^* shrinks but $\hat{f}$ grows, this region of misunderstanding grows and so does the relative size of the equilibrium. This makes sense: The greater the misunderstanding, the more surprise torture.

The Interrogator's own full information threshold $\hat{f}$ is likely to be higher than the Detainee's. Indeed, we know from Proposition 7.2 that f^* is less than one-half and from Proposition 7.3 that $\hat{f}$ is greater than or equal to one-half. In fact, Observation 7.3 tells us that the two thresholds, the two beliefs, will be the same only in the special case when the Interrogator has understood perfectly the information's value. All other cases open up the possibility for surprise torture.

As a result, a detainee will believe the interrogator believes he has revealed all he knows "before" or more quickly than the interrogator herself. Indeed, an interrogator's job is to be skeptical, to try and get every last drop of valuable information out of the detainee. So there is likely to be some daylight between f^* and $\hat{f}$, making room for f to fall in between and sustain this equilibrium. In other words:

Implication 8.2 (**Surprise Torture Is Likely**). *Surprise torture—torture of a detainee after he has provided information, even if it was all of it—is likely.*

The implication for real-world torture is that the lower the quality or quantity (or both) of background information, the less interrogators know about a detainee, the more likely is surprise torture. There is something a bit perverse here as well. Presumably, intelligence agencies and their interrogators are most concerned about the information about which they know the least. It can be scarier not knowing what you don't know than knowing you don't know some specific threat.

Indeed, this was the implication of Defense Secretary Donald Rumsfeld's (in)famous dismissal of a question about Iraq and weapons of mass destruction (WMDs) during a February 2002 press conference. Asked about whether there was "any evidence to indicate that Iraq has attempted to or is willing to supply terrorists with weapons of mass destruction," Rumsfeld tried to brush off the question by saying the following:

> Reports that say that something hasn't happened are always interesting to me, because as we know, there are known knowns; there are things we know we know. We also know there are known unknowns; that is to say we know there are some things we do not know. But there are also unknown unknowns—the ones we don't know we don't know. And if one looks throughout the history of our country and other free countries, it is the latter category that tend to be the difficult ones. And so people who have the omniscience that they can say with high certainty that something has not happened or is not being tried, have capabilities that are … They can do things I can't do (laughter).[3]

Rumsfeld was, understandably, not the first government security official to think this way and will not be the last. If torture is used to find the "unknown unknowns," however, then surprise torture is more likely. Information will be misinterpreted, and detainees will not be believed even if they have given up important information, even everything they know. In other words:

Implication 8.3 (**Information Importance Increases Surprise Torture**). *The more important the information (in terms of unknown unknowns), the more likely the use of "unnecessary" torture (from the proponents' point of view) because the value of information is less well understood.*

Innocent Detainee Recognition Threshold, p^*

Finally, consider p^*, the Interrogator's belief that the Detainee is Innocent (and not Resistant) after having received "no information." As this threshold increases (moves to the back of the cube), the region gets bigger. This too makes sense;

for values of p above the threshold, the Interrogator does not want to torture, thinking she has the wrong man. The more hesitant she is to believe that "no information" means an Innocent Detainee rather than a Resistant one, the more likely she is to torture and so the space for the equilibrium increases to the back of the cube.

We know, however, from Proposition 7.2 that if the Pragmatic Interrogator believes that it is more likely that the Detainee she faces is Cooperative than both of the other two types, then p^* is less than one-half and likely closer to zero. Consequently, the back boundary of the dark-gray surprise torture region is under one-half and likely closer to zero (the front of the parameter space). In other words, the equilibrium exists only if the Interrogator believes that the probability the Detainee is Innocent after "no information" is very small. This is indeed likely to be the case.

SUBSTANTIVE INTERPRETATION

Substantively, this formal result covers two outcomes in the real world in terms of the Cooperative Detainee. In the first, the Cooperative Detainee has revealed all his information in order to avoid torture. Nevertheless, he is tortured afterward either because the Interrogator does not understand that the information is valuable or because she believes that he is not telling all he knows (or a combination of the two). Even according to the pragmatic model of torture for intelligence only, this torture is unjustified because a Detainee who has revealed all of his valuable information should not be tortured.

In the second substantive outcome or interpretation of this equilibrium, the Cooperative Detainee has revealed some information, but not everything he knows, and is tortured afterward. There is still surprise here—the Cooperative Detainee thought the Interrogator believed he had revealed all his information and so wouldn't be tortured—but it is not the same sort of surprise one would feel if one had truly revealed everything and continued to be tortured. According to the pragmatic model, this torture is justified because a Detainee with valuable information is holding some of it back, refusing to reveal it. (Keep in mind, however, that an Innocent Detainee is tortured in this equilibrium as well.)

Note that the two cases are necessarily observationally equivalent to the Interrogator. The fundamental and unsolvable epistemological problem of interrogations generally—with or without torture—is the inability of the Interrogator to know what is "inside" a Detainee's mind. Interrogators can never know whether a Detainee, even a very cooperative and productive one, has revealed all he knows.

For a case in the real world to match the surprise torture outcome, it must meet the following conditions:

1. The detainee possessed information sought by the interrogator.
2. The detainee was subjected to objective and not leading questioning.
3. The detainee gave up some or all of her valuable information but was tortured afterward from ignorance and/or disbelief on the part of the interrogator.

*   *   *

REAL-WORLD CASE: SHEILA CASSIDY

The story of Sheila Cassidy, an English doctor tortured by Pinochet's secret police in 1975, meets all three criteria.[4]

On December 4, 1971, tired of the "rat race" of British medical life, Doctor Cassidy set sail for Chile on a cargo ship. She studied Spanish, passed her medical exams, and eventually found work in an urban hospital. It was not long, however, before her growing religious inclinations moved her closer to the Catholic church and she decided to work in a shantytown clinic where she could provide more basic medical services to the poor. Her work and increasing commitment to the Catholic church (she decided to become a nun at one point) led her to befriend many priests and nuns, both Chilean and in the large missionary community.

On October 21, 1975, a Catholic priest asked her whether she was willing to treat a man who had been wounded in the leg by a bullet. The priest did not identify the man, but Cassidy knew it was one of the men from a leftist revolutionary party who were being hunted down by the Pinochet military dictatorship. The man faced certain torture and perhaps death at the hands of the Chilean secret police, the Dirección de Inteligencia Nacional or DINA, if he sought help at a hospital. Cassidy was apolitical, though she was increasingly aware of the misery and hardship imposed by Pinochet's martial law, and says in her memoirs that she decided to help simply because she was a doctor and doctors treat the injured and ill.

Cassidy did the best she could with limited resources to care for the wounded fugitive, Nelson Gutierrez, in the convent where he had taken clandestine refuge. It was difficult to control the infection and she saw him several times over a period of days. Eventually, he was spirited away (ultimately finding asylum in the residence of the Papal Nuncio), and Cassidy went back to her work at the clinic.

On November 1, 1975, Cassidy was visiting the house of another priest, looking in on a sick nun. She heard a blood-curdling scream and ran downstairs to find

Enriquetta, the housekeeper, face down in a pool of blood with a large wound in her back. No sooner had Cassidy reached Enriquetta than machine gun fire from the street began to rip up the house. Plainclothes DINA agents entered the house and demanded her name. When she replied "Sheila," they said, "she's the one we want," and after searching the house they bundled her into a car, slapped her, tied a blindfold on her, and drove off.

It wasn't long before the car pulled into the courtyard of a colonial-era villa, Villa Grimaldi, now infamous as a major DINA torture center. Cassidy was taken to a room with a desk, a chair, a bare metal bunk frame, and what she would later call "an electric box," with wire leads snaking from it. In disbelief at her situation, she initially refused to comply with their orders to undress, but relented after they started ripping the clothes from her. They tied her fast to the lower bunk bed, directly to the metal frame, her weight supported by the metal mesh.

And then they started shocking her. This was the infamous *parilla*, the "grill." She tried to scream but they had forced a rag into her mouth. With the pain coursing throughout her entire body, they began the interrogation.

"Where did you treat Gutierrez?"
"Who asked you to treat him?" (Cassidy 1977, p. 174).

These (objective) questions let Cassidy know that DINA did not know about the priests' involvement in particular and the role of the church more generally and she resolved to keep it that way by lying to her torturers.[5] Two thoughts helped her withstand the pain. The first was the conviction that British officials would soon rescue her. The second was the knowledge that the lives of her friends depended on her.

And so, in response to their questions—"Why did they ask you?" "Where does he work?" "Who owned the house?" "What does he do?" "How did they contact you?"—and in between bouts of painful shocks, she began to make up answers. Finally, though, she could not come up with a street name and thus offered to take them there. At this point, she had no plan other than to stop the pain.

They drove her around the area she had lied about but after a while discovered she'd been lying to them. Angry at having been played and the precious time they'd lost, they promised another round of the *parilla* and drove her back to Villa Grimaldi. Still, she had bought the fugitives and the priests precious time. Moreover, it so happens that the fictional house she described matched a house in the neighborhood they were searching. As a result, they actually thought they had found the house and mounted a raid, only to discover that they had been misled. This demonstrates dramatically how even objective questioning can, when combined with torture, lead to false information and wasted time.

Back at Villa Grimaldi, they put one of the electrical clips in her vagina and cranked up the current. The resulting pain was "appalling" and the questions came so fast she was unable to make up answers to them. In her words, "they broke me." Even so, she told the truth only "little by little," telling "them as little as [she] could" to minimize the number of people in danger (Cassidy 1977, p. 188).

The trouble for Cassidy was that her tormenters refused to believe her. They refused to believe that nuns and priests could be mixed up with Marxist revolutionaries. This "disbelief was very hard to bear" because she "received many gratuitous shocks" for another hour or more and "there seemed no escape from the white hot sea of pain" (Cassidy 1977, p. 189).

Eventually the DINA torturers believed Cassidy and they searched the convent. They found neither the priests nor their main quarries, Gutierrez and revolutionary leader Andres Pascal Allende, and about this they were not happy. She was returned to Villa Grimaldi but this time she was interrogated by two senior officers in an office. They did not torture her and asked about the whereabouts of Gutierrez and Allende. She told them that Gutierrez had received asylum in the Papal Nuncio and that she didn't know where Allende had fled.

They refused to believe she didn't know because they assumed she was working with the MIR. They refused to believe her protestation that she only treated Gutierrez because it was her medical duty. And yet, when she told one interrogator that she would even have treated him if he were wounded, he said he believed her.

That did not stop him, however, from sending her to the *parilla* for a third time.

The pain was worse. They went back to the events of the day to see if they could find any leads. Eventually they hit upon a question that led Cassidy to say that a priest was going to try and find asylum for Allende. In her words, this was "the last information that I had" (Cassidy 1977, p. 192).

While DINA officers went out to find the priest, she was taken before senior officers again. Again suspicious that a church group could be involved, they hit her in the face and threatened to keep torturing her on the *parilla*, saying she would eventually give in. She was even tied to the bed again, but was not shocked any more.

Two months after her arrest, signed statements, and detention in various centers, she was released and returned to England.

BACK TO THE MODEL

Here, then, is an illustration of the surprise torture equilibrium. In the model, the Interrogator continues to torture after "information" either because she doesn't understand the information is valuable or because she believes the Detainee is holding more information back. The former belief is the u parameter or variable, while the latter belief is the f variable. Translating Cassidy's situation back into the language of the model, the value of u for the DINA interrogators was low; in their religious world view, good Catholic nuns and priests would never associate with godless Marxist revolutionaries and so they discounted her information.[6]

Remember that u is between zero and one, so a low value, a value approaching zero, reduces the value of the denominator. As the denominator gets smaller, the value of the whole threshold f gets bigger. This pushes the threshold to the top of the axis, so that the space occupied by torture is greater. More values of f fall under the threshold and thus support torture. The DINA's estimation of u pushed the threshold up, moving it past the maximum of Cassidy's belief f^*, and they tortured her despite the fact that she gave them the information they wanted.

Cassidy's case is like many others under Pinochet. Like French paratroopers in Algiers, DINA wasted no time with other techniques and immediately began torturing. As has been widely documented, torture under Pinochet was widespread, with concentration camps and torture centers set up all over Chile for anyone suspected of anti-regime activity (Muñoz 2008, p. 47; also Ensalaco 2011). The DINA intelligence gathering system relied on torture; as a result, reputation costs r for failing to torture a suspect who did not immediately give up information must have been high.

Even if r were not that high, however, it is clear from the huge apparatus of detention, torture, and summary execution to Pinochet's own bland dismissals that the costs of using torture c and a were very low. This is perhaps nowhere better illustrated than by DINA's reaction to the Italian government's policy of granting asylum to Chileans who fled to the Italian embassy. After DINA tortured an opposition leader by the name of Lumi Videla to death, they threw her abused body over the wall of the Italian embassy in Santiago (Ensalaco 2011, p. 78).

Given the ferocity of the regime's desire to root out any opposition, as well as the fact that they intended to execute many of those who did not die under torture, it is not surprising that the information hiding threshold $\hat{f}$ was very high. Moreover, given the sheer number of victims swept up by DINA and other Chilean torture units, it would be surprising if they always interpreted the information they received correctly—that is, that u approached 1.

There was also another factor at work here, however. Her torturers' inability to accept her information as valuable stemmed not from a lack of background information or context in which to place it, but rather from a world view that simply couldn't square priests and nuns acting in support of leftists. While the

Chilean clergy did not directly and openly oppose the regime, many did become active in human rights and became a thorn in the regime's side. It should not have been such a surprise to DINA, but their own ideology blinded them to the possibility. It is easy to imagine how this conflict between world view and the facts in front of an interrogator might generalize to other contexts and conflicts.

As for Cassidy, she clearly assumed they would believe her when she told the truth. She also appears to have believed that her interrogators were pragmatic, that they would stop torturing once she gave them the information they sought. This may partly be due to the fact that she was not a professional operative or even active in the opposition; she just treated one man. Others may have been less confident that the DINA interrogators were Pragmatic and not Sadistic. It may also be the case that the threshold q dropped over time. She says she resisted initially to give others as much time to get away and only gave up information once she thought enough time had passed that they were more likely to be safe. In other words, the value of her information (to her), v, was very valuable at first, pushing her threshold up, but fell over time, causing the threshold at which point she would tell the truth to drop as well.

*   *   *

The argument thus far has shown that:

1. EITs are torture and the effectiveness of interrogational torture is an open question. (Chapter 2)
2. The Bush program approximates closely the ideal model of interrogational torture and includes limits on torture; the Bush and ideal models provide benchmarks for comparison with the game theory models to come. (Chapter 3)
3. The Bush model generates strange, quixotic outcomes. (Chapter 4)
4. The Bush interrogational torture program is more realistically modeled as objective and leading question variants of an incomplete information game, with three types of detainees, two types of interrogators, and uncertainty about the amount and value of information provided. (Chapter 5)
5. By positing a set of Detainee strategies, calculating the Interrogator's expected utility using Bayes' Rule to identify her best response, and checking for incentives to deviate by any of the Detainee types, it is possible to derive a perfect Bayesian equilibrium in which a Detainee is tortured after providing information. (Chapter 6)

6. The RIT model generates nine perfect Bayesian equilibria, the formal and empirical characteristics of which generate important observations, propositions, and implications, including:

   (a) The Interrogator's thresholds for believing that a Detainee is Innocent after "no information" are less than one-half, with $\hat{p}$ close to one-half and p^* closer to zero.

   (b) The Interrogator's information hiding threshold under objective questioning $\hat{f}$ is greater than or equal to one-half, whereas her information hiding threshold under leading questioning $\tilde{f}$ as well as the Detainee's version f^* of $\hat{f}$ are a little less than one-half.

   (c) Objective questioning (potentially) provides better information, but is necessarily accompanied by more torture, than leading questioning, which, however, provides less valuable information.

   (d) All things being equal, interrogators are more likely to get less valuable information than highly valuable information.

   (Chapter 7)

7. Surprise torture of a Cooperative Detainee—even if he has provided all his information—is not only likely, but perversely more likely

   (a) the more willing the Detainee is to divulge information and

   (b) the more important the information is in terms of "unknown unknowns."

   (Chapter 8)

The next step in the argument is to examine and interpret the *ambiguous information, selective torture* and *false confirmation, selective torture* equilibria.

Ambiguous Information and False Confirmation

While the CIA believes al-Libi fabricated information, the CIA cannot
determine whether, or what portions of, the original statements or the
later recants are true or false.

—CIA OFFICER, *Report of the Select Committee on Intelligence on Postwar Findings
about Iraq's WMD Programs and Links to Terrorism*

The two equilibria discussed in this chapter occur under leading questioning
only. In the *ambiguous information, selective torture* equilibrium, both the Cooperative and Innocent Detainee types play "information" while the Interrogator
plays "no torture" after "information" and "torture" after "no information." The
false confirmation, selective torture equilibrium is similar to the *ambiguous information equilibrium*, except that in this case only the Innocent Detainee is sufficiently
confident that the Interrogator is Pragmatic and chooses "information," falsely
confirming what the Interrogator wants to hear. The Interrogator is satisfied with
the confirmation and thus does not torture after "information." The Interrogator
tortures after "no information," however, so the Cooperative and Resistant Detainees are tortured in this equilibrium. We consider the features of each before
discussing the substantive interpretation, a real-world case, and then returning to
the model.

AMBIGUOUS INFORMATION

The Cooperative and Innocent Detainees play "information" because their
belief that the Interrogator is Pragmatic is greater than their (individual

and independent) thresholds $q \geq \hat{q}$ and $q \geq q^*$, respectively. The Interrogator chooses not to torture because the Detainee's confirmation has satisfied her threshold ($\tilde{f}$). She tortures after "no information" because there is no chance an Innocent Detainee played this move. Only a Resistant Detainee does not provide confirmation in this equilibrium.

The information is ambiguous because the Interrogator has asked a leading question and has received the confirmation she wanted, but does not know whether it came from a Cooperative Detainee who could provide real confirmation or from an Innocent Detainee who would confirm anything so as to avoid torture. Since both Detainee types confirm whatever the Interrogator says, their responses provide no new information. Everything was the same as it was, based on the accuracy of the question. If the assumption embedded in the question was accurate, confirmation cements it (unwittingly in the case of the Innocent Detainee); if it was inaccurate, confirmation cements that false information.[1]

Equilibrium Features

Figure 9.1 depicts the *ambiguous information, selective torture equilibrium,* with the darker- and lighter-shaded areas representing the moves "information" by the Cooperative and Innocent Detainees, respectively. The dotted area covers the portion of the parameter space supporting torture. In the surprise torture equilibrium, there were two information hiding thresholds, the Interrogator's actual belief ($\hat{f}$) and the belief the Detainee thinks is the Interrogator's (f^*). In this

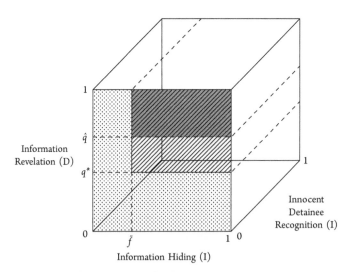

Figure 9.1 Ambiguous Information, Selective Torture Equilibrium

equilibrium there is only one because there is no possibility for misunderstanding under leading questioning and so the parameter capturing possible misunderstanding (u) drops out of the payoffs and the resulting equation for the threshold.

There are, however, two versions of the information revelation threshold, one for the Cooperative Detainee $(\hat{q})$ and one for the Innocent Detainee (q^*). Finally, note that there is no Innocent Detainee recognition threshold $(\hat{p}$ or $p^*)$. The reason for this is that, in this equilibrium, the probability the Detainee is Innocent after observing "no information" is zero; only the Resistant Detainee chooses "no information" in this equilibrium. As a result, this equilibrium occupies the two-dimensional plane on the face of Figure 9.1 rather than a rectangular solid.

INFORMATION REVELATION THRESHOLDS, $\hat{q}$ AND q^*

Since both the (knowledgeable) Cooperative and (nonknowledgeable) Innocent Detainees provide information under leading questioning in this equilibrium, each has an information revelation threshold. As we noted in Chapter 7, there were no solid grounds to constrain these independent thresholds and they could lie anywhere along the vertical q axis. I have set the Innocent Detainee's threshold q^* below the Cooperative Detainee's threshold $\hat{q}$ only to distinguish them. Nothing depends on this ordering, however, and it could be that the situation is reversed or that the thresholds are equal. The point for our purposes is that the equilibrium space is the region north of the lowest threshold.

As they increase, the equilibrium space shrinks. As the Detainees become more suspicious that the Interrogator will torture them anyway, even if they provide exactly the confirmation sought by the Interrogator, they become less likely to provide that confirmation. Conversely, the more the Interrogator is able to convince the Detainees that she will not torture if only the Detainee supplies her with the answer she wants to hear, lowering the thresholds, the more the equilibrium space grows.

Perversely, then, the more a detainee accepts the interrogator's logic of torture—no information results in torture, but pleasing the interrogator means avoiding it—the greater the chances are for ambiguous information. In other words:

Implication 9.1 (**Torture's Logic and Ambiguous Information**). *Everything else being equal, the more the logic of torture works as its proponents envision, the greater the likelihood of ambiguous information elicited by the interrogator under leading questioning.*

We can also think about the threshold and the logic of torture mathematically. Given that, all else being equal, the thresholds $\hat{q}$ and q^* go down as the torture costs k imposed on them increase, it follows that the space supporting ambiguous information increases. We have, that is, confirmed the common sense intuition:

Implication 9.2 (**Brutality and Ambiguous Information**). *Everything else being equal, as the brutality of torture increases, the greater the likelihood of ambiguous information elicited by the interrogator under leading questioning.*

INFORMATION HIDING THRESHOLD, $\tilde{f}$

"Hiding" information may seem contradictory under leading questioning as compared to objective questioning. In the latter, the interrogator must decide at one point that she is satisfied with the information provided by the detainee, not knowing what the total possible amount and quality are, and thus stops torturing. In the former, the interrogator tells the detainee exactly what she wants to hear, so the "total possible amounts" (if not the quality) of information is what the *interrogator* decides to ask, *not* what the detainee actually *knows*.

The interrogator must, however, still be satisfied with what she has heard before she stops torturing. Her satisfaction will depend both on what the detainee is willing to confirm and, crucially, on what she wants confirmed. The higher her demands, the more she wants confirmed, the higher her threshold.

This can also be seen in the individual parameters constituting the threshold: $\tilde{f} = \frac{p_C(r-c)+p_I(-a-c)}{p_C(r+a)}$. First, as we have said repeatedly, the Interrogator's prior probability the Detainee is Cooperative p_C is likely to be high, whereas the prior probability the Detainee is Innocent p_I is likely to be low. Of all the costs in $\tilde{f}$, the one of most concern to interrogators and their employers is r, the reputation or credibility costs from not using torture on uncooperative detainees. As we have said, the torture cost c is likely to be very low, as is the "unnecessary" torture cost a (keeping in mind $a > r$). Combined with a low probability the Detainee is Innocent, we know from Proposition 7.4 that $\tilde{f}$ approaches one-half.

Even so, recalling Proposition 7.4, the upper limit to $\tilde{f}$ remains under one-half. This pushes the equilibrium region to the left side of the parameter space, covering more area on the face, as captured in Figure 9.1. This means more area for ambiguous information and reduces the area covered by torture (to the left of the threshold). As the threshold approaches one-half, ambiguous information decreases, but the space occupied by torture increases. In other words, the more the Interrogator demands in terms of confirmation (the higher the threshold), the more likely the use of torture, even under leading questioning, suggesting the following implication:

Implication 9.3 (**Torture Persists under Leading Questioning**). *Leading questioning will not eliminate torture; the higher the interrogator's demand for confirmation, the more torture.*

FALSE CONFIRMATION, SELECTIVE TORTURE

The *false confirmation, selective torture* equilibrium is the other equilibrium which occurs under leading questioning only. This time only the Innocent Detainee plays "information," falsely confirming what the Interrogator wants to hear. The Cooperative Detainee believes that the Interrogator is Sadistic and not Pragmatic ($q < \hat{q}$) or suspects that the Interrogator is Pragmatic, but will believe that the Detainee is still withholding information and so will torture anyway ($q \geq \hat{q}$ and $f < f^*$) and as a result chooses "no information." (Remember that although the Cooperative and Innocent Detainees have the same preference ordering, their beliefs can differ.) The Interrogator has received the confirmation she wanted with "information" and so does not torture. The Interrogator does, however, torture the Cooperative and Resistant Detainee types after "no information."

Since the Detainee providing the confirmation in this equilibrium is known to be Innocent, the confirmation provided by the Detainee cannot be objectively correct, accurate confirmation. At best, if the questions asked are accurate, the confirmation is unwittingly true. If the questions are inaccurate or misleading or based on erroneous information, then the confirmation will be as well. In either case, the confirmation provides no new information.

Equilibrium Features

Figure 9.2 presents the equilibrium, showing the Innocent Detainee's information revelation threshold. The darker-shaded area above q^* is the region covered by the Innocent Detainee's confirmation (choice of "information"). The area covered by dots represents the torture of the Cooperative and Resistant Detainees.

INFORMATION REVELATION THRESHOLD, q^*
We have discussed the effects of the Cooperative and Innocent Detainee thresholds under leading questioning above, in the context of the ambiguous information, selective torture equilibrium. The only difference here is that the Cooperative Detainee's belief falls below $\hat{q}$ or is above it, but his belief that the Interrogator will be satisfied with his confirmation falls below his threshold f^*.

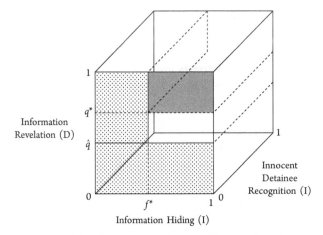

Figure 9.2 False Confirmation, Selective Torture Equilibrium

In short, a Cooperative Detainee's suspicion and mistrust of the Interrogator helps sustain this equilibrium. If he was not suspicious and distrustful, he would choose information, collapsing the equilibrium.

As we said above, the Innocent Detainee does trust the Interrogator and is willing to falsely confirm what she asks of him. Indeed, the more he trusts her (the lower the threshold), the greater the area supporting false information. In other words, we have the exact same implication (9.1) for false information as we did for ambiguous information:

Implication 9.4 (**Torture's Logic and False Information**). *Everything else being equal, the more the logic of torture works as its proponents envision, the greater the likelihood of false information via confirmation of inaccurate leading questioning.*

Indeed, there is the same parallel with the ambiguous information equilibrium in terms of torture's severity as well. Thus, we also confirm the common-sense intuition that more brutality leads to more false information:

Implication 9.5 (**Brutality and False Information**). *All else being equal, increasing the brutality of torture of an innocent detainee under leading questioning increases the likelihood of false information.*

Substantive Interpretation

The substantive interpretation of these equilibria is that the Interrogator has asked a leading question and has received the answer she wanted to hear. In the first equilibrium she does not know whether the confirmation provided is coming from a Cooperative Detainee with knowledge or falsely confirmed by an Innocent Detainee trying to escape torture. In the second case she is certain that the Detainee is Innocent, but gets the confirmation she seeks. Note that this equilibrium also captures the case when an Interrogator has asked a leading question which is false, a Cooperative Detainee willing to provide information has refused to confirm the falsely premised question, and the Detainee is tortured for it!

Rather than thinking about Detainees as being purely Cooperative or Innocent, one way of thinking about this is to imagine their knowledge or ignorance with respect to different types of information. So, for example, a Detainee may have information on locations (safe houses, weapons caches, training camps) but not names or plots. Such a Detainee would be knowledgeable (either Cooperative or Resistant) with respect to the former, but Innocent with respect to the latter. Asking leading questions might result in ambiguous information since some of the information would be correct, but other information would not be. This sort of case would provide a real-world example of these equilibria. Thus, for a case in the real world to match them, it must meet the following conditions:

1. The detainee was subjected to leading and not objective questioning.
2. The detainee confirmed the interrogator's leading questions.
3. The ultimate value of some of the information was false and other was unclear.
4. The detainee was not tortured afterward.

*   *   *

Real-World Case: Ibn al-Shaykh al-Libi

Ali Mohammed al-Fakheri, better known by his *nom de guerre*, Ibn al-Shaykh al-Libi, provides just such a case.[2]

Born in Libya, al-Libi fought with the *mujahideen* against the Soviets in Afghanistan and by the 9/11 attacks had become the internal emir, or chief, of the Khalden jihadist training camp.[3] He fled following the U.S. invasion and was picked up in Pakistan sometime at the end of 2001. After about two weeks he was turned over to the Americans and taken to an interrogation and detention facility at Bagram airbase outside Kabul in Afghanistan.

A pair of FBI agents were the first to interrogate him. One, Russell Fincher, was a devout Christian and he quickly established a rapport with al-Libi, praying with him and talking about Jesus and Mohammed. In more than 80 hours of interviewing al-Libi, Fincher and his colleague got al-Libi talking—after having read him his Miranda rights. According to Fincher and Jack Cloonan, who read Fincher's reports back in the FBI's New York field office, al-Libi provided information on Zacarias Moussaoui, the so-called 20th hijacker, and Richard Reid, the "shoe bomber."[4] The Justice Department was building cases against both men at the time. There was even some hope al-Libi would cut a deal and work with the prosecution. He provided details about the operation of the jihadist training camps in Afghanistan. He told his FBI interrogators over warm coffee in a cold office about a plot to bomb the U.S. embassy in Aden, Yemen. Although it was in its final stages, the plot was foiled. Asked about Al Qaeda's connections with foreign governments, however, he made no mention of Iraq.

Despite the information he allegedly provided, the CIA thought he was holding out and demanded to take over the interrogation from the FBI. It was al-Libi, then, two months before the capture of Abu Zubaydah, who became the first political football in the contest between the FBI and the CIA as to who would lead the interrogations of terrorist suspects. The CIA's victory in that game and a harbinger of what was to come was communicated to al-Libi in dramatic fashion. A CIA officer who would later receive a reprimand from the Agency for threatening a different (and blindfolded) detainee with an unloaded gun and a power drill, interrupted a session with Fincher and told al-Libi he was going to be sent to Egypt.[5] The officer promised he would "find [al-Libi's] mother and . . . fuck her" (Isikoff and Corn 2007, p. 121).

Placed on the cold concrete floor with his socks, shoes, and gloves taken away, it took al-Libi only 15 minutes to decide he

> would fabricate any information the interrogators wanted in order to gain better treatment and avoid being handed over to [Egypt]. According to al-Libi, after his decision to fabricate information for debriefers, he "lied about being a member of al-Qa'ida. Although he considered himself close to, but not a member of, al-Qa'ida, he knew enough about the senior members, organization and operations to claim to be a member." "Once al-Libi started fabricating information," he claimed, "his treatment improved and he experienced no further physical pressures from the Americans" (United States Senate 2006, pp. 79–80).

The CIA did not stay satisfied for long, however, and soon guards tied al-Libi to a stretcher, duct-taped his feet, hands, and mouth, hooded him, and tossed him in the back of a pickup. The truck was driven straight into the bowels of a cargo plane which took off for Cairo.

The Egyptians made it clear what was in store for him if he did not provide information on future operations. Al-Libi claims not to have known about any other future attacks but said he began to make them up to avoid torture.

His interrogators pushed his creativity to the limits, he said, when they demanded to know about Al Qaeda's connections with Iraq. Unsuccessful in telling them what they wanted, they put him in a small box for about 17 hours. When he still failed to say something they wanted to hear, they knocked him down and punched him for a quarter of an hour.

He then concocted a story about three Al Qaeda members going to Iraq to learn about nuclear weapons. He said he supplied the names of actual Al Qaeda members in order to make his lies more believable. Believable they were, and he was rewarded with food. Some days later, however, the interrogators wanted information on connections between Al Qaeda and anthrax and biological weapons training in Iraq. Al-Libi claims he was once again unable to craft a story because he didn't even understand the term "biological" and didn't know what a biological weapon even was. The beatings ensued once again (United States Senate 2006, pp. 79–82).

Receiving these reports back from the Egyptians, the Defense Intelligence Agency in February 2002 wrote up a report, a "Defense Intelligence Terrorism Summary," that questioned the credibility of the claims made by al-Libi about Saddam Hussein's support for training Al Qaeda in WMDs. Instead, the report stated: "[I]t is more likely this individual is intentionally misleading the debriefers. Ibn al-Shaykh has been undergoing debriefs for several weeks and may be describing scenarios to the debriefers that he knows will retain their interest" (United States Senate 2006, p. 77).

As is now well known, this did not prevent "President Bush, Vice President Dick Cheney, and other officials [from] repeatedly cit[ing] the information provided by Mr. Libi as 'credible' evidence that Iraq was training Al Qaeda members in the use of explosives and illicit weapons" (Jehl 2005a). Bush, for example, claimed "in a major speech in Cincinnati in October 2002 that 'we've learned that Iraq has trained Al Qaeda members in bomb making and poisons and gases'" (Jehl 2005a). Of course, we know now these claims were false.

In February 2003 al-Libi was returned to the Americans and transferred to Guantanamo. When questioned again by the CIA one year later, "Al-Libi claimed that he fabricated 'all information regarding al-Qa'ida's sending representatives to Iraq to try to obtain WMD assistance.' Al-Libi claimed that to the best of his knowledge al-Qa'ida never sent any individuals into Iraq for any kind of support in chemical or biological weapons, as he had claimed previously" (United States Senate 2006, pp. 79–80). As a result, the CIA reissued the intelligence reports with the recantation, in essence withdrawing the intelligence as untrustworthy (Isikoff and Hosenball 2005).

When asked why he backtracked on his earlier statements, al-Libi replied this way: "They were killing me. I had to tell them something" (Isikoff and Corn 2007, 124).

The ambiguity of the information received by al-Libi is captured nicely by the entry in History Commons, "an open-content participatory journalism" website akin to Wikipedia but focusing on events and containing supporting links to newspapers, documents, and other sources. It should be treated with caution and I have not relied on it for the account above, but an entry connected with al-Libi is apposite: "Provides Mix of Valid, False Information."[6]

Of course, the key is how the CIA officials charged with evaluating intelligence from interrogations interpreted the information from al-Libi. As the epigraph to this chapter states, "a CIA officer explained that while CIA believes al-Libi fabricated information, the CIA cannot determine whether, or what portions of, the original statements or the later recants are true or false" (United States Senate 2006, p. 108). According to a "senior U.S. intelligence official, Al-Libi 'changed his story, and we're still in the process of trying to determine what's right and what's not right' from his information. 'He told us one thing at one time and another at another time.' The official said that 'the CIA did not know whether he was telling the truth' about there being no connection with Iraq" (Priest 2004).

And finally there is former CIA Director George Tenet himself, who used the al-Libi "information" to support the Iraq war. Tenet put it this way in his memoir:

> He clearly lied. We just don't know when. Did he lie when he first said that al-Qa'ida members received training in Iraq or did he lie when he said they did not? In my mind, either case might still be true. The fact is, we don't know which story is true, and since we don't know, we can assume nothing (Tenet and Harlow 2007, pp. 353–354).

BACK TO THE MODEL

It would appear that al-Libi should never have been a case study in this book at all, but rather in a book on how at least some terrorists immediately start singing to the FBI (Weiser 2014). It was only when the CIA demanded more, began asking leading questions, and threatened torture to get it that his case became relevant here.

In terms of the thresholds, q^* was apparently rather low; al-Libi didn't have to spend more than a quarter-hour in a cold cell before deciding to try and please his captors with whatever they wanted to hear in return for better treatment. His CIA and Egyptian interrogators, however, apparently had a higher threshold $\tilde{f}$. Their threshold was high in two ways.

First, the interrogators had a high hurdle for what would satisfy them. They wanted to hear very specific "facts" confirming Al Qaeda's pursuit of WMDs from Iraq and tortured him until they got them. Second, while al-Libi was willing to provide them with whatever they wanted to hear, his own ignorance of the subject matter made it difficult for him to give them what they wanted.

It is worthwhile pointing out that the RIT model excluded by assumption the possibility that a Detainee's response to a leading question might fail to be understood by the Interrogator (that was why the u variable dropped out of the payoffs). We have in the al-Libi case a failure on the other side, not incorporated directly into the model because we gave the benefit of the doubt to torture proponents: a failure of the Detainee to understand an Interrogator's question, even though it is a leading one. (Since it was not in the model, it was left out of Implication 9.3.) Presumably this would be a more common occurrence in objective questioning, but we see it even here. A failure to understand the question means that the Detainee effectively plays "no information" and is tortured until he does understand it—and falsely confirms it.

Viewing the al-Libi case through the lens of the model also captures something else of importance. It has been widely known for a while now that neoconservatives within the Bush administration led by Vice President Cheney were bent on invading Iraq no later than early 2002, whether or not Iraq had WMDs or links to Al Qaeda, as secret memos summarizing the Bush administration's thinking and prepared for top UK policy makers illustrate (Ricketts 2002, Rycroft 2002). The problem was, the memos point out, that Bush administration hawks needed evidence linking Iraq to Al Qaeda's pursuit of WMDs for justification. To this degree, the hawks could care less whether or not al-Libi was "innocent" of this knowledge. What they wanted was confirmation.

Both of the equilibria in this chapter express this idea in Figures 9.1 and 9.2. The equilibria are planes on the front surface of the parameter space and not three-dimensional solids because there is no chance the Detainee is Innocent after observing "no information." The Interrogator believes a Detainee who confirms what she wants to hear is either Innocent for sure (in the false confirmation equilibrium) or either Innocent or Cooperative (in the ambiguous information equilibrium)—and she doesn't care either way.

To this degree, the two "bad" information equilibria are special cases of bad information in terms of these Interrogator beliefs. It is important to note that this does not at all mean that this surface is the only region colonized by bad information in the model. We have seen this already, though we have not made much of it in our focus on the Cooperative and Innocent types of Detainees. In both these two equilibria and the surprise torture equilibrium in the last chapter, a Resistant Detainee may be providing false information in one interpretation of the move "not reveal information." As we shall see below, however, this will be the case not just for the Resistant Detainee.

*   *   *

The argument thus far has shown that:

1. EITs are torture, and the effectiveness of interrogational torture is an open question. (Chapter 2)
2. The Bush program approximates closely the ideal model of interrogational torture and includes limits on torture; the Bush and ideal models provide benchmarks for comparison with the game theory models to come. (Chapter 3)
3. The Bush model generates strange, quixotic outcomes. (Chapter 4)
4. The Bush interrogational torture program is more realistically modeled as objective and leading question variants of an incomplete information game, with three types of detainees, two types of interrogators, and uncertainty about the amount and value of information provided. (Chapter 5)
5. By positing a set of Detainee strategies, calculating the Interrogator's expected utility using Bayes' Rule to identify her best response, and checking for incentives to deviate by any of the Detainee types, it is possible to derive a perfect Bayesian equilibrium in which a Detainee is tortured after providing information. (Chapter 6)
6. The RIT model generates nine perfect Bayesian equilibria, the formal and empirical characteristics of which generate important observations, propositions, and implications, including:
   (a) The Interrogator's thresholds for believing that a Detainee is Innocent after "no information" are less than one-half, with $\hat{p}$ close to one-half and p^* closer to 0.
   (b) The Interrogator's information hiding threshold under objective questioning $\hat{f}$ is greater than or equal to one-half, whereas her information hiding threshold under leading questioning $\tilde{f}$ as well as the Detainee's version f^* of $\hat{f}$ are a little less than one-half.
   (c) Objective questioning (potentially) provides better information, but is necessarily accompanied by more torture, than leading questioning, which, however, provides less valuable information.
   (d) All things being equal, interrogators are more likely to get less valuable information than highly valuable information.
   (Chapter 7)
7. Surprise torture of a Cooperative Detainee—even if he has provided all his information—is not only likely, but perversely more likely
   (a) the more willing the Detainee is to divulge information and
   (b) the more important the information is in terms of "unknown unknowns."
   (Chapter 8)

8. The perversity under objective questioning persists under leading questioning, namely
   (a) the more the Innocent Detainee believes Interrogator promises of no torture in exchange for confirmation, the more likely is ambiguous and false information.
   (b) the more brutal the torture, the more likely is ambiguous and false information.
   (c) the more important the confirmation is to the Interrogator and the more difficult it is for the Detainee to understand what is being asked, the greater the likelihood of torture.
   (d) leading questioning will not eliminate torture; the higher the interrogator's demand for confirmation, the more torture.
   (Chapter 9)

The next step in the argument is to examine and interpret the *valuable information, selective torture equilibrium.*

Valuable Information, Selective Torture

Ennigkeit's . . . forceful and intensive threat . . . caused [Gäfgen] to fear
even harsher measures. He did not want to expose himself to those . . . .
—German court document in the case of Magnus Gäfgen

There are three additional pairs of equilibria in the RIT game, one each under
objective and leading questioning. They are "pairs" because each member of the
pair calls for the same set of actions in both questioning types, but the beliefs
supporting those actions differ across the questioning types. Since substantively
they call for the same set of observable actions, we will consider each pair together. This chapter considers the first of these pairs: the *valuable information,
selective torture equilibrium*. The next chapter examines the two pairs in which no
information is provided, one in which the detainees are tortured and the other in
which they are not.

EQUILIBRIUM FEATURES

In the *valuable information, selective torture equilibrium*, the Cooperative Detainee
provides information satisfying the Interrogator, who therefore does not torture afterward. Just as in the *valuable information, surprise torture equilibrium*,
the Cooperative Detainee is confident both that the Interrogator is pragmatic
$(q \geq \hat{q})$ and that the Interrogator will believe that the Detainee has told everything he knows $(f > f^*)$ and so decides to play "information." In the leading
questioning version, the Innocent Detainee also has the move "information" but

does not believe that it is sufficiently likely that the Interrogator is Pragmatic, $q < q^*$ and thus refuses to lie and confirm what the Interrogator wants to hear.

The Interrogator chooses not to torture after "information" in this equilibrium because she believes that the Detainee has in fact revealed everything he knows ($f > \hat{f}$, under objective questioning) or she wants him to confirm ($f > f^*$, under leading questioning). The Interrogator tortures after "no information" because she thinks that it is unlikely that the Detainee is Innocent rather than Resistant when a Detainee fails to reveal anything valuable ($p < p^*$). In other words, the equilibrium depends on torturing an Innocent Detainee for telling the truth of his innocence.

Thus, the only differences between the objective and leading question variants of this equilibrium are the addition of the Innocent Detainee's beliefs $q < q^*$ and the change in the Interrogator's information hiding threshold from $\hat{f}$ under objective questioning to f^* under leading questioning. The latter change is due to the fact that, under leading questioning, the information clarity parameter u drops out from the Interrogator's payoffs and so the resulting threshold derived from them. That makes it identical to the Detainee's version under objective questioning, f^*.

Figure 10.1 presents the equilibrium in the parameter space, with the dots again representing the region covered by torture. The thresholds for both questioning variants are in their usual places, but the gray-shaded region in the northwest corner is the equilibrium under objective questioning only. In the leading questioning variant, the shaded volume would expand to the left, colonizing the region between f^* and $\hat{f}$ but still staying north of $\hat{q}$ and to the front of p^*. Given that the pragmatic justification for interrogational torture rests on

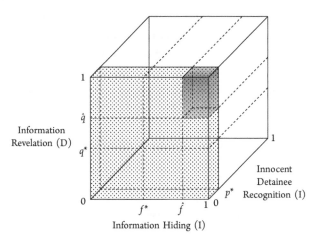

Figure 10.1 Valuable Information, Selective Torture Equilibrium

the claim that it provides actual intelligence—that is, new, valuable information unknown and unknowable prior to questioning and torture—we concentrate on the objective variant of the equilibrium in what follows. Note that under objective questioning the dots fill the entire volume to the front of p^*, including the valuable information region, because even in that region an Innocent Detainee is tortured for telling the truth.

Information Revelation Threshold $\hat{q}$

The equilibrium is bounded by the Cooperative Detainee's information revelation threshold $\hat{q}$, the information hiding threshold $\hat{f}$, and the Innocent Detainee recognition threshold p^*. Take the information revelation threshold $\hat{q}$ first. As $\hat{q}$ drops, as the Cooperative Detainee's willingness to talk increases, the equilibrium region expands, with "information" occupying more volume and "torture" (of a Cooperative Detainee) occupying less volume. Conversely, a Cooperative Detainee with a higher threshold is less willing to divulge information, even under threat of torture, and so the equilibrium volume shrinks, opening up more space for torture of a Cooperative Detainee.

So we have four elements at work here: the value of the Cooperative Detainee's information v, the intensity or severity of the torture k, the size of the region occupied by (and so the likelihood or frequency of) information (of some quality) above $\hat{q}$, and finally, the complementary region on the q axis below $\hat{q}$, which is the size of the volume taken up by (and thus the frequency of) torture of a Cooperative Detainee who does not provide information. Considering only this q dimension, then, and holding the amount of torture constant, an expansion of the equilibrium region along the q axis perforce means less valuable information. That is, for a given level of torture (k), and $\hat{f}, f^*$, and p^* held constant, the only way for the region to expand, for the equilibrium to occupy a greater proportion of the parameter space, is for the value of information v to drop. If we hold v constant instead of k, then the only way for the region to expand to occupy a greater proportion of the parameter space and thus be more likely is for the costs (brutality) of torture k to increase. In other words, torture must become more severe. There are, in other words, multiple trade-offs:

1. As information value increases,
    (a) the likelihood of getting information decreases and
    (b) the frequency of torture increases
2. As information value decreases,
    (a) the likelihood of getting information increases and
    (b) the frequency of torture decreases

3. As torture severity increases,
   (a) the likelihood of getting information increases and
   (b) the frequency of torture decreases
4. As torture severity decreases,
   (a) the likelihood of getting information decreases and
   (b) the frequency of torture increases

Trade-off 1a and its complement trade-off 2a are restatements of Implication 7.2: Everything else being equal, the more valuable the information possessed by the Cooperative Detainee, the higher the value of $\hat{q}$ and the less likely he is to reveal it. The less valuable the information, the lower the value of $\hat{q}$ and the more likely he is to reveal it. As we said in Chapter 7, this is of course true for interrogations without torture. The point bears repeating that torture does not do any better.

Now consider trade-offs 1b and 2b. Higher-value information (a higher v) pushes up $\hat{q}$ and thus the lower bound of the equilibrium. As it does, as the darker-shaded region moves toward the top, the volume below it is replaced by torture of the Cooperative Detainee. (Remember that an Innocent Detainee as well as a Resistant Detainee is tortured in the entire space to the front of p^*.) Thus, as accords with intuition, more valuable information is accompanied by more torture.

Finally, take a look at the second set of trade-offs 3 and 4 associated with torture severity. Consistent with the assumption granted to proponents, namely that torture compels information from a Cooperative Detainee, more brutal torture means that information is more likely, whereas less brutal torture reduces that likelihood (trade-offs 3a and 4a). Notice, though, that there is also a less obvious trade-off. All else being equal, an increase in torture severity means less frequent torture of Cooperative Detainees (i.e., more space occupied by information, less by torture), while a decrease in severity results in less information and more torture (trade-offs 3b and 4b). But this means that the pragmatic goal of infrequent and minimally brutal torture in obtaining information is unobtainable, with the following important implication:

Implication 10.1 (**Torture Frequency–Brutality Trade-off**). *Everything else being equal, increasing the likelihood of information requires either less frequent torture or less brutal torture; it is not possible to minimize both.*

Putting these multiple but related trade-offs together, we have the following implication:

Implication 10.2 (**Information Value–Brutality Trade-off**). *Everything else being equal, eliciting information is more likely (the equilibrium region* *expands to a greater proportion of the parameter space) only if the information becomes less valuable or the torture becomes more brutal, not both.*

Information Hiding Threshold $\hat{f}$

Now take a look at $\hat{f}$. The lower the value of $\hat{f}$, the more room there is for an f satisfying the Interrogator, making her willing to forgo torture, but also increasing the possibility of the Detainee getting away without revealing some information. That is, the more "lenient" she is, the lower her expectations of what she expects the Detainee to reveal to her, the larger the equilibrium region, and the less torture is employed. The more suspicious the Interrogator is that the Detainee has not revealed all of his information, the higher the value of $\hat{f}$; that is, the more it moves to the right and the less likely it is that there is an f exceeding it. In other words, the less lenient she is, the higher her expectations for what counts as "cooperation," the smaller the equilibrium region, and the greater the space supporting torture.

Imagine grabbing $\hat{f}$ and sliding it to the left (i.e., lowering it). As you did, the gray-shaded region would grow and the region to the left would shrink, resulting in:

1. an expansion of the information region
2. more information hiding
3. less torture of a Cooperative Detainee

Now slide it back to the right. As you do, the gray-shaded region shrinks and the region to the left grows, resulting in:

1. a reduction of the information region
2. less information hiding
3. more torture of a Cooperative Detainee

There is thus another set of trade-offs, this time between the frequency with which information is obtained, the frequency of information hiding, and the frequency of torture:

Implication 10.3 (**Information–Torture Trade-off**). *Everything else being equal, eliciting information is more likely (the equilibrium region expands to a greater proportion of the parameter space), and torture of a cooperative detainee less frequent, only if the standard of detainee cooperation is lowered, thereby increasing information hiding.*

From Proposition 7.3 in Chapter 7 we know that $\hat{f}$ is greater than or equal to one-half; the Interrogator will have a high threshold. The point at which she says to herself "ok, that's all he's got, I can stop now" will be a high hurdle. This pushes the equilibrium region to the right, shrinking it along the f axis.

Innocent Detainee Recognition Threshold p^*

Finally, consider p^*, the Interrogator's Innocent Detainee recognition threshold. If the updated probability the Detainee is Innocent upon observing "no information" is above p^*, the Interrogator chooses "not torture." For probabilities below p^*, the Interrogator chooses "torture." The *valuable information, selective torture equilibrium* requires the latter. Thus, the higher this threshold (the more the Interrogator thinks that a Detainee who fails to provide information is Resistant, not Innocent), the greater the volume occupied by both "information" and torture of an Innocent Detainee in this equilibrium. As p^* goes down, as the space supporting the belief that a "no information" Detainee is Resistant shrinks (i.e., the space supporting the Detainee is Innocent grows), both the "information" and "torture innocents" regions shrink toward the face of the parameter space. In other words, it is not possible to have one without the other:

> *Implication* 10.4 (**Information–Torture of Innocents Trade-off**). *Everything else being equal, an increase in information is inevitably accompanied by an increase in innocent torture; a decrease in innocent torture is accompanied by a decrease in information.*

From Proposition 7.2, p^* is less than one-half, restricting the equilibrium region to something under the front half of the parameter space. The lower the prior probability p_R, the closer the value of p^* to 0, leaving less room for "information" and "no torture" of a Cooperative Detainee. The more the Interrogator believes everyone breaks—as is likely—the lower the value of p^*.[1]

In other words, the assumption that real-life interrogators will believe that almost no innocent detainees end up manacled to a chair in a secret prison (i.e., p_I is vanishingly low) and that "everybody breaks, bro" (i.e., p_R is very low and p_C is high) decreases the volume of the equilibrium region. We have, in other words, a strange and even paradoxical implication:

> *Implication* 10.5 (**Torture–Information Paradox**). *Everything else being equal, the very assumptions driving an interrogational torture program—the most likely detainee has information and will reveal it under (the threat of [more])*

torture, very few detainees cannot be "broken," and the chances of a detainee being innocent are virtually zero—all make valuable information less, not more, likely.

*   *   *

With these general considerations in mind, we now turn to the case studies. We noted above that this equilibrium covers two cases in the real world, one in which the detainee hides some information, but it is enough to satisfy the interrogator, and one in which the detainee truly does reveal all of his information and satisfies the Interrogator. We consider examples of each.

INFORMATION HIDING: PACHA WAZIR

For a case in the real world to match the information hiding outcome pertaining to a Cooperative Detainee, it must meet the following conditions:

1. The detainee was cooperative (i.e., had information).
2. The detainee was subjected to objective or leading questioning.
3. The detainee gave up some but not all of his valuable information.
4. The cooperative detainee was not tortured afterward.

The ideal case illustrating this equilibrium is one in which there is a Detainee known to possess some valuable information. He is not tortured, but knows that torture is likely if he does not give up his information. He is questioned, without torture, and provides information. The Interrogator believes that the Detainee has provided all the information he has and so does not torture him. We know in hindsight that, in fact, he was hiding still more information which he never divulged.

These criteria, particularly the last one, make it difficult to find a case in the public domain which fits this bill perfectly. But we can come close with the story of an Afghan banker named Pacha Wazir.[2]

Wazir, known also by the honorific Haji Wazir since he had made the pilgrimage (*haj*) to Mecca, came from one of the most prominent families in Jalalabad, Afghanistan. Wealthy, portly, and sporting a "fastidiously trimmed beard," he maintained a "palatial" home in Dubai and was married with seven children (Suskind 2006, p. 160). Wazir ran a successful currency exchange business, several banks, and wire transfer stations, as well as a chain of informal money transfer stations called *hawalas* with his brother. His operations covered South Asia and Europe and he maintained additional offices in Dubai and in Pakistan.

One of his clients was Al Qaeda.

At least that was what both Canadian and U.S. intelligence suspected. The Canadian Security Intelligence Service (CSIS) linked a terrorist suspect they were monitoring, Mohamed Harkat, to Wazir (Canadian Security Intelligence Service 2009; Federal Court of Canada 2010). As for the United States, Wazir was considered a potential source of terrorist financing by several government agencies and departments. The FBI had asked banking authorities in Dubai, whom they were helping to set up tighter auditing and other financial monitoring and controls, to look into Wazir. The information that came back in the summer of 2002 was alarming: The FBI believed that Wazir "was responsible for handling a startling $67 million in assets for al Qaeda in just over two years" (Suskind 2006, p. 145). Nevertheless, the FBI did not feel it had enough evidence of laundering through U.S. banks and institutions in order to prosecute him in the United States.

The CIA, however, had a back-up plan for Wazir: "to own him" (Suskind 2006, p. 146). The FBI was told to back off while the CIA prepared its plans. Those plans were moved up abruptly by the diligence of United Arab Emirates (UAE) central bankers, who froze Wazir's assets. Wazir inquired why; and when he was told the FBI was investigating him, he traveled to Dubai on his own accord to meet with them and clear up what he claimed was a misunderstanding. The FBI delayed him a day, enough time to get in a CIA snatch team.

The CIA team grabbed him in his own driveway as he was about to leave for his meeting with the FBI. They kept him in the U.A.E. for the initial interrogation, but he wasn't talking. To up the pressure on him and see if they could get information out of his brother, the CIA kidnapped Wazir's brother in Germany and spirited him out of the country. Neither, however, provided any information. It wasn't long before Pacha Wazir was on his way to a CIA black site outside Rabat, Morocco.[3]

Wazir, of course, didn't know he was in Morocco. He must have known he was somewhere in North Africa, given the Arabic accents and the occasional French he heard spoken around him. But he discovered quickly that the main interrogator was an American. The American was unhappy with Wazir's answers and shouted at him in between coughing fits.

Soon, though, the American was replaced with another European-looking interrogator who spoke Arabic and French. "Jacques," as the man introduced himself, was actually Glenn Carle, a career CIA case officer who had been sent to work with the Moroccans and interrogate Wazir.

At his first interrogation of Wazir, Carle found him "terrified," though he had not been tortured (Carle 2011, pp. 69, 70). As we have seen, in mid-2002, the full-blown EIT program, with its conditioning, standard, and enhanced techniques, had not yet been established. Thus, though Wazir was no doubt hooded and shackled during his rendition flight, he had apparently not been subjected to the full panoply of conditioning that would become standard in short order: sleep deprivation, nakedness, stress positions, etc.

Still, Wazir would have been told that no one knew where he was and he would have known the reputation for torture that most of the intelligence services had throughout North Africa and the Middle East. Thus, although he had not been tortured, he certainly feared it could happen. Though Carle himself opposed torture, and never used it during his interrogation of Wazir, he did not disabuse Wazir of this possibility. In other words, Wazir knew that torture was a possible "move" by his interrogators, even if it might not be Carle doing it himself.

Carle recalls that when he first started working on the Wazir case, he found that "the assessment that was made of [Wazir] was quite compelling and . . . accepted it . . . I knew my colleagues to be hard-working and careful and that they reviewed their assessments regularly and the assessment was that [Wazir] was one of the top players in Al-Qaeda" (Leopold 2011). "He had been involved in activities of legitimate concern to the CIA, because they did touch upon al-Qa'ida activities. That's a fact" (Ackerman 2011). Consequently, in Carle's view, "[a]t the moment he was rendered it seemed the right decision to interrogate him and bore down into his activities. Huge effort had gone into his case, and the information appeared strong. It looked as though we had a chance to strike a truly damaging blow to Al Qaeda" (Horton 2011a).

To this day, Carle believes that Wazir "was not a random individual who knew nothing . . . he knew information relevant for our counter-terrorism operations— he was not a complete innocent" (Horton 2011a). Certainly the CIA and other government officials (FBI, Treasury) believed that Wazir possessed valuable information. In short, it appears fairly clear that Wazir was no Innocent Detainee; the question was whether he would cooperate or not.

Carle attempted to induce cooperation using the same techniques he had used as a case officer to get people to betray their countries: a combination of rapport, assessing Wazir's motivations, and manipulating, stressing, and disorienting him (verbally) (Carle 2011, p. 67). The goal was to help Wazir reason his own way to wanting to cooperate. Although he was initially a little ambivalent about whether some of the disorienting methods were torture (e.g., disrupting sleep patterns), Carle ruled out physical torture from the beginning and the "milder" disorienting methods early on (Carle 2011, pp. 26, 67, 138–139). As Carle later put it in an interview, "from my first second of involvement in the [Wazir] operation I simply would not allow or have anything to do with any physical coercive measure. I would not do it" (Ackerman 2011).

This did not prevent Carle from "keep[ing] him fearful that [Carle] controlled his fate" (Ackerman 2011). Indeed, in places he went further. He once warned Wazir that "others were not as nice, or as patient, as [Carle] was" (Carle 2011, p. 74).

The result was, according to Carle, successful. "The information he provided was useful. ... [Wazir] knew things we did not, and needed to know" (Carle 2011, p. 85). Indeed, Carle estimated that he provided "85–90 percent of what he knew" (Carle 2011, p. 109). "He answered truthfully—most of the time. He continued to pretend ignorance on some topics where my colleagues and I believed he had information" (Carle 2011, p. 109). "He withheld information about certain aspects of al-Qa'ida operations" (Carle 2011, p. 115). Still, "in the end, ... I decided he was, fundamentally, straight with me. Never totally, but fundamentally, yes." Wazir "was truthful, innocent, disingenuous, and complicit simultaneously" (Ackerman 2011).

Carle attributes extracting the information to his rapport-based technique, "rather than seeking to cow or humiliate him" (Horton 2011a). While it is clear that Carle did not take the humiliation/psychological "regression" tack that would come to characterize the EIT program, it is impossible to know whether his success was due to rapport alone and/or the possibility things could get worse. Given Wazir's initial reluctance to talk, it seems reasonable to think that the possibility of torture had some influence.

Carle also came to believe that Wazir was not the high-level Al Qaeda operative the CIA had believed, let alone bin Laden's banker (Canadian Security Intelligence Service 2009, pp. 23–24). The CIA had "erroneously inflated [Wazir]'s importance and role." He "was more like a train conductor who sells a criminal a ticket" not "part of the al-Qa'ida network" and so "not quite what we believed" (Carle 2011, pp. 133, 135).

He simply did not "have the critical information, or close ties with Al Qaeda, that the Agency believed he had and that had justified his rendition. ... he was less directly involved with Al Qaeda than we had assessed him to be; and he was no terrorist. ... [H]e was fundamentally a businessman; I do not believe he was actively colluding with Al Qaeda. I came to believe him when he said that he vehemently opposed Al Qaeda's theology and acts. ... It was the wrong decision to continue to hold him for eight years after we had established that many of our assumptions were simply wrong" (Horton 2011a).

The men and women nearly 4,000 miles away on the plushly carpeted, wood-paneled seventh floor of CIA headquarters could not have disagreed more. They were convinced that Wazir was hiding valuable information: They wanted the remaining "10 to 15 percent" (Carle 2011, p. 109). The exact same information which Carle interpreted as demonstrating Wazir's lack of knowledge "convinced Headquarters that he was dissembling" (Carle 2011, p. 145). They pressured Carle at every step of the interrogation; "the order was to do whatever it took to get him to talk ... and to do so now" (Carle 2011, p. 64). Finally, they became fed up and decided to render him again, this time to the notorious "Salt Pit," the CIA black site prison in an old brick factory on the outskirts of Kabul.

This time he got the full treatment by the ninja-clad CIA snatch team: forcible sodomy, shackles, and hood. There he would end up being tortured by other CIA officers under orders from Langley. Whether or not he gave up further information is unknown. He was released in February 2010, eight years after his capture. No charges against him were ever filed.

NO INFORMATION HIDING: MAGNUS GÄFGEN

For a case in the real world to match the no information hiding outcome, it must meet the following conditions:

1. The detainee was cooperative (i.e., had information and was willing to give it up to avoid torture).
2. The detainee was subjected to objective or leading questioning.
3. The detainee gave up all of his valuable information (as far as we can tell).
4. The cooperative detainee was not tortured afterward.

*   *   *

While there may very well be cases from the CIA or other terrorist interrogations, none to my knowledge has been made public. There is, however, a case from Germany which matches the no information hiding version of the valuable information equilibrium perfectly: that of Magnus Gäfgen, a German law student and devout Catholic.[4]

On Monday, September 29, 2002, at 4:25 in the afternoon, Gäfgen and his girlfriend had just parked their car in a basement parking garage at the Rhein-Main airport in Frankfurt when they were yanked from their seats by police commandos in plainclothes. The commandos threw them to the ground and cuffed them, yelling, "Where is the boy?!"

The boy was Jakob von Metzler, the toothy, smiling 11-year-old son of one of the oldest banking families in Europe. On the morning of September 27, 2002, he had said good-bye to his buddies and got on bus number 35 near his school in Frankfurt am Main. It was the last day of school before the fall break and he was looking forward to going on vacation with his family. Normally he got off at a bus stop just 100 meters from the family villa next to Park Louisa in the Frankfurt City Forest, to walk the rest of the way home. He never made it.

A ransom note did, however. It was discovered on the villa property at 12:40 pm the same day by a domestic servant. The Metzlers complied with the demands for a million euros in used, unmarked, small denominations stuffed in Aldi shopping bags. Precisely as the note demanded, they put the bags next to the signpost at the northbound tram stop "Oberschweinstiege" of line 14 at 12:49 am on Monday, September 29. They had also, however, contacted the police, and the drop-off location was under surveillance when the money was picked up at 1:00 am.

The police followed the young man who picked up the money. Hoping he would lead them to the boy, they continued to shadow him on Monday, as he drove around Frankfurt with his girlfriend, depositing the ransom money into his account at various bank branches, buying a vacation for two to the Canary Islands, and taking a test drive in a C-class Mercedes and then ordering it, using some of the ransom money for the down payment. When, however, he drove that afternoon to the airport at Frankfurt, they arrested him.

The police had already identified him as Magnus Gäfgen. Gäfgen was studying criminal law at Wolfgang Goethe-Universität in Frankfurt. Born and raised in Frankfurt, he had been active in Catholic youth groups since he was 16 and had completed his civil service duty working in a nursing home.[5] They knew, too, that he knew Jakob through his girlfriend's circle of friends.

Following a brief stop at a hospital to clean up some abrasions on his face, Gäfgen was taken to police headquarters. Detective M., a veteran investigator of kidnappings, brought Gäfgen to his office and immediately started questioning him about the whereabouts of the boy.[6] Confronted with the fact that the police had seen him pick up the money and deposit it into his account, Gäfgen first said that someone had offered him 20,000 euros to pick up the bags. He professed, though, to know nothing about the boy or his fate. Detective M. tried to build trust with Gäfgen by sitting next to him and using his first name. Upon being told that the media knew of the kidnapping, Gäfgen said "hopefully the child is still alive" (Landgericht Frankfurt am Main 2003, p. 17). Detective M. showed Gäfgen pictures of the boy and talked about the parents' fear, but nothing worked. Gäfgen provided no information on Jakob's location.

Detective M. then wrote down on a slip of paper three questions and put it in front of Gäfgen:

Is the boy alone somewhere?
Is the boy being guarded/under supervision?
Is the boy no longer alive?

He told Gäfgen he was going to turn around and asked Gäfgen to put an "X" next to the question corresponding to the boy's condition. Gäfgen put an "X" next to "guarded."

Based on this and the fact that the police had mistakenly thought that half of the ransom money was missing from Gäfgen's apartment, the police believed that Gäfgen had accomplices. He was asked more questions, but refused to answer them. Between 11:30 and midnight he spoke to an "on call" defense lawyer and afterward said he was prepared to say where Jakob was. He told the police that Jakob was in one of the many little cottages on the Langener Waldsee, a recreational lake about 10 miles south of Frankfurt, describing the cottage and the surroundings in some detail.

The detectives pressed him about his accomplices. Gäfgen then falsely accused a pair of brothers he had known when he was younger and with whom he had fallen out. At 1:00 am, Gäfgen asked to stop and go to bed. The detectives agreed and Gäfgen promised to speak further to Detective M. in the morning.

Meanwhile, overnight, a thousand police and dogs were dispatched to the Langener Waldsee to search for Jakob. SWAT teams raided the houses of the brothers in the early morning darkness, immediately asking where the boy was before taking them to the police station for more intensive questioning. They denied any involvement in the kidnapping.

Deputy police chief Wolfgang Daschner arrived at police headquarters at 6:30 am on Tuesday, October 1. He had slept little the night before, worrying about Jakob and how to rescue him. Having heard an update about where things stood from one of his section leaders at 6:35, Daschner called Detective Ennigkeit and Detective Mü. into an adjoining room and informed them he "intended to order the application of direct coercion" (Landgericht Frankfurt am Main 2005, pp. 9–10).

Daschner calmly set out his reasoning. He did not expect much from the brothers fingered by Gäfgen because it appeared by then that Gäfgen had lied. The child's life was in danger, with no food or water for three days. "Gäfgen must therefore be induced to divulge the boy's whereabouts" (Landgericht Frankfurt am Main 2005, p. 10). If it were available, a truth serum could be administered by syringe. Having explained his reasoning, Daschner ordered that Gäfgen be threatened with torture, given a chance to talk, and then, under medical supervision, be subjected to renewed questioning under the infliction of pain not causing bodily injury. Detectives Mü. and Ennigkeit were told to make the necessary preparations.

Detective Mü. was "perplexed," believing that the use of force was unlawful even in these "extra-legal circumstances" (Landgericht Frankfurt am Main 2005, p. 10). He also thought that there were alternatives which would work, such as confronting Gäfgen with Jakob's family members.

Despite these misgivings, Detective Mü. began preparations and at 6:50 called the chief of the SWAT team. Detective Mü. asked whether he had anyone in his unit prepared to "torture" Gäfgen. The SWAT leader was so taken aback by this word and the request that he said nothing and hung up the phone. He immediately discussed the request with his unit leaders, and all agreed such an act and order would be illegal.

Five minutes after calling the SWAT team, Detective Mü. ordered a subordinate to summon the police doctor in the building. At 7:00 am, Detective Mü. called a meeting of the section leaders of the kidnapping command center, including Detective Ennigkeit. Detective Mü. relayed Daschner's order and began a discussion. Daschner's order provoked much concern and dismay, with many detectives arguing that there was no legal basis for such an order and that any confession thus obtained would not hold up in court. The SWAT team leader said he could not give such an order to anyone in his unit; if he did, it "would put the good reputation of his unit in doubt" (Landgericht Frankfurt am Main 2005, p. 11). Another said that the use of force wouldn't work. Moreover, there were better alternatives and they should stick to the current plan to confront Gäfgen with family members. One detective, "R," did say that his conscience made him support Daschner's plan—even if it was illegal—as a last resort, if all other avenues had been exhausted. They concluded their discussion with an agreement to stick to their plan, including further questioning of the brothers and the search at the Langener Waldsee. Hurting Gäfgen was to be done, if at all, only when they had taken all other possible steps.

Twenty minutes later, at 8:00 am, Daschner called several of the group into his office, demanding angrily and loudly to know why his order had not been carried out. They relayed their unified misgivings about Daschner's order and explained their plan and hopes of success. Daschner asked the SWAT team leader why he couldn't find anyone to carry out the torture. Minimizing the significance, Daschner provided an example of what he was talking about: "twisting over the thumb and wrists" or "pressure" "in particular spots" such as the ear, which would cause "pain, a lot of pain" that would induce Gäfgen to talk "in a very short time" (Landgericht Frankfurt am Main 2005, p. 13; Dahlkamp 2004).

The SWAT leader said that such an order could not be given and that no one in his unit was prepared to carry it out. Upon Daschner's continued pressing, the SWAT leader said that there was one person who might do it, but he was on vacation. Daschner then demanded that he be flown by helicopter back to Frankfurt, and Daschner would speak to him personally.[7]

Simultaneously, the detectives had confronted Gäfgen with his mother. Gäfgen told her that he had been blackmailed and said nothing about the whereabouts of the child.

At 8:30 am Daschner called Ennigkeit into his office. Daschner instructed Ennigkeit to question Gäfgen again, to appeal to his conscience and the acute mortal danger Jakob was in. If Gäfgen still refused to provide any information, then Gäfgen should be told that he could expect direct force to be used against him. He should be threatened that he will be questioned again while being inflicted with pain under a doctor's supervision. He would also be informed that the torture would cause no permanent damage. It was clear to both Daschner and Ennigkeit that the threat must be "intensive and intimidating" given both the urgency of the situation and Gäfgen's "stubborn resistance" (Landgericht Frankfurt am Main 2005, p. 14). Daschner also let Ennigkeit know that the man willing and able to carry out the torture if necessary was being flown by helicopter from his vacation. The entire conversation lasted only a few minutes.

About ten minutes later, the police doctor arrived at the command center, was informed by Detective Mü. of the situation and Daschner's plan, and asked whether he was prepared to participate medically. The doctor said yes. When Detective Mü. notified Daschner by telephone about the doctor's readiness, Daschner responded that he had already ordered Ennigkeit to threaten Gäfgen.

Indeed, by that point, Ennigkeit was already sitting alone with Gäfgen in the interrogation room. He sat down across from the law student, face to face, a foot away, and told him that the police were going on the assumption that Jakob's life was in danger and that it would be to Gäfgen's "advantage" to reveal the location of the child. If he continued to remain silent or provide false information, the police were prepared to inflict pain on him, with a doctor present and with no lasting bodily harm, in order to get him to reveal details that could save the child's life (Landgericht Frankfurt am Main 2005, p. 16). They were also considering administering a truth serum.

Ennigkeit spoke "intensively and forcefully" (Landgericht Frankfurt am Main 2005, p. 16). The detective added that a special officer was on his way by helicopter "who could inflict pain on him that he would never forget" (Landgericht Frankfurt am Main 2005, p. 16). As he said this last part, he made a circling motion with his hand, imitating the rotors spinning. Ennigkeit concluded by saying that he hoped that this and Gäfgen's conscience would cause him to change his mind and "provide truthful information" (Landgericht Frankfurt am Main 2005, p. 16).[8]

> The threat made an impression on [Gäfgen]. He had not been moved by the appeal to his conscience and the possibility for leniency.... The threat scared him ... Ennigkeit's ... forceful and intensive threat ... caused him to fear even harsher measures. He did not want to expose himself to those (Landgericht Frankfurt am Main 2005, p. 17).

It took fewer than ten minutes for Gäfgen to say where they could find the boy.

Gäfgen himself was driven to the location, a small pond near the town of Birstein, to point out exactly where Jakob was. The police found Jakob precisely where Gäfgen said he would be: in shallow water under a dock, wrapped in a plastic bag and duvet cover.

No one ever ended up laying a hand on Magnus Gäfgen; the threat had worked. He had revealed all his information under objective questioning and the threat of torture, but it was too late for Jakob von Metzler. Gäfgen later confessed (without torture) that after "intensively thinking things through" in the planning stages of the kidnapping, he had decided that Jakob "must die" if his plan was to succeed (Landgericht Frankfurt am Main 2003, pp. 10, 11). The boy already lay murdered in Gäfgen's trunk while the ransom note was being thrown onto the Metzler property.

BACK TO THE MODEL

In both the Wazir and Gäfgen cases, p^* was low. In the Wazir case, this was true for both Carle and his CIA bosses back in Langley; neither thought that Wazir was an innocent somehow accidentally caught up in the program. Canadian intelligence and the United States' own investigation linked him to Al Qaeda financing. In the Gäfgen case, the fact that Gäfgen picked up the money made it clear to the police right away that he was somehow involved; and after they quickly ruled out other suspects, it became just as clear that he had acted alone and knew Jakob's location.

The other thresholds differed across the two cases and even within the Wazir case. Wazir's threshold $\hat{q}$ was apparently high, at least during the time spent with Carle at the CIA's Moroccan black site. While he revealed a lot of information—as much as 90% of what Carle believed he possessed—he did not reveal it all. For Carle this was enough; it satisfied his threshold $\hat{f}$.

It was not enough for CIA officials back in Langley; their version of $\hat{f}$ was higher than Carle's. They expected more out of Wazir. One reason may have been related to the clarity parameter u. Wazir's exact role in Al Qaeda financing was just never that clear. A Canadian federal court looked into the Wazir case during a related proceeding and found not only that "the public evidence concerning Hadje Wazir being linked to bin Laden is also inconclusive" but also that it couldn't be sure that a Wazir associated with Al Qaeda financing was even the same person as Pacha Wazir (Federal Court of Canada 2010, pp. 345, §259). In the court's words:

> As to whether Hadje and Pacha Wazir are one and the same or not, the Court notes that these names are common in Pakistan. The evidence is therefore also inconclusive in that regard (Federal Court of Canada 2010, p. 345, §260).

This lack of clarity may have also figured into CIA estimates of what they thought Wazir might be hiding. They not only wanted the last 10–15%, but also were convinced that the last hidden information was very valuable, an assessment not shared by Carle. In other words, Langley thought that the v Wazir was not revealing must be very high. The only way to bring down Wazir's $\hat{q}$ to the point of talking was to torture more. And so they shipped him off to the Salt Pit. Whether or not he provided more valuable and accurate intelligence, we just do not know.

In Gäfgen's case, $\hat{f}$ was also very high, if only because the police wanted only one very specific piece of information from their suspect: Jakob's location. Gäfgen's threshold $\hat{q}$, however, was apparently very low. All it took from Detective Ennigkeit was talking about a "specialist" in administering pain and a whirring of his fingers to cause Gäfgen to tell the truth.

*   *   *

The argument thus far has shown that:

1. EITs are torture and the effectiveness of interrogational torture is an open question. (Chapter 2)
2. The Bush program approximates closely the ideal model of interrogational torture and includes limits on torture; the Bush and ideal models provide benchmarks for comparison with the game theory models to come. (Chapter 3)
3. The Bush model generates strange, quixotic outcomes. (Chapter 4)
4. The Bush interrogational torture program is more realistically modeled as objective and leading question variants of an incomplete information game, with three types of detainees, two types of interrogators, and uncertainty about the amount and value of information provided. (Chapter 5)
5. By positing a set of Detainee strategies, calculating the Interrogator's expected utility using Bayes' Rule to identify her best response, and checking for incentives to deviate by any of the Detainee types, it is possible to derive a perfect Bayesian equilibrium in which a Detainee is tortured after providing information. (Chapter 6)
6. The RIT model generates nine perfect Bayesian equilibria, the formal and empirical characteristics of which generate important observations, propositions, and implications, including:
   (a) The Interrogator's thresholds for believing that a Detainee is Innocent after "no information" are less than one-half, with $\hat{p}$ close to one-half and p^* closer to zero.
   (b) The Interrogator's information hiding threshold under objective questioning $\hat{f}$ is greater than or equal to one-half, whereas her information hiding threshold under leading questioning $\tilde{f}$ as well as the Detainee's version f^* of $\hat{f}$ are a little less than one-half.

(c) Objective questioning (potentially) provides better information, but is necessarily accompanied by more torture, than leading questioning, which, however, provides less valuable information.

(d) All things being equal, interrogators are more likely to get less valuable information than highly valuable information.

(Chapter 7)

7. Surprise torture of a Cooperative Detainee—even if he has provided all his information—is not only likely, but perversely more likely

(a) the more willing the Detainee is to divulge information and

(b) the more important the information is in terms of "unknown unknowns."

(Chapter 8)

8. The perversity under objective questioning persists under leading questioning, namely

(a) the more the Innocent Detainee believes Interrogator promises of no torture in exchange for confirmation, the more likely is ambiguous and false information.

(b) the more brutal the torture, the more likely is ambiguous and false information.

(c) the more important the confirmation is to the interrogator and the more difficult it is for the detainee to understand what is being asked, the greater the likelihood of torture.

(d) leading questioning will not eliminate torture; the higher the interrogator's demand for confirmation, the more torture.

(Chapter 9)

9. The *valuable information, selective torture* equilibrium reveals four further trade-offs and a paradox:

(a) Everything else being equal, eliciting information

    i. requires either more frequent or more brutal torture,

    ii. is more likely when the information is less valuable or the torture is more severe, but not both,

    iii. is more likely when the standard of cooperation is lowered, even though it increases the likelihood of information hiding,

    iv. is necessarily accompanied by innocent torture; decreasing the likelihood of innocent torture requires decreasing the likelihood of information.

(b) the very assumptions justifying interrogational torture paradoxically make it less reliable in terms of the likelihood of getting valuable information.

(Chapter 10)

The next step in the argument is to examine and interpret the *no information, torture* and *no information, no torture* equilibria.

Torturing Innocents, Resisting Torture

Each blow stupefied me a little more, but at the same time confirmed me in my decision not to give way to these brutes . . . I remained silent. "He's playing games with us! Put his head under again!"

—HENRI ALLEG AND HIS TORTURER, *La Question*, 1957

In the two (sets of) equilibria discussed in this chapter, no Detainee type provides information to the Interrogator. In one set, the Interrogator tortures in response; in the other she does not. Each occurs under both types of questioning. In this chapter we examine both sets, organizing the discussion by the actions underlying them, rather than by questioning type.

NO INFORMATION, TORTURE

In the *no information, torture equilibrium*, Cooperative and Innocent Detainees do not reveal information, either because they believe they will be tortured anyway (see Appendix A for the full set of beliefs) or because the Innocent Detainee does not have the move to reveal information under objective questioning. Either way, the Interrogator believes that the Detainee is hiding information rather than Innocent $(p < \hat{p})$ and so tortures.

Equilibrium Features

The relevant thresholds in this equilibrium are thus the information revelation threshold(s) $\hat{q}$ and, in the case of leading questioning, q^* for the Innocent

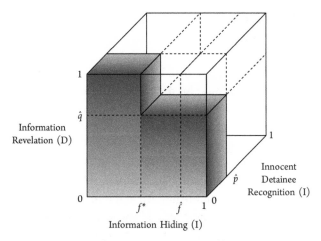

Figure 11.1 No Information, Torture Equilibrium

Detainee, the Innocent Detainee recognition threshold $\hat{p}$, and the information hiding threshold f^*. The way in which they bound the equilibrium is depicted in gray in Figure 11.1, with all the thresholds placed in their usual locations based on their theoretical or empirical properties discussed in Chapter 7. The white space behind the gray-shaded area (everything greater than or equal to $\hat{p}$) is the next (and final) equilibrium we discuss later in the chapter: the *no information, no torture equilibrium*.

The Detainee q thresholds provide the upper bound or "roof" of the equilibrium. The Cooperative Detainee believes the Interrogator will torture anyway and so refuses to give up what he knows, whether the questioning is objective or leading. In the latter case, the Innocent Detainee has the option of talking, but also believes he will be tortured anyway and so maintains his innocence. What about the area to the north of $\hat{q}$?

In this region, the Cooperative Detainee does believe that Interrogator is Pragmatic, but also believes that the Interrogator will torture anyway because she (the Interrogator) will think he has more information to provide or is willing to confirm $(f < f^*)$. Finally, the Interrogator's Innocent Detainee recognition threshold $\hat{p}$ encloses the "back end" of the equilibrium. The Interrogator has observed "no information," and her belief that this is due to an Innocent Detainee is below her threshold $\hat{p}$. She's too worried it's a Resistant Detainee trying to get away with hiding the information and so she tortures.

Although we have said (Observation 7.2) that f^* is likely to approach one-half from the zero side, the greater the degree of confidence the Detainee has that the Interrogator will believe he has revealed all his information (i.e., as f^* drops), the more the upper part of the region shrinks to the left. (This also assumes that the Detainee believes that the Interrogator is Pragmatic [i.e., $q \geq \hat{q}$].)

The less confident she is, the more it moves toward one-half, expanding the upper part of the region to its maximum.[1]

The situation is similar for the Innocent Detainee recognition threshold $\hat{p}$. It also is less than, but close to, one-half. Lowering it so that the region is reduced requires the Interrogator to lower his threshold, to be more willing to believe that the Detainee is Innocent after observing "no information." The less willing she is to believe this, as seems empirically likely, the more the threshold pushes toward one-half, expanding the region.

Now consider how the movement of Detainee information revelation thresholds $\hat{q}$ and q^* affect this equilibrium. The more valuable the information v to the Cooperative Detainee and the more important it is to the Innocent Detainee not to falsely confess l, the higher this threshold and so the larger the region. The region can shrink so that torture without information takes up less total space in two ways.

First, the information value v (or desire not to falsely confess l) might be lower. The less valuable the information, the more willing the Cooperative Detainee is to reveal it—that is, the lower the threshold, pushing the region down. The same is true for the Innocent Detainee's desire not to falsely implicate himself. Second, the Interrogator can drive down the threshold by increasing the severity of the torture, k. In other words, you can get less torture overall with more severe torture or you can get less severe torture but at the expense of expanding the region. This is the same conclusion we came to in Implication 10.1, since the "no information" region is just the complement of the "valuable information" region in that equilibrium.

Substantive Interpretation

This equilibrium corresponds to a very important outcome in the real world: A detainee fails to provide valuable information and is tortured. It remains forever unclear whether the torture was "justified" because the detainee actually possessed the valuable information or was unjustified even according to the pragmatic view because the detainee was innocent or cooperative but innocent (i.e., ignorant) of that particular piece of information. Even in the former case, it is forever unclear whether more (severe) torture would have compelled the hidden information because the detainee was cooperative or whether no amount of torture would have wrung the information out of him (because he was Resistant).

For a case in the real world to match the "no information, torture" outcome, it must meet the following conditions:

1. The detainee was any of the three types.
2. The detainee was subjected to objective or leading questioning.

3. The detainee gave up no or very little valuable information.

4. The detainee was tortured afterward.

We have already seen a real-world case with Pacha Wazir after he was taken out of Carle's hands and rendered to the Salt Pit in Afghanistan. In the view of CIA headquarters, he had not provided the information they sought and so was tortured at the Salt Pit. The other cases to explore are the Resistant and Innocent types, particularly since, as we have seen, both are tortured in other equilibria for playing "no information." We have cases clearly illustrating each type: Khaled El-Masri, an innocent unemployed German car salesman kidnapped by the CIA and tortured in black sites in Morocco and Afghanistan, and Henri Alleg, a French newspaper editor and journalist tortured by French paratroopers during the Battle of Algiers in 1957.

Torturing Innocents: Khaled El-Masri

On the last day of 2003, El-Masri left Ulm, Germany, on a long bus ride to Skopje, Macedonia, where he planned to take a short vacation.[2] At 3:00 that afternoon the bus crossed from Serbia into Macedonia. Border guards there considered El-Masri's new German passport suspicious and took him off the bus to look through his baggage and question him further about connections to Islamic groups and terrorism. He denied any connection. After seven hours, a group of armed men in plainclothes drove him in a convoy of three cars to the Skopski Merak Hotel in the Macedonian capital, across the street from the zoo.

A nine-member Macedonian security team held him in a room on the top floor for the next 23 days, with three of them present at all times. He was interrogated constantly. They repeatedly denied his requests to speak with someone from the German Embassy. He began a hunger strike on day 13 and didn't eat another bite for the next ten days. At one point, he angrily tried to walk out of the hotel room, but the Macedonian officers drew their pistols and motioned him away from the door.

On January 22, 2004, a thousand miles away on a Spanish resort island in the Mediterranean, a seven-member CIA rendition team and three contract pilots were also staying at a hotel, the five-star luxury Marriot Club Son Antem. The next morning, one of them enjoyed a massage at the spa and by the afternoon, the entire team, two of whom were women, had checked out of the hotel individually and assembled at the Palma de Majorca airport. At 5:40 they took off in the CIA-contracted Boeing 737 jet, tail number N313P, and landed in Skopje just over two hours later.

Around the time the CIA jet was landing, El-Masri was asked to make a video statement that he had not been harmed and was then blindfolded, handcuffed, put into a waiting jeep, and driven to the airport. He sat alone in a chair, still blindfolded and still handcuffed, ostensibly waiting for a medical exam before being returned to Germany.

Suddenly two people pulled his arms back hard and others began to beat him from all sides. They cut his clothes away from his body and threw him on the floor. With a boot on his naked back holding him to the floor, someone forced a suppository into his anus. This done, they jerked him back to his feet, bound his feet together, and removed his blindfold. There was an immediate flash of a camera. As his vision cleared, he saw seven or eight men around him, clad in black, including black ski masks. They put a diaper and then a tracksuit on him. They shackled his feet and hands and attached both to a belt around his waist. They put pads over his eyes, a blindfold over that, and earmuffs over his ears before hooding him. They marched him (he shuffled with the short shackles) to the waiting Boeing, and once inside he was thrown face down onto the floor. His cuffs and foot shackles were detached from his belt just long enough to pull and manacle him into a spread eagle position. He could detect no seats, and it felt like what he imagined a cargo plane was like. They gave him at least two injections and he was unconscious for most of the flight to Kabul via Baghdad.

On landing he was put in a room long enough that he began to think from the newspapers there that he was in Afghanistan. Then they put him in the trunk of a car and drove for ten minutes. He awoke to find he was in a small, filthy, concrete cell furnished with a threadbare military-issue blanket and rags of clothes bundled into a pillow. A dirty plastic bottle contained yellow, foul-smelling water for drinking. There was one small window, high on the wall. Previous occupants had scratched in Arabic and Farsi on the walls. El-Masri had arrived at the Salt Pit, the brick factory converted into a secret CIA prison near the Bagram military airfield.

Later that same night, masked men took him for a medical exam, including taking photos of him naked and a blood sample. The doctor was also masked and dismissed his complaints about the water. The masked men came for him later the same night and took him from his cell to an interrogation room. All his interrogators were also masked. After four interrogations over four days, they deemed his refusal to acknowledge any connection with, or having information on, 9/11 hijacker Mohammed Atta or other terrorists as uncooperative. He was left alone in his cell for three weeks, let out only three times a day to use the toilet. The food gave him diarrhea.

Finally, with some of the other prisoners, he decided to try a hunger strike in March. Although others eventually gave in, El-Masri refused all food for 37 days, drinking only the stagnant water. After he refused their requests to end the strike, on April 10, 2004, his captors ended it for him. Four masked men entered his cell and shackled him in handcuffs and manacles and then carried him to the interrogation room. After binding him to a chair, one of the men pulled his head back and a doctor pushed a tube up his nostril and down his throat, force feeding him from a funnel at the other end. They threatened to keep doing it if El-Masri didn't eat. Eventually, they agreed to give him better food and water and books to read and he agreed to end the strike.

On May 16, while still recovering from the hunger strike, "Sam," a tall, blond Westerner who spoke German with a northern accent, interrogated El-Masri and later promised that he would be going back to Germany. When nothing happened for several days, El-Masri started another hunger strike. Then, on May 28, 2004, he was blindfolded, handcuffed, and driven away from the prison. He heard a plane land while he was locked in a cargo container. The door opened and he was ordered to change into his old clothes. When he had done so, he was again blindfolded, the earmuffs were put on, and he was taken to the waiting plane. They chained him to his seat.

After landing some hours later, his manacles were exchanged for a rope binding his hands but the blindfold remained. He was put into a car with several men. Over the course of the next seven or eight hours, the car drove over rough and bumpy roads, up and down mountains, changing drivers and passengers several times. There was almost no talking. Then the car stopped and he was taken out.

When they removed his blindfold, he could see that it was dark and they had pulled off a deserted stretch of a dirt road. They returned his passport and suitcase to him and untied the rope around his wrists. They pointed to a path and told him to start walking and not to look back.

His spine tingled as he walked, and he wondered whether they were going to shoot him in the back.

But he did as they instructed and when he rounded a bend, three Albanian border guards were waiting for him with a packed lunch. They drove him to the airport in Tirana, Albania's capital. After paying for his own ticket back to Germany, they shepherded him through customs and immigration with no inspections and put him on a plane to Frankfurt. When he arrived in Frankfurt— unkempt, long hair, shaggy beard, and sixty pounds lighter—the German officer at passport control demanded to see other documents because he looked so different from the passport photo taken just eight months earlier.

The reason for his release? His name had been confused with a Khalid al-Masri with suspected connections to terrorists because of a transliteration error. Even so, many in the CIA said the agency should wait until the Germans checked out his passport before rendering him. The Al Qaeda unit head at the CIA— the hard-charging red-headed woman behind the "Maya" character in the film *Zero Dark Thirty*—overruled them, however. She had a "hunch" El-Masri was involved in terrorism (Grey 2006, p. 94).[3]

Resisting Torture: Henri Alleg

A little before four o'clock in the afternoon on June 12, 1957, Henri Alleg knocked on the door of a friend's third-floor apartment in Algiers.[4] It was opened not by his friend Maurice Audin, but by a detective. Alleg ran back down the stairs trying to escape. He had nearly made it to the street when the detective caught up with him. With the revolver at his back, he walked back up to Audin's apartment. The detective put in a quick call to the "paras"—paratroopers—and by four o'clock, they and the police had arrived. The lieutenant from the 10th Paratrooper Division considered Alleg an "excellent catch," for Alleg was the former editor-in-chief of the banned *Alger Républicain*, a left-wing daily supportive of Algerian independence.

In truth, Alleg was not surprised the moment had come. He had gone underground eight months before, not much more than a year after the *Alger Républicain* had been banned by the French authorities and after his co-workers were starting to be rounded up by the police and paras. But he had continued to write on behalf of Algerian independence in the communist daily *l'Humanité* from his various places in hiding.

The paras wanted to know who was doing that hiding and where. The lieutenant asked him exactly that before they had even cuffed him. Alleg's response was "That I won't tell you!" (Alleg, Calder, and Sartre 2006, p. 38).

He was led handcuffed down the stairs to a passenger car waiting across the street. The barrel of the guard's submachine gun poked into his ribs during the ride into the upper part of Algiers. They stopped at a construction site near the El-Biar Square. Alleg was taken out of the car and marched across the courtyard in front of a large apartment building under construction, then into the building itself and up the stairs.

There were no handrails on the steps. Rebar poked out from the bare ends of unfinished concrete walls. Electrical wires hung from the ceilings. Guards shoved disheveled prisoners up and down stairs and in and out of rooms. Several stories up, Alleg's guards took him into what might one day be someone's living room. They took off his handcuffs and a different lieutenant waiting there handed him a pencil and paper. He politely told Alleg to write down who protected him, what he had been doing, with whom he had met, and so on. Alleg responded,

"I have nothing else to say to you. I shall write nothing and don't count on me to betray those who have had the courage to hide me" (Alleg, Calder, and Sartre 2006, p. 40).

A young sunburned para in a blue beret then fetched him down one floor to the kitchen. There, next to the sink and oven, he was ordered to undress. At first he refused, but when they said they would do it by force if necessary, he complied. Naked, he was ordered to lie down on a vomit-covered wooden plank and his ankles and wrists were fastened to the plank by leather straps. The short and sunburned soldier stood over him, confidently telling him that "Everybody talks. You'll have to tell us everything—and not only a little bit of the truth, but everything!" (Alleg, Calder, and Sartre 2006, p. 41). He started to shiver and the blue berets thought he was afraid. No, he said, he was just cold.

A captain then joined the two lieutenants and the four enlisted men in the kitchen. Upon Alleg's refusal to say anything more, they lifted him into the adjoining room where the light was better. The soldiers then brought in boxes for the officers to sit on. The lieutenant who had arrested him showed Alleg the *gégène*, the field telephone. Alleg had written about others who had suffered from it and was all too aware of what would happen next. All he said, however, was a demand that the paras follow proper procedures in charging him and to address him appropriately—using the formal "*vous*" rather than the informal "*tu*" they had used up to that point.

A sergeant sat on his chest and showed Alleg the alligator clips leading from the *gégène*. Then he attached one clip to Alleg's earlobe and the other to his finger, both on his right side. The first shock felt like lightning exploding next to his head, and he jumped against his bonds and screamed. The lieutenant timed the cadence of his question—"Where have you been hiding?"—with the shocks of the telephone.

Alleg's answer, however, did not bear on the question, instead telling the lieutenant that he would regret torturing.

This did not make the lieutenant happy at all, and he turned the dial to its maximum. Despite this, Alleg still did not talk, and it wasn't because they had stuffed his shirt into his mouth to muffle his screams. The sergeant moved one of the clips to Alleg's penis to see if that might compel him to reveal his hiding place. Its only effect, however, was to cause such convulsions that they had to retie his straps.

So they tried other tricks. They stripped the wire and taped it across the width of his chest. They doused him with cold water for direct discomfort as well as to increase the effects of the electricity. The spectators drank beer. Alleg didn't talk.

They untied him from the plank and began to beat him while some were sent to fetch his friend Audin from another building. They showed him a battered Audin, who told Alleg that "It's hard, Henri," before he was taken away (Alleg, Calder, and Sartre 2006, p. 41). Alleg's continued refusal to talk began to frustrate the paras. The other lieutenant continued to beat him, moving from fists and knees to a piece of lumber.

He was taken back to the room with the *gégène* and tied to the plank once again. This time, however, they used a larger machine and Alleg could feel the difference, as his entire body spasmed. Still he did not talk.

Now he was asked if he knew "how to swim" and was carried on the plank to the kitchen. The end with his head rested over the sink and a couple of paras held up the end with his feet. The paras jammed a wooden wedge between his teeth and wrapped a rag around his mouth and nose. The para told him that when he was ready to talk, he should move his fingers.

Water flowed from the tap through a rubber hose onto the rag, soaking it.

At first he was able to snatch a breath or two and keep some of the water out of his throat. But it didn't last long.

> I had the impression of drowning, and a terrible agony, that of death itself, took possession of me. . . . In spite of myself, the fingers of my two hands shook uncontrollably (Alleg, Calder, and Sartre 2006, p. 49).

The paras misinterpreted this involuntary movement as willingness to talk and removed the rag in triumph. Alleg gulped in air as the captain pounded his stomach to expel the water Alleg had swallowed. When they realized he was staying silent, they put him back under.

Three times he experienced "the terrible moment where [he] felt [himself] losing consciousness, while at the same time fighting with all [his] powers not to die." The first two times they brought him back from the brink, and he managed to both gasp for air and throw up water at the same time. The third time he blacked out.

He never again moved his hands.

When he regained consciousness, he found himself on the floor of the adjoining room, naked but removed from the plank. The paras pulled him up off the floor and began to beat him like a punching bag, tossing him back and forth between them. Then they tied his feet and suspended him by his feet from a shelf in the kitchen. One of the paras then lit a piece of paper like a torch and burned Alleg's penis with it. They moved to other parts of Alleg's body, his legs, his nipples. They beat him. They stepped on his fingers trailing on the hard floor.

After a while of this, he was half-dragged, half-carried to a cell. He crawled onto the mattress, but was stabbed when he put his weight on it. A guard outside the door laughed that he had put barbed wire in it. But his colleague recognized what Alleg had accomplished. "All the same, he has gained a night for his friends to get away" (Alleg, Calder, and Sartre 2006, p. 52).

The next day they gave him several more sessions with the *gégène*. Frustrated with Alleg's continued refusal to talk, they stuck the wire into the back of his mouth. Once the shocks began, the paras didn't even need to hold the wire; the current caused Alleg's jaw to clench shut and his teeth held the wire in place, no matter how hard he tried to open his mouth. He felt like his eyeballs were being pushed out of their sockets from the inside. Smashing his head against the concrete brought some relief, but the shocks continued for a while longer.

He didn't talk.

Sometime later they began to burn him again, scorching his nipples and the bottom of his swollen feet. He said nothing. Furious, they beat him. He said nothing. They tempted him with water, knowing the electricity had made him desperately thirsty. He said nothing. They punched him in the face. He said nothing. More shocks. He said nothing.

Later a high-ranking officer came to see him and offered to take Alleg back to France if he told what he knew; if Alleg refused he would "disappear" (Alleg, Calder, and Sartre 2006, p. 65). Alleg's response?

"Too bad" (Alleg, Calder, and Sartre 2006, p. 65).

The officer told him his only option now was suicide and walked out.

Back in his cell, Alleg heard the screams of a woman being tortured nearby. For a while he thought he recognized his wife's voice and that the paras had followed through on their threat to torture her to get him to talk. He stayed silent in his cell.

At one point he splashed water on his face and a guard mockingly asked him whether he was feeling better. Alleg replied, "Yes, you'll soon be able to start on me again" (Alleg, Calder, and Sartre 2006, p. 71).

They didn't though, not really. They tried a "truth serum," but that didn't work either. Henri Alleg never talked. He was transferred to another prison and eventually escaped his torturers, spending time in Czechoslovakia before making his way back to France.

Back to the Model

That El-Masri was innocent and had nothing to do with Al Qaeda or terrorism is now beyond dispute, though the United States has never apologized or recognized his claims and, in fact, used its diplomatic muscle to deter the nominally independent German judiciary from pursuing criminal action against the United States.[5] During his captivity, El-Masri was apparently asked leading questions about his connections with the 9/11 hijacker Mohammed Atta and other terrorists. His resistance was remarkably powerful, suggesting his aversion against falsely implicating himself *l* was high, something also supported by his multiple hunger strikes. If he was asked objective questions, he could not have provided satisfactory answers to them and so was tortured.

Henri Alleg, in contrast, was no innocent swept up in the paratrooper's broad net. His refusal to provide the information sought by the paras was met with multiple tortures, some very similar to the CIA and others well beyond what we know the CIA practiced, including electrical shocks and burning. And yet he never talked.

It is worthwhile noting that because of the peculiarity of these cases, we happen to have the background information necessary to establish their type (Innocent and Resistant, respectively). To an Interrogator at the time, however, their behavior was observationally equivalent. Alleg = El-Masri.

NO INFORMATION, NO TORTURE

In this equilibrium, no Detainee provides information but the Interrogator does not torture because she believes the Detainee is Innocent and not Cooperative or Resistant (i.e. $p \geq \hat{p}$). The ideal outcome here is if the Detainee is in fact Innocent, for he is not tortured for telling the truth. If, however, he does have information, then he got away with hiding it. From the proponents' point of view, this is particularly problematic if the Detainee was Cooperative, because he likely would have given up at least some of his information had the Interrogator tortured.

Equilibrium Features

There is only one threshold to consider in this equilibrium and that is the Interrogator's innocent detainee recognition threshold $\hat{p}$. The reason for this is that the Detainee does not need to form beliefs about whether the Interrogator is Pragmatic nor what his information hiding threshold might be because the Interrogator does not torture after "no information." No type of detainee can do any better than this, and so none of them provides information. Since $\hat{p} \lessapprox \frac{1}{2}$, this equilibrium must take up more than half of the entire equilibrium space, as illustrated in Figure 11.2.

This means that most of the parameter space is taken up by detainees who were questioned and threatened with torture but gave no information, and were never tortured. This makes sense theoretically, given that we built in disincentives to torture in order to give the pragmatic account, to give proponents, the best possible case they can make. But does it make sense empirically? How does this correspond to the real world?

For a case in the real world to match the "no information, no torture" outcome, it must meet the following conditions:

1. The Detainee was any of the three types.
2. The Detainee was subjected to objective or leading questioning.
3. The Detainee gave up no valuable information.
4. The Detainee was not tortured afterward.

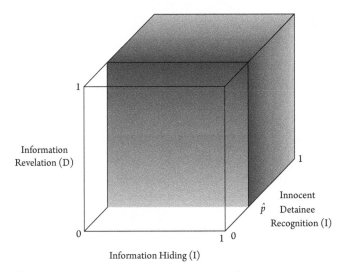

Figure 11.2 No Information, No Torture Equilibrium

What do we have that corresponds to this case?

Not much, unfortunately.

The problem is this. Once torture becomes an interrogation tool, it tends to be used. By the time a detainee ended up at a CIA black site, he had already been tortured and would continue to be tortured by the conditions of confinement and perhaps "standard" techniques—whether or not he was ever subjected to EITs. We just don't have good accounts of someone who was brought before an interrogator in a torture program, questioned, threatened with torture, and provided no or misleading information and who was not tortured afterward because he was deemed innocent. Some must surely exist, but they are apparently few and far between.

We might think we could include some cases of military interrogations in Iraq and Afghanistan. In some of those cases, of course, detainees were actually threatened with torture and were actually tortured. In many others, though, military interrogators followed the old norms and never threatened torture (Alexander 2011; Alexander and Bruning 2008). What if at least some of those detainees feared they would be tortured if they did not satisfy their captors, even though their interrogators never had any intention whatsoever to do so, even if they refused to provide information? No doubt many of these detainees were not tortured despite having provided no information. This isn't really close enough to qualify as cases for our model, though. We are modeling what happens when interrogators (their bosses!) decide to use torture to extract information. This element is missing from the non-torturous military interrogation cases and we are left wanting for examples. We return to this problem in Chapter 13.

*   *   *

The argument thus far has shown that:

1. EITs are torture and the effectiveness of interrogational torture is an open question. (Chapter 2)
2. The Bush program approximates closely the ideal model of interrogational torture and includes limits on torture; the Bush and ideal models provide benchmarks for comparison with the game theory models to come. (Chapter 3)
3. The Bush model generates strange, quixotic outcomes. (Chapter 4)
4. The Bush interrogational torture program is more realistically modeled as objective and leading question variants of an incomplete information game, with three types of detainees, two types of interrogators, and uncertainty about the amount and value of information provided. (Chapter 5)
5. By positing a set of Detainee strategies, calculating the Interrogator's expected utility using Bayes' Rule to identify her best response, and checking for incentives to deviate by any of the Detainee types, it is possible to derive a perfect Bayesian equilibrium in which a Detainee is tortured after providing information. (Chapter 6)
6. The RIT model generates nine perfect Bayesian equilibria, the formal and empirical characteristics of which generate important observations, propositions, and implications, including:
   (a) The Interrogator's thresholds for believing that a Detainee is Innocent after "no information" are less than one-half, with $\hat{p}$ close to one-half and p^* closer to zero.
   (b) The Interrogator's information hiding threshold under objective questioning $\hat{f}$ is greater than or equal to one-half, whereas her information hiding threshold under leading questioning $\tilde{f}$ as well as the Detainee's version f^* of $\hat{f}$ are a little less than one-half.
   (c) Objective questioning (potentially) provides better information, but is necessarily accompanied by more torture, than leading questioning, which, however, provides less valuable information.
   (d) All things begin equal, Interrogators are more likely to get less valuable information than highly valuable information.
   (Chapter 7)

7. Surprise torture of a Cooperative Detainee—even if he has provided all his information—is not only likely, but perversely more likely
   (a) the more willing the Detainee is to divulge information and
   (b) the more important the information is in terms of "unknown unknowns."
   (Chapter 8)
8. The perversity under objective questioning persists under leading questioning, namely:
   (a) The more the Innocent Detainee believes Interrogator promises of no torture in exchange for confirmation, the more likely is ambiguous and false information.
   (b) The more brutal the torture, the more likely is ambiguous and false information.
   (c) The more important the confirmation is to the Interrogator and the more difficult it is for the Detainee to understand what is being asked, the greater the likelihood of torture.
   (d) Leading questioning will not eliminate torture; the higher the Interrogator's demand for confirmation, the more torture.
   (Chapter 9)
9. The *valuable information, selective torture* equilibrium reveals four further trade-offs and a paradox:
   (a) Everything else being equal, eliciting information
      i. requires either more frequent or more brutal torture,
      ii. is more likely when the information is less valuable or the torture is more severe, but not both,
      iii. is more likely when the standard of cooperation is lowered, even though it increases the likelihood of information hiding,
      iv. is necessarily accompanied by innocent torture; decreasing the likelihood of innocent torture requires decreasing the likelihood of information.
   (b) The very assumptions justifying interrogational torture paradoxically make it less reliable in terms of the likelihood of getting valuable information.
   (Chapter 10)
10. From the two equilibria in which no Detainee provides information we learn that:
    (a) Everything else being equal, torture becomes less likely (the equilibrium region shrinks to a smaller proportion of the parameter space) after "no information" only if the information becomes less valuable or the torture becomes more severe, not both.

(b) It is difficult to find real-world cases in which detainees subjected
    to the threat of torture in interrogations were not tortured after
    failing to provide information.
(Chapter 11)

The next step in the argument is to summarize the results of our inquiry and
compare them to the benchmarks from Chapter 3.

Torture's Garden

Wherever you go there is more pain, more torture, more blood flowing
and draining through the soil . . . more terror and more hell.
—MIRBEAU, *Le Jardin des Supplices*, 1899

In Octave Mirbeau's disturbing *fin de siècle* novel, there is a garden with many
different tortures. We too have found torture's garden to be extraordinarily
verdant. It contains all varieties of information. False information. Ambiguous
information. Partially and fully valuable information. No information at all. Torture also blooms well there. Torture of detainees who hide information. Torture
of detainees who hide no information and have given all the information they
have. Torture of innocents. Torture of those from whom it cannot compel
information.

We are now ready to harvest this fruit and assess the claims made by torture
proponents in Chapter 3. That is, we can collect the observations, propositions,
and implications over the past six chapters and compare them to the four sets of
benchmarks set by torture proponents. Recall that each benchmark has two components, a *predictive* component that tells us what will emerge from the model as
well as a *normative* component that tells us the standard against which we compare what actually does emerge from the model. Thus, meeting the normative
benchmark depends on satisfying the predictive benchmark; a failure to achieve
the prediction means that the normative standard has not been met. A failure to
meet these normative standards, in turn, would mean that the pragmatic model
fails to satisfy even its own criteria for justifying interrogational torture. As a
result, for each set of benchmarks—information reliability, torture frequency,
torture severity, and the torture justification outcome—we examine first the predictive benchmark and then use those results to assess the normative benchmark.

Since we have run through all the equilibria, we start with the last benchmark, the pragmatic model's Torture Justification Outcome.

TORTURE JUSTIFICATION OUTCOME

Recall the predictive component of Benchmark 4 from Chapter 3 stating the ideal outcome sketched by proponents of the Bush program:

> Benchmark 4 **Torture Justification Outcome (TJO)**: *A minimum degree (severity) and amount (frequency) of torture is used against only the most resistant detainees with valuable information, who give up all, or nearly all, that valuable information. Neither cooperative detainees who have provided all their information nor innocent detainees are tortured.*

In order to compare this prediction against the results of RIT, we need to first translate it into game theoretic language and the terms of the RIT model. This gives us the following:

> Benchmark 4' **Torture Justification Equilibrium (TJE)**: *Supported by a reasonable set of beliefs, the following strategies will constitute an equilibrium under objective questioning in the RIT model: the Cooperative Detainee plays "information," the Innocent Detainee plays "no information" (i.e., tells the truth), and the Pragmatic Interrogator plays "no torture" after both actions ("information" and "no information").*

Setting aside for the moment what we mean by "reasonable" beliefs, we can begin our search for an equilibrium matching the TJE by eliminating any equilibria in which no valuable information is provided. This leaves the *valuable information–surprise torture* equilibrium under objective questioning and the two *valuable information–selective torture* equilibria, one under objective and one under leading questioning. In principle, since leading questioning provides no new information and no new intelligence, assessing the claims about information made by the pragmatic model should require us to stick to equilibria under objective questioning. For the sake of argument, however, we can set this aside for the moment and what we will say applies to both questioning types.

Recall that there are two interpretations of both the surprise torture and valuable information equilibria, one in which the Cooperative Detainee genuinely has revealed all he knows (full disclosure) and one in which he is still hiding information (partial disclosure). Each interpretation applies to both equilibria; in one he is tortured (*valuable information, surprise torture*), whereas in the other he is not (*valuable information, selective torture*). The full-disclosure interpretation of the surprise torture equilibrium we should eliminate for torturing a Cooperative Detainee after having provided all his information because it conflicts with the TJO and the TJE's prohibition on this torture. It makes no difference in what follows, however, whether we include or exclude it.

Strictly speaking, the second interpretation (partial disclosure) of the surprise torture equilibrium might also be ruled out by the TJE because the Cooperative Detainee is tortured, but only because we do not specify whether the information disclosed is full or partial in stating the TJE. It seems unfair to proponents to eliminate this equilibrium since a detainee with information has refused to provide it all and is tortured. This is a justifiable outcome on the pragmatic view.

We might also eliminate the partial disclosure interpretation of the valuable information equilibrium because it means that a detainee got away with hiding information. We can, though, grant this too to torture proponents, for it changes nothing in what follows.

Thus, both the partial disclosure interpretation of the *valuable information–surprise torture* equilibrium and both interpretations of the *valuable information–selective torture* equilibrium come closest to the pragmatic ideal.

Closest, but not close enough. An Innocent Detainee is still tortured for telling the truth in both sets of equilibria.

The reason is that the Interrogator believes the failure to reveal information signals a Resistant—not an Innocent—Detainee $(p < p^*)$, who is then tortured. The Interrogator must torture after failing to receive valuable information in order to compel valuable information from those willing to give it up under the threat of torture. This holds for the *valuable information–surprise torture* equilibrium and for the two *valuable information–selective torture* equilibria, one under objective and one under leading questioning. We thus have the following proposition:

Proposition 12.1 (**Necessary Torture of Innocents**). *In order for interrogational torture ever to generate any valuable information, innocent detainees must be tortured for telling the truth.*

Indeed, we know from Implication 10.4 that the likelihoods of information and torture of innocents inevitably track each other. Expanding the information region expands the region supporting torture of innocents; reducing the torture of innocents means reducing the likelihood of valuable information. As a result, the TJE of Benchmark 4′ does not exist:

Proposition 12.2 (**TJE Impossibility**). *The set of strategies defining the pragmatic model's torture justification equilibrium (TJE)—the Cooperative Detainee* plays "information," the Innocent Detainee plays "no information" (i.e., tells the truth), and the Pragmatic Interrogator plays "no torture" after both actions ("information" and "no information")—does not occur in equilibrium for any set of beliefs.

Information from torture is possible (albeit under very unlikely conditions, as we will see), but only if innocents are tortured. It is possible to avoid torturing innocents, but then no valuable information is forthcoming. Not both. Moreover, from Implication 10.1 we also know that it is impossible to minimize both the frequency and brutality of torture in eliciting information, as the TJO benchmark requires: "A minimum degree (severity) and amount (frequency) of torture is used . . . ."

Thus, the ideal outcome of torture proponents is just that: a quixotic ideal that fails to reflect reality of interrogational torture. Interrogational torture fails to satisfy the predictive condition of Benchmark 4. Now recall the normative part of the TJO benchmark:

Benchmark 4 **Torture Justification Outcome**: *Torture in interrogations is justified if and only if torture*

1. *is not used against cooperating detainees who have provided all their information (Cooperatives),*
2. *is not used against innocent detainees (Innocents),*
3. *does not exceed the minimum frequency (Total Frequency) and severity (Severity) "necessary," and*
4. *(the threat of) torture generates all, or nearly all, the valuable information possessed by knowledgeable detainees (Information).*

All four conditions must be met for the program to meet the proponents' benchmark. A violation of any one condition renders the program a failure.

Proposition 12.2 shows that the last, *Information*, condition is satisfied only if the *Innocents* condition is violated. The latter condition cannot be satisfied if the *Information* condition is to be satisfied. It is not possible to both elicit information and avoid torturing innocents. The surprise torture equilibrium and the fact that it is likely (Implications 8.1 and 8.2) violate the *Cooperatives* condition. Proposition 12.5 shows that torture is likely to exceed restraints and guidelines on severity, violating the *Severity* condition. We return to the questions of torture frequency and severity in more detail below, but what we have seen thus far is sufficient to show that, using its own model and its own logic, the pragmatic model of interrogational torture fails to meet its own normative standard justifying the practice.

INFORMATION RELIABILITY

Perhaps this seems too strong to some. Even if the *ideal* outcome does not oc-cur in equilibrium, (some) torture proponents may be willing to accept (many? some? a few?) innocents being tortured as long as the program provides good information overall. On this view, the program would be a success if it met the predictive and normative parts of the *Information Reliability* benchmark, even if it failed to achieve the ideal outcome claimed for it. Recall that the predictive part of this benchmark is:

> *Benchmark* 1 **Information Reliability**: *Most detainees have information and give up (nearly) all of it so that the ratio of clear and valuable information to all information will be high.*

We can assess this prediction in two ways, by looking at the set of RIT equilib-ria and outcomes and by using the parameter space to examine the set of beliefs supporting the prediction. Starting with the former, there are nine total equilibria of the two versions of the game (leading and objective questioning), but three of these equilibria call for the same actions by the Detainee and the Interrogator. Thus, there are six behaviorally distinct equilibria. Since there are also two sub-stantive interpretations (full and partial disclosure) of two of the six equilibria (*valuable information, surprise torture* and *valuable information, selective torture*), there are eight total outcomes.

Valuable information occurs in three of the nine total equilibria and four of the eight substantive outcomes of the RIT model. If we were to imagine for the moment that all the equilibria are equally likely, then your chances of ending up with valuable information are as low as one in three and no higher than a coin flip. Remember too that this includes the leading questioning version of the valuable information, selective torture equilibrium. Were we to exclude it since it provides no new information or intelligence, then those numbers drop further, to a low of just over two in ten equilibria. If any of these numbers were the chances your car would start on a cold morning, it's unlikely you would tell your friends you have a reliable car.

But perhaps some equilibria are just unlikely in terms of the beliefs required to sustain them. Perhaps we should just focus on the equilibria in which valuable information is provided. We can once again deploy the parameter space "cube" to assist us. Since introducing the parameter space in Chapter 7, we have thought about the equilibrium regions in the following way. A large region is supported by a greater range of beliefs than a smaller region. This means that, for any equi-librium, an increase in its size means that a greater proportion of possible beliefs sustain it. This, in turn, suggests that it is more likely; it can occur for a wider range of conditions. Benchmark 1 predicts, then, that equilibria with valuable information should take up a large proportion of the parameter space.

As we just discussed, the only two equilibria with valuable information are *valuable information, surprise torture* and *valuable information, selective torture*. Once again, since leading questioning provides no new information, strictly speaking the leading questioning version of the valuable information, selective torture equilibrium does not satisfy reliability Benchmark 1. For the purposes of the illustration and the discussion below, we will speak primarily about the objective questioning version, but what we will say applies equally to the leading questioning version.

We have already placed these equilibria individually in the parameter space in Chapters 8 and 10. Figure 12.1 places them together in that space.

Take a look first at the darker-shaded region supporting valuable information, selective torture, recalling that this region is defined by $\hat{f}$, p^*, and $\hat{q}$. From Observation 7.1 and Propositions 7.1 and 7.2, we know that both $\hat{p}$ and p^* are less than one-half (i.e., toward the front), with $\hat{p}$ approaching that value and p^* approaching zero the more the Interrogator believes everyone breaks—as is likely.

From Proposition 7.3, we know that as the cost of torture to the Interrogator c approaches zero and the additional cost of unnecessary torture drops (as a approaches r), again, as is likely, the Interrogator's information hiding threshold $\hat{f}$ is greater than or equal to one-half (i.e., on the right side). The final threshold $\hat{q}$ we cannot constrain because, as we said in Chapter 7, there are neither formal mathematical nor good empirical grounds to do so. As a result, Figure 12.1 bounds the valuable information region using what we know about $\hat{f}$ and p^* and

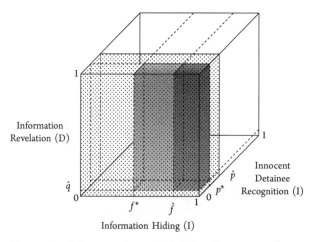

Figure 12.1 Maximum Extent, Valuable Information and Torture

assuming a $\hat{q}$ most favorable to proponents, that is, very low so the region is about as large as it can be. It is worth noting that in order for the threshold to be this low, either the information must be of very low value (low v) or the torture must be very brutal (high k) (or both).

Now take a look at the lighter-shaded region to its left. This is the volume supporting valuable information in the surprise torture equilibrium. The only threshold differences here are the addition of f^*, which forms the left-hand boundary of the equilibrium whereas $\hat{f}$ forms the right-hand side, dividing the two equilibria. The dotted region occupying the volume to the front of $\hat{p}$ is the region in which either the Cooperative or Innocent Detainee (or both) is tortured in at least one of the equilibria in the model. The blank space to the back of $\hat{p}$ is occupied by no torture. We return to these last two regions shortly.

Sticking with information reliability for the moment, what does Figure 12.1 suggest about the likelihood of getting valuable information from torture?

Don't hold your breath.

The lighter- and darker-shaded regions together are at about their maximums and they take up a relatively small proportion of the parameter space. Moreover, we are including the surprise torture equilibrium, which means that the information comes at the price of torturing both innocents and those who have provided information—maybe all of it. Nor would it help to put the leading question variant of the valuable information, selective torture equilibrium into the space. That equilibrium simply occupies the exact same space currently occupied by the two equilibria in Figure 12.1; it would not increase the total space occupied by valuable information. (And the information from leading questioning is not as valuable anyway.)

Since even at their maximum volume the two equilibria including valuable information take up a relatively small proportion of the parameter space, they occur for only narrow ranges of values on two of the three belief axes. Now recall that, to keep the model tractable, we gave the Detainee only two moves, "information" and "no information." We gave the move "no information" three interpretations: (1) truthful, accurate, but nonvaluable information, (2) false and misleading information, and (3) no information whatsoever.

Thus, the complementary volume (everything outside the gray-shaded boxes) represents some mix of no information and false and misleading information, as Figure 12.2 more clearly illustrates. This is the minimum extent of no/false information; as $\hat{q}$ rises, the white box representing information shrinks toward the top. The vacated space is colonized by more of the gray "no information." It is also important to note that this volume does not represent the absence of information or the bad information from a Resistant Detainee, which we expect to get all the time by assumption. Nor is it even only bad information from

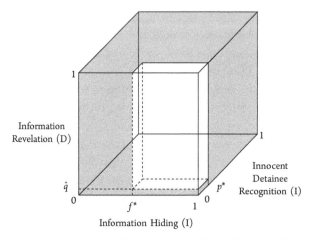

Figure 12.2 Minimum Extent, False and No Information by Cooperative Detainee

false confirmation by an Innocent Detainee attempting to avoid torture. This is the lack of information or the elicitation of misleading information from a Cooperative Detainee—that is, a Detainee who *does* have valuable information and is willing to give it up under the right conditions.

In short, torture in interrogations does not predictably, reliably generate valuable information. This, together with the relative rarity of valuable information among the set of all equilibria, gives us the following proposition:

Proposition 12.3 (**Information Unreliability**). *The ratio of valuable information to all other information under interrogational torture is low, with a mixture of no information, nonvaluable information, and false information dominating the parameter space.*

Moreover, other implications support and explain why. We know from Implication 7.2, for example, that, all things being equal, interrogators are more likely to get less valuable information than highly valuable information from torture, no different from interrogations without torture. This directly contradicts proponents' claims that torture is justified precisely because it *does* do better. Although increasing the brutality of torture (raising k) increases the likelihood of valuable information, we know from Implications 9.2 and 9.5 that it also increases the likelihood of ambiguous and false information elicited by the Interrogator under leading questioning. The Torture–Information Paradox in Implication 10.5 reveals that the very same assumptions motivating states to torture for information are likely to make the elicitation of valuable information *less*, not more, reliable.

As the Information Reliability benchmark makes clear, the normative standard for information reliability depends on interrogational torture predictably generating reliable information:

Benchmark 1 **Information Reliability**: *Interrogational torture is successful if and only if detainees give up (nearly) all their information so that the ratio of clear and valuable information to all information is high (Information).*

Proposition 12.3 as well as Implications 7.2, 9.2, 9.5, and 10.5 demonstrate that the pragmatic model fails to meet its own normative Information Reliability standard. Interrogational torture is not reliable in generating valuable information, despite the claims of proponents.

The only possible justification for interrogational torture is that it is effective in reliably generating reliable information. This is a necessary (if not necessarily sufficient) condition for the practice ever to be justified. The failure to meet this condition refutes the pragmatic justification of torture for information.

TORTURE FREQUENCY

We have just shown that the "end" part of the "end justifies the means" logic of interrogational torture fails to live up to the pragmatic model. What about the "means" part of the calculus? The pragmatic model claims that torture will be very limited, visited upon just a small fraction of detainees. More precisely, according to the predictive part of the Torture Frequency benchmark, we have the following:

Benchmark 2 **Torture Frequency**: *Torture will be employed infrequently, just on a few particularly resistant detainees who refuse to provide information, so that:*

1. *the total frequency of torture is low (Total Frequency),*
2. *Cooperative detainees are not tortured after they have provided all their information (Cooperatives),*
3. *Innocent detainees are not tortured for telling the truth (Innocents).*

Proposition 12.1 already showed that the Innocents condition is violated. The *valuable information, surprise torture equilibrium* and the fact that it is likely (Implication 8.2) together demonstrate that the Cooperatives condition is violated.

How about the Total Frequency condition? It is admittedly a bit vague, but then so are proponents and their claims. Presumably there should be few detainees who are tortured in both absolute and relative terms. In other words, if torture is a last resort for hardened terrorists, then we should expect not just that the total number of detainees tortured should be small, but also that this number should be a small proportion of all detainees *questioned*. After all, many detainees are not hardened and cooperate. There will even be innocents who should be weeded out of the program before they are ever tortured.

So the Total Frequency condition requires that the proportion of those tortured in this reference population should be very small. In terms of the model, this suggests that torture should take up a very small proportion of the parameter space and should figure in few of the model's equilibria. So how does this prediction fare?

Not very well.

Take another look at Figure 12.1 and the region filled with dots. This is the volume to the front of the interrogator's innocent detainee recognition threshold $\hat{p}$. As we said above when introducing the figure, there is some form of "unnecessary" torture in this region, either of an Innocent detainee or of a Cooperative Detainee who has provided all his information, or both. This is why, for example, it covers the shaded regions where valuable information is provided. Even in the *valuable information, selective torture equilibrium,* where the Cooperative Detainee providing information is not tortured, the Innocent Detainee *is* tortured for failing to answer the Interrogator's questions satisfactorily.

Recall from Proposition 7.1 and the discussion thereafter that $\hat{p} \lesssim \frac{1}{2}$. This means that torture takes up just under half of the entire parameter space. This is far greater than the tiny fraction that one would expect from the claims of proponents and the Total Frequency condition of the Torture Frequency benchmark. Also remember that the entire parameter space includes the cases where the Interrogator is in general willing to torture if Detainees don't talk but lets them go without having provided information because she thinks they are innocent (i.e., $p > \hat{p}$). If we restrict our attention to the region in which Interrogators think a Detainee providing no information is *not* innocent, as would seem likely, then this "unnecessary" torture takes up the *entire* space. In other words, the choice of reference population makes no difference. In both cases the prediction in the Total Frequency condition is incorrect; torture occurs with greater frequency than predicted by proponents.

What if we look not at the thresholds and range of beliefs represented by the parameter space but instead at the range of equilibria and outcomes in which there is "unnecessary" or "unjustifiable" torture? As a reminder, "unnecessary" and "unjustifiable" mean here unnecessary and unjustifiable in the eyes of torture *proponents*, not *opponents*. The benchmark requires that there should be few, if any, equilibria supporting such "unnecessary" or "unjustifiable" torture. How accurate is this prediction?

Not very.

In seven of the eight substantive outcomes the Resistant Detainee is tortured for failing to provide information, even though it has no effect on him. This does not count against the pragmatic model, however, for on that view such torture is justified. How about what proponents themselves consider "unjustifiable" torture?

Five of the eight substantive outcomes entail such "unjustifiable" torture on the pragmatic view. Knowledgeable Detainees are tortured, for example, after they have provided all the information they possess, contra the Cooperatives condition. Innocent Detainees are tortured for telling the truth, contra the Innocents condition. In two of the remaining three outcomes, the Innocent Detainee falsely confesses under leading questioning and the threat of torture.

Moreover, the more important the information (in terms of unknown unknowns), the more likely is "unnecessary" torture (from the proponents' point of view) because the value of information is less well understood (Implication 8.3). Even under leading questioning, the more important that confirmation is to the Interrogator, the more likely is torture of an Innocent Detainee (Implication 9.3). There is only one outcome in which neither a Cooperative nor an Innocent Detainee is tortured unjustifiably or falsely confesses (the *no information, no torture equilibrium*), but in that equilibrium both the Cooperative and Resistant Detainees get away without providing any information. Indeed, this is the *only* outcome of the eight in which there is no torture at all.

Drawing on our observations about both the proportion of the parameter space taken up by torture as well as "unjustified" torture's frequency among the set of outcomes, we can state the following proposition:

Proposition 12.4 (**Torture's Slippery Slope 1**). *Once torture is admitted as an interrogation technique, it will exceed the limits and controls imposed on it and become more frequent than proponents expect.*

Recall now the normative part of the Torture Frequency benchmark:

Benchmark 2 **Torture Frequency**: *Interrogational torture is successful if and only if torture is not employed too frequently:*

1. *the total frequency of torture is low (Total Frequency),*
2. *Cooperative detainees are not tortured after they have provided all their information (Cooperatives),*
3. *Innocent detainees are not tortured for telling the truth (Innocents).*

Proposition 12.4 demonstrates that the Total Frequency condition is violated as well. This, along with having demonstrated that the Cooperatives and Innocents conditions are also violated, shows that interrogational torture fails to satisfy the pragmatic model's normative standard for Torture Frequency. Interrogational torture results in more torture than even proponents anticipate and are willing to accept.

TORTURE SEVERITY

The pragmatic model places restrictions not just on *who* is tortured, but also on *how* those who are tortured are tortured. In particular, there are restrictions on the range of acceptable techniques as well as on the intensity or severity of those techniques. The result is the predictive component of the Torture Severity benchmark:

> Benchmark 3 **Torture Severity**: *When torture is employed, its severity will approximate the minimum degree necessary to compel valuable information.*

Now proponents might, again with some justification within their pragmatic model, say "minimum degree" cannot be interpreted too literally or it becomes a strawman easily taken apart. Fair enough, but neither can it be so loose as to be a Jello-man impervious to examination because it is too slippery to nail down. This will not matter if the model comes down clearly one way or the other. Let's see.

Although the RIT model does not make the severity of torture one of the moves by the Interrogator, it is still possible to assess Benchmark 3 by examining another feature of the model: the Detainee's information revelation threshold $\hat{q}$ in Figure 12.1. This threshold along the vertical q axis is the point at which the Detainee switches from "no information" (below the threshold) to "information" (above the threshold). Recall that the threshold, mathematically derived from the model but also intuitively compelling, is the ratio of the value of information v to the costs of torture k, or $\frac{v}{k}$ (both to the Detainee). Once again, it takes little familiarity with mathematics to see that this fraction (and so the threshold) increases as the value of information increases and/or the torture costs decrease. As the threshold increases, the space in which valuable information is provided to the Interrogator, the bottom surface of the darkest-shaded valuable information region in Figure 12.1, shrinks toward the top of the cube.

The job of an Interrogator using torture is to lower the threshold, to drive it down so that the Detainee talks "earlier" and the valuable information region moves toward the bottom, increasing its volume in absolute terms and relatively in terms of the total parameter space. How can the Interrogator do this? She has no control over the value of information, but she does have control over the torture costs to the Detainee.

In fact that's *all* she has control over. She knows different human beings respond differently to the same torture so she will not know the value of k for any particular technique on any particular detainee. But she does know ("believe" is more accurate) that increasing the severity (i.e., ratcheting up k) of that particular technique for that particular detainee will lower the threshold. If she does it enough, she may tip the Detainee over the threshold to "information." This is the inescapable and brutal logic of torture anytime and everywhere it is practiced. In other words we have:

Proposition 12.5 (**Torture's Slippery Slope 2**). *Once torture is admitted as an interrogation technique, the strategic incentives facing the interrogator result in increasingly brutal forms of torture.*

In all likelihood, then, even a tightly controlled and regulated interrogational torture program will fail to match the predictive benchmark for torture severity and thus also fail to match the pragmatic model's normative benchmark on limits on torture:

Benchmark 3 **Torture Severity**: *The program succeeds if and only if torture is not employed too severely—well beyond the minimum degree necessary to compel valuable information.*

Interrogational torture will result not only in too much torture, but severity exceeding limits and restrictions and thus reaching the level of abuse as defined by proponents themselves.

CONCLUSION

The outcomes derived from following the proponents' own logic of interrogational torture fail to match their predictions. As a result, interrogational torture fails to meet the four normative benchmarks identified by torture proponents as justifying the practice. The information generated by torture is unreliable, but torture will be more frequent and brutal than even proponents envision and would accept.

*   *   *

This completes the argument:

1. EITs are torture and the effectiveness of interrogational torture is an open question. (Chapter 2)
2. The Bush program approximates closely the ideal model of interrogational torture and includes limits on torture; the Bush and ideal models provide benchmarks for comparison with the game theory models to come. (Chapter 3)
3. The Bush model generates strange, quixotic outcomes. (Chapter 4)
4. The Bush interrogational torture program is more realistically modeled as objective and leading question variants of an incomplete information game, with three types of detainees, two types of interrogators, and uncertainty about the amount and value of information provided. (Chapter 5)
5. By positing a set of Detainee strategies, calculating the Interrogator's expected utility using Bayes' Rule to identify her best response, and checking for incentives to deviate by any of the Detainee types, it is possible to derive a perfect Bayesian equilibrium in which a Detainee is tortured after providing information. (Chapter 6)
6. The RIT model generates nine perfect Bayesian equilibria, the formal and empirical characteristics of which generate important observations, propositions, and implications, including:
   (a) The Interrogator's thresholds for believing that a Detainee is Innocent after "no information" are less than one-half, with $\hat{p}$ close to one-half and p^* closer to zero.
   (b) The Interrogator's information hiding threshold under objective questioning $\hat{f}$ is greater than or equal to one-half, whereas her information hiding threshold under leading questioning $\tilde{f}$ as well as the Detainee's version f^* of $\hat{f}$ are a little less than one-half.
   (c) Objective questioning (potentially) provides better information, but is necessarily accompanied by more torture, than leading questioning, which, however, provides less valuable information.
   (d) All things being equal, Interrogators are more likely to get less valuable information than highly valuable information.
   (Chapter 7)
7. Surprise torture of a Cooperative Detainee—even if he has provided all his information—is not only likely, but perversely more likely

(a) the more willing the Detainee is to divulge information and

(b) the more important the information is in terms of "unknown unknowns."

(Chapter 8)

8. The perversity under objective questioning persists under leading questioning, namely:

  (a) The more the Innocent Detainee believes Interrogator promises of no torture in exchange for confirmation, the more likely is ambiguous and false information.

  (b) The more brutal the torture, the more likely is ambiguous and false information.

  (c) The more important the confirmation is to the Interrogator and the more difficult it is for the Detainee to understand what is being asked, the greater the likelihood of torture.

  (d) Leading questioning will not eliminate torture; the higher the interrogator's demand for confirmation, the more torture.

  (Chapter 9)

9. The *valuable information, selective torture* equilibrium reveals four further trade-offs and a paradox:

  (a) Everything else being equal, eliciting information

    i. requires either more frequent or more brutal torture,

    ii. is more likely when the information is less valuable or the torture is more severe, but not both,

    iii. is more likely when the standard of cooperation is lowered, even though it increases the likelihood of information hiding,

    iv. is necessarily accompanied by innocent torture; decreasing the likelihood of innocent torture requires decreasing the likelihood of information.

  (b) The very assumptions justifying interrogational torture paradoxically make it less reliable in terms of the likelihood of getting valuable information.

  (Chapter 10)

10. From the two equilibria in which no Detainee provides information we learn that:

  (a) Everything else being equal, torture becomes less likely (the equilibrium region shrinks to a smaller proportion of the parameter space) after "no information" only if the information becomes less valuable or the torture becomes more severe, not both.

(b) It is difficult to find real-world cases in which detainees subjected to the threat of torture in interrogations were not tortured after failing to provide information.

(Chapter 11)

11. The results of the model violate the pragmatic model's necessary conditions for justifying the practice—the ideal outcome never obtains, information is unreliable in both senses of the term, and torture will be both more frequent and more brutal than proponents expect and are willing to accept—thus refuting the pragmatic argument for interrogational torture. (Chapter 12)

Torture's Confession

The real bottom line for any model is whether we find it useful and illuminating.

—MICHAEL LAVER, *Private Desires, Political Action*

Interrogational torture does not work. President Bush thought it worked. So did his Vice President, Dick Cheney, his Defense Secretary, Donald Rumsfeld, and his CIA Director, Robert Gates. Supreme Court Justice Anthony Scalia thinks it works. The creators of Jack Bauer and the television show *24* as well as the more recent film *Zero Dark Thirty* think it works. Many Americans think it works. Even many liberal college professors and others opposed to torture on other grounds think it works. For anyone who has ever had so much as a root canal, it sure seems like it *should* work.

But it does not. Interrogational torture generates bad information. It results in false information by innocent detainees. It results in ambiguous information of unclear value. It results in no information at all. Does saying it does not work mean it can never work? No. It can work. Under conditions that hardly ever obtain in the real world, it can work (but only if we're willing to torture innocent detainees). Can you put out a fire with gasoline? Yes you can, but, as my brother-in-law physicist says, it is not recommended.[1]

There may not be much useful information, but there will be a lot of torture. Torture of innocent detainees. Torture of detainees with information to try and get more information, whether they have more or not. And the torture will be nasty torture too. The slippery slope created by the incentives given to the interrogator means that torture will exceed even the limits and constraints placed on it by those who support its limited use. The ugliness of torture just keeps getting uglier.

We did not reach these conclusions by assuming our interrogators are a bunch of sadists. We did not reach these conclusions by assuming that interrogators are susceptible to dehumanizing social–psychological effects à la what happened at Abu Ghraib. We did not even reach these conclusions by assuming that an organizational culture pushes interrogators to adopt a "willing to do what it takes" mentality or professional incentives geared to favor the quantity of information over its quality.

We reached these conclusions by assuming that our interrogators were basically "good guys" and "good women." They preferred not to torture, especially an innocent detainee or a detainee who has told all he knew, and were only willing to do so as a last resort. So we did not "rig the game" in advance to get a lot of torture. If anything, we rigged it to get less torture. We gave not only the Bush program but torture proponents generally the best shot they could take to justify their position. And so, from relatively weak assumptions (i.e., reasonable ones favorable to proponents), we arrive at a powerful and important conclusion about what happens when humans torture other humans for information: Good guys get bad information with ugly methods.

IMPLICATIONS

In Chapter 3 we said that if the Bush model closely approximated the ideal model espoused by pragmatic legal theorists and philosophers, then a test of that model is simultaneously a test of the ideal pragmatic model. By the end of that chapter we said that the Bush model did indeed approximate that pragmatic model. Over the course of the next nine chapters we have seen that the Bush model fails. Since the Bush model qualifies as a crucial test of the ideal principle, the pragmatically normative model justifying interrogational torture, the failure of the Bush model is a failure of that legal–theoretical and philosophical justification. Torture cannot be justified.

We cannot torture. No matter what. In real life, it is never just one person and a bomb. Interrogational torture always becomes a government program, with all that entails. Torture really does sit on a slippery slope. Innocents will be tortured, as will detainees who have information but who have provided it all. Resistant detainees will be subjected to increasingly brutal tortures, to no avail. Some information may emerge, but it will be muddled and clouded by false and misleading information. In many cases, there will be no information at all.

Some will say we must torture even if there is a small chance it will work. No. There are some things we cannot do because they run too much against the grain of our character. As Senator John McCain said on the floor of the Senate, the CIA torture program "stained our national honor."[2]

We know right now we risk the death of more of our men and women in uniform by refusing to use biological and chemical weapons and flamethrowers. We permit hundreds of thousands of people a year to die—knowing we could prevent those deaths—because we hold other things dear. According to Harvard University's School of Public Health, 467,000 Americans die from smoking every year and another 64,000 from alcohol use (Danaei et al. 2009). We do not ban cigarettes or alcohol. According to the U.S. Centers for Disease Control and Prevention, about 30,000 Americans die every year from gunshot wounds.[3] We haven't tried to change the Second Amendment to the Constitution. The United Nations World Food Program estimates that approximately 3.1 million children under five die worldwide from undernourishment.[4] We do not radically reorient our foreign policy aid programs. Do we risk other deaths by forswearing torture? Possibly, but probably not. But we also gain by not swelling the ranks of suicide bombers and staying true to our character (Pape 2015).

THE LOGIC OF INTERROGATIONAL TORTURE

We have found that the pragmatic model claiming to justify interrogational torture fails. We can do more, however. We can say just *why* and *how* it fails. Doing so in this section paves the way for saying something more broadly about the role of formal modeling in political philosophy in the next section.

The logic motivating interrogational torture is a simple binary relation between torture and information. No torture, no information. Some torture, some information. Lots of torture, lots of information. Yet proponents of interrogational torture argue that it is possible to employ limited, targeted torture to get lots of valuable information. They want to have their cake and eat it too. We have seen that they cannot. From Chapters 6 to 12 we have seen precisely the opposite: torture exceeding its limits, restraints, and controls but resulting in little valuable information. Instead of minimal torture and maximal valuable information, we see the opposite: maximal torture, minimal valuable information.

Why?

Why Interrogational Torture Fails

The answer is found in the modifications we made from the BIT to the RIT models. The main difference between the RIT model of Chapter 5 and the BIT model of Chapter 4 is the addition of several uncertainties facing the Detainee and the Interrogator, namely those surrounding Detainee and Interrogator types, the clarity of the information, and the degree of information hiding. We found it necessary to include these elements missing from the BIT model in order to better represent the reality of interrogational torture. Indeed, we found that leaving them out resulted in quixotic outcomes far removed from reality.

From Chapter 8 forward we also found that including them resulted in outcomes which do, in fact, reflect reality. (I return to the problem of the *no information, no torture equilibrium* below.) They reflect that reality because the real world of interrogational torture is much more complex and messy than the BIT model admits.

By including the possibility of resistant and innocent detainees in addition to the cooperative type, we see how the combination of leading questioning and torture leads to ambiguous and false information. We see how innocent detainees with no information look identical to resistant detainees who never give up their information. By including the possibility of a sadistic interrogator we come to understand why even cooperative and innocent detainees who might otherwise provide information do not, fearing they will be tortured anyway. By including the possibility that the interrogator misperceives valuable information as nonvaluable, we show how detainees can be subjected to surprise torture even after they have provided valuable information. By modeling explicitly the common-sense idea that interrogators have some threshold of information disclosure that will satisfy them—a threshold unknown and unknowable by the detainee—we explain refusal by a nominally cooperative detainee to reveal information, surprise torture after providing information, and information satisfying the interrogator and no torture. Finally, by building questioning type (objective versus leading) into the moves and payoffs of the players, we demonstrate a range of problems with interrogational torture, from false and ambiguous information to the trade-offs between questioning type, information, and torture.

Inevitable Trade-off Between Information and Torture

This last example of a trade-off points to something deeper. The reason torture proponents cannot have their cake and eat it too is due to the "double maximand" problem, perhaps made most famous by the utilitarian philosopher Jeremy Bentham. Bentham thought the goal of legislation and public policy was the "greatest happiness of the greatest number" of people (Bentham 1891, p. 93). The trouble is that one cannot maximize both goals simultaneously. There are inevitable trade-offs between them. Kymlicka (2002, p. 50) provides a nice illustration of this problem. Say there are two distributions, each assigning different units of happiness via some public policy to a population of three people. Distribution A assigns 10 to each, while distribution B assigns 20 to persons 1 and 2 but nothing to person 3. Distribution A provides happiness to the greatest number (all three get something), while distribution B provides the greatest (total) happiness (of 40 as opposed to 30).

From Chapter 7 forward, we have seen analogous versions of this problem in the multiple trade-offs between information value and frequency on the one hand and torture frequency and brutality on the other hand. In our case, the problem is simultaneously minimizing torture (maximizing the humanity of an inhumane system) and maximizing information.

From Implication 7.1 we know that there is a trade-off between information and torture across questioning types. All else being equal, leading questioning results in less frequent torture but poorer information; objective questioning results in more frequent torture and better-quality (new) information. It is simply not possible to limit torture's frequency and still get valuable information as opposed to mimicked confirmation.

Implication 10.2 suggests a related, but distinct, trade-off. Everything else being equal, eliciting information is more likely only if the information becomes less valuable or the torture becomes more severe, not both. There is, in other words, a fundamental, over-arching trade-off between the predictability or likelihood of getting valuable information and minimizing torture. You can increase the reliability of information or you can minimize the brutality of torture. One or the other, but not both simultaneously.

There is a related trade-off between the likelihood of information hiding and torture. Consistent with the logic and incentives of interrogational torture, interrogators will torture if they believe that the detainee is hiding more information. Implication 10.3 tells us that, everything else being equal, eliciting information is more likely (the equilibrium region expands to a greater proportion of the parameter space), and torture of a cooperative detainee less frequent (the torture of an innocent stays the same), only if the standard of detainee cooperation is lowered, thereby increasing information hiding.

We saw all this visually in the discussion of the volume occupied by torture in Figure 12.1. Imagine you have a slider for each of the thresholds $\hat{q}, \hat{f}$, and $\hat{p}$. Your task is to try and maximize the volume supporting valuable information, taking one axis at a time.

Start with $\hat{q}$ and imagine it's in the middle, halfway between 0 and 1. In order to increase the volume occupied by valuable information along the q axis—that is, to increase its frequency by pushing $\hat{q}$ down—torture must become more brutal (higher k) or the information less valuable (lower v). On the other hand, reducing torture severity means reducing the likelihood of information. For torture's information reliability to go up, so must torture. (Of course we have seen above that even at its maximum possible degree of reliability, torture remains unreliable.) Proponents cannot escape the brutal pain–information logic of interrogational torture.

Now move to $\hat{f}$, keeping in mind that interrogators torture if they believe detainees are hiding information (i.e., to the left of $\hat{f}$). If you slide $\hat{f}$ to the left, you increase the space in which cooperative detainees provide information and are not tortured, but only because you've lowered the standard of what you consider full disclosure. This increases the chances of information hiding. In other words, you increase the chances of getting some information and not torturing, but also the chances of missing information.

Finally, grab the p^* threshold. In order to increase the reliability of torture (i.e., expand the valuable information region), you must push it toward the back, as close as possible to its maximum of less than one-half. As you do so, you simultaneously increase the region supporting the torture of an innocent detainee. Reducing the chances of torturing an innocent requires reducing the reliability of information (in the sense the predictability of getting information).

In short, interrogational torture is inevitably accompanied by trade-offs between information on the one hand and torture on the other hand (Table 13.1). It is simply not possible to limit torture and still get valuable information. This is why we see the same results every time, everywhere it has been practiced throughout history.

Paradoxes and Perversities

There is more. Whereas the trade-offs just discussed are consistent with the brutal pain–information calculus of interrogational torture—and inconsistent with the claims of limited torture, lots of information—there are also relations which run counter to our intuition, which are even paradoxical.

The more a detainee believes in the logic of torture, the more he believes that interrogators are pragmatic and do not torture gratuitously, the more likely is:

1. surprise torture of a cooperating detainee (Implication 8.1)
2. ambiguous information (Implication 9.1)
3. false information (Implication 9.4)

in addition to the expected valuable information.

Table 13.1. INFORMATION–TORTURE TRADE-OFFS

For...	either...	or...
Increased information likelihood	torture is worse	information is less valuable
High-value information	torture is worse	information is less likely
Reduced frequency of torture	torture is worse	information is less valuable
Reduced severity of torture	torture is more frequent	information is less valuable

Finally, from Implication 10.5, everything else being equal, the very assumptions driving an interrogational torture program—the most likely detainee has information and will reveal it under (the threat of [more]) torture, very few detainees cannot be "broken," and the chances of a detainee being innocent are virtually zero—all make valuable information *less*, not more, likely.

Despite the easy but mistaken tendency to think of interrogational torture in one-off, ticking time bomb situations, it is a government program. It is a *system* of torture. The unavoidable and inevitable messiness and uncertainty accompanying such a system or government program with many interrogators and detainees results in the failure of the pragmatic model. A rigorous and systematic analysis of those results reveals the inevitable trade-offs between information and torture causing that failure. It discloses perversities and paradoxes as twisted and contorted as the bodies subject to its practice.

FORMAL MODELS AND POLITICAL PHILOSOPHY

In demonstrating not only that interrogational torture cannot live up to the claims made for it by its proponents, but also why it fails to do so by interrogating its inner logic, we cash out the claim I made in Chapter 1 that applying game theory to interrogational torture is not just useful, but powerful. It is helpful at this point to step back and think about the formal argument here in the larger context of formal models and political theory, in two somewhat different ways. The first draws on an analogy to the philosopher John Stuart Mill's four grounds supporting the "liberty of thought and expression" (Mill 1972 [1859], pp. 78–113). The second reflects on the different uses to which models are put. Both sets of considerations reinforce the value of modeling interrogational torture.

J.S. Mill and Challenging Dogma

Mill, a utilitarian philosopher like Bentham, was a staunch defender of free speech, especially speech and expression that ran contrary to popular opinion. He was motivated in part by an Aristotelian impulse that viewed the exercise of reason in public discourse as virtuous activity, as an end in itself. But he was also motivated by the conviction that effective public discourse must be rational—that is, founded on reason and truth rather than dogma and prejudice.

The pragmatic model of interrogational torture is rife with such received opinion, dogma, and prejudice, much of it based on intuition. Mill identified four ways in which free expression confronting popular opinion is a means to the goal of rational discourse and understanding. The same grounds Mill found for confronting public opinion apply to our confrontation of the proponents' view with the analytical model.

First, we do not want to assume that what we think we know, either from observation or via intuition, is *all* there is to know. That would assume a sort of infallibility of observation and intuition in terms of completeness or comprehensiveness. The fact is, our intuitions and even our casual observations might be missing something.

An example of this is the surprise torture equilibrium. Though the history of, and commentary on, torture is replete with many different cases, there is little attention given as a separate category to those cases where detainees have provided all their information but continue to be tortured, whereas this is not true for the torture of innocents or other categories. Similarly, the effects of the clarity of the information to the interrogator has received no systematic treatment. In short, game theory helps us avoid what at the outset we called the dangerous seduction of intuition. Intuition tells us we already know instinctively everything there is to know about interrogational torture. Intuition is wrong.

Second, our intuitions may be only partially correct; our observations may be incomplete or tell us only part of the story. To assume otherwise is to assume a different sort of infallibility, an infallibility of accuracy about what we do know, rather than the comprehensiveness or extent of what we know. Intuition, for example, would tell us that everyone breaks. Just contemplating what it might be like to be waterboarded or put in a confinement box for hours on end tends to reaffirm that belief via intuition. We also have observations in the form of historical accounts and case studies that confirm this belief. And yet, Henri Alleg, Jeremiah Denton, and many, many others show us that real life is not so straightforward. Some people really do resist the most horrific pain and psychological disruption and never talk or instead provide intentionally misleading information. Game theory helps illuminate this outcome as well.

Moreover, some of those partially true intuitions can lead to surprising, unforeseen truths. Take, for example, leading questioning. Nearly everyone who has written about torture emphasizes false confessions and false information, especially under leading questioning. The RIT model shows not only how false confession and confirmation emerge from leading questioning, but also ambiguous information, which has not been systematically discussed.

Mill's third ground is perhaps most directly related. He notes that even if some commonly held opinion is fully true,

> unless it is suffered to be, and actually is, vigorously and earnestly contested, it will, by most of those who receive it, be held in the manner of a prejudice, with little comprehension or feeling of its rational grounds (Mill 1972 [1859], p. 112).

There is already far too much prejudice on all sides of the torture debate, with precious "little comprehension." Game theory supplies the rational grounds or firmament for the intuitions which do withstand scrutiny and a systematic, logical explanation for what we observe.

We see, for example, how a cooperative detainee's willingness to divulge information can be represented as the ratio of the value of the information to the costs of torture. This simple mathematical expression is derived mathematically, logically, deductively from the model but also corresponds to our intuitions about how both the value of information and pain of torture are related to the detainee's decision whether or not to talk. Those intuitions are informed by real cases and also guide the logic of the proponents' pragmatic model. The mathematical expression also lays bare the interrogator's incentive to keep torturing to drive down the threshold and make the detainee willing to talk.

Finally with respect to Mill, there is the danger that received opinion left unchallenged may become "dogma," "a mere formal profession, inefficacious for good, but cumbering the ground" (Mill 1972 [1859], p. 112). We see this in the case of torture, with opponents claiming that torture never works and proponents saying it always does, each ignoring the anecdotes advanced by the other. The formal RIT model provides clarification and explication of the conditions under which such claims are (not) true.

Using—Not Believing—Models

A second approach to considering the value of modeling interrogational torture examines the way we use them. As Laver (1997, p. 7) puts it in the epigraph to this chapter, "[t]he real bottom line for any model is whether we find it useful and illuminating." In other words, models are used for various purposes and should be assessed by how well they achieve those purposes (Clarke and Primo 2007, p. 742). The closer the correspondence to the object they model, the better they will do. Clarke and Primo (2007, pp. 742–744) identify five uses of models, four of which are relevant here: structural, generative, explicative, and predictive. We will also identify an additional use not included in their typology.[5]

The first use is *structural*, according to which the purpose is to gather known but distinct empirical regularities within one analytical framework. The idea is that there are disparate, disconnected findings or facts which can be generated from and explained in terms of (i.e., structured by) one coherent and unifying logical account. The RIT model is structural insofar as it explains how we get the variety of outcomes we see in the real world of interrogational torture from a single set of assumptions about detainees and interrogators and what each knows and believes.

Several, but not all, of the outcomes in Chapters 8 to 11 have been discussed widely by historians, philosophers, and legal scholars, each emphasizing
a different reason or cause. Some have mentioned many of the outcomes, also
referring to different causes. None has explained all of them via one consistent, logical framework. Aristotle and Ulpian discuss both resistant prisoners who
never reveal information and innocents who falsely confess, as does Beccaria
(Aristotle 350, pp. I, 15; Pennington 2008; Beccaria 1764). The Catholic saint
Augustine, in contrast, ignores the former case and mentions the danger of the
latter, but says the successful cases of confession justify the practice (Augustine
1984, p. 860). The RIT model organizes and explains these diverse outcomes in
terms of different combinations of Detainee types and different values for important parameters in the model: questioning type, clarity of information, and
others.

The purpose of a *generative* model is to "generate interesting and nonobvious
statements," "counterintuitive results which are unanticipated prior to the model
being solved" (Clarke and Primo 2007, p. 744; also Laver 1997, p. 7). In other
words, whereas structural models help us understand better the wide and disparate array of things we already know, generative models give us new perspective
on, and insight into, existing problems or phenomena. The RIT model serves this
purpose as well.

In fact, one needs only review the short passages on torture from Aristotle
and Augustine to Beccaria to see that those reflecting on torture tend to focus
on just three outcomes: Innocents who provide false confirmation of questions
or false confessions, those who say nothing and hold out, and those who provide valuable information or a confession. There is little discussion of surprise
torture or ambiguous information, both generated by RIT. Other examples of
new insights include Implication 8.1—the more willing a Cooperative Detainee
is to provide information, the more likely he is to be tortured after having
provided it—and Implication 8.3—the more important the information (in
terms of unknown unknowns), the more likely is "unnecessary" torture (from
the proponents' point of view) because the value of information is less well
understood.

Explicative models, as the name suggests, explicate or "explore the putative
causal mechanisms underlying phenomena of interest" (Clarke and Primo 2007,
p. 744). Substituting in brackets the relevant factors for interrogational torture,
a causal mechanism is "a process in which a causal variable of interest ... [tor-
ture] ... influences an outcome [revealing information]. The identification of
a causal mechanism requires the specification of an intermediate variable or a
mediator [e.g., the detainee's belief that the interrogator will not torture after
providing information] that lies on the causal pathway between the [causal] and
outcome variables" (Imai et al. 2011, p. 765).

The RIT model pursues this purpose as well, demonstrating, for example, how the ratio of information value to the cost of torture determines a Cooperative Detainee's decision to provide information or not. Another example is how a difference between the Detainee's and the Interrogator's information hiding thresholds leads to surprise torture.

The last model in the Clarke and Primo (2007, p. 743) typology is *predictive*, models used to "[f]orecast events or outcomes." The power of a predictive model is thus based on the range and accuracy of its predictions. The more powerful the model, the closer the correspondence between its predictions and what we see in the world, that is, empirical data. It won't be missing anything and won't get anything wrong. The traditional method for assessing this correspondence is data collection and analysis.

The RIT model is predictive in a slightly different way. As we discovered in Chapter 1, the data just do not exist to test systematically the RIT (or any other) model's predictions in this traditional way. Even so, there should be a minimal sort of correspondence between the model and world. The predictions of the model should not conflict with what we do know about interrogational torture from the dribs and drabs of data over the millennia. Whatever predictions made by the model we should find in the world, and there should be no important outcomes in the world missing from the model.

To this degree, Howes (2012, pp. 20, 23) and other critics miss the point when they say that rational choice models tell us nothing new and "simply formalize what others have already said." Presumably it would count against a model if it did *not* generate the outcomes we commonly see. A useful model accounts for all the cases we observe in the real world, does not miss any cases in the real world, and does not generate implausible outcomes we fail to observe. And, indeed, this is the case for the RIT model.

With one exception. You may recall that we found it difficult to identify a real-world case corresponding to the *no information, no torture equilibrium*. What generates this outcome? The credit we extended to the proponent model that interrogators sometimes believe detainees are innocent after the move "no information" $(p \geq \hat{p})$. We made that assumption in order to both better reflect reality (innocents are swept up in torture programs) and give the benefit of the doubt to proponents that our interrogators do not torture willy-nilly and especially do not want to torture innocents.

It might be, then, that our assumption about interrogators is wrong. In the real world perhaps they really *are* willing to torture innocents. Maybe. There is another, more charitable and, in my view, more likely explanation. It is that the entire system of interrogational torture—the incentives facing interrogators, their own understandable motivation to root out the bad guys, the organizational culture, the pressure from higher-ups, psychological biases—together constitute a perfect storm making it extremely unlikely a detainee swept up in the system could claim innocence and be believed. Thus the model helps us gain new insight into why we apparently do not see this outcome very frequently in reality. As Clarke and Primo (2012, p. 95) put it, "it is sometimes necessary to write down models that produce outcomes that are at odds with empirical experience in order to better understand that experience."

But RIT is also predictive in a different way. It generates predictions (equilibrium outcomes) to be assessed not just against what we see in the real world, but also against the predictions of the normative, pragmatic model of interrogational torture advanced by proponents. This is our final, fifth use of models, one we might add to Clarke and Primo (2007)'s list. This use we might call *empirically substitutive*. The pragmatic model of interrogational torture depends on twin empirical claims (it is effective in generating valuable information while minimizing torture) which cannot be verified empirically. The predictions of the RIT model substitute for those empirical tests, permitting us to assess the pragmatic model in the absence of data.

To this degree, RIT, like other formal models, is a helpful "tool for probing reality" (Brady 2004, p. 297). Our probing of the reality of interrogational torture has provided little support for the claims and justifications of proponents. Interrogational torture necessarily results in increasingly frequent and brutal torture, including of innocents, but fails to reliably yield valuable information. Torture games have no winners.

Postscript

This is nasty work, I tell you, but it goes with the job. We didn't try to come up with some sort of new idea for the guy. Everything happened like those clumsy films prepared him for, everything happened just like he expected: and *this* is always the surprise.

—Imre Kertész, *Detektívtörténet*

On December 9, 2014, the Senate Select Committee on Intelligence released the long-anticipated, redacted summary of its report on the CIA's detention and interrogation program. The 525-page document (hereafter *report*), with over 2,700 footnotes referencing secret CIA cables, emails, reports, interviews, and other documents, presents the Findings and Conclusions as well as an Executive Summary of the 6,700-plus-page full study (which remains classified) (United States Senate 2014a).[1] Republican members of the committee, then in the minority, submitted their own minority report disagreeing with the majority's findings (United States Senate 2014b). The CIA also responded with a redacted version of its June 2013 response to the report (Central Intelligence Agency 2014).

The game theoretic model on which this book is based, including the predictions that torture is ineffective yet more brutal than even proponents expect, was published in an academic journal in March 2012, more than two years before the release of the Senate report (Schiemann 2012a). The chapters you just finished reading were also largely written before the report's release.[2]

The claim I made at the outset about the lack of systematic data still holds. The minority report by Republicans on the committee and the CIA's objections in its own response demonstrate that there is no agreement even on what constitutes good evidence, so we still do not have the sort of rigorous test that can convince either side in the debate. Moreover, the sheer sizes of the summary and the responses—not to mention their complexities—prevent a full analysis here.

Nevertheless, even a brief examination is worthwhile. Bush administration and CIA officials have long claimed that the program was a success in terms of both information and adhering to the guidelines. The RIT model contradicts these claims. Given that the RIT outcomes and propositions reflecting the logic of interrogational torture were derived more than two years *before* the report was released, the report and the responses provide new and independent data to compare against both the Bush benchmarks and the RIT model's predictions. Table PS.1 distills the differing predictions from previous chapters and pairs them side by side. They guide our examination of the report and the responses to it.

TORTURE OF INNOCENTS

The universe, or total population, of detainees in the CIA program was at least 119 (United States Senate 2014*a*, p. 40).[3] Of these 119, nearly one in four (26 or 22%) were wrongfully held according to the CIA's *own* guidelines and the President's September 17, 2001, Memorandum of Notification authorizing covert action by the CIA (United States Senate 2014*a*, pp. 41–43, 109, 135–136, 154, 159, 458). These included:

1. Two innocent men detained as leverage against family members; one of these men was described by the CIA as "intellectually challenged"
2. Two innocent men falsely accused by KSM under torture
3. Two of the CIA's own sources who had actually sought out the CIA to volunteer information
4. An innocent man falsely accused because of a "blood feud"
5. An innocent man the CIA later said was "at the wrong place at the wrong time"
6. Several cases of mistaken identity similar to that of Khaled El-Masri, sometimes based on translation errors

Table PS.1. PREDICTIONS FOR SENATE REPORT

Prediction	Bush Model	RIT Model
Innocent detainees tortured	No	Yes
Cooperative detainees tortured	No	Yes
Frequency of torture	Low	High
Severity of torture	Minimum necessary	Exceed limits
Information	Predictably reliable	Unreliable, poor

Two of these innocent men (Gul Rahman and Laid Ben Dohman Saidi, aka Abu Hudhaifa) were subjected to the enhanced torture methods. The report notes that this figure of 26 is also a conservative estimate insofar as it does not include those about whom there was internal CIA debate nor those who were later released when the CIA no longer considered them a threat. Nor does it include multiple detainees the CIA had detained by other countries because they did not meet the CIA's criteria (United States Senate 2014a, pp. 41–43, 87).

The Republican members of the committee contest none of the foregoing. Indeed, their response is completely silent on the question of innocent men tortured by the CIA. Neither "innocent" nor any of its cognates and synonyms appear anywhere in the Republican report. Of the 26 wrongfully detained mentioned by the majority, the Republican response mentions only two of them by name, Haji Ghalgi (detained for leverage against a relative) and Hayatullah Haqqani (wrong place, wrong time) (United States Senate 2014b, p. 57). The Republican report says of the former only that he fabricated information and of the latter only that he did not provide fabricated information, both under "noncoercive interrogations." It is unclear what the Republican committee members mean by "noncoercive," since the rendition process and conditioning techniques—not to speak of the standard techniques—qualify as torture. The Republican report does include innocents implicitly—in the numbers of those who failed to generate information without the enhanced techniques. In other words, an innocent man's failure to provide the information he does not have counts *against* the effectiveness of "noncoercive" interrogations!

For its part, the CIA admits in its official response that at least six detainees did not meet its own standard and were wrongfully detained (Central Intelligence Agency 2014, p. 75). Some of the other detentions, however, it claims, were "reasonable" under the standard at the time. This includes the "mentally challenged" brother who, after all, was released "in a matter of weeks," even if the release of "[m]ost took three to six months" (Central Intelligence Agency 2014, pp. 52–53).

The excuse offered by the CIA was that "the national priority was preventing attacks" (Central Intelligence Agency 2014, pp. 76–77). Those of us old enough to remember those early months after 9/11 know that this is both absolutely true and utterly beside the point. To say that pressure to prevent an attack caused the detention (and torture) of innocents is to *explain why* it happened; it does not say that it did *not* happen.

In short, there is no doubt or argument that the CIA tortured innocent people, matching the RIT prediction in Proposition 12.1, not the Bush prediction. This violates the Innocents condition of the Torture Frequency benchmark. Evidence from the CIA program contradicts proponents' standards and claims that innocents should not and will not be tortured.

TORTURE OF COOPERATIVE DETAINEES

This criterion would seem difficult to assess because, as we have repeatedly argued, one can never know whether a detainee has more information in his head. If he continues to hide information, then that torture is justified on the pragmatic model. If, however, the CIA *itself* comes to the conclusion that a detainee has no more information despite being tortured, then that torture is unnecessary according to the pragmatic model (and the CIA's own standards). Ideally we would look at the case histories of the other 93 detainees who the Senate study agrees met the standard for detention and so actually had information to provide.

We do not, however, have this information systematically set out for any of them. Instead we have some information on some of them. If this information supports the benchmark—no Cooperative Detainees were tortured "unnecessarily" or "unjustifiably"—then it could still be the case that other detainee histories might not support the benchmark. But we would never know. If, however, there *are* significant instances of such unnecessary torture, then that is *sufficient* to indicate that the benchmark is not met. Consider two cases, Abu Zubaydah (United States Senate 2014*a*, pp. 51–63, 66–73, 230–236) and Abd al-Rahim al-Nashiri (United States Senate 2014*a*, pp. 92–99).

Abu Zubaydah provided information "on al-Qa'ida activities, plans, capabilities, and relationships, in addition to information on its leadership structure, including personalities, decision-making processes, training, and tactics. Abu Zubaydah provided the same type of information prior to, during, and after the use of the CIA's enhanced interrogation techniques" (United States Senate 2014*a*, p. 232). Zubaydah's failure to provide "detailed and verifiable information on terrorist operations planned against the United States, including the names, phone numbers, email addresses, weapon caches, and safe houses" resulted in, after a 47-day isolation period, the "non-stop use of the CIA's enhanced interrogation techniques" (combinations of shackling, hooding, diapering, nudity, slaps and attention grabs, walling, stress positions, waterboard, small and large confinement boxes [the latter presented as a coffin], white noise, dietary and temperature manipulation, sleep deprivation, and death threats) "24 hours a day" for nearly three weeks.

"After the use of the CIA's enhanced interrogation techniques ended, CIA personnel at the detention site concluded that Abu Zubaydah had been truthful and that he did not possess any new terrorist threat information" (United States Senate 2014*a*, p. 71). "At no point during or after the use of the CIA's enhanced interrogation techniques did Abu Zubaydah provide information on al-Qa'ida cells in the United States or operational plans for terrorist attacks against the United States" (United States Senate 2014*a*, p. 234). As a result of the failure to provide this information, the interrogation team flipped the rationale for using the techniques: "the interrogation team later deemed the use of the CIA's enhanced interrogation techniques a success, not because it resulted in critical threat information, but because it provided further evidence that Abu Zubaydah had not been withholding the aforementioned information from the interrogators." Neither the Republican nor the CIA responses contest the report's claim that Abu Zubaydah never provided information under torture on cells or operational plans in the United States. (They do claim other information was provided, which we address below.)

Abd al-Rahim al-Nashiri provided information to a foreign government after his capture in the United Arab Emirates in mid-October 2002 including "details on multiple terrorist plots in which he was involved prior to his detention, [such as] the attacks against the USS Cole and the MV Limburg, plans to sink oil tankers in the Strait of Hormuz, plans to attack warships docked at ports in Dubai and Jeddah, and his casing of a Dubai amusement park" (United States Senate 2014a, p. 99). Intelligence reports with this information were disseminated throughout the CIA. Nevertheless, the next month he was rendered by the CIA first to the Salt Pit in Afghanistan for a short period before moving on to the black site in Thailand, where he was subjected to EITs, including waterboarding at least three times. When the Thai site was shut down, he was transferred with Abu Zubaydah to the CIA's black site in Poland. There he was subjected to EITs during four periods: December 5–8, 2002, December 27, 2002, to January 1, 2003, January 9–10, 2003, and January 15–27, 2003.

The EITs were administered over the objections of the officers on the ground in Poland, who determined that al-Nashiri was cooperative and not resisting answering their questions (United States Senate 2014a, p. 498). Headquarters, however, was adamant: "[I]t is inconceivable to us that al-Nashiri cannot provide us concrete leads ... When we are able to capture other terrorists based on his leads and to thwart future plots based on his reporting, we will have much more confidence that he is, indeed, genuinely cooperative on some level" (United States Senate 2014a, p. 94). The on-again, off-again pattern of EITs reflects this back and forth, with the local officers deeming al-Nashiri compliant after each period of EIT use and the headquarters criticizing them for making "sweeping statements" about al-Nashiri's compliance and ordering more torture.

The torture included a range of authorized techniques as well as some unauthorized ones, including:

> vertical shackling for two and one-half days, far exceeding the four hour maximum, racking a pistol near his head and running a cordless drill near him while blindfolded, telling him "[w]e could get your mother in here," and "[w]e can bring your family in here," pinning him down on his stomach with his head below his torso and forcibly injecting Ensure into his rectum, slapping him on the back of the head, keeping him nude during periods of vertical shackling, and putting him in improvised stress positions

that required the intervention of a medical officer who feared al-Nashiri's shoulders might start to dislocate (United States Senate 2014a, pp. 95–99, 513–514).

Al-Nashiri never provided the information that the CIA's lead analysts at headquarters believed he possessed, namely "perishable threat information to help [the CIA] thwart future attacks and capture additional operatives" (United States Senate 2014a, p. 99). Contractor psychologist and interrogator Jessen himself concluded in October 2004, 21 months after the final documented use of torture, that al-Nishiri provided "essentially no actionable information" and "the probability that he has much more to contribute is low" (United States Senate 2014a, p. 99).

The CIA response does not challenge the claim in the report that al-Nishiri never provided threat information during or following the use of EITs. Al-Nishiri's name does not even appear in the Republican response.

The report contains other instances of such unnecessary torture of coopera-tive detainees, but what we have found so far is sufficient to show that the CIA's program tortured cooperative detainees long after they had no more informa-tion to provide. This confirms Implication 8.2 that cooperative detainees will be tortured for information they do not have and so matches the RIT model's prediction, not the Bush model's. In other words, the CIA program violated the Cooperatives condition of the Torture Frequency benchmark. Note that the failure to satisfy these conditions, along with those referring to innocent de-tainees above, entails a failure to satisfy the prediction of the ideal outcome in the Torture Justification Outcome benchmark. In other words, without having yet examined whether or not the program generated valuable information, we have already shown that the CIA program failed to live up to the ideal espoused by torture proponents.

TOTAL FREQUENCY OF TORTURE

The Total Frequency condition of the Torture Frequency benchmark predicts that the total frequency of torture will be low. We can assess this overall frequency of torture in the CIA program in several ways. Torture exceeds the threshold of low frequency if:

1. Any techniques were employed on those who did not "qualify" for the program (completely innocent or "wrongfully held" according to the CIA's own standards) (Wrongful).
2. Unauthorized techniques were employed on those who did qualify (Unauthorized).

3. Authorized techniques were employed on those who did qualify without giving them a chance to cooperate or even after they had cooperated (*Immediate*).
4. Authorized techniques were employed on those who did qualify without the required approval for specific techniques (*Unapproved*).
5. The total number and proportion of detainees in program subjected to torture is high (*Total Frequency*).

We might also include longer or more frequent or intense use of authorized techniques against those who did qualify, but these are better discussed below in terms of torture severity.

First, we have already seen that nearly a quarter of detainees were subjected to some form of torture without cause because they were wrongfully held. Using torture on those who did not qualify according to the CIA's own standards by definition means that it was used more frequently than permitted, satisfying condition *Wrongful*.

Second, the Senate study documents, and the CIA does not deny, that the agency used some unapproved techniques on detainees who did "qualify" for the CIA program, satisfying condition *Unauthorized*.

The torture of al-Nishiri described above is a clear example. The CIA apparently put "pressure on [an] artery" and performed "mock executions" on other detainees (United States Senate 2014a, p. 216). Abu Zubaydah was warned somewhat obliquely to "keep in mind" the "welfare" of his family, while contract torture psychologists Jessen and Mitchell threatened KSM much more directly. On KSM's first day at the black site in Poland, they told him that "if anything happens in the United States, '[they] were going to kill [his] children'." A picture of his sons hung up in his cell amplified their message (United States Senate 2014a, p. 513, also pp. 11, 111, 117).

The CIA never listed "rectal hydration" or "rectal feeding" in their list of techniques, and the CIA leadership continues to maintain with a straight face that they are "well acknowledged medical technique[s] to address pressing health issues" (Central Intelligence Agency 2014, p. 79). (The Republican minority response ignores rectal feeding/hydration entirely.) Rectal feeding was indeed "well acknowledged" as a last-ditch medical procedure—a century ago (Short and Bywaters 1913). Its medical use, however, faded into history along with mercury cures, drilling holes in the skull, bloodletting, and the urine treatment (don't ask). As anyone who has visited a hospital or even seen one on TV knows, modern medicine uses either an IV infusion or nasogastric tubes (i.e., through the nose).

The reason "[r]ectal hydration is almost never practiced in medicine [is] because oral and intravenous routes of fluid administration are more effective . . . The large colon has the capacity to absorb fluids, but has a very

limited capacity to absorb nutrients with the exception of glucose and elec-
trolytes. Pureed food and nutritional supplements, such as Ensure, should never
be administered rectally."[4] CIA medical officials, of course, knew this very well,
with one medical officer at a black site considering normal "IV infusion as safe
and effective." The CIA's chief interrogator stated frankly the real purpose: to
demonstrate the interrogator's "total control over the detainee" (United States
Senate 2014a, pp. 126, 108).

Third, although the guidelines required and the CIA told Congress that the
techniques would be applied only after detainees refused an initial opportunity to cooperate and only in a graduated fashion until they cooperated, the
report found that "detainees who were subjected to the CIA's enhanced interrogation techniques were usually subjected to the techniques immediately
after being rendered to CIA custody" (United States Senate 2014a, p. 9). Indeed, by my count working through the report, a minimum of over one in
four (10) were subjected to enhanced torture immediately, without being given
an opportunity to cooperate. Some of these had even already declared to the
CIA their intent to cooperate. Others had already provided valuable information prior to rendition (United States Senate 2014a, pp. 9–10, 103, 459),
including nearly one in three subjected to EITs (12 of 39), satisfying condition
Immediate.

In one case, the CIA had doubts about whether an Arsala Khan was the
person they were seeking. The solution was to go straight to torture "to make
a better assessment regarding [his] willingness to start talking, or assess *if
[Khan] is in fact the man we are looking for*" (United States Senate 2014a,
p. 458) (my emphasis). After a month of "extensive use of" EITs so that
he could barely speak and had hallucinations his family members were being mauled by dogs, "'the CIA concluded that [...] Khan does not appear
to be the subject involved in ... current plans or activities against U.S. personnel or facilities,' and recommended that he be released to his village with
a cash payment." He was nevertheless held by the U.S. military for another
four years. The reason for his kidnapping and torture? He had been falsely accused by someone with a vendetta against him (United States Senate 2014a,
pp. 42, 136).

Fourth, the CIA employed generally approved techniques on many detainees
without the required authorization from CIA headquarters for that particular
detainee. For example, the Senate study found that 17 of the 39 detainees who
were subjected to the enhanced techniques had it done to them without the required headquarters approval—44% of all those receiving EITs (United States
Senate 2014a, p. 127).[5] Some of these techniques, such as nudity, dietary manipulation, and water dousing, were not approved at the time they were employed.
In other cases, generally authorized techniques were used on detainees who had

been ordered to undergo other enhanced techniques. In short, it is clear that the CIA program satisfied condition *Unapproved*.

Walling, for example, was employed against Abu Hazim in addition to other enhanced techniques such as dousing with water and sleep deprivation. Walling was not approved because Hazim had broken his foot during his capture. He was also forced into standing sleep deprivation, despite approval for seated sleep deprivation only. Abd al-Karim also broke a foot attempting to escape his captors and so was not supposed to have received some of the techniques. He was nevertheless subjected to cramped confinement, various stress positions, walling, and standing sleep deprivation (United States Senate 2014*a*, pp. 138–139).

Fifth and finally, consider the last condition, *Total Frequency*. Begin by recalling that the total (minimum) population of detainees in the CIA program was 119. There were (again a minimum of) 39 detainees subjected to EITs (i.e., torture beyond the rendition/conditioning and the standard technique). Thus, on the most conservative (i.e., favorable to proponents) counting possible, one in three detainees in the program were tortured.

The problem is that the conditioning and standard techniques—isolation, nudity, sleep deprivation, various stress positions, cold water dousing, food manipulation (reduction), use of loud music or white noise, temperature manipulation, and the use of diapers—also constitute torture, as we saw in Chapter 2. Of course the rendition process itself, with sensory deprivation, nudity, and forcible sodomy, constituted torture in its own right. Assuming the standard rendition protocol was followed for all CIA captives, fully 100% of the detainees in the program were tortured in one way or another.

Any way you look at it, torture was very frequent, confirming the first Slippery Slope proposition (12.4) that once torture is admitted as an interrogation technique, it will exceed the limits and controls imposed on it and become more frequent than proponents expect. Thus, the results of the CIA program match the RIT model prediction and fail to match the Bush model prediction, violating the Torture Frequency benchmark. In terms of the frequency of torture, then, the CIA program lived up to neither the actual Bush program nor the ideal model of proponents.

TORTURE SEVERITY

Although the logic of interrogational torture requires more (brutal) torture to extract information, the pragmatic model's Torture Severity benchmark argues that its severity will approximate the minimum degree necessary to compel valuable information. Torture proponents are a little vague on exactly what this means and, to be fair, as we said in Chapter 12, we cannot pin this down too closely.

Even so, if there are clear-cut cases of torture beyond the program's own limits, then this is a problem. This can happen in five ways:

1. Particularly brutal unauthorized techniques (*Unauthorized*)
2. Authorized techniques employed longer than permitted (*Duration*)
3. Authorized techniques employed more frequently than permitted (*Frequency*)
4. Authorized techniques employed more intensely or severely than permitted (*Severity*)
5. Authorized techniques employed in combinations violating guidelines (*Combinations*)

We have already seen the brutality of some of the unauthorized techniques, with rectal hydration/feeding at the top of the list. Five Detainees were subjected to rectal feeding/hydration. One of them, Mustafa al-Hawsawi, was later determined to have acquired "hemorrhoids, an anal fissure, and symptomatic rectal prolapse" (United States Senate 2014a, p. 126). Several detainees were told they would never leave the black sites alive (United States Senate 2014a, p. 11). Detainees were forcibly immersed in ice water baths or hosed with cold water while standing and shackled to the ceiling before being taken to cells with temperatures as low as 59 degrees Fahrenheit (United States Senate 2014a, p. 131). One CIA psychologist recalled hearing Abu Hudhaifa "gasp out loud several times as he was placed in the tub" of ice water (United States Senate 2014a, p. 445). Although the CIA reported to the Justice Department that lights were always on for security, in fact they often kept detainees in total darkness. This method they apparently discovered by accident. One day interrogators found Ramzi bin al-Shibh "cowering in the corner, shivering" after his cell light had gone out. Consequently, his interrogators "decided to use darkness as an interrogation technique." He was then subjected to nude standing sleep deprivation, his hands shackled over his head, his feet manacled, "in total darkness" (United States Senate 2014a, p. 448).

In other cases, interrogators employed authorized techniques, but employed them in unauthorized ways: longer, more frequently, more intensely, or in combinations other than guidelines and interrogation plans permitted. The Senate report is replete with such instances. Consider just the following two cases:

Ridha al-Najjar was arrested in Karachi, Pakistan, in May 2002 and detained by a foreign government. Within weeks he offered up information on al-Kuwaiti, Bin Laden's courier (United States Senate 2014a, p. 408). Nevertheless, he was rendered to CIA black sites, eventually ending up at the Salt Pit in Afghanistan. In early August 2002, the CIA began subjecting him to "loud music, nutritionally sufficient but poor food, sleep deprivation, and hooding" (United States Senate

2014a, p. 79). A little over a month later, his CIA interrogators deemed him "clearly a broken man ... on the verge of a complete breakdown" and willing to do whatever the CIA wanted.

That, however, did not stop the torture. When a military legal officer visited in November, he noted that the interrogation plan for al-Najjar included "isolation in total darkness; lowering the quality of his food; keeping him at an uncomfortable temperature (cold); [playing music] 24 hours a day; and keeping him shackled and hooded." He had also had his hands handcuffed over his head for 22 hours a day for two straight days, with a diaper substituting for a toilet (United States Senate 2014a, p. 79). The CIA produced one intelligence report from him following his detention and interrogations (United States Senate 2014a, p. 80).

Abu Ja'far al-Iraqi was transferred to CIA custody from the U.S. military in September 2005 (United States Senate 2014a, p. 174). On December 1, 2005, CIA Director Porter Goss authorized using EITs on al-Iraqi because the "CIA believes that Abu Ja'far possesses considerable operational information about Abu Mu'sab al-Zarqawi (the leader of Al Qaeda in Iraq)."[6] As a result, al-Iraqi

> was subjected to nudity, dietary manipulation, insult slaps, abdominal slaps, attention grasps, facial holds, walling, stress positions, and water dousing with 44 degree Fahrenheit water for 18 minutes. He was shackled in the standing position for 54 hours as part of sleep deprivation, and experienced swelling in his lower legs requiring blood thinner and spiral ace bandages. He was moved to a sitting position, and his sleep deprivation was extended to 78 hours. After the swelling subsided, he was provided with more blood thinner and was returned to the standing position. The sleep deprivation was extended to 102 hours. After four hours of sleep, Abu Ja'far al-Iraqi was subjected to an additional 52 hours of sleep deprivation, after which CIA Headquarters informed interrogators that eight hours was the minimum rest period between sleep deprivation sessions exceeding 48 hours. In addition to the swelling, Abu Ja'far al-Iraqi also experienced an edema [swelling] on his head due to walling, abrasions on his neck, and blisters on his ankles from shackles (United States Senate 2014a, p. 175).

It is easy to find more examples. KSM ingested so much water during waterboarding sessions that his stomach was "distended" and water gushed out of his mouth when interrogators pressed down on his stomach.[7] At one point, a medical officer instructed interrogators to add salt to the water to prevent "water intoxication" and "electrolyte dilution." A medical officer on site described the sessions as "a series of near drownings" (United States Senate 2014a, p. 112). At the Salt Pit, Gul Rahman was subjected to "48 hours of sleep deprivation, auditory overload, total darkness, isolation, a cold shower, and rough treatment [i.e., dragged naked and hooded through the hallways while being punched and slapped]" before being shackled to the wall in a way that forced him to lie on the bare concrete floor, dressed in nothing but a sweatshirt. He was found dead from hypothermia the next day (United States Senate 2014a, p. 80). The study found that "detainees who were subjected to the CIA's enhanced interrogation techniques and extended isolation exhibited psychological and behavioral issues, including hallucinations, paranoia, insomnia, and attempts at self-harm and self-mutilation" (United States Senate 2014a, p. 11).

Consistent with its breezy indifference to the torture of innocents, the Republican response is also silent on the CIA program's abuses in terms of severity. It makes no attempt to counter the claims made in the Senate report. There is no mention in the Republican response of hallucinations, water dousing, rectal hydration/feeding, threats to detainees and their families, or other abuses documented in the Senate report.

The CIA admits to having "erred" in the use of some techniques, plays down other violations as problems with the program early on which were corrected later, or charges the Senate report with leaving out "clarifying detail." But the "most important" rebuttal is that Congress had been briefed about all this anyway (Central Intelligence Agency 2014, p. 78). The CIA response challenges only four claims about brutality: hallucinations from sleep deprivation, water dousing, rectal feeding/hydration, and waterboarding.

Hallucinations, the CIA argues, were rare and did not really matter anyway since they went away when detainees were eventually permitted to sleep. The agency's response also simply repeated the claim that interrogators stopped sleep deprivation when detainees hallucinated, ignoring the Senate's documentation of Hassan Ghul's continued sleep deprivation despite hallucinations (United States Senate 2014a, p. 158).

Water dousing, the CIA admits, was a problem at the Salt Pit due to cold temperatures, but this was corrected later at other sites (Central Intelligence Agency 2014, p. 79). The CIA response does not address the documented cases where water dousing was employed in such a way that—in the words of one CIA interrogator—"can easily approximate waterboarding." Indeed, Abu Hazim's water dousing included a cloth over his mouth and water poured directly on his face. A medical officer removed the cloth when Hazim's face "turned blue" (United States Senate 2014a, pp. 132–133).

The CIA ignores rectal feeding entirely in its response. As we have seen, it claims that rectal hydration was both necessary and an established medical practice. A two-minute Internet search or brief conversation with any doctor will tell you that the claim that rectal hydration is "more efficient than a naso-gastric tube" is absurdly false. The claim that it was necessary for hydrating "noncompliant" detainees because needles and nasogastric tubes were dangerous is hard to square with the "total control" of the Detainees in theory and in practice (United States Senate 2014a, p. 513). It's also hard to square with logic: Would *you* be more compliant with rectal hydration as compared to an IV or nasogastric tube? In any case, the Senate report points out that

> the assertion [by the CIA in its response] that Majid Khan was "unco-operative" prior to rectal rehydration and rectal feeding is inaccurate. As described in CIA records, prior to being subjected to rectal rehydration and rectal feeding, Majid Khan cooperated with the nasogastric feedings and was permitted to infuse the fluids and nutrients himself (United States Senate 2014a, p. 141).

Khan would later engage in self-destructive behavior, including attempts to cut "his wrist," "a vein in the top of his foot," and the skin on his elbow "using a filed toothbrush." He also tried to "chew into his arm at the inner elbow" (United States Senate 2014a, p. 141).

Finally, the CIA also admits that it used waterboarding in ways that deviated from the guidelines (but not the "principles" authorizing the technique). It mentions KSM's waterboarding in particular and suggests that part of the problem was how "adept" he was at "resisting the technique" (Central Intelligence Agency 2014, p. 79).[8] Indeed, one CIA cable from KSM's detention at the Polish black site in March 2003 accused KSM of lying in order to get himself tortured!

> [T]he enhanced measures resulting from his lying in [sic] details could be a resistance strategy to keep the interrogation from threatening issues ... [KSM's] apparent willingness to provoke and incur the use of enhanced measures may represent a calculated strategy to either: (A) re-direct the course of the interrogation; or (B) to attempt to cultivate some doubt that he had knowledge of any current or future operations against the US (United States Senate 2014a, p. 118).

In any event, the CIA dismisses the relevance of the waterboard problems since "only three detainees" were waterboarded (Central Intelligence Agency 2014, p. 79). Unfortunately, there is strong evidence that, in fact, the CIA waterboarded additional detainees. First, there are the cases of water dousing becoming "indistinguishable" from waterboarding discussed above. Second, the CIA was "unable to explain" "a CIA photograph of a wooden waterboard ... surrounded by buckets, ... a bottle of unknown pink solution (filled two thirds of the way to the top), and a watering can resting on the [waterboard's] wooden beams" at a time and detention site where no waterboarding was ever approved (United States

Senate 2014*a*, p. 132). Finally, the Senate report gives credence to a September 2012 report by Human Rights Watch alleging the waterboarding of CIA detainee Mohammed Shoroeiya, aka Abd al-Karim, at the same detention site as the photograph (United States Senate 2014*a*, p. 133).[9]

In short, the CIA rebuttal fails to counter the obvious conclusion: The CIA program also slid down the second Slippery Slope (Proposition 12.5): Once torture is admitted as an interrogation technique, the strategic incentives facing the interrogator result in increasingly brutal forms of torture. This again matches the RIT model's prediction and fails to meet the pragmatic model's Torture Severity benchmark and thus the Severity condition of the Torture Justification Outcome as well. The CIA program, like those that went before it, could not escape the inevitable consequences of introducing torture into an interrogation room.

INFORMATION RELIABILITY

The last benchmark is the most important for torture proponents. Some of these proponents may be willing to accept the torture of innocents, of cooperative detainees, of torture surpassing all limits on frequency and brutality as long as it can be counted on to produce the necessary valuable information. Indeed, the only possible argument that can be made for the practice is that it works, that it satisfies the Information Reliability benchmark:

> Benchmark 1 **Information Reliability**: *Most detainees have information and give up (nearly) all of it so that the ratio of clear and valuable information to all information will be high.*

Only if this prediction is met can interrogational torture be defended even in these proponents' eyes.

The trouble is—even leaving aside the fact that it is far from clear that "most" detainees had valuable information—that this is the most difficult benchmark to assess. It would take an entire book of its own to trace out the claims and counterclaims about who knew what and gave up what part of it when and under which circumstances. Figuring how important some bit of information was on its own as compared to its place in the larger context compounds the problem. Nor do the redactions in the report and responses make this any easier.

Luckily we have another option, one similar to the strategy we adopted in assessing the other benchmarks. We need to see if there is any evidence of an obvious failure to satisfy the benchmarks. If we find instead that there are few instances of detainees providing no information or fabricated information under torture, if we find that only torture could reliably (predictably) generate reliable (good, actionable, previously unknown threat) information from these detainees, then the Information Reliability benchmark is satisfied by the data we have available. If the opposite is true, if the torture frequently resulted in no information or false information and not valuable information which was otherwise unobtainable, then that is sufficient to demonstrate that the CIA program failed to meet the pragmatic model's own criterion of success.

No Information

Muhammad Rahim, the last detainee in the program, was captured in Pakistan on June 25, 2007. The CIA thought he would likely know information about Al Qaeda, including the location of Osama bin Laden, and rendered him to a black site in Afghanistan. When he "declined" to offer up any information on threats to the United States or the locations of Al Qaeda leaders, a team of four CIA interrogators began torturing him. The methods included facial slaps, abdominal slaps, the facial hold, eight different periods of extended sleep deprivation while shackled in a standing position in a diaper and a pair of shorts, and a diet of water and liquid Ensure. He provided "historical information" but nothing about the whereabouts of Al Qaeda leaders in questioning during his interrogation. At one point he was left isolated in his cell with "minimal contact" for six weeks. He still didn't talk.

His interrogators reported back to headquarters that Rahim's behavior had "demonstrated that the physical corrective measures available to [interrogators] have become predictable and bearable." A high-ranking officer in the Counterterrorism Center thought the harsh measures were a bad idea since it made a detainee who withstood them to "believe [they] had won." The CIA never disseminated any intelligence reports based on information from Rahim (United States Senate 2014a, pp. 189–194).

The Abu Ja'far al-Iraqi case discussed just above provides another example. Here is what was originally put into a draft of the President's daily briefing (PDB) from the CIA following his torture: Abu Ja'far al-Iraqi provided "almost no information that could be used to locate former colleagues or disrupt attack plots." This statement was later deleted at the urging of an al-Iraqi interrogator, who worried "[i]f we allow the Director to give this PDB, as it is written, to the President, I would imagine the President would say, 'You asked me to risk my presidency on your interrogations, and now you give me this that implies the interrogations are not working. Why do we bother?' We think the tone of the PDB should be tweaked" (United States Senate 2014a, p. 175).

Even the poster boys for the CIA program, Abu Zubaydah and KSM, withheld some vital information at the same time they provided other intelligence. Both "denied any significant connection between al-Kuwaiti [a suspected courier] and [bin Laden]," though the CIA later determined that they had information and so had withheld it (United States Senate 2014a, p. 420). Abu Faraj al-Libi, Ammar al-Baluchi, and Khalid bin Attash also almost certainly withheld information they possessed on the suspected bin Laden courier (United States Senate 2014a, pp. 404–426).

KSM provided information on a plot to target various U.S. and other Western locations and interests in Karachi, Pakistan, but only after confronted with evidence that two Al Qaeda operatives had been captured (Khallad bin Attash and Ammar al-Baluchi) (United States Senate 2014a, pp. 265–272). During the period he was subjected to EITs, KSM had been silent on these plots. A bitter CIA cable said that the Al Qaeda unit at headquarters was "disappointed" and this "long-standing omission [was] a serious concern, especially as this omission may well have cost American lives had Pakistani authorities not been diligent in following up on unrelated criminal leads" (United States Senate 2014a, p. 272). KSM was joined by Ramzi bin al-Shibh, Ammar al-Baluchi, and Khallad bin Attash in withholding information about another plot to attack Heathrow Airport and Canary Wharf in London (United States Senate 2014a, p. 326). And so on.

These cases illustrate a broader finding of the Senate investigation: Seven of the 39 detainees subjected to the enhanced torture methods provided no information whatsoever during their time in CIA detention. In other words, the CIA disseminated exactly "zero intelligence reports . . . based on information" these seven detainees provided under torture (United States Senate 2014a, pp. 9, 25). Considering only this figure, the enhanced torture techniques, the ones the United States really needed to use to get vital information otherwise unobtainable, were 82% reliable in getting *any kind* of information out of a detainee worth reporting (and we shall see that a good deal of it will turn out to be false). That's a B–. Perhaps this is acceptable if you're just looking to pass Psych 101 and graduate, but would it be acceptable if it were your car's reliability? Would you fly an airline that crashes "only" 18% of the time? Whether or not the United States of America should torture people seems closer in importance to the airline example than it does to the "passing Psych 101" example.

The Republican response reflects a different view, opining that a 82% success rate "sounds pretty good" (United States Senate 2014b, p. 55). In any case, they say, it is better than the 57.5% success rate they calculate for the 80 detainees not subjected to EITs. Even if this constituted an accurate comparison (it does not, as we shall see), the relative comparison is a disturbing defense of torture. Is simply doing better good enough to justify torture? How much better is better enough?

More problematic is the fact that the 57.5% is an inaccurate figure for comparison, for three reasons. First, either bizarrely or disingenuously, this calculation reflects the failure of *innocents* subjected to other, non-EIT torture methods, to provide the information they never had! Of the 80 detainees not subjected to EITs, 34 did not provide information, generating the Republican 57.5% effectiveness rate. The problem is that this 80 includes at least 24 detainees who were wrongfully held (the other two wrongfully held detainees were subjected to EITs). This means that they did not have the information the CIA thought they did—making it *impossible* for them to have provided good information. (Of course they could have provided false information, but the same is true of those who supplied information under EITs. We return to information quality below.) These 26 innocent detainees should be dropped from the Republican calculation (24 from the no-EITs group and two from the EITs group).

More precisely, we should drop them from the count of the detainees in each group (no-EITs and EITs) who provided no information. Of the 39 detainees subjected to EITs, seven provided no information. Since two of these 39 were innocent, it stands to reason that we should drop them from the seven who did not provide information. This reduces the number of non-information-providing detainees in the EIT group to five (from seven).

We do the same thing for the group not subjected to EITs. According to the Republican response, 34 of the 80 in this group did not provide information. From the total of 26 innocents, 24 were in this non-EIT group (the other two were subjected to EITs). Again, it stands to reason that these 24 innocents could not have provided information and so should be subtracted from the non-information-providing group of 34, leaving 10. Table PS.2 sets out these corrected figures in parentheses, along with the corrected success and failure rates calculated using the method in the Republican response.

As you can see, the effectiveness rate of EITs went up a bit, from 82% to 86%, as a result of dropping the two innocent detainees from the "no information" column. Once, however, the innocent detainees who by definition could not have provided information are subtracted from the "no information" count of the non-EIT group, the success rate of non-EITs shoots up to the old EIT proportion of 82%. These rates are both commonsensically and statistically indistinguishable.[10]

Table PS.2. CORRECTED INFORMATION RATES

		Information		
		Yes	*No*	*Total*
Techniques	*EITs*	86% (32)	14% (5)	37
	No EITs	82% (46)	18% (10)	56
	Total	78	15	93

Second, more importantly, as we have already shown, the 80 detainees who did not receive EITs were still tortured, just not tortured to quite the same degree. The division into "enhanced," "standard," and "conditioning" is an arbitrary one. Indeed, some techniques were initially not on any list, then classified as standard, and then became enhanced. We might just as well break out the numbers by rectal feeding or waterboarding, since those were the worst of the worst in many eyes. The point is that everyone in the program was forcibly sodomized, hooded, manacled, kept nude, and had their diets manipulated to one degree or another. The appropriate comparison, then, would actually be to *entirely* noncoercive interrogations, such as those conducted by military and FBI interrogators throughout American history, including against Al Qaeda in Iraq and Afghanistan. Unfortunately we do not have these data (and anyway they would suffer from the same epistemological and empirical problems we covered in Chapter 2).

Third, this counting method also ignores the fact that the detainees receiving EITs were more likely to have more, and more valuable, information. That is *why* they qualified for enhanced torture after all. If detainees were equally likely to talk (i.e., whether or not they had been tortured with the enhanced techniques, as we saw in the corrected figures just now), then it is not surprising at all that those receiving EITs would generate more reports. By definition, they had more information to give. While it is no doubt true that they may have wanted to hide that information even more, it is just as true that your ability to hide information is unrelated to, independent of, how much information you happen to have.

Suppose we set all these problems aside and compare the total number of detainees who provided information resulting in disseminated reports to those associated with no reports. If we do this, the overall success rate of the program drops to 66% (78 of 119). That's a solid D. Keep this up and you won't graduate.

The Republican response rightly points out that the number of reports is less important than the quality of what was provided. In their words, the "true test of effectiveness is the value of what was obtained—not how much or how little was obtained" (United States Senate 2014*b*, p. 55). They make this point to dismiss the Senate's claims about the failure rate (18% of EITs, 33% of the total). Fair enough. Before we turn to the quality of the information coming out of the CIA program, however, note that this shift in attention does not entirely do away with the problem of those providing no information.

What about the value of the information which was never elicited from those who withheld it? An argument justifying torture as the only possible way to get "vital ... otherwise unavailable actionable intelligence" cannot simply dismiss those cases in which the techniques failed to get that intelligence (United States Senate 2014*a*, p. 322). It may be that the information kept hidden by detainees who don't reveal information is much more valuable than the information which is obtained. Maybe not. The point is we do not know.

In any event, Republicans are absolutely right that it is important to look at information quality in addition to information quantity. Information can be good (unique, actionable intelligence on important threats or key enemies), neutral (nonuniquely, corroborative, confirmatory of out-of-date information), or bad (fabricated or false information which misleads or misdirects attention away from true plots, persons, locations, etc.). Obviously good is what interrogators are after. Neutral can be helpful, but is just as obviously of lower value. Moreover, proponents and the pragmatic model (rightly) do not justify torture on the basis that it merely provides corroborative or historical information. Bad is doubly bad. Bad information not only means not getting the vital, actionable threat information, but also entails actually moving further away from it, devoting time and resources in a direction which will ultimately prove fruitless and provide a greater advantage to the enemy. A reliable and effective interrogational torture program should have lots of good information, some neutral information, and very little bad information. Let's start with the latter.

False Information

Based on a misreading of information from another tortured detainee, CIA headquarters directed the interrogators in Poland to press KSM on his plot to recruit African-American converts in the United States for terrorist attacks.

> On March 21, 2003, KSM was waterboarded for failing to confirm interrogators' suspicions that KSM sought to recruit individuals from among the African American Muslim community. KSM then stated that he had talked with Issa about contacting African American Muslim groups prior to September 11, 2001. The next day KSM was waterboarded for failing to provide more information on the recruitment of African American Muslims. One hour after the waterboarding session, KSM stated that he tasked Issa "to make contact with black U.S. citizen converts to Islam in Montana," and that he instructed Issa to use his ties to Shaykh Abu Hamza al-Masri, a U.K.-based Imam, to facilitate his recruitment efforts (United States Senate 2014a, p. 294).

This (and other fabricated) information "required extensive FBI investigations." Less than two months after providing this threat "information," the FBI hosted a conference on the investigations following up on KSM's leads, including attempts by Al Qaeda to recruit terrorists in the United States (United States Senate 2014a, p. 511). A little over a year later in June 2003, perhaps confronted with the FBI's failure to turn up anything in Montana, KSM acknowledged that he fabricated the story about Abu Issa al-Britani and Montana because he was "under 'enhanced measures' when he made these claims and simply told his interrogators what he thought they wanted to hear."

CIA headquarters, however, considered KSM's retractions to be "another resistance/manipulation ploy" and "convenient excuses" and thus instructed CIA interrogators at the Polish black site "to get KSM to reveal ... the key contact person in Montana." By the end of the month, the bin Laden unit at CIA headquarters finally agreed that KSM's reporting about African American Muslims in Montana was "an outright fabrication." And, indeed, "no individuals related to KSM's reporting were ever identified in Montana" (United States Senate 2014a, pp. 294–295). The FBI had wasted precious resources on a wild goose chase as a result of KSM's tortured false information.

The Senate report is full of other information fabricated by KSM, including some which led to the capture and detention of innocent men, and is worth examining (United States Senate 2014a, e.g., pp. 240–241, 296, 511). How about other detainees? Following two days of enhanced torture in May 2003, Ammar al-Baluchi told his interrogators that he had provided false information the previous day (United States Senate 2014a, p. 414). Hambali, a Southeast Asian operative captured in the summer of 2003, provided information and was deemed cooperative from the beginning but was nevertheless subjected to enhanced torture. Within four months he had recanted his earlier information. The CIA itself believed those retractions (United States Senate 2014a, pp. 134–135). The reason?

Hambali reported that

> through statements read to him and constant repetition of questions, he was made aware of what type of answers his questioners wanted. [Hambali] said he merely gave answers that were similar to what was being asked and what he inferred the interrogator or debriefer wanted, and when the pressure subsided or he was told that the information he gave was okay, [Hambali] knew that he had provided the answer that was being sought (United States Senate 2014a, pp. 134, 282–283).

In other words, the CIA had engaged in leading questioning and got the answers it wanted. The result was false information.

Abu Bakr al-Filistini, aka Samr al-Barq, was being subjected to enhanced torture on August 1, 2003, under suspicion of involvement in a plot to make anthrax. He nevertheless told his interrogators that "we never made anthrax." His interrogators were not happy and told him "that the harsh treatment would not stop until he 'told the truth.' " "[C]rying ... al-Barq then said 'I made the anthrax.' " When his interrogators asked if he was lying, he admitted he was. "After CIA interrogators 'demonstrated the penalty for lying,' al-Barq again stated 'I made the anthrax' and then immediately recanted, and then again stated that he made anthrax. Two days later, al-Barq stated that he had lied about the anthrax production 'only because he thought that was what interrogators wanted'" (United States Senate 2014a, p. 109).

With respect to the CIA's main claim that enhanced torture provided the information which led to bin Laden, the Senate found that

> information from CIA detainees subjected to the CIA's enhanced interrogation techniques—to include CIA detainees who had clear links to Abu Ahmad al-Kuwaiti based on a large body of intelligence reporting—provided . . . intentionally misleading . . . fabricated, inconsistent, and generally unreliable information on Abu Ahmad al-Kuwaiti throughout their detention (United States Senate 2014a, pp. 405, 413–419, 425).

There were other cases where the information provided should have been suspect. The torture of Arsala Khan resulted in one intelligence report which was based on information he provided while hallucinating that his interrogators had given his family to dogs who were mauling and killing them (United States Senate 2014a, p. 135). Muhammed Rahim threatened to provide false information if his interrogators continued to torture him (United States Senate 2014a, pp. 190–191).

The CIA response devotes surprisingly little space to the fabricated or otherwise inaccurate information generated from torture. In the only specific case it addresses directly, the CIA claims that Hambali told the truth under torture and it was his recantation which was a lie (Central Intelligence Agency 2014, p. 50). The Senate examined these claims and found that "the CIA's June 2013 Response is incongruent with the assessment of CIA interrogators at the time," quoting from the CIA's own cables (United States Senate 2014a, pp. 283, 509). The CIA's more general defense is that they put disclaimers on reports dissemination information from detainees and issued retractions when appropriate (Central Intelligence Agency 2014, pp. 51–55). These caveats and disclaimers, however, apparently did not prevent the CIA, FBI, and other agencies from chasing down false leads nor prevent the CIA from arresting innocent people. The retractions do not mention that the fabricated information came from torture.

The CIA response does, however, point to a successful uncovering of fabricated information via torture. In July 2004 Janat Gul was rendered into CIA detention on the basis of a CIA source who fingered Gul as having information on Al Qaeda plans to launch a pre-election attack against the United States. The CIA subjected Gul to enhanced torture, "including continuous sleep deprivation, facial holds, attention grasps, facial slaps, stress positions, and walling." He eventually "experienced auditory and visual hallucinations ... [telling] CIA officers that he saw 'his wife and children in the mirror and had heard their voices in the white noise.'" He later "asked to die, or just be killed." Although his interrogators began to believe Gul did not possess the information, headquarters ordered the enhanced torture be continued. He never provided any threat information (United States Senate 2014a, pp. 161–163).

But, the CIA claims, this is actually a *success*. Why?

Because Gul's denials of knowledge under torture of any threat helped the CIA figure out that its original source had fabricated information. In other words, torturing someone without information is fine as long as it helps uncover the lies of the people who identified the tortured person.

The Republican response dismisses the importance of false and fabricated information more explicitly. "Fabrication is simply not a good measure of 'effectiveness,' because detainees are often strongly motivated to protect the identities of their terrorist colleagues and the details of their terrorist operations" (United States Senate 2014b, p. 57). For a response smugly scornful of the Senate report's "logical" flaws and "faulty premises," this is an odd locution (United States Senate 2014b, pp. 55–58). It says that because detainees have strong motivation to protect information, false information is a bad measure of effectiveness. This makes no sense. False information's validity as a measure of effectiveness has to do with what we mean by "effective" (actionable, critical, etc.); the motivations inside the heads of detainees have no bearing on that meaning.

What the Republican response is trying to say is the same thing the CIA said: We should not be surprised; detainees lie whether or not you torture them.[11] This is, of course, true, but it undermines the rationale for the CIA torture program, which is that the methods were the one way to obtain "otherwise unavailable actionable intelligence" (for a list of the many occasions on which the CIA used this and cognate justifications, see United States Senate [2014a pp. 198–200, footnotes 1,050 and 1,051; pp. 321–322, footnote 1,667, and section III of the report]). The claim of torture proponents is that torture is necessary precisely because it gets us the information we would otherwise *not* get. Not the false and fabricated information we get from nontorturous methods, but the actionable intelligence we need. *That* is what "effective" means. The CIA also moves the goalposts much closer to the ball when it rewrites history to say that "[t]he purpose of the program was to minimize what was withheld with the understanding that obtaining complete disclosures from detainees in every case was not possible" (Central Intelligence Agency 2014, p. 51).[12]

The Republican response also attempts to defend the frequency of false information with the averral that "fabricated information can sometimes turn out to be highly significant" (United States Senate 2014b, p. 57). This is logic unencumbered by reason. First, the CIA in particular and interrogators more generally often do not figure out until (much) later that the statements were fabrications. In the meantime the information is taken at face value, with all that implies, which means that, at least for a while, fabricated information *is* a problem. Second, suppose we grant that "sometimes" (the right combination of) fabrications will (eventually) turn out to be significant. Do we start torturing knowing full well we will get bad information but hoping that "sometimes" the lies they tell us might somehow make sense later? Is this a sufficiently strong reason to torture? It is certainly far weaker than the justifications originally provided by the CIA and its proponents, let alone those of philosophers and legal scholars.

Good Information . . . Just not from Torture

Now it could be that despite the problems with no information and fabricated, false information, there was so much good information generated from torture in terms of both quantity and quality that it overwhelmed these problems. In order to assess this question, the Senate selected "20 of the most frequent and prominent examples of purported counterterrorism successes that the CIA has attributed to the use of its enhanced interrogation techniques." The committee examined the contemporaneous cables, emails, intelligence reports, and other documents to assess whether or not it was the CIA's use of enhanced torture which resulted in "unique, otherwise unavailable intelligence that led to the capture of specific terrorists and the 'thwarting' of specific plots" (United States Senate 2014a, pp. 249–251). This review identified the following problems (United States Senate 2014a, pp. 9–10):

1. In some cases there was no relationship between the cited counterterrorism success and any information provided by detainees during or after the use of the CIA's enhanced interrogation techniques.
2. In the remaining cases, the CIA inaccurately claimed that specific, otherwise unavailable information was acquired from a CIA detainee as a result of the CIA's enhanced interrogation techniques, when in fact the information was either
   (a) corroborative of information already available to the CIA or other elements of the U.S. intelligence community from sources other than the CIA detainee, and was therefore not otherwise unavailable, or
   (b) acquired from the CIA detainee prior to the use of the CIA's enhanced interrogation techniques.

3. Examples provided by the CIA included numerous factual inaccuracies.
4. The CIA consistently omitted the significant amount of relevant intelligence obtained from sources other than CIA detainees who had been subjected to the CIA's enhanced interrogation techniques—leaving the false impression the CIA was acquiring unique information from the use of the techniques.
5. Some of the plots that the CIA claimed to have "disrupted" as a result of the CIA's enhanced interrogation techniques were assessed by intelligence and law enforcement officials as being infeasible or ideas that were never operationalized.

The Republican minority on the committee and the CIA, of course, dispute these claims. Partly they do so, as we have seen, by simply moving the goalposts and redefining what counts as good information, on occasion in Orwellian terms. Thus, corroborative information, repeating information previously provided while not under torture, and even false information are counted as good and useful. But only in part. The Republican and CIA responses also challenge the committee's report on minute details of what Detainees revealed when and under what circumstances.

Sorting out who is right is extraordinarily difficult. The devil really is in the details of the combined 828 pages and 3,623 footnotes. Consequently, we examine here just one example illustrating the contested nature of claims about reliability: the capture of Jose Padilla.

Jose Padilla is a former Chicago gang member who converted to Islam in prison. He was later radicalized and in 2001 he traveled to Pakistan and Afghanistan to wage jihad and trained in explosives and other terrorist methods. On May 8, 2002, he was arrested upon landing in Chicago.

What was he plotting and how was he identified?

Initially he was thought to be plotting some sort of nuclear attack. The fact is, the attack plan was dismissed by the CIA itself before Padilla was even arrested as "cockamamie" (the plan called for "placing liquid uranium hexaflouride [sic] in a bucket, attaching it to a six foot rope, and swinging it around [the] head as fast as possible for 45 minutes," something a physicist told the CIA would kill anyone trying to do it). Nevertheless, the CIA admits that it improperly continued to refer to this "Dirty Bomb" plot as late as 2007 in connection with Padilla (United States Senate 2014a, p. 252; Central Intelligence Agency 2014, p. 44). What was eventually discovered was that he was sent to the United States to try and blow up buildings with natural gas. The CIA has claimed that Padilla's identity and involvement in this plot were discovered only after the CIA tortured Abu Zubaydah with the enhanced techniques (United States Senate 2014a, pp. 252–253).

According to the committee's report, "the CIA's enhanced interrogation techniques played no role in the identification of Jose Padilla or the thwarting of the Dirty Bomb or Tall Buildings plotting." In addition to the fact that the CIA already had information on Padilla sufficient to stop him and his plotting and the information Zubaydah supplied was not sufficient by itself to locate Padilla, the committee asserts that Abu Zubaydah "provided this information to FBI special agents who were using rapport-building techniques, in April 2002, more than three months prior" to the application of enhanced torture methods in August (United States Senate 2014a, pp. 256–257).

In its June 2013 response, the CIA contested the committee's claim that their existing information on Padilla was sufficient to have apprehended him without the additional information provided by Zubaydah (Central Intelligence Agency 2014, p. 44). Although, as the "chief of the Abu Zubaydah Task Force" herself put it in 2002, "AZ's info alone would never have allowed us to find [Jose Padilla]," it seems reasonable to conclude that the information was of *some* value. The real question is how it was procured, and the CIA also challenged the committee's claim that Zubaydah had not been subjected to EITs when he provided the information. The agency noted that interrogators had already subjected Zubaydah to sleep deprivation (Central Intelligence Agency 2014, p. 88). The Republican response adds to this by asserting that Zubaydah's treatment also "included nudity, liquid diet, [and] sensory deprivation" (United States Senate 2014b, pp. 68–69). They cite sleep deprivation in particular as "play[ing] a significant role in Abu Zubaydah's identification of Jose Padilla" (United States Senate 2014b, pp. 15–16).

In other words, much hinges on exactly what was done to Abu Zubaydah leading up to when he provided the information on Padilla. Here is the apparent sequence of events, reconstructed from all three sources: United States Senate (2014a, pp. 54–56, 251–264), United States Senate (2014b, pp. 68–70), and Central Intelligence Agency (2014, pp. 87–88).

On the evening of April 15, 2002, the CIA team transferred a sedated Abu Zubaydah back to the black site from the hospital. He woke up at 11:00 pm. Constant questioning in rotating shifts of CIA and FBI agents kept him awake for the next 76 hours. On April 17 he provided information to his FBI interrogators about Al Qaeda, KSM (whom he had previously identified to FBI agents as the "mastermind" of the 9/11 attacks), and "general information on extremists in Pakistan." At 3:00 am on April 19, 2002, he was permitted to sleep for three hours because he could no longer focus on the questions submitted to him and was providing "incoherent" answers. Interrogators woke him up at 6:00 am and began questioning him again.

Forty hours and thirty minutes later, at 10:30 pm on April 20, 2002, the FBI team began their interrogation shift. They allowed Zubaydah to sleep for two hours as well as eat, pray, and receive a medical checkup. Shortly thereafter, they confronted Zubaydah with emails showing that Zubaydah had sent two men to KSM. Zubaydah then told the FBI that two men had come to him with their plot to blow up a nuclear device in the United States. Zubaydah dismissed it as implausible (Padilla would later say that Zubaydah "chuckled" at the idea), but sent them to KSM for something that might work. Although he did not know their names, he provided physical descriptions of the pair. This information was similar to other reporting they had on Jose Padilla and within hours the CIA cabled back these connections to headquarters. The United States issued a travel alert for Padilla; and when he boarded a plane in Zurich two weeks later, an undercover FBI special agent boarded with him, watching him on the flight to Chicago, where they arrested him.

So what can we make of this? In terms of pure lack of sleep, two hours of sleep in a little under two days is not a lot, but it's not too different from pulling a couple of all-nighters the night before a paper is due. Indeed, a CIA cable from the black site compared the "limited sleep" (note, not sleep deprivation) to that endured by medical students (United States Senate 2014a, p. 256). Moreover, Zubaydah had slept shortly before providing the information to the FBI and not to the CIA interrogators of the previous shift, before he slept. One might just as easily conclude that it was *sleep*, and not sleep deprivation, which generated the information.

In any case, the limited sleep regimen imposed on Abu Zubaydah in the second half of April 2002 was certainly a far cry from the degree of sleep deprivation that he would face four months later, in August. It was also very different from what is implied by the Republican response, which emphasizes the total amount of sleep and wakefulness over the entire April 19–21, 2002, period. This conceals the fact that Zubaydah gave up the information after having just slept.

It is also important to point out that the *way* in which Zubaydah was kept awake differed greatly from what would follow. He was kept awake by continuous questioning, not vertical or other shackling in stress positions hooded in a diaper, let alone cold water dousing or other techniques used to keep detainees awake. Nor was nudity or dietary manipulation the same as would later be the case. He was covered by a towel while the FBI questioned him. They gave him Coke and tea (United States Senate 2014a, p. 256). Finally, the questioning process itself was much different than the ways in which interrogators would later question detainees during the techniques, while shackled and perhaps hooded, dousing them with water, slapping them, walling them.

In short, the "enhanced" techniques to which Abu Zubaydah was subjected were very different from those eventually earning the euphemism. There is no denying they departed from normal FBI and military practice. There is also no denying, however, that they fail to qualify as an adequate example of the torture eventually practiced. If the Senate report was, as the Republican response argues, too "absolute" in its claims of ineffectiveness in this case, then the Republican response commits the same sin. The circumstances are far too ambiguous—at best—to qualify as the "direct refutation" claimed for it (United States Senate 2014b, p. 70). No "fatal flaw" or "analytical chain reaction" ensues (United States Senate 2014b, p. 62). Indeed, a senior CIA officer stated that "Padilla and the dirty bomb plot was prior to enhanced and he never really gave us actionable intel to get them" (United States Senate 2014a, p. 261).

Moreover, both the CIA and Republican responses, and even the Senate's own report, fail to mention several other relevant facts explaining Zubaydah's cooperation on the 21st despite his treatment. First, adopting the Republican's more "chronological" "analytical methodology," Zubaydah had already been cooperating with the FBI agents at the site and in the hospital before the CIA began torturing him upon his return from the hospital on the 15th (United States Senate 2014b, p. 61). He started to clam up under the new regimen. When he did offer information, it was to the FBI, using their questioning approach, not the CIA's, as even the Republican response admits. Zubaydah recognized a photograph of Ramzi bin al-Shibh on the 18th and provided the name to his FBI interrogators (United States Senate 2014b, p. 72). After the FBI left, the CIA itself deemed Zubaydah less compliant. Indeed, they considered him so uncooperative they put him in isolation for a month and a half before subjecting him to full-blown enhanced torture including waterboarding for 19 straight days.

As a matter of fact, if the techniques were so necessary and effective, this is where one would expect to find the CIA and the Republican response listing off the new unique and valuable information gained. What do we find?

Although the Republican response claims that the August enhanced torture yielded "a significant amount of important information" from Zubaydah, they provide only two examples, one from August 20 and one from August 21, a few days before the CIA stopped using the enhanced torture methods.

On August 20, Zubaydah was asked how he would get back in touch with senior Al Qaeda operatives if he were released. He replied that he would seek out a "well-known associate of Hassan Ghul." This associate could put him in touch with Ghul and other senior Al Qaeda associates (United States Senate 2014b, p. 74). The CIA claims that this was "unique information" without which the capture of terrorist Ramzi bin al-Shibh "would not have occurred" (Central Intelligence Agency 2014, pp. 106–107). The Republican response echoes this interpretation, arguing that there is a "direct causal connection" between this information and the accidental capture of bin al-Shibh in a raid by Pakistani authorities (United States Senate 2014*b*, p. 75).

"Direct causal connection" is too strong by half. First, for the causal distance from the information to the ultimate capture of bin al-Shibh, the number and length of the causal links matter. There is a direct causal link between the Big Bang and my sitting at my desk writing these words, but it's pretty distant. Second, and more importantly, the connection is not direct at all. As the Senate report documents in detail, both the CIA and the Pakistani authorities were already well aware of the associate's connection to Ghul and had even already raided his house and questioned him. Zubaydah's corroboratory— not at all "unique"—information simply confirmed the associate's importance. Moreover, the Pakistani safe house raids did not target bin al-Shibh; he was picked up fortuitously. That's not exactly "direct" (United States Senate 2014*a*, pp. 347–350).

On August 21, 2002, CIA interrogators showed Zubaydah several photos of suspected terrorists. He recognized Ramzi bin al-Shibh and said that he worked with KSM. The CIA labeled this "significant new details" in cables at the time (United States Senate 2014*a*, p. 76). The problem is that there wasn't much new to the CIA in this information. Not only was bin al-Shibh's close association with KSM already known to the CIA from other sources, but Zubaydah himself had already told his interrogators about their association (United States Senate 2014*a*, p. 346). Even the Republican response's own narrative demonstrates this. They point out that on May 19 and 20, before the 47 days of isolation and 19 days of brutal torture in August, Zubaydah had (1) identified another photo of him as "al-Shiba" and (2) stated that he was always with KSM. In the words of the Republican response, Zubaydah simply "confirmed" under torture what he had already said without the enhanced torture back in May (United States Senate 2014*b*, pp. 72–73). There was no previously unknown, new information here, let alone anything actionable. As "[p]articipants in the interrogation of Abu Zubaydah" put it, Abu Zubaydah "probably reached the point of cooperation even prior to the August institution of 'enhanced' measures—a development missed because of the narrow focus of the questioning. In any event there was no evidence that the waterboard produced time-perishable information which otherwise would have been unobtainable" (United States Senate 2014*a*, p. 234).

In short, we have seen the failure of detainees to provide any information at all, to provide false and misleading information, and to provide some corroborative information, including information that confirms what the *same* detainee had already provided without torture. The examples cited here are not the only instances. The Senate report is full of others. And while the CIA and

Republican responses are able to point to some minor and corroborative information provided under torture, there is no instance anything near to the sort of
information supporting the pragmatic model's claims of reliably generating reliable (valuable) information on imminent threats. Thus, the Bush program failed
to meet the Information Reliability benchmark—*the only possible justification for
interrogational torture.*

These appendices contain formal descriptions and arguments associated with the RIT model in Chapters 5 through 12, including proofs of the equilibria (A), comparative statics analyses of the thresholds (B), and relevant observations and proofs of propositions (C).

The RIT Model

This appendix contains the formal description of the RIT game and proofs of the pure strategy perfect Bayesian equilibria.

A.1 THE GAME

The game, reproduced as Figure A.1, begins with two independent moves by Nature. The first move selects the Detainee's type, D_j, from the space {*Cooperative, Resistant, Innocent*}, $\{D_C, D_R, D_I\}$, with the common prior probability distribution p_C, p_R, and p_I, where p_j, is the probability the Detainee is type j, and $p_C + p_R + p_I = 1$. Nature's second move selects the Interrogator's type, I_k, from the space {*Pragmatic, Sadistic*}, $\{I_P, I_S\}$ with the common prior probability distribution q_P and q_S, where q_k, is the probability the Interrogator is type k, and $q_P + q_S = 1$.

The Interrogator can engage in two kinds of questioning: objective or leading. Under objective questioning, the Interrogator does not tell the Detainee what she wants to hear. Under leading questioning, the Interrogator does let the Detainee know what would please her. In the leading questioning version, then, each D_j chooses a strategy from $\{i, \bar{i}\}$, where i is reveal valuable information ("Information" in Figure A.1) and $\bar{i}$ is not reveal valuable information ("~Information" in Figure A.1). Move $\bar{i}$ is equivalent to keeping silent as well as providing information which is not valuable.

Under objective questioning, when the Interrogator does not reveal what she wants to hear, D_I has move $\bar{i}$ only. Strategies for D_j are given as $(\alpha_1, \alpha_2, \alpha_3)$ indicating that D_C chooses (α_1), D_R chooses (α_2), and D_I chooses (α_3).

Following D_j's move, each Interrogator type I_k chooses to torture (t) or not torture $(\bar{t})$ from $\{t, \bar{t}\}$, with (β_1, β_2) denoting that I_P chooses β_1 when it observes i and chooses β_2 when it observes $\bar{i}$ and likewise for I_S with (γ_1, γ_2).

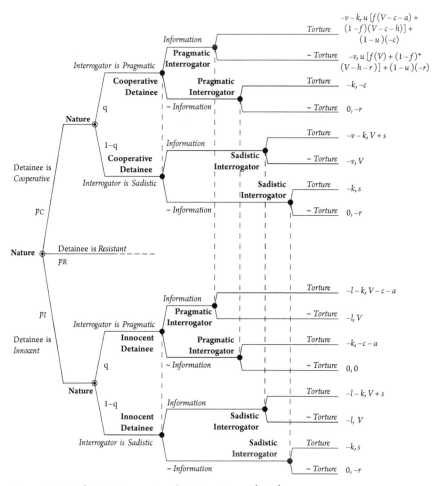

Figure A.1 Realistic Interrogational Torture Game (RIT)

Let $\mu_{x,y}$ denote I_k's beliefs about the Detainee type y at her x information set, i.e., $(x, y) \in \{i, \bar{i}\} \times \{C, R, I\}$. As examples, $\mu_{i,C}$ is the Interrogator's updated belief that the Detainee is Cooperative after observing "information" and $\mu_{\bar{i},I}$ is the Interrogator's updated belief that the Detainee is Innocent after observing "no information."

Both the Cooperative and Resistant Detainees pay costs $-v, v > 0$ for i and receive a payoff of 0 for $\bar{i}$. They also suffer costs $-k, k > 0$ if they are tortured by the Interrogator and receive a payoff of 0 for no torture. The preference orderings for each are: $D_C = 0 > -v > -k > -v - k$ and $D_R = 0 > -k > -v > -v - k$. Since, as we shall see, $\bar{i}$ is the Resistant Detainee's dominant strategy, the $\frac{v}{k}$ threshold pertains to the Cooperative Detainee only and so it is unnecessary to index the costs k to each type. The Innocent Detainee's payoff ordering is identical to that of the Cooperative Detainee, with l taking the place of v for the cost of i.

Both Interrogator types pay a cost $-r$, $r > 0$ if they fail to torture after move $\bar{i}$ from a knowledgeable (Cooperative or Resistant) Detainee and 0 for not torturing after move $\bar{i}$ from an Innocent Detainee. I_P bears a cost $-c$, $c > 0$ for torturing any D_i and an additional cost $-a$, $a > 0$ (with $-c > -r > -a$), for "unnecessary" torture of an Innocent Detainee who chooses $\bar{i}$ (i.e., tells the truth) or of any Detainee who chooses i. In contrast, I_S receives a benefit s, $s > 0$ to torture after any move by D_i.

Both Interrogator types receive a payoff of V for a Cooperative Detainee's move i under objective questioning that provides all the information they have to the Interrogator; for fractions less than full information, the Interrogators receive a payoff of $V - h$. Since the value of i is uncertain, the Interrogators have only the common prior belief that i provides V with probability f and $V - h$ with probability $1 - f$, with $f \in (0, 1)$.

In the objective questioning variant of the model, i is perceived by I_P as i with probability u and is perceived as the nonvaluable $\bar{i}$ with probability $1 - u$, $u \in (0, 1]$. This uncertainty is I_P's private information; the Detainee assumes that the Interrogator recognizes i as valuable ($u = 1$) and plays accordingly. I_P assumes that the prior belief u is common knowledge and plays accordingly. Three points of clarification are in order here. First, the Interrogator's perception (with probability $1 - u$) of the information as nonvaluable does not change her information set. Although her payoffs are the same as those of the $\bar{i}$ information set ($-c$ after torture and $-r$ after no torture), she knows she is receiving some type of information from a Cooperative Detainee. She must, however, decide whether or not to torture prior to fully understanding the information's value. Second, the uncertainty captured by u occurs under objective questioning only—there is no uncertainty over the value of information under leading questioning. Third, the Interrogator's belief about whether i is valuable (u) is independent of the Interrogator's belief about whether the Detainee is hiding information (f).

A.2 PROOFS OF EQUILIBRIA

This section contains the proofs and formal statements of the equilibria discussed in Chapter 8 and beyond. I solve for pure strategy perfect Bayesian equilibria. I make the following knifepoint assumptions to rule out indifference between strategy choices for D_j and I_P: If payoff-indifferent between choosing i and $\bar{i}$, D_C and D_I prefer i; if payoff-indifferent between t and $\bar{t}$, I_P prefers $\bar{t}$.

A.2.1 Objective Questioning

Under objective questioning, I_P's payoffs after i are weighted by u, $u \in (0, 1]$ but any D_i playing i believes $u = 1$. Since $\bar{i}$ dominates i for D_R, and D_I only has move $\bar{i}$ under objective questioning, there are only two pure strategies to consider, $(i,\bar{i},i)$ and $(\bar{i},i,\bar{i})$.

A.2.1.1 $\{i, \bar{i}, i\}$

Suppose D_i plays the strategy $(i, \bar{i}, i)$; using Bayes' Theorem, I_P's beliefs at the i information set are $\mu_{i,C} = 1$, $\mu_{i,R} = 0$, $\mu_{i,I} = 0$ and at the $\bar{i}$ information set are $\mu_{\bar{i},C} = 0$, $\mu_{\bar{i},R} = \frac{p_R}{p_R + p_I}$, $\mu_{\bar{i},I} = \frac{p_I}{p_R + p_I}$. Given these beliefs, the expected utility of t at the i information set is $uV - uh - ufa + ufh - c$. The expected utility of $\bar{t}$ at the i information set is $uV - uh + ufh + ufr - r$. I_P therefore prefers to torture after i for

$$u < \frac{r - c}{f(r + a)} \equiv \hat{u}. \tag{A.1}$$

Solving for f, we obtain

$$f < \frac{r - c}{u(r + a)} \equiv \hat{f}. \tag{A.2}$$

These are the *information recognition* and *information hiding thresholds*, respectively. Recalling the Detainee's assumption that any i is recognized with certainty ($u = 1$), it will be useful to define the Detainee's belief about the Interrogator's information hiding threshold as

$$f < \frac{r - c}{r + a} \equiv f^*. \tag{A.3}$$

I_P's expected utility for t at her $\bar{i}$ information set is $-c - \frac{p_I}{p_R + p_I}(a)$. Her expected utility for $\bar{t}$ after $\bar{i}$ is $\frac{p_R}{p_R + p_I}(-r)$. I_P therefore plays t after $\bar{i}$ for

$$p_I < \frac{r - c}{c + a} p_R \equiv p^*. \tag{A.4}$$

This is an *innocent detainee recognition threshold*. By simple inspection of equations (A.2) and (A.3), it is clear that $f^* \le \hat{f}$ for all $u, u \in (0, 1]$. Equations (A.2), (A.3), and (A.4) thus define six subcases.

A.2.1.1.1 $f < f^* \le \hat{f}$ and $p < p^*$

For this combination of beliefs, I_P plays (t, t). I_S always prefers torture to not torture. It remains to check whether $(i, \bar{i}, i)$ is D_i's best response to these choices. The strategy $\bar{i}$ dominates i for D_R; and under objective questioning, $\bar{i}$ is D_I's only strategy so they will not deviate. Because $f < f^*$, D_C would anticipate I_P's response of t after i, providing D_C with an incentive to switch to $\bar{i}$. Consequently, this set of strategies and beliefs cannot constitute a PBE.

A.2.1.1.2 $f^* < f < \hat{f}$ and $p < p^*$

For this combination of beliefs, I_P plays (t, t). I_S always prefers torture to not torture. It remains to check whether $(i, \bar{i}, \bar{i})$ is D_i's best response to these choices. The strategy $\bar{i}$ dominates i for D_R and under objective questioning $\bar{i}$ is D_I's only strategy so they will not deviate. Because D_C believes that $f^* < f$, he believes that I_P plays $\bar{t}$ rather than t after i. For D_C, the expected utility of i is $q(-v) + (1 - q)(-v - k) \Leftrightarrow -qv - v - k + qv + qk$, or $qk - v - k$ and the expected utility of $\bar{i}$ is $-kq + (1 - q) - k$ or $-k$. Thus, D_C prefers i to $\bar{i}$ for $qk - v - k \geq k \Leftrightarrow qk \geq v$, or

$$q \geq \frac{v}{k} \equiv \hat{q}. \tag{A.5}$$

This is the Cooperative Detainee's *information revelation threshold*. With no incentive to deviate to $\bar{i}$, the strategy profile $\{i, \bar{i}, \bar{i}\}$; (t, t), (t, t): $q \geq \hat{q}$, $f^* < f < \hat{f}$; $(\mu_i, \mu_{\bar{i}})\}$ for $\mu_{i,C} = 1, \mu_{\bar{i},I} = p < p^*$ constitutes a PBE. This is the *valuable information, surprise torture equilibrium*.

A.2.1.1.3 $f^* \leq \hat{f} < f$ and $p < p^*$

For this combination of beliefs, I_P chooses $(\bar{t}, t)$ and I_S chooses (t, t). It remains to check whether $(i, \bar{i}, \bar{i})$ is D_i's best response to these choices. From equation (A.5), D_C prefers i to $\bar{i}$ for $q \geq \hat{q}$. The strategy $\bar{i}$ dominates i for D_R; and under objective questioning, $\bar{i}$ is D_I's only strategy so they will not deviate. Thus, the strategy profile $\{i, \bar{i}, \bar{i}\}$; $(\bar{t}, t)$, (t, t): $q \geq \hat{q}, f^* \leq \hat{f} < f$; $(\mu_i, \mu_{\bar{i}})\}$ for $\mu_{i,C} = 1, \mu_{\bar{i},I} = p < p^*$ constitutes a PBE. This is a *valuable information, selective torture equilibrium*.

A.2.1.1.4 $f < f^* < \hat{f}$ and $p \geq p^*$

For this combination of beliefs, I_P plays $(t, \bar{t})$. I_S always prefers torture to not torture. It remains to check whether $(i, \bar{i}, \bar{i})$ is D_i's best response to these choices. The strategy $\bar{i}$ dominates i for D_R; and under objective questioning, $\bar{i}$ is D_I's only strategy so they will not deviate. Because $f < f^*$, D_C would anticipate I_P's response of t after i. Since I_P plays $\bar{t}$ after $\bar{i}$, D_C has an incentive to deviate to $\bar{i}$ and so this strategy profile and belief combination cannot be part of a PBE.

A.2.1.1.5 $f^* < f < \hat{f}$ and $p \geq p^*$

For this combination of beliefs, I_P plays $(t, \bar{t})$. I_S always prefers torture to not torture. It remains to check whether $(i, \bar{i}, \bar{i})$ is D_i's best response to these choices. The strategy $\bar{i}$ dominates i for D_R; and under objective questioning, $\bar{i}$ is D_I's only strategy, so they will not deviate. Because D_C believes that $f^* < f$, he believes I_P plays $\bar{t}$ rather than t after $\bar{i}$. D_C nevertheless has an incentive to deviate because I_P

plays $\bar{t}$ after $\bar{i}$, making $\bar{i}$ preferable to i for any q and preventing this strategy profile and combination of beliefs from constituting a PBE.

A.2.1.1.6 $f^* \leq \hat{f} < f$ and $p \geq p^*$

For this combination of beliefs, I_P plays $(\bar{t}, \bar{t})$. I_S always prefers torture to not torture. Since I_P plays $\bar{t}$ after $\bar{i}$, D_C has an incentive to deviate to $\bar{i}$ and so this strategy profile and belief combination cannot be part of a PBE.

A.2.1.2 $\{\bar{i}, \bar{i}, \bar{i}\}$

Suppose D_i plays the strategy $(\bar{i}, \bar{i}, \bar{i})$; using Bayes' Theorem, I_P's beliefs at the $\bar{i}$ information set are p_C, p_R, and p_I. Given these beliefs, I_P's expected utility from t after $\bar{i}$ is $-c - p_I a$. Her expected utility from $\bar{t}$ after $\bar{i}$ is $-r(p_C + p_R)$. Thus I_P plays t after $\bar{i}$ for

$$p_I < \frac{r - c}{r + a} \equiv \hat{p}. \tag{A.6}$$

This is the other *innocent detainee recognition threshold*, providing two cases.

A.2.1.2.1 $p < \hat{p}$

For this set of I_P beliefs, I_P plays t; I_S chooses the dominant strategy t. It remains to check whether $(\bar{i}, \bar{i}, \bar{i})$ is D_i's best response to these choices. The strategy $\bar{i}$ dominates i for D_R; and under objective questioning, $\bar{i}$ is D_I's only strategy, so they will not deviate. Under objective questioning, only D_C can play i, so, applying the Intuitive Criterion, $\mu_{i,C} = 1$ (Cho and Kreps 1987). This is identical to Case A.2.1.1 above, so the expected utility of t and $\bar{t}$ are given by $uV - uh - ufa + ufh - c$ and $uV - uh + ufh + ufr - r$, respectively. From equation (A.2), I_P therefore prefers to torture after i if its off-path beliefs satisfy

$$f < \frac{r - c}{u(r + a)} \equiv \hat{f}. \tag{A.2}$$

Further, for this off-path move to prevent D_C's deviation, D_C must believe that I_P will play t after i—that is, $f < f^* \leq \hat{f}$. Thus, the strategy profile $\{(\bar{i}, \bar{i}, \bar{i}); (t, t), (t, t): (q < \hat{q}$ or $q \geq \hat{q}$ and $f < f^* \leq \hat{f}); (\mu_i, \mu_{\bar{i}})\}$ for $\mu_{i,C} = 1$ and $\mu_{\bar{i},I} = p < \hat{p}$ is a PBE. This is the *no information, torture equilibrium*.

A.2.1.2.2 $p \geq \hat{p}$

For this set of I_P beliefs, I_P plays $\bar{t}$ after $\bar{i}$; I_S chooses the dominant strategy (t, t). It remains to check whether $(\bar{i}, \bar{i}, \bar{i})$ is D_i's best response to these choices. No D_i can do better, and so the strategy profile $\{(\bar{i}, \bar{i}, \bar{i}); (\beta_1, \bar{t}), (t, t) : (q \in (0, 1)); \mu_i, \mu_{\bar{i}}\}$ for $\mu_i = 0$ and $\mu_{\bar{i},I} = p \geq \hat{p}$ is a PBE. This is the *no information, no torture equilibrium*.

A.2.2 Leading Questioning

In this case the Interrogator's approach is leading questioning, causing u to drop out of I_P's payoffs and making strategy i now available to D_I. Because $\bar{i}$ continues to dominate i for D_R, there are four pure strategies to consider: $\{i, \bar{i}, i\}$, $\{i, \bar{i}, \bar{i}\}$, $\{\bar{i}, \bar{i}, i\}$, and $\{\bar{i}, \bar{i}, \bar{i}\}$.

A.2.2.1 $\{i, \bar{i}, i\}$

Suppose D_i plays the strategy $(i, \bar{i}, i)$; using Bayes' Theorem, I_P's beliefs at the i information set are $\mu_{i,C} = \frac{p_C}{p_C + p_I}$, $\mu_{i,R} = 0$, $\mu_{i,I} = \frac{p_I}{p_C + p_I}$ and at the $\bar{i}$ information set are $\mu_{\bar{i},C} = 0$, $\mu_{\bar{i},R} = 1$, $\mu_{\bar{i},I} = 0$. Given these beliefs, I_P's expected utility for t after i is $V + \frac{-p_C c - p_C h - p_C f a + p_C f h - p_I c - p_I a}{p_C + p_I}$. The expected utility for $\bar{t}$ is $V + \frac{-p_C h - p_C r + p_C f h + p_C f r}{p_C + p_I}$. I_P therefore plays t after i for

$$f < \frac{p_C(r - c) + p_I(-a - c)}{p_C(r + a)} \equiv \tilde{f}. \tag{A.7}$$

This is the *information hiding threshold* under leading questioning. I_P's expected utilities after $\bar{i}$ are $-c$ for t and $-r$ for $\bar{t}$, so I_P plays t after $\bar{i}$. There are thus two cases based on $\tilde{f}$.

A.2.2.1.1 $f < \tilde{f}$

For this set of beliefs, I_P plays (t, t). I_S always prefers torture to not torture. It remains to check whether $(i, \bar{i}, i)$ is D_i's best response to these choices. The strategy $\bar{i}$ dominates i for D_R. Both D_C and D_I, however, can do better by switching to $\bar{i}$ for any q, and this combination of beliefs and strategies cannot be part of a PBE.

A.2.2.1.2 $f > \tilde{f}$

For this set of beliefs, I_P plays $(\bar{t}, t)$. I_S always prefers torture to not torture. It remains to check whether $(i, \bar{i}, i)$ is D_i's best response to these choices. The strategy $\bar{i}$ dominates i for D_R. From equation (A.5) earlier, we know that D_C prefers i to $\bar{i}$ for $q \geq \hat{q}$. For D_I, the expected utility of i is $qk - l - k$ and the expected utility of $\bar{i}$ is $-k$. Thus, D_I prefers i to $\bar{i}$ for

$$q > \frac{l}{k} \equiv q^*. \tag{A.8}$$

This is the *innocent detainee's information revelation threshold*. Thus, the strategy profile $\{(i, \bar{i}, i), (\bar{t}, t), (t, t) : q \geq \hat{q}$ and $q \geq q^*; f > \tilde{f}; (\mu_i, \mu_{\bar{i}})\}$ for $\mu_{i,C} = \frac{p_C}{p_C + p_I}$, $\mu_{i,I} = \frac{p_I}{p_C + p_I}$, and $\mu_{\bar{i},R} = 1$ is a PBE. This is the *ambiguous information, selective torture equilibrium*.

A.2.2.2 $\{\bar{i}, \bar{i}, i\}$

Suppose D_i plays the strategy $(\bar{i}, \bar{i}, i)$; using Bayes' Theorem, I_P's beliefs at the i information set are $\mu_{i,C} = 0$, $\mu_{i,R} = 0$, $\mu_{i,I} = 1$ and at the $\bar{i}$ information set are $\mu_{\bar{i},C} = \frac{p_C}{p_C + p_R}$, $\mu_{\bar{i},R} = \frac{p_R}{p_C + p_R}$, $\mu_{\bar{i},I} = 0$. Given these beliefs, I_P's expected utility for t after i is $V - c - a$ and his expected utility for $\bar{t}$ is V.

I_P's expected utility for t after $\bar{i}$ is $-c$ and his expected utility for $\bar{t}$ is $-r$, so I_P chooses $(\bar{t}, t)$. I_S chooses (t, t). It remains to check whether $(\bar{i}, \bar{i}, i)$ is D_i's best response to these choices. From equation (A.5), D_C prefers $\bar{i}$ to i when i is not pivotal to avoid torture, which happens when $q < \hat{q}$ and when $q \geq \hat{q}$ and $f < f^*$. The strategy $\bar{i}$ dominates i for D_R. From case A.2.2.1.2, D_I prefers i to $\bar{i}$ for $q \geq q^*$.

Thus, the strategy profile $\{(\bar{i}, \bar{i}, i); (\bar{t}, t), (\bar{t}, \bar{t}) : q < \hat{q}, q \geq \hat{q}$ and $f < f^*$, and $q \geq q^*; (\mu_i, \mu_{\bar{i}})\}$ for $\mu_{r,I} = 1$, $\mu_{\bar{i},C} = \frac{p_C}{p_C + p_R}$, and $\mu_{\bar{i},R} = \frac{p_R}{p_C + p_R}$ constitutes a PBE. This is a *false confirmation, selective torture equilibrium.*

A.2.2.3 $\{i, \bar{i}, \bar{i}\}$

This set of strategies on the part of D_i is identical to case A.2.1.1, where D_I had move $\bar{i}$ only. Therefore, I_P's beliefs at the i information set are $\mu_{i,C} = 1$, $\mu_{i,R} = 0$, $\mu_{i,I} = 0$ and at the $\bar{i}$ information set are $\mu_{\bar{i},C} = 0$, $\mu_{\bar{i},R} = \frac{p_R}{p_R + p_I}$, $\mu_{\bar{i},I} = \frac{p_I}{p_R + p_I}$.

Recalling that u drops from I_P's payoffs under leading questioning, the expected utility of t at the i information set is $V - c - h - fa + fh$. The expected utility of $\bar{t}$ at the i information set is $V - h - r + fh + fr$. Identical to equation (A.3) above, I_P therefore prefers to torture after i if

$$f < \frac{r - c}{r + a} \equiv f^*. \tag{A.3}$$

It likewise follows from case A.2.1.1 that I_P's expected utility for t at her $\bar{i}$ information set is $-c - \frac{p_I}{p_R + p_I}(a)$ and her expected utility for $\bar{t}$ after $\bar{i}$ is $-\frac{p_R}{p_R + p_I}(r)$ and so, from equation (A.4), I_P plays t after $\bar{i}$ for

$$p_I < \frac{r - c}{c + a} p_R \equiv p^*. \tag{A.4}$$

This defines four subcases.

A.2.2.3.1 $f < f^*$ and $p < p^*$

For this combination of beliefs, I_P chooses (t, t) and I_S chooses (t, t). It remains to check whether $(i, \bar{i}, \bar{i})$ is D_i's best response to these choices. Since I_P plays t after i, D_C has an incentive to deviate to $\bar{i}$, and this strategy profile and belief combination cannot be part of a PBE.

A.2.2.3.2 $f > f^*$ and $p < p^*$

For this combination of beliefs, I_P chooses $(\bar{t}, t)$ and I_S chooses (t, t). It remains to check whether $(i, \bar{i}, \bar{i})$ is D_i's best response to these choices. From equation (A.5), D_C prefers i to $\bar{i}$ for $q \geq \hat{q}$. Strategy $\bar{i}$ dominates i for D_R. From equation (A.8), D_I prefers $\bar{i}$ to i for $q \leq q^*$.

Thus, the strategy profile $\{(i, \bar{i}, \bar{i}); (\bar{t}, t), (t, t) : q \geq \hat{q}, q < q^*, f > f^*; (\mu_i, \mu_{\bar{i}})\}$ for $\mu_{i,C} = 1$ and $\mu_{\bar{i},I} = p < p^*$ constitutes a PBE. This is a *valuable information, selective torture equilibrium*.

A.2.2.3.3 $f < f^*$ and $p > p^*$

For this combination of beliefs, I_P chooses $(t, \bar{t})$ and I_S chooses (t, t). But since I_P plays $\bar{t}$ after $\bar{i}$, D_C has an incentive to switch to $\bar{i}$, and this strategy profile and set of beliefs cannot be part of a PBE.

A.2.2.3.4 $f > f^*$ and $p > p^*$

I_P chooses $(\bar{t}, \bar{t})$ and I_S chooses (t, t). Again, since I_P plays $\bar{t}$ after $\bar{i}$, D_C has an incentive to switch to $\bar{i}$, and this strategy profile and set of beliefs cannot be part of a PBE.

A.2.2.4 $\{i, \bar{i}, \bar{i}\}$

Once again, this strategy profile is identical to its counterpart under objective questioning in A.2.1.2, but, given that D_I now has move i in addition to move $\bar{i}$, it is necessary to check whether D_I would deviate in each of the two subcases of A.2.1.2 defined by equation (A.6), $\hat{p} \equiv \frac{r-c}{r+a}$.

A.2.2.4.1 $p < \hat{p}$

For this set of I_P beliefs, I_P plays t; I_S chooses the dominant strategy t. It remains to check whether $\bar{i}$ is the best response for both D_C and D_I under leading questioning. By equation (A.5), D_C prefers $\bar{i}$ to i for $q < \hat{q}$ and thus will not deviate; the same is true for D_I for $q < q*$.

For $f < f^*$, D_C expects I_P to play t after i and so will not deviate to i even for $q \geq \hat{q}$. For $q \geq \hat{q}$ and $f > f^*$, however, D_C expects I_P to play $\bar{t}$ after i and thus has an incentive to deviate to i. D_I also has an incentive to deviate for $q \geq q^*$.

To prevent deviation to i by D_C and D_I, I_P would have to play t after i. Since under leading questioning, both D_C and D_I can choose i but D_R never does so, let $\mu_{i,C}$ be I_P's off-path belief that the Detainee is D_C, and $1 - \mu_{i,C}$ be I_P's off-path belief that the Detainee is D_I, upon observing i.

The expected utility of t is $V - c - a - \mu fa - \mu h - \mu fh + \mu a$. The expected utility of $\bar{t}$ is $\mu V - \mu h - \mu r + \mu fh + \mu fr + V$. I_P therefore prefers to torture after i for off-path beliefs satisfying

$$\mu_{i,C} > \frac{c+a}{(1-f)(a+r)} \equiv \mu_i^*. \tag{A.9}$$

This off-path belief is a real constraint (i.e., $\mu_{i,C}^* \in (0,1)$) for

$$f < \frac{r-c}{r+a} \equiv \hat{p}. \tag{A.6}$$

Thus, the strategy profile $\{(\bar{\imath}, \bar{\imath}, \bar{\imath}); (t,t), (t,t) : (q < \hat{q} \text{ and } q < q^*) \text{ or } (q \geq \hat{q}$ and $q \geq q^*$ and $f < f^*)$ or $(q \geq \hat{q}$ and $q < q^*$ and $f < f^*)$ or $(q < \hat{q}$ and $q \geq q^*$ and $f < f^*)$ with $(\mu_i, \mu_{\bar{\imath}})\}$ for $\mu_{i,C} > \mu_i^*$ and $\mu_{\bar{\imath},I} = p < \hat{p}$ is a PBE. This is the *no information, torture equilibrium*.

A.2.2.4.2 $p \geq \hat{p}$
For this set of I_P beliefs, I_P plays $(\beta_1, \bar{t})$; I_S chooses the dominant strategy (t,t). It remains to check whether $(\bar{\imath}, \bar{\imath}, \bar{\imath})$ is D_i's best response to these choices. No D_i can do better and so the strategy profile $\{(\bar{\imath}, \bar{\imath}, \bar{\imath}); (\beta_1, \bar{t}), (t,t)\} : q \in (0,1); (\mu_i, \mu_{\bar{\imath}})$ for $\mu_{\bar{\imath},I} = p \geq \hat{p}$ is a PBE. This is the *no information, no torture equilibrium*. $\square$

Comparative Statics Analysis

This appendix supports the comparative statics results in Chapter 7 by establishing the signs of the derivatives of the thresholds in Appendix A.2 with respect to their component parameters.

B.1 FROM EQUATION (A.5), $\hat{q} = \dfrac{v}{k}$

$$\frac{\partial \hat{q}}{\partial v} = \frac{1}{k} > 0,$$

$$\frac{\partial \hat{q}}{\partial k} = -\frac{1}{k^2} < 0.$$

B.2 FROM EQUATION (A.2), $\hat{f} = \dfrac{r - c}{u(r + a)}$

$$\frac{\partial \hat{f}}{\partial r} = \frac{a + c}{u(r + a)^2} > 0,$$

$$\frac{\partial \hat{f}}{\partial c} = -\frac{1}{u(r + a)} < 0,$$

$$\frac{\partial \hat{f}}{\partial a} = -\frac{r - c}{u(r + a)^2} < 0,$$

$$\frac{\partial \hat{f}}{\partial u} = -\frac{r - c}{u^2(r + a)} < 0.$$

B.3 FROM EQUATION (A.3), $f^* = \dfrac{r-c}{r+a}$

$$\frac{\partial f^*}{\partial r} = \frac{a+c}{(r+a)^2} > 0,$$

$$\frac{\partial f^*}{\partial c} = -\frac{1}{r+a} < 0,$$

$$\frac{\partial f^*}{\partial a} = \frac{c-r}{(r+a)^2} < 0.$$

B.4 FROM EQUATION (A.4), $p_I < \dfrac{r-c}{c+a}p_R \equiv p^*$

$$\frac{\partial p^*}{\partial r} = \frac{p_R}{c+a} > 0,$$

$$\frac{\partial p^*}{\partial c} = -p_R\frac{r+a}{(c+a)^2} < 0,$$

$$\frac{\partial p^*}{\partial a} = -p_R\frac{r-c}{(c+a)^2} < 0,$$

$$\frac{\partial p^*}{\partial p_R} = \frac{r-c}{a+c} > 0.$$

B.5 FROM EQUATION (A.6), $p_I < \dfrac{r-c}{r+a} \equiv \hat{p}$

$$\frac{\partial \hat{p}}{\partial r} = \frac{a+c}{(a+r)^2} > 0,$$

$$\frac{\partial \hat{p}}{\partial c} = -\frac{1}{r+a} < 0,$$

$$\frac{\partial \hat{p}}{\partial a} = \frac{c-r}{(r+a)^2} < 0.$$

B.6 FROM EQUATION (A.7), $f < \dfrac{p_C(r-c) + p_I(-a-c)}{p_C(r+a)} \equiv \tilde{f}$

$$\frac{\partial \tilde{f}}{\partial r} = \frac{(p_C + p_I)(a+c)}{p_c(r+a)^2} > 0,$$

$$\frac{\partial \tilde{f}}{\partial c} = -\frac{p_C + p_I}{p_c(r+a)} < 0,$$

$$\frac{\partial \tilde{f}}{\partial a} = \frac{(p_I + p_C)(c-r)}{p_C(r+a)^2} < 0,$$

$$\frac{\partial \tilde{f}}{\partial p_C} = \frac{p_I(a+c)}{p_C^2(r+a)} > 0,$$

$$\frac{\partial \tilde{f}}{\partial p_I} = -\frac{a+c}{p_C(r+a)} < 0.$$

Observations and Propositions

This appendix makes several observations and proves the relevant propositions from Chapter 7, following the order of presentation in the text after making two observations not in the text but which will prove useful in proving a proposition below.

C.1 OBSERVATION C.1

Observation C.1 $\frac{1}{2} < w = \frac{a+c}{a+r} < 1.$

Let $w \equiv \frac{a+c}{a+r}$. Since $c < r$, $w < 1$. Claiming $\frac{a+c}{a+r} > \frac{1}{2}$ implies that $2a + 2c > a + r$, which becomes $a + c > r - c$. This is true since $a > r$ and $c > 0$.

C.2 OBSERVATION C.2

Observation C.2 If $p_C > p_I \geq p_R$ or if $p_C > p_R \geq p_I$, then $p_R < \frac{1}{2}$.

Proof
By assumption, p_C, p_R, and p_I are positive and $p_C + p_R + p_I = 1$. Suppose that $p_C > p_I \geq p_R$ or $p_C > p_R \geq p_I$ and suppose that $p_R \geq \frac{1}{2}$. Since $p_C > p_R$, this implies $p_C > \frac{1}{2}$. But this means $p_C + p_R > 1$, which contradicts $p_C + p_R + p_I = 1$. □

C.3 OBSERVATION 7.1: $\hat{p} < \frac{1}{2}$

The Interrogator's innocent detainee recognition threshold $\hat{p}$ is less than one-half.

Given $a > r > c, \hat{p} = \frac{r-c}{r+a} < \frac{r}{2r} = \frac{1}{2}$.

C.4 PROPOSITION 7.1: $\hat{p} \lessapprox \frac{1}{2}$

As c approaches zero and a approaches r, the Interrogator's innocent detainee recognition threshold $\hat{p}$ approaches one-half from below.

Given $a > r > c$, for $a \to r$ and $c \to 0$, $\hat{p} = \frac{r-c}{r+a} \lessapprox \frac{r}{r+a} \lessapprox \frac{r}{2r} = \frac{1}{2}$.

C.5 PROPOSITION 7.2: $p^* < \frac{1}{2}$

If the Pragmatic Interrogator believes it more likely that the Detainee she faces is Cooperative than both of the other two types, then the innocent detainee recognition threshold p^* is less than one-half: If $p_C > p_I \geq p_R$ or if $p_C > p_R \geq p_I$, then $p^* < \frac{1}{2}$.

Proof
First, by Observation 7.1, $\hat{p} < \frac{1}{2}$. Note that $p^* < \hat{p}$ if and only if $\frac{r-c}{c+a}p_R < \frac{r-c}{r+a}$, which is equivalent to $p_R < \frac{a+c}{a+r} = w$. Since, by Observation C.1, $w > \frac{1}{2}$, and, by Observation C.2, $p_R < \frac{1}{2}$, we have $p_R < w$. Thus $p^* < \hat{p}$ and so by Observation 7.1, $p^* < \frac{1}{2}$. $\qquad\square$

C.6 PROPOSITION 7.3: $\hat{f} \geq \frac{1}{2}$

As c approaches zero and as a approaches r, the Interrogator's information hiding threshold $\hat{f}$ is greater than one-half.

Proof
Recall that $\hat{f} \equiv \frac{r-c}{u(r+a)}$. Note that $\frac{r-c}{u(r+a)} \geq \frac{1}{2}$ if and only if $\frac{2(r-c)}{u(r+a)} \geq 1$. Rearranging some terms gives us $2(r-c) \geq u(r+a)$. Solving for u, we have $u \leq \frac{2(r-c)}{r+a}$. Given $0 < c < r < a$, as assumed, for $c \to 0$ and $a \to r$, $u \leq \frac{2(r-c)}{r+a} \approx u \leq \frac{2r}{2r}$. This is equivalent to $u \leq 1$, which is true for $u \in (0, 1]$, as assumed. $\qquad\square$

C.7 OBSERVATION 7.2: $f^* \lesssim \frac{1}{2}$

The Detainee's version of the Interrogator's information hiding threshold f^* approaches one-half from below.

Since $f^* = \hat{p} = \frac{r-c}{r+a}$ and by Observation C.4 $\hat{p} \lesssim \frac{1}{2}$, it follows immediately that $f^* \lesssim \frac{1}{2}$.

C.8 OBSERVATION 7.3: $f^* \leq \hat{f}$

The Interrogator's and the Detainee's beliefs will "agree" on the information hiding threshold f only in the special case when the Interrogator has understood perfectly the information's value; all other cases open up the possibility for surprise torture.

By simple inspection of $f^* = \frac{r-c}{r+a}$ and $\hat{f} = \frac{r-c}{u(r+a)}$, it is clear that $f^* \leq \hat{f}$ for all $u \in (0, 1]$, as assumed, and that $\frac{r-c}{r+a} = \frac{r-c}{u(r+a)}$ if and only if $u = 1$.

C.9 PROPOSITION 7.4: $\tilde{f} \lesssim \frac{1}{2}$

As both p_I and c approach zero and as a approaches r, the Interrogator's information hiding threshold $\tilde{f}$ approaches one-half from below.

Proof
Recall that $\tilde{f} \equiv \frac{p_C(r-c) + p_I(-a-c)}{p_C(r+a)}$. Suppose $\tilde{f} \geq \frac{1}{2}$. This implies $2\left(\frac{p_C(r-c) + p_I(-a-c)}{p_C(r+a)}\right) \geq 1$. Simplifying yields $2p_Cr - 2p_Cc - 2p_Ia - 2p_Ic \geq p_Cr + p_Ca$. Rearrange some terms and we have $p_Cr - 2p_Cc - 2p_Ia - 2p_Ic \geq p_Ca$. Given $a > r$ as assumed, this is a contradiction, and so $\tilde{f} < \frac{1}{2}$. Given $0 < c < r < a$ as assumed, when $p_I \to 0, c \to 0$ and $a \to r$, $\frac{p_C(r-c) + p_I(-a-c)}{p_C(r+a)} \to \frac{p_C(r)}{p_C(2r)} = \frac{1}{2}$. □

C.10 PROPOSITION 7.5: FOR $p_i > 0$, $\tilde{f} < f^* \leq \hat{f}$

If there is a positive probability that the Detainee is Innocent, the Interrogator's information hiding threshold $\tilde{f}$ under leading questioning is less than the Detainee's version under objective questioning: For $p_I > 0, \tilde{f} < f^* \leq \hat{f}$.

Proof

Note first that by observation 7.3, $f^* \leq \hat{f}$. Recall the definitions $\tilde{f} \equiv \frac{p_C(r-c) + p_I(-a-c)}{p_C(r+a)}$ and $f^* \equiv \frac{r-c}{r+a}$. Note that $\tilde{f} < f^*$ if and only if $\frac{p_C(r-c) + p_I(-a-c)}{p_C(r+a)} < \frac{r-c}{r+a}$. Simplifying the right side of the inequality yields $\frac{p_C(r-c) + p_I(-a-c)}{p_C} < r-c$. Simplifying the left side gives us $p_C(r-c) + p_I(-a-c) < p_C(r-c)$. Rearrange some terms and we have $p_I(-a-c) < 0$, which is true for $p_I \in (0, 1]$ and $a, c > 0$. □

Preface

1. In truth the math really is not that hard, just some algebra and basic calculus in addition to the steps for solving the game. I know this because otherwise I would not have been able to do it. I am neither a game theorist nor a mathematician. This is probably also a good time to make it clear to any readers with training in game theory that the model makes no contribution to game theory. My goal is to say something about interrogational torture, and game theory is just a tool to that end. For more on the technical details associated with the model, see Appendices A to C.

Chapter 1

1. The following narrative of events is based on: McGirk, Calabresi, and Shannon (2002); Shane (2008); Risen (2006); Soufan (2011, 2009); Johnston (2006); Mayer (2008); Suskind (2006); Tenet and Harlow (2007); Rodriguez Jr and Harlow (2012); Thiessen (2010); Rizzo (2014); Grey (2006); McDermott and Meyer (2012); United States Senate (2014a).

2. According to one report, he occupied his days "masturbating like a monkey in the zoo. ... He didn't care that they were watching him" (Mayer 2008, p. 175). It is unclear, however, whether this type of behavior predated, or was the consequence of, his confinement. Former Bush speech writer Marc Thiessen interprets Zubaydah's masturbation as "resistance" to interrogation, providing a new rationale for adolescent boys everywhere (Thiessen 2010, p. 87).

3. Zubaydah's own account to the International Committee of the Red Cross largely corroborates these accounts (International Committee of the Red Cross 2007, pp. 29–32).

4. And still does in modern French. *La Question* is the simple title of Henri Alleg's memoir of the torture he suffered at the hands of French paratroopers in Algeria (Alleg, Calder, and Sartre 2006).

5. See http://en.wikipedia.org/wiki/Genghis_Khan.

6. Respondents were placed into these groups based on how they responded to questions on whether harsh interrogation methods are effective and whether they are

justified. A methodology statement with question wording is available at http://publicmind.fdu.edu/2011/torture/.

7.   Available at http://www.huffingtonpost.com/2012/12/14/torture-poll-2012_n_2301492.html.

8.   Available at http://www.huffingtonpost.com/2014/12/12/torture-report-poll_n_6316126.html.

9.   See, for example, the exchange surrounding my article in the March 2012 issue of *Political Research Quarterly*.

10.   I fully recognize that formal logic and mathematics are themselves preeminent vehicles for making many people's eyes glaze over and dream longingly of cleaning underneath the refrigerator, but bear with me for a bit.

11.   You can see the scene here: http://www.youtube.com/watch?v=CemLiSI5ox8. Whatever the other merits of the film, this is a terrible attempt at game theory. First, there are only four brunettes and five guys. Second, it never considers the preferences of the women and thus the likelihood of success with the blonde or any of the brunettes. This is not just sexist, but also ignores a pretty important part of the strategic dynamic. Finally, Hollywood actually gets the solution wrong! Nash himself would never have proposed this solution, and we will see why in a moment.

12.   *Law and Order SVU* aficionados, however, will notice that I am faithful to the basic storyline and even much of the actual dialog of the original episode; only the jail sentences are contrived.

13.   Technically speaking, it's a Nash equilibrium, named after the same John Nash of *A Beautiful Mind*.

14.   Though it may have been a game attempt at convincing his friends in order to provide an opening for himself, as one friend seems to suspect: "Nash, if this is some way for you to get the blonde on your own, you can go to hell."

15.   You can see the painting of waterboarding at http://en.wikipedia.org/wiki/Vann_Nath.

16.   See http://www.thisweekinpalestine.com/details.php?catid=20&id=2761&edid=168. *Shabeh* (also writteen *shabach*) is a favorite stress position torture of the Israeli security forces.

17.   "FACTBOX—New US consumer financial bureau has wide powers," Reuters, September 14, 2010. Available at http://blogs.reuters.com/financial-regulatory-forum/2010/09/14/factbox-new-us-consumer-financial-bureau-has-wide-powers/. Accessed June 29, 2012.

18.   See http://www.consumerfinance.gov/credit-cards/credit-card-act/feb2011-factsheet/.

CHAPTER 2

1.   The following quotes liberally from Wallach (2006, pp. 482–484).

2.   The following narrative of events is based on Coffman's testimony from the trial transcript in the author's possession (Coffman 1983, pp. 202–247). I am grateful to Dinah Olaniyan, Dennis Dimsey, and Scott Woodward for their assistance obtaining the relevant transcripts from this case.

3.   A "trusty" was an inmate the prison staff used to perform menial tasks and, in an earlier time, control and administer punishments to other prisoners. Although

outlawed by the 1970s, the system persisted in Texas for another decade. See http://en.wikipedia.org/wiki/Trusty_system.

4. The following narrative of events is based on Hicks's testimony from the trial transcript in the author's possession (Hicks 1983, pp. 9–91).

5. So obvious it hits you between the eyes.

6. See http://gawker.com/5866267/this-is-what-a-cia-black-site-looks-like.

7. Huffington Post/YouGov, December 10–11, 2014. Poll results available here: http://www.huffingtonpost.com/2014/12/12/torture-report-poll_n_6316126. html. Methodology statement available here: http://data.huffingtonpost.com/ yougov/methodology.

8. See http://www.cbsnews.com/news/torture-and-reaction-to-the-senate-intelligence-report/.

9. See http://faculty.cua.edu/pennington/PenningtonTortureEssay.htm.

10. Let's bracket for the moment how on earth such scales might be constructed.

11. The burden on torture proponents is higher; presumably we would not support interrogational torture if it is just a coin flip whether it works or not.

12. I'm grateful to Ken Benoit for clarifying this point.

13. Knowing contextual information about the detainee, such as rank and role in Al Qaeda, will help with, but not solve, this problem.

14. ABC News/Washington Post, December 16, 2014, http://www.washingtonpost. com/world/national-security/new-poll-finds-majority-of-americans-believe-torture-justified-after-911-attacks/2014/12/16/f6ee1208-847c-11e4-9534-f79a23c40e6c_story.html; CBS News, December 11–14, 2014, http://www. cbsnews.com/news/torture-and-reaction-to-the-senate-intelligence-report/; Pew Research Center, December 11–14, 2014, http://www.people-press.org/ 2014/12/15/about-half-see-cia-interrogation-methods-as-justified/; Huffington Post/YouGov, December 10–11, 2014, http://www.huffingtonpost.com/ 2014/12/12/torture-report-poll_n_6316126.html.

CHAPTER 3

1. Swiftian, but not entirely unrealistic: http://dcmo.defense.gov/about/ mission-and-vision.html. Over the top, but not by much: Jose Rodriquez, the former head of the program, refers to "sharing best practices with other intelligence collectors" (Rodriquez Jr and Harlow 2012, p. 147). A February 2003 CIA memo on the program stated that "resources are critical to the success of the Program's ability to meet identified customer requirements," supported "oversight of all activities to ensure quality control," and predicted "increased demand for more HVT program services" (Central Intelligence Agency 2003a, p. 13).

2. For some on the academic left, it also makes me somehow complicit in aiding and abetting torture. For a rebuttal to this view employing a "discourse" of reason, logic, and empirical evidence see Schiemann (2012b).

3. I am grateful to an anonymous reviewer for suggesting that I clarify this point and for suggestions about the tone elsewhere in the book.

4. Bentham's own views changed over the years and were somewhat contradictory. See Davies (2012), who examines Bentham's unpublished writings on torture.

5. This is not the place to explore them, but there are other utilitarian arguments for torture (e.g., Allhoff 2006 and Kershnar 2010) as well as utilitarian arguments against torture (e.g., Arrigo 2004, Brecher 2007, Bufacchi and Arrigo 2006, and Morgan 2000).

6. This contradicts their claim that torture is effective. Moreover, the mathematical expression they chose (but did not justify) for the threshold does not work in the way they apparently believe. If there is no chance the person with the information is the actual wrongdoer, the threshold equals zero. If there is no chance that any other alternatives to torture will work, which is the entire reason why they argue that torture is needed, the threshold is actually undefined (there is a zero in the denominator).

7. Dershowitz is very defensive about being labeled a proponent of torture, since his goal is to minimize the practice, but the fact of the matter is that his "conditional normative position" would enshrine it in law and it is not a mischaracterization of his position to say so (Dershowitz 2003, p. 277).

8. Posner also argues that "sleep deprivation, close confinement in chilly or dirty cells, bright lights (the old 'third degree'), shouting, threats, truth serums, and lies" could fall below torture and be "merely coercive" (Posner 2004, p. 292).

9. If the FISA courts and the courts nominally supervising the NSA phone and internet surveillance programs are any indication, and I think they are, Posner may well be right.

10. It seems to me that Krauthammer is to be applauded here for avoiding euphemisms such as "enhanced interrogations." Krauthammer is advocating inhumane treatment and doesn't shrink from it. As he puts it, "moral honesty is essential."

11. On CIA association with torture in Latin America see Karl (2011), McCoy (2006, Chapter 3), Otterman (2007, Chapters 5–6), and Quigley (2011). On renditions pre-9/11 see Mayer (2008, Chapter 6, pp. 101–138).

12. See Central Intelligence Agency (2003d).

13. See Levin (2004), Bradbury (2005a), Bradbury (2005b), and Bradbury (2005c).

14. The memo did not rule out other techniques; and, as we will see, other documents show other techniques were included in the Standard list.

15. Other techniques were also possible, subject to "specific approval" (Central Intelligence Agency 2003c, p. 2).

16. A later memo on waterboarding expanded this responsibility so that "[a]ny member of the interrogation team"—not just the medical officer—"has the obligation to voice concern, and if necessary to halt" waterboarding "in the event a detainee were to be perceived as unable to withstand the affects [sic] of the waterboard for any reason" (Central Intelligence Agency 2005, p. 3).

17. The draft guidelines dated September 2003 are reproduced as Appendix F in Central Intelligence Agency (2004c, pp. 147–158). The September 2003 and December 2004 guidelines differ somewhat. Partly this appears to be due to rewriting and different redaction decisions, but there also appear to be some shifts in policy. In general, the 2003 version is harsher, with diapering and a standard sleep deprivation length of 72 hours as opposed to 48 hours in 2003. In 2004, water dousing is listed among the enhanced techniques whereas it is a standard technique in 2003.

18. See also Central Intelligence Agency (2004a, pp. 2–3).

19.   This is evident in other CIA documents as well. "Sleep deprivation will end sooner if the medical or psychologist observer finds contraindications to continued sleep deprivation" (Central Intelligence Agency 2004a, pp. 14–16). "Any member of the interrogation team has the obligation to voice concern, and if necessary to halt" waterboarding "in the event a detainee were to be perceived as unable to withstand the affects [sic] of the waterboard for any reason" (Central Intelligence Agency 2005, p. 3).

20.   Other category II techniques were similar to the CIA torture program: isolation, light and sound deprivation, food manipulation, forced nakedness, forced grooming (e.g., forced shaving), and manipulation of phobias such as the use of dogs.

21.   At least in the United States. Some of them may be subject to arrest if they travel abroad.

22.   Yoo is now a law professor at the University of California, Berkeley and Bybee is a federal judge.

23.   The "additional techniques" were isolation, prolonged interrogations (e.g., 20 hours per day), prolonged standing, sleep deprivation, physical training, face slap/stomach slap, removal of clothing, and inducing anxiety via aversions (e.g., dogs) (Danner 2004, pp. 191–192). Not all of these were actually employed.

24.   For a more technical treatment of this ratio idea and interrogational torture as an "epistemic system," see Koppl (2005, pp. 91, 94). See Rumney (2006, p. 481) for an empirical approach to reliability. For the reasons stated in the Chapter 2, the empirical approach to this question seems, to me, a dead end.

Chapter 4

1.   At the risk of being overly repetitive, if we had empirical data, we could assess how torture actually *does* work and compare those findings to our benchmarks.

2.   This chapter and much of those that follow will read as perhaps even more cold and calculating. The logic of torture advocated by proponents is a brutal one, and we will reproduce that logic to assess whether it works as they claim.

3.   One of my regrets concerning the article that launched this project was not having the space to explain fully the subtitle: "How Good Guys Get Bad Information with Ugly Methods." I meant "guys" in the colloquial, "we're all on the same team" sense, not in the strictly gender-identification sense. It is very clear from CIA documents, memoirs, and detainee testimonials that key analysts, debriefers, interrogators, and rendition "ninja" team members were female. I'll also continue to capitalize Interrogator and Detainee to refer to players in the game as opposed to interrogators or detainees generally.

4.   Two points are in order here. First, a sequential move game is equivalent to a simultaneous move game if players are ignorant of the other player's choice. If you've moved before me but I have no idea what you've done, then it's the same thing as if we choose at the same moment. This is another difference from the original *Law and Order SVU* episode in which Deborah thought that Carlo had already moved, making it sequential, not simultaneous. Second, in the case of the Prisoners' Dilemma, the sequence does not matter anyway, since "rat out" is a dominant

strategy for both players: Each is better off choosing it no matter what the other player does. As we'll see, in truly sequential games without a dominant strategy, the timing of moves can make a big difference.

5. In the original article I used the terms "weak" and "strong" respectively for these detainee types. Although I was simply following language used by writers on torture from the ancients forward and not making value judgments, I now consider it a mistake, regret it, and thus will use the more descriptive terms "Cooperative" and "Resistant" in this book.

6. I should make a quick note of caution here. It just so happens that both players receive a payoff of two in this outcome, but this is purely coincidental and has no bearing on solving the game. Their payoffs are completely independent.

7. The technical definition of a subgame is a part of the original game such that the complete history of the game to that point is *common knowledge* (both players know it, each knows the other knows it, each knows that the other knows that they know it, and so on). In our example, the two nodes where the Interrogator moves (after "information" and after "no information") are subgames, as is the entire game.

8. You may have noticed that, to keep things moving, we did not check to see whether the other two possible strategy profiles—{"information", ("no torture","no torture")} and {"no information", ("torture","no torture")}—constitute Nash equilibria. You can check for yourself, but I can also save you the trouble and tell you that they are are not.

9. See http://www.huffingtonpost.com/2014/03/28/jeremiah-denton-dead-dies_n_5050132.html

10. This is not mere speculation; according to two former CIA officials, it actually happened at the secret CIA prison in Poland. A CIA debriefer told KSM that she knew everything about him and that he shouldn't lie to her. KSM's response? He leaned back in his chair and replied, "Then why are you here?" (Goldman 2013).

CHAPTER 5

1. These player types correspond closely to the player types in Wantchekon and Healy (1999).

2. I thank former military interrogator Matthew Alexander for pointing this out to me.

3. Technically, it transforms the game from one of incomplete information to one of imperfect information.

4. For the exceedingly nerdy, some more game theory jargon: Decision nodes connected by a dashed line are *information sets*—that is, a set of nodes at which a player has identical moves and does not know at which of these nodes she is moving. See Gibbons (1992, pp. 119–120).

5. Unfortunately for the innocent, however, a strict adherence to this rule meant there was no way to end their torment by falsely confessing. Roth (1964, pp. 99–104) relates the awful suffering of Elvira del Campo in 16th-century Toledo, who begged her torturers to tell her to what she should confess.

6. If you are risk-seeking, you would actually be willing to pay more, whereas if you are risk-averse, you would be willing to play only if you paid even less than $5.50.

7. Since the weights are equal in this case, .5 and .5, it's actually a regular average. We want to leave open the possibility, however, that the probabilities and thus the weights will be different, resulting in a weighted average.

8. In order to keep the notation as simple as possible, I have not indexed v and k for the Cooperative and Resistant types. This will not be a problem since the Resistant type always plays "no information" and so the thresholds involving v and k are always those of the Cooperative type. See Appendix A.

9. If you don't have a kid in middle or high school and thus haven't been forced recently to go back over algebra, we can multiply both sides of the inequality by -1 and change the direction of the inequality, and the relationship remains the same without the negatives.

10. The quote is taken from Hayek's Nobel Prize in economics acceptance speech, December 11, 1974, available at http://www.nobelprize.org/nobel_prizes/economic-sciences/laureates/1974/hayek-lecture.html.

11. It is well known, for example, that many torturers suffer psychological trauma as the result of their activities (Atkinson 2007; Fanon 1963, pp. 264–270; Rejali 2007, pp. 524–526).

12. Recall too that there are two versions of the game, one assuming leading questioning and one assuming objective questioning.

13. Note that this does not change the Pragmatic Interrogator's information set. Although her payoffs are the same as those of the "no information" information set ($-c$ after torture and $-r$ after no torture), she knows she is receiving some type of information from a Cooperative Detainee. She must, however, decide whether or not to torture prior to fully understanding the information's value. I am grateful to Livio Di Lonardo for forcing me to clarify this point.

Chapter 6

1. For the non-card players: Diamonds and hearts are red, clubs and spades are black.

2. Speaking loosely, a PBE is an equilibrium in which beliefs and strategies are in a sort of harmony: The beliefs are consistent with the strategies in that equilibrium and the strategies are optimal, given player beliefs. For a clear introduction and step-by-step example, see Gates and Humes (1997, pp. 113–139); for a more technical but still accessible statement, see Gibbons (1992, pp. 175–183). For a fascinating look at the origins and real-world practical uses of Bayes' Rule, see McGrayne (2011).

3. In the RIT game, the Detainee never observes a move by the Interrogator and thus calculates his expected utility in the normal way.

4. The other three are: (*no info, info, info*), (*info, info, no info*), (*no info, info, no info*).

5. A pure strategy is a strategy a player plays with probability 1. There are also *mixed strategies*, probabilistic combinations of pure strategies such as ($\frac{1}{3}$ *torture*, $\frac{2}{3}$ *don't torture*). If you've played rock–paper–scissors and kept your opponent guessing by mixing up which one you threw, then you've played a mixed strategy before. To keep things more realistic and tractable, we will solve for only pure strategy equilibria.

6. We only care about the actions of the Pragmatic Interrogator because that type matches up with the pragmatic model. Again, we need a Sadistic Interrogator in

the game because it affects the Detainee's behavior (as we will see shortly), but we want to examine the actions of the Pragmatic type.

7. Another way to think about this is that the other two branches are weighted with zero probability, making everything zero, so you'd just be putting in 0s for the Resistant and Innocent terms in the addition part of your expected value equation.

8. Note the similarity to real-life interrogations: Resistant and Innocent Detainees are observationally equivalent to Interrogators in terms of the information they (fail to) provide.

9. Your updated beliefs are known in Bayesian terminology as "posteriors."

10. Actually u cannot be zero, since by assumption u is strictly greater than zero but less than or equal to one, that is, $u \in (0, 1]$. The reason for this is that if $u = 0$, that is equivalent to "no information," which is covered by the other move. But you get the idea that as u approaches zero, the value of the information also goes down.

11. We explore the implications of this relationship in more detail in Chapter 7.

12. Or almost all of them. There is an additional step necessary for assessing the plausibility of equilibria in which all three Detainee types play "no information": specifying beliefs off the equilibrium path. The basic idea of calculating expected utility is the same, but going over that here without an example would take us too far astray. See Gibbons (1992, pp. 175–183).

Chapter 7

1. In a formal mathematical proof, a proposition might be a theorem, if it is important, or a lemma, if it is an intermediate step to proving a theorem but of little intrinsic interest. Both because the math employed here is so straightforward and because I sometimes rely on empirical assumptions, I stick to the more modest "proposition." For more on these terms see Moore and Siegel (2013, p. 22).

2. Recall from Chapter 6 that f^* is the Detainee's version of $\hat{f}$. The threshold $\tilde{f}$ has the same function as $\hat{f}$ under leading questioning. We also derived the Innocent Detainee recognition threshold p^* in the last chapter; $\hat{p} = \frac{r-c}{r+a}$ is the version of the Innocent Detainee recognition threshold in the *no information, torture equilibrium*. See Appendix A.

3. Nerdily: $f^* \leq \hat{f}$ for all $u, u \in (0, 1]$.

4. This is called a proof by contradiction.

5. Keep in mind that we are speaking about the prior probability f and not one of the f thresholds.

Chapter 8

1. Since the Sadistic Interrogator always plays torture and we are only interested in the actions of the Pragmatic Interrogator, we can ignore her behavior from now on.

2. This does not mean that there will be less torture overall, however; it simply means that the dark-gray region narrows toward $\hat{f}$. The space to the left of that region continues to be covered by torture of Innocent and Resistant Detainees.

3. Available at http://opinionator.blogs.nytimes.com/2014/03/25/the-certainty-of-donald-rumsfeld-part-1/?_php=true&_type=blogs&_r=0.

4. The following account is based primarily on Cassidy's memoir (Cassidy 1977), but see also Ensalaco (2011, pp. 78–81) as well as Cassidy's testimony before the International Commission of Inquiry in to the Crimes of the Military Junta in Chile, Helsinki, March 28th–29th, 1976, available at http://www.blest.eu/biblio/arrests/cap4.html.

5. This passage is also startlingly clear evidence of strategically rational thinking, despite just having been subjected to electrical shocks.

6. Later on, DINA officers spoke to some nuns at the convent and the nuns denied any fugitives having been in the house. When Cassidy protested they were lying, the DINA officer said to her: "But a nun would not lie, *doctora*" (Cassidy 1977, p. 191).

Chapter 9

1. Presumably there would be other costs to unwitting confirmation by an innocent detainee, if that confirmation leads the interrogator to believe the detainee possesses valuable information and pressures him into revealing other information which is false or misleading.

2. The following draws on Jehl (2005a), Priest (2004), Jehl (2005b), Isikoff and Hosenball (2005), Gardham (2009), Human Rights Watch (2012), Isikoff and Corn (2007), United States Senate (2006), and Human Rights Watch (2012).

3. Abu Zubaydah was its external emir. The camp appears not to have been directly under bin Laden's control, but it trained fighters for jihadist causes.

4. Moussaoui, arrested in August 2001, was alleged to have been a possible back-up in the 9/11 attacks and received a life sentence. Reid is an Australian citizen who tried and failed to set off explosives hidden in the heel of his shoe mid-flight from Paris to Miami on December 20, 2001.

5. The officer left the CIA after the reprimand but was rehired as a contractor. See History Commons, available at http://www.historycommons.org/entity.jsp?entity=_albert__1 as well as United States Senate (2014a, pp. 94–96, 450).

6. See http://www.historycommons.org/searchResults.jsp?searchtext=Ibn+al-Shaykh+al-Libi&events=on&entities=on&articles=on&topics=on&timelines=on&projects=on&titles=on&descriptions=on&dosearch=on&search=Go.

Chapter 10

1. We can see this in another way. Recall that the Interrogator will torture when the probability the Detainee is Innocent after "no information" is below p^*, or $p_I < \frac{r-c}{c+a} p_R$. A little algebraic manipulation tells us another way of saying this, namely that the Interrogator will torture when the odds of an Innocent to a Resistant Detainee, $\frac{p_I}{p_R}$, are below $\frac{r-c}{c+a}$. We have been assuming that c approaches 0 and a approaches r. If so, then the right side $\frac{r-c}{c+a}$ approaches 1. Thus the condition $\frac{p_I}{p_R} < \frac{r-c}{c+a}$ is met as long as $p_I < p_R$, as we have also been assuming. $p_I > p_R$ would violate this condition and the Interrogator would switch to "no torture" because it is sufficiently likely that "no information" came from an Innocent Detainee.

2. The following account draws on Ackerman (2011), Carle (2011), Horton (2011a), Horton (2011b), Leopold (2011), and Suskind (2006). You may notice that the Canadian Intelligence Service report document comes from a group dedicated to

exonerating a Canadian suspected of ties to terrorism, Mohamed Harkat, and could therefore reasonably be seen as suspect. I cross checked this document with references in Canadian court documents, which make it clear that this document was made available to Mr. Harkat during legal proceedings and so is authentic. See, for example, Federal Court of Canada (2010, p. 279, §65).

3. The postscript to the Dubai part of this story is that the CIA then kidnapped off the street two employees of Wazir's bank in Karachi on their way home from work. When they declined a CIA offer to cooperate with them, the two were also rendered to a black site. The following morning two CIA operatives opened the bank, pretending to be distant cousins filling in while the proprietors were away.

4. The following draws on Landgericht Frankfurt am Main (2003), Landgericht Frankfurt am Main (2005), European Court of Human Rights (2010), Dahlkamp et al. (2004). I gleaned some additional, incidental, details from the German TV documentary, "Jakob von Metzler—Tod eines Bankiersohns," Philipp Engel, *Die großen Kriminalfälle*, Season 7, Episode 1, December 1, 2008. Available at: http://www.youtube.com/watch?v=NlSEQCx2JiI. For the debate about torture this stirred in Germany, see Beestermöller and Brunkhorst (2006).

5. At the time, *Zivildienst* was an alternative to military conscription for conscientious objectors.

6. German court documents identify some tangentially involved people by the first letter of their last name only.

7. It turned out later that this person was a martial arts instructor for the police.

8. Neither Daschner nor Ennigkeit denies ordering and making these threats. Gäfgen later claimed that Ennigkeit "further threatened to lock him in a cell with two huge black men who would sexually abuse him. The officer also hit him several times on the chest with his hand and shook him so that, on one occasion, his head hit the wall" (European Court of Human Rights 2010, p. 4). No courts have substantiated Gäfgen's claims.

Chapter 11

1. It is also worth recalling from Chapter 8 that there is still surprise torture to the right of f^* under objective questioning.

2. The following narrative relies on El-Masri (2005), European Court of Human Rights (2006), Meek (2005), Grey (2006), Priest (2005).

3. The case of Algerian Laid Saidi was perhaps even worse. Saidi was picked up on the basis of a telephone recording in which he was overheard to speak cryptically about "airplanes." He was renditioned the usual CIA way to "the dark prison," another prison in Afghanistan, where he was chained naked in stress positions, was subjected to loud music in almost total darkness, and had cold water thrown on him. Eventually his interrogators played the tape for him. It turns out that he was discussing "tires" and not "planes." The analyst misunderstood the plural "at-tirat" for "tayarat". See http://www.nytimes.com/2006/07/07/world/africa/07algeria. html?ei=5090&en=17b76be0aba70618&ex=1309924800&partner=rssuserland& emc=rss&pagewanted=all&_r=0.

4. The following narrative relies on Alleg's memoirs (Alleg, Calder, and Sartre 2006; Alleg 2012). For background context on the civil war in Algeria and the role of

French torture, see Aussaresses (2004), Branche (2007), Branche (2001), Evans (2011), Horne (1977), Morgan (2007), Rejali (2007, 480ff).

5. For the U.S. diplomatic threats see the series of cables on Wikileaks summarizing the back and forth with German authorities, https://search.wikileaks. org/plusd/cables/07BERLIN200_a.html, https://wikileaks.org/plusd/cables/ 07BERLIN230_a.html, https://wikileaks.org/plusd/cables/07BERLIN242_a. html, https://wikileaks.org/plusd/cables/07BERLIN730_a.html.

CHAPTER 13

1. The vapors above liquid gasoline are actually what burn, not the liquid itself. The trouble is that there is usually a lot of vapor where there is liquid gasoline.

2. The transcript is available at http://www.mccain.senate.gov/public/index.cfm/ 2014/12/floor-statement-by-sen-mccain-on-senate-intelligence-committee-report-on-cia-interrogation-methods.

3. Data from the U.S. Centers for Disease Control and Prevention WISQARS database. Available at http://webappa.cdc.gov/cgi-bin/broker.exe.

4. See http://www.wfp.org/hunger/stats.

5. In a subsequent work, Clarke and Primo (2012) alter their typology somewhat. Although I do draw on this later work, I find the first typology more helpful for my purposes.

POSTSCRIPT

1. The Forward, Findings, and Summary each have their own numbering within the combined pdf. All page references below are pdf pages, not the original document pages.

2. The only exceptions are some details in the narrative of Abu Zubaydah at the beginning of Chapter 1 and a few other scattered references.

3. The report explains why this is a conservative estimate and that the CIA itself admits it is still unsure just how many detainees were in the program (Central Intelligence Agency 2014, p. 75).

4. For this, and several other reactions by physicians to the CIA method, see https:// s3.amazonaws.com/PHR_other/fact-sheet-rectal-hydration-and-rectal-feeding. pdf.

5. Although the CIA argues in its June 2013 response that the Senate report "overstates the number of instances" in several ways (Central Intelligence Agency 2014, pp. 81–82), the Senate report rejects these claims, showing that it used very conservative counting rules for such instances (United States Senate 2014a, pp. 127–129).

6. There is some irony here. Zarqawi was later located and killed by U.S. forces using noncoercive interrogation techniques on sources in Iraq. See Alexander and Bruning (2008).

7. This contrasts sharply with Thiessen's torture apologia, in which he explicitly distances the CIA's waterboarding technique from "true torture" partly on the basis that the distention and stomach-pressing was not part of the CIA program (Thiessen 2010, p. 131ff).

8. This, however, contradicts other official CIA claims as well as apologists of the program such as Bush speech writer Marc Thiessen that waterboarding *always* worked (Thiessen 2010, p. 102). To be fair, Thiessen may well have been misled by his CIA informants.

9. The HRW report, "Delivered into Enemy Hands," is available at http://www.hrw.org/reports/2012/09/05/delivered-enemy-hands.

10. Statistically: $z = .56$, $p = .289$, one-tailed test.

11. Once again the Republican response counts an innocent detainee's response to the lesser torture methods against the effectiveness of those methods. Despite the fact that the CIA itself admits that Haji Ghalgi was only used as " 'useful leverage' against a family member" (United States Senate 2014*a*, p. 42), the Republican response includes him in the list of "deceptive detainees" who were subjected to the "noncoercive" methods (United States Senate 2014*b*, p. 57).

12. The Republican response moved the goalposts right in front of the ball and very far from the original justification for the program, defining "performance metrics" including, among others, "improved information sharing" (United States Senate 2014*b*, p. 59).

REFERENCES

Ackerman, Spencer. 2011. "Some Will Call Me a Torturer: CIA Man Reveals Secret Jail." *wired.com*, July 1, 2011. Available at http://www.wired.com/2011/07/am-i-a-torturer/all/1.

Alabama State Legislature. 1881. "Testimony Taken by the Joint Special Committee of the Session of 1880–81 to Inquire into the Condition and Treatment of Convicts of the State." In the author's possession.

Alexander, M. and J.R. Bruning. 2008. *How to Break a Terrorist: The US Interrogators Who Used Brains, not Brutality, to Take Down the Deadliest Man in Iraq*. New York: Free Press.

Alexander, Matthew. 2011. *Kill or Capture: How a Special Operations Task Force Took Down a Notorious Al Qaeda Terrorist*. New York: St. Martin's Press.

Alleg, Henri, J. Calder, and J.P. Sartre. 2006. *The Question*. Lincoln, NE: Bison Books.

Alleg, Henri. 1960. *La Question*. Paris: Les Éditions de Minuit.

Alleg, Henri, trans. Gila Walker. 2012. *The Algerian Memoirs: Days of Hope and Combat*. New York: Seagull Books.

Allhoff, Fritz. 2006. "A Defense of Torture: Separation of Cases, Ticking Time-Bombs, and Moral Justification." *International Journal of Applied Philosophy* 19(2):243–264.

Aristotle. 350. *On Rhetoric*. Available at http://classics.mit.edu/Aristotle/rhetoric.html. Accessed on June 30, 2012.

Arrigo, Jean Maria. 2004. "A Utilitarian Argument Against Torture Interrogation of Terrorists." *Science and Engineering Ethics* 10(3):543–572.

Atkinson, Keith. 2007. "The Torturer's Tale." In *The Phenomenon of Torture: Readings and Commentary*, ed. William F. Schulz. Philadelphia: University of Pennsylvania Press, pp. 104–109.

Augustine, Saint. 1984. *Concerning the City of God against the Pagans*. New York: Penguin.

Aussaresses, Paul. 2004. *The Battle of the Casbah: Terrorism and Counterterrorism in Algeria 1955–1957*. New York: Enigma Books.

Bagaric, Mirko and Julie Clarke. 2007. *Torture: When the Unthinkable Is Morally Permissible*. Albany State University of New York Press.

Beccaria, Cesare. 1872. *An Essay on Crimes and Punishments*. Albany, NY: W.O. Little and Co.

Beestermöller, Gerhard and Hauke Brunkhorst. 2006. *Rückkehr der Folter: der Rechtsstaat im Zwielicht?* München: C.H. Beck.

Bentham, Jeremy, F.C. Montague ed. 1891. *A Fragment on Government.* London: Oxford University Press.

Boal, Mark. 2011. "Zero Dark Thirty." Script, Sony Pictures. Available at http://flash. sonypictures.com/shared/movies/zerodarkthirty/zdt_script.pdf.

Bowden, Mark. 2003. "The Dark Art of Interrogation." *The Atlantic Monthly* 292(3):51–76.

Bradbury, Steven G. 2005a. "Memorandum for John A. Rizzo, Senior Deputy General Counsel of the Central Intelligence Agency. Application of 18 U.S.C. §§2340–2340A to Certain Techniques that May Be Used in the Interrogation of a High Value al Qaeda Detainee." May 10, Washington D.C.: Office of Legal Counsel, Department of Justice.

Bradbury, Steven G. 2005b. "Memorandum for John A. Rizzo, Senior Deputy General Counsel of the Central Intelligence Agency. Application of 18 U.S.C. §§2340–2340A to the Combined Use of Certain Techniques in the Interrogation of High Value al Qaeda Detainees." May 10, Washington D.C.: Office of Legal Counsel, Department of Justice.

Bradbury, Steven G. 2005c. "Memorandum for John A. Rizzo, Senior Deputy General Counsel of the Central Intelligence Agency. Application of United States Obligations Under Article 16 of the Convention Against Torture to Certain Techniques that May Be Used in the Interrogation of High Value al Qaeda Detainees." May 30, Washington D.C.: Office of Legal Counsel, Department of Justice.

Brady, H.E. 2004. "Introduction." *Perspectives on Politics* 2(02):295–300.

Branche, Raphaëlle. 2001. *La Torture et l'armee pendant la guerre d'Algérie, 1954–1962.* Paris: Gallimard.

Branche, Raphaëlle. 2007. "Torture of Terrorists? Use of Torture in a 'War Against Terrorism:' Justifications, Methods and Effects: The Case of France in Algeria, 1954– 1962." *International Review of the Red Cross* 89(3):543–560.

Brecher, Bob. 2007. *Torture and the Ticking Bomb.* Malden, MA: Wiley-Blackwell.

Bufacchi, Vittorio and Jean Arrigo. 2006. "Torture, Terrorism and the State: A Refutation of the Ticking-Bomb Argument." *Journal of Applied Philosophy* 23(3):355–373.

Bush, George W. 2011. *Decision Points.* New York: Random House.

Bybee, Jay S. 2002. "Memorandum for John Rizzo, Acting General Counsel of the Central Intelligence Agency. Interrogation of al Qaeda Operative." August 1, Washington D.C.: Office of Legal Counsel, Department of Justice.

Canadian Security Intelligence Service. 2009. "Summary of the Security Intelligence Report in relation to Mohamed HARKAT." Ottawa: Canadian Security Intelligence Service, February 6, 2009. Available at: http://www.justiceforharkat.com/download. php?view.197.

Carle, Glenn. 2011. *The Interrogator: An Education.* New York: Nation Books.

Cassidy, Sheila. 1977. *Audacity to Believe.* New York: HarperCollins.

Central Intelligence Agency. 1983. "Human Resource Exploitation Training Manual." Washington D.C.: Central Intelligence Agency. Available at http://www.gwu.edu/~ nsarchiv/NSAEBB/NSAEBB27/02-01.htm.

Central Intelligence Agency. 2003a. "CIA Memo re: Enhanced Interrogation Program, February 25, 2003." Washington D.C.: Central Intelligence Agency. Available at:

ACLU, The Torture Database, ACLU-RDI 4612, http://www.thetorturedatabase. org/files/foia_subsite/pdfs/CIA000507.pdf.

Central Intelligence Agency. 2003b. "Guidelines on Confinement Conditions for CIA Detainees, January 28, 2003." Washington D.C.: Central Intelligence Agency. Available at ACLU, The Torture Database, ACLU-RDI 4561, http://www. thetorturedatabase.org/files/foia_subsite/pdfs/DOJOLC001040.pdf.

Central Intelligence Agency. 2003c. "Guidelines on Interrogations Conducted Pursuant to the [redacted], January 28, 2003." Washington D.C.: Central Intelligence Agency. Available at: ACLU, The Torture Database, ACLU-RDI 4562, http://www. thetorturedatabase.org/files/foia_subsite/pdfs/CIA000559.pdf.

Central Intelligence Agency. 2003d. "Psychological Assessment of Zain al-Abedin al-Abideen Muhammad Hassan, a.k.a. Abu Zubaydah." Washington D.C.: Central Intelligence Agency. Available at: http://www.aclu.org/files/torturefoia/released/ 082409/cia_ig/oig39.pdf.

Central Intelligence Agency. 2004a. "Background Paper on CIA's Combined Use of Interrogation Techniques, December 30, 2004." Washington D.C.: Central Intelligence Agency. Available at CIA-OIG, ACLU, The Torture Database, ACLU-RDI 4586, http://www.thetorturedatabase.org/files/foia_subsite/pdfs/DOJOLC001126.pdf.

Central Intelligence Agency. 2004b. "OMS Guidelines on Medical and Psychological Support to Detainee Rendition, Interrogation, and Detention, December 1, 2004." Washington D.C.: Central Intelligence Agency. Available at ACLU, The Torture Database, ACLU-RDI 4587, http://www.thetorturedatabase.org/files/foia_subsite/ pdfs/DOJOLC001145.pdf.

Central Intelligence Agency. 2004c. "Special Review: Counterterrorism Detention and Interrogation Activities (Office of the Inspector General, CIA), May 7, 2004." Washington D.C.: Central Intelligence Agency Office of Inspector General. Available at ACLU, The Torture Database, CIA-OIG, ACLU-RDI 4611, http://www. thetorturedatabase.org/files/foia_subsite/pdfs/CIA000349.pdf.

Central Intelligence Agency. 2004d. "Waterboarding Guidelines, August 5, 2004." Washington D.C.: Central Intelligence Agency. Available at ACLU, The Torture Database, ACLU-RDI 4579, http://www.thetorturedatabase.org/files/foia_subsite/pdfs/ DOJOLC001095.pdf.

Central Intelligence Agency. 2005. "Horizontal Sleep Deprivation, April 22, 2005." Washington D.C.: Central Intelligence Agency. Available at ACLU, The Torture Database, ACLU-RDI 4588, http://www.thetorturedatabase.org/files/foia_subsite/ pdfs/DOJOLC001180.pdf.

Central Intelligence Agency. 2014. "CIA Comments on the Select Committee on Intelligence Report on the Rendition, Detention, and Interrogation Program." Washington D.C.: Central Intelligence Agency. Director of Central Intelligence. June 27, 2013. Released December 9, 2014. Available at https://www.cia.gov/library/reports/ CIAs_June2013_Response_to_the_SSCI_Study_on_the_Former_Detention_ and_Interrogation_Program.pdf.

Cervantes, Miguel. 1605. Don Quixote. John Ormsby, trans. Available at: http://www. online-literature.com/cervantes/don_quixote/12/.

Cheney, Dick and Liz Cheney. 2012. In My Time: A Personal and Political Memoir. New York: Simon and Schuster.

Cho, In-Koo and David M. Kreps. 1987. "Signaling games and stable equilibria." *The Quarterly Journal of Economics* 102(2) (May): 179–221.

Clarke, Kevin A. and David M. Primo. 2007. "Modernizing Political Science: A Model-Based Approach." *Perspectives on Politics* 5(04):741–753.

Clarke, Kevin A. and David M. Primo. 2012. *A Model Discipline: Political Science and the Logic of Representations.* New York: Oxford University Press.

Coffman, Kevin. 1983. "U.S. v. James C. Parker, John Glover, Carl Lee, Floyd Allen Baker, Docket No. H-83-66, (U.S. District Court, Southern District of Texas, Houston Division, September 1, 1983) ("Transcript of Trial, Volume III")." In the author's possession.

Conroy, John. 2000. *Unspeakable Acts, Ordinary People: The Dynamics of Torture.* Berkeley, CA: University of California Press.

Criminal Investigation Division, U.S. Army. 1971, August 23. "Final Report of Investigation, 70-CID-121-00802, Carmon et al." Col. Henry Tufts Archives, Labadie Collection, Hatcher Library, University of Michigan.

Dahlkamp, Jürgen, Gisela Friedrichsen, Felix Kurz, Caroline Schmidt, and Andreas Wassermann. 2004. "Machen Sie das!" *Der Spiegel,* 47, November 15, 2004. Available at: http://www.spiegel.de/spiegel/print/d-36625699.html.

Danaei, Goodarz, Eric L. Ding, Dariush Mozaffarian, Ben Taylor, Jürgen Rehm, Christopher J.L. Murray, and Majid Ezzati. 2009. "The Preventable Causes of Death in the United States: Comparative Risk Assessment of Dietary, Lifestyle, and Metabolic Risk Factors." *PLoS Medicine* 6(4):e1000058.

Danner, Mark. 2004. *Torture and Truth: America, Abu Ghraib, and the War on Terror.* New York: New York Review of Books.

Davies, Jeremy. 2012. "The Fire-Raisers: Bentham and Torture." *19: Interdisciplinary Studies in the Long Nineteenth Century,* 15. Available at http://www.19.bbk.ac.uk/index.php/19/article/view/643/866.

Department of Defense. 2003. "Counter-Resistance Techniques in the War on Terrorism." Washington D.C.: Secretary of Defense, April 16. Available at http://www.defense.gov/news/jun2004/d20040622doc9.pdf.

Department of Justice, Office of Professional Responsibility. 2009. "Report. Investigation into the Office of Legal Counsel's Memoranda Concerning Issues Relating to the Central Intelligence Agency's Use of "Enhanced Interrogation Techniques" on Suspected Terrorists." July 29, Washington D.C.: Office of Professional Responsibility, Department of Justice.

Department of the Army. 1992. "FM 34-52 Intelligence Interrogation." Washington D.C.: Headquarters, Department of the Army.

Dershowitz, Alan M. 2002. *Why Terrorism Works: Understanding the Threat, Responding to the Challenge.* New Haven, CT: Yale University Press.

Dershowitz, Alan M. 2003. "The Torture Warrant: A Response to Professor Strauss." *New York Law School Law Review* 48:275–294.

Dixit, Avinash K., Susan Skeath and David H.J. Reiley. 2009. *Games of Strategy.* New York: W. W. Norton & Company Incorporated.

East India Company. 1665. *A True Relation of the Unjust, Cruell, and Barbarous Proceedings Against the English at Amboyna, in the East Indies, by the Neatherlandish Governour, and Council There.* Tho. Mabb, for William Hope at the Anchor.

Eco, Umberto. 1983. *The Name of the Rose*. William Weaver, trans. San Diego: Harcourt Brace Jovanovich.

Ekeland, Ivar. 2006. *The Best of All Possible Worlds: Mathematics and Destiny*. Chicago: University of Chicago Press.

El-Masri, Khaled. 2005. "Khaled El-Masri v. George J. Tenet; Premier Executive, Transport Services, Inc.; Keeler and Tate Management LLC; Aero Contractors Limited, Does 1-20, Complaint. United States District Court for the Eastern District of Virginia, Alexandria Division. December 6, 2005." Available at https://www.aclu.org/sites/default/files/images/extraordinaryrendition/asset_upload_file829_22211.pdf.

Ensalaco, Mark. 2011. *Chile Under Pinochet: Recovering the Truth*. Philadelphia: University of Pennsylvania Press.

European Court of Human Rights. 2006. *Case of El-Masri v. The Former Yugoslav Republic of Macedonia. Judgment. Application no. 39630/09, December 13, 2012*. Strasbourg: European Court of Human Rights. Available at http://hudoc.echr.coe.int/sites/eng/pages/search.aspx?i=001-115621#{%22itemid%22:[%22001-115621%22]}.

European Court of Human Rights. 2010. "Judgment, Case of Gäfgen v. Germany (Application no. 22978/05), June 1, 2010." Available at http://hudoc.echr.coe.int/sites/eng/pages/search.aspx?i=001-99015#{%22itemid%22:[%22001-99015%22]}.

Evans, Martin. 2011. *Algeria: France's Undeclared War*. New York: Oxford University Press.

Fanon, Frantz. 1963. *The Wretched of the Earth*. New York: Grove Press.

Federal Court of Canada. 2010. "Harkat (Re), 2010 FC 1241, [2012] 3 F.C.R. 251." Office of the Commissioner for Federal Judicial Affairs Canada, December 9, 2010, Available at: http://recueil.fja-cmf.gc.ca/eng/2012/2010fc1241.html.

Gardham, Duncan. 2009. "Al-Qaeda chief commits suicide in Libyan prison, report says." *The Telegraph*, May 11. Available at http://www.telegraph.co.uk/news/worldnews/africaandindianocean/libya/5310168/Al-Qaeda-chief-commits-suicide-in-Libyan-prison-report-says.html.

Gates, Scott and Brian D. Humes. 1997. *Games, Information, and Politics: Applying Game Theoretic Models to Political Science*. Ann Arbor: University of Michigan Press.

Gibbons, Robert. 1992. *Game Theory for Applied Economists*. Princeton: Princeton University Press.

Goldman, Adam. 2013. "The hidden history of the CIA's prison in Poland." *Washington Post*, January 23. Available at http://www.washingtonpost.com/world/national-security/the-hidden-history-of-the-cias-prison-in-poland/2014/01/23/b77f6ea2-7c6f-11e3-95c6-0a7aa80874bc_story.html.

Grey, Stephen. 2006. *Ghost Plane: The True Story of the CIA Torture Program*. New York: St. Martin's Press.

Haas, M. 2009. *George W. Bush, War Criminal?: The Bush Administration's Liability for 269 War Crimes*. Westport: Praeger.

Hansen, Leroy. 1953. "General's Cousin Tells of Tortures." *Tucson Daily Citizen*, August 6, 1953, p.17. Available at http://newspaperarchive.com/tucson-daily-citizen/1953-08-06/page-17.

Haynes II, William J. 2002. "Action Memo. Counter-Resistance Techniques." November 27, Washington D.C.: General Counsel, Department of Defense.

Hicks, David. 1983. "U.S. v. James C. Parker, John Glover, Carl Lee, Floyd Allen Baker, Docket No. H-83-66 (U.S. District Court, Southern District of Texas, Houston Division, September 1, 1983) ("Transcript of Trial, Volume V")." In the author's possession.

Hobbes, Thomas. 1839. *Elements of Philosophy.* Available at: https://archive.org/details/englishworkstho21hobbgoog.

Homza, Lu Ann. 2006. *The Spanish Inquisition, 1478–1614: An Anthology of Sources.* Cambridge, MA: Hackett Publishing.

Horne, Alistair. 1977. *A Savage War of Peace: Algeria 1954–1962.* New York: Viking Press.

Horton, Scott. 2011a. "The Interrogator: Six Questions for Glenn Carle." *Harpers Magazine,* July 5, 2011. Available at http://harpers.org/blog/2011/07/unredacting-the-interrogator/.

Horton, Scott. 2011b. "Unredacting 'The Interrogator'." *Harpers Magazine,* July 5, 2011. Available at http://harpers.org/blog/2011/07/unredacting-the-interrogator/.

Howes, Dustin Ells. 2012. "Torture Is Not a Game: On the Limitations and Dangers of Rational Choice Methods." *Political Research Quarterly* 65(1):20–27.

Human Rights Watch. 2012. "Delivered Into Enemy Hands: US-Led Abuse and Rendition of Opponents to Gaddafi's Libya." http://www.hrw.org/reports/2012/09/05/delivered-enemy-hands.

Ignatieff, Michael. 2005. "Moral Prohibition at a Price." In *Torture: Does It Make Us Safer? Is It Ever OK? A Human Rights Perspective,* pp. 18–27. Kenneth Roth and Minky Worden, eds. New York: The New Press/Human Rights Watch.

Imai, Kosuke, Luke Keele, Dustin Tingley, and Teppei Yamamoto. 2011. "Unpacking the Black Box of Causality: Learning about Causal Mechanisms from Experimental and Observational Studies." *American Political Science Review* 105(04):765–789.

International Committee of the Red Cross. 2007. ICRC Report on the Treatment of Fourteen 'High Value Detainees' in CIA Custody. Washington, DC: International Committee of the Red Cross.

Isikoff, Michael and David Corn. 2007. *Hubris: The Inside Story of Spin, Scandal, and the Selling of the Iraq War.* New York: Random House.

Isikoff, Michael and Mark Hosenball. 2005. "Al-Libi's Tall Tales." *Newsweek,* November 10. Available at http://web.archive.org/web/20051126201544/http://www.msnbc.msn.com/id/9991919/site/newsweek/.

Jehl, Douglas. 2005a. "A Tortured Past." *New York Times,* December 9. Available at http://www.nytimes.com/2005/12/09/politics/09intel.html.

Jehl, Douglas. 2005b. "Report Warned Bush Team About Intelligence Suspicions." *New York Times,* November 5. Available at http://www.informationclearinghouse.info/article10887.htm.

Johnston, David. 2006. "At a Secret Interrogation, Dispute Flared Over Tactics." *New York Times,* September 10. Available at http://www.nytimes.com/2006/09/10/washington/10detain.html?pagewanted=all&_r=0.

Karl, Terry Lynn. 2011. "U. S. Foreign Policy, Deniability, and the Political "Utility" of State Terror: The Case of El Salvador." In *The United States and Torture: Interrogation, Incarceration, and Abuse,* ed. Marjorie Cohn. pp. 69–95. New York: New York University Press.

Kennedy, Thomas E. 2010. *In the Company of Angels: A Novel.* New York: Bloomsbury Publishing.

Kershnar, Stephen. 2010. "For Interrogational Torture." *International Journal of Applied Philosophy* 19(2):223–241.

Kertész, Imre. 2009. *Detektívtörténet.* Budapest: Magvető.

Koppl, R. 2005. "Epistemic Systems." *Episteme, A Journal of Social Epistemology* 2(2):91–106.

Krauthammer, Charles. 2004. "The Truth about Torture." In *Torture: A Collection*, ed. Sanford Levinson. Oxford: Oxford University Press, pp. 307–316.

Kymlicka, Will. 2002. *Contemporary Political Philosophy: An Introduction.* New York: Oxford University Press.

Landgericht Frankfurt am Main. 2003. *Urteil vom 28. Juli 2003 5/22 Ks 2/03 3490 Js 230118/02.* Frankfurt am Main: Landgericht. Available at http://openjur.de/u/168232.html.

Landgericht Frankfurt am Main. 2005. *Schriftliche Urteilsgründe in der Strafsache gegen Wolfgang Daschner, 15.02.05.* Frankfurt am Main: Landgericht. Document in the author's possession.

Langbein, John H. 1978. "Torture and Plea Bargaining." *The University of Chicago Law Review* 46(1):3–22.

Langbein, John H. 2006. *Torture and the Law of Proof: Europe and England in the Ancien Regime.* Chicago: University of Chicago Press.

Laver, Michael. 1997. *Private Desires, Political Action: An Invitation to the Politics of Rational Choice.* New York: SAGE Publications.

Lea, Henry Charles and Edward Peters. 1973. *Torture.* Philadelphia: University of Pennsylvania Press.

Leopold, Jason. 2011. "CIA Kidnapped, Tortured "the Wrong Guy," Says Former Agency Operative Glenn Carle." *truth-out.org,* October 22, 2011. Available at http://www.truth-out.org/news/item/4154:cia-kidnapped-tortured-the-wrong-guy-says-former-agency-operative-glenn-carle.

Levin, Daniel. 2004. "Memorandum for James B. Comey, Deputy Attorney General, Legal Standards Applicable under 18 U.S.C. §§2340–2340A." December 30. Washington D.C.: Office of Legal Counsel, Department of Justice.

Lichtbau, Eric and Eric Schmitt. 2011. "U.S. Widens Inquiries Into 2 Jail Deaths." *New York Times,* June 30. Available at http://www.nytimes.com/2011/07/01/us/politics/01DETAIN.html?pagewanted=all.

Lichtbau, Eric and Scott Shane. 2010. "Report Faults 2 Authors of Bush Terror Memos." *New York Times,* February 19. Available at http://www.nytimes.com/2010/02/20/us/politics/20justice.html?adxnnl=1&adxnnlx=1383307210-PVRt4FKt/7HcLVQXnin2cg.

Llorente, Juan A. and Gabriel H. Lovett. 1967. *A Critical History of the Inquisition of Spain.* Williamstown, MA: John Lilburne Co.

Mackey, C. and G. Miller. 2004. *The Interrogators: Inside the Secret War Against Al Qaeda.* New York: Little, Brown and Company.

Marty, Dick. 2006. *Alleged Secret Detentions and Unlawful Inter-state Transfers of Detainees Involving Council of Europe Member States.* Doc. 10957, June 12, 2006. Strasbourg:

Council of Europe, Parliamentary Assembly. Available at http://www.assembly.coe.int/CommitteeDocs/2007/ENMarty_09072007.htm.

Mayer, Jane. 2008. *The Dark Side: The Inside Story of How the War on Terror Turned into a War on American Ideals.* New York: Random House.

McCarthy, Andrew C. 2006. "Torture: Thinking about the Unthinkable." In *The Torture Debate in America*, ed. Karen J. Greenberg. New York: Cambridge University Press, pp. 98–110.

McCoy, Alfred W. 2006. *A Question of Torture: CIA Interrogation, from the Cold War to the War on Terror.* New York: Henry Holt and Company.

McDermott, Terry and Josh Meyer. 2012. *The Hunt for KSM: Inside the Pursuit and Takedown of the Real 9/11 Mastermind, Khalid Sheikh Mohammed.* New York: Little, Brown.

McGirk, T., M. Calabresi, and E. Shannon. 2002. "Anatomy of a Raid." *Time* 159(15):40–42.

McGrayne, Sharon Bertsch. 2011. *The Theory that Would Not Die: How Bayes' Rule Cracked the Enigma Code, Hunted Down Russian Submarines, & Emerged Triumphant from Two Centuries of Controversy.* New Haven: Yale University Press.

Meek, James. 2005. "They Beat Me from All Sides." *The Guardian*, January 13. Available at: http://www.theguardian.com/world/2005/jan/14/usa.germany.

Mill, John Stuart. 1972 [1859]. *On Liberty.* London: Dent Everyman's Library.

Mirbeau, Octave. 1899. *Les Jardins des Supplices.* Paris: Bibliothèque-Charpentier.

Moore, Will H. and David A. Siegel. 2013. *A Mathematics Course for Political and Social Research.* Princeton: Princeton University Press.

Morgan, Rod. 2000. "The Utilitarian Justification of Torture: Denial, Desert and Disinformation." *Punishment & Society* 2(2):181–196.

Morgan, Ted. 2007. *My Battle of Algiers: A Memoir.* New York: HarperCollins.

Muñoz, Heraldo. 2008. *The Dictator's Shadow: Life Under Augusto Pinochet.* New York: Basic Books.

Nelson, Craig. 2003. *The First Heroes.* New York: Penguin.

Nelson, Deborah. 2008. *The War Behind Me: Vietnam Veterans Confront the Truth about U.S. War Crimes.* New York: Basic Books.

Nelson, Deborah and Nick Turse. 2006. "A Tortured Past." *Los Angeles Times*, August 20, 2006. Available at http://www.latimes.com/news/nationworld/nation/la-na-vietnam20aug20,0,4709695.story?page=4&coll=la-home-headlines.

Ohlin, J.D. 2010. "The Torture Lawyers." *Harvard International Law Journal* 51:193.

Otterman, Michael. 2007. *American Torture: From the Cold War to Abu Ghraib and Beyond.* Melbourne: Melbourne University Publishing.

Pape, Robert. 2015. "The Strategic Costs of Torture." Unpublished manuscript, University of Chicago.

Parry, John. 2010. "Do the 'Torture Lawyers' Have Guilty Minds?: A Response to Jens Ohlin." *Harvard International Law Journal Online* 51:23, Lewis & Clark Law School Legal Studies Research Paper No. 2010-16.

Parry, John T. 2004. "Escalation and Necessity: Defining Torture at Home and Abroad." In *Torture: A Collection*, ed. Sanford Levinson. Oxford: Oxford University Press pp. 145–164.

Pennington, Kenneth. 2008. "Torture and Fear: Enemies of Justice." *Rivista internazionale di diritto comune* 19(8):8.

Peters, Edward. 1973. Bibliographical Note. In *Torture*, ed. Henry Charles Lea and Edward Peters. Philadelphia: University of Pennsylvania Press.

Peters, Edward. 1999. *Torture*. Philadelphia: University of Pennsylvania Press.

Pfiffner, James P. 2010. *Torture as Public Policy: Restoring U.S. Credibility on the World Stage*. Boulder, CO: Paradigm Publishers.

Pfiffner, James P. 2014. "The Efficacy of Coercive Interrogation." In *Examining Torture: Empirical Studies of State Repression*, ed. Tracy Lightcap and James P. Pfiffner. New York: Palgrave Macmillan, pp. 127–158.

Phifer, Jerald. 2002. "Memorandum for Commander, Joint Task Force 170, Request for Approval of Counter-Resistance Techniques." Department of Defense, Joint Task Force 170, Guantanamo Bay, Cuba, October 11.

Posner, Eric A. and Adrian Vermeule. 2006. "Should Coercive Interrogation Be Legal?" *Michigan Law Review* 104(4):671–707.

Posner, Richard A. 2004. "Torture, Terrorism, and Interrogation." In *Torture: A Collection*, ed. Sanford Levinson. Oxford: Oxford University Press, pp. 291–298.

Priest, Dana. 2004. "Al Qaeda-Iraq Link Recanted." *Washington Post,* August 1. Available at http://www.washingtonpost.com/wp-dyn/articles/A30909-2004Jul31.html.

Priest, Dana. 2005. "Wrongful Imprisonment: Anatomy of a CIA Mistake." *Washington Post,* December 4. Available at http://www.washingtonpost.com/wp-dyn/content/article/2005/12/03/AR2005120301476.html.

Quigley, Bill. 2011. "Torture and Human Rights Abuses at the School of Americas-WHINSEC." In *The United States and Torture: Interrogation, Incarceration, and Abuse,* ed. Marjorie Cohn. pp. 53–67. New York: New York University Press.

Rejali, Darius M. 2007. *Torture and Democracy*. Princeton: Princeton University Press.

Ricketts, Peter. 2002. "Iraq: Advice for the Prime Minister." London. Letter to Prime Minister Tony Blair, PR 121, March 22, 2002. Available at: http://www.comw.org/warreport/fulltext/0203ricketts.pdf.

Risen, James. 2006. *State of War: The Secret History of the CIA and the Bush Administration*. New York: Free Press.

Rizzo, John. 2014. *Company Man: Thirty Years of Controversy and Crisis in the CIA*. New York: Scribner.

Rodriguez Jr, Jose A. and Bill Harlow. 2012. *Hard Measures: How Aggressive CIA Actions After 9/11 Saved American Lives*. New York: Threshold Editions.

Roth, Cecil. 1964. *The Spanish Inquisition*. New York: W. W. Norton & Company.

Rumney, P.N.S. 2006. "Is Coercive Interrogation of Terrorist Suspects Effective—A Response to Bagaric and Clarke." *University of San Francisco Law Review* 40:479.

Rycroft, Matthew. 2002. "Iraq: Prime Minister's Meeting, 23 July." London. Letter to David Manning, S 195 /02, July 23, 2002. Available at http://nsarchive.gwu.edu/NSAEBB/NSAEBB328/II-Doc14.pdf.

Salter, Mark and John McCain. 1999. *Faith of My Fathers*. Random House.

Scarry, Elaine. 1985. *The Body in Pain: The Making and Unmaking of the World*. New York: Oxford University Press.

Scharf, M.P. 2010. "The Torture Lawyers." *Duke Journal of Comparative & International Law* 20:389–473.

Schelling, Thomas C. 1966. *Arms and Influence*. New Haven: Yale University Press.

Schiemann, John W. 2012*a*. "Interrogational Torture: Or How Good Guys Get Bad Information with Ugly Methods." *Political Research Quarterly* 65(1):3–19.

Schiemann, John W. 2012*b*. "Political Theory Is Not a Game: On the Dangers of Detached and Inhuman Normative Theory." *Political Research Quarterly* 65(1):28–33.

Schwarz, Frederick A.O. and Aziz Z. Huq. 2013. *Unchecked and Unbalanced: Presidential Power in a Time of Terror*. New York: New Press.

Shane, Scott. 2008. "Inside a 9/11 Mastermind's Interrogation." *New York Times*, June 22. Available at http://www.nytimes.com/2008/06/22/washington/22ksm.html?pagewanted=all&_r=0.

Shane, Scott. 2012. "No Charges Filed on Harsh Tactics Used by the C.I.A." *New York Times*, August 30. Available at http://www.nytimes.com/2012/08/31/us/holder-rules-out-prosecutions-in-cia-interrogations.html.

Short, A. Rendle and H.W. Bywaters. 1913. "Amino Acids and Sugars in Rectal Feeding." *British Medical Journal* 1(2739):1361–1367.

Silverman, Lisa. 2001. *Tortured Subjects: Pain, Truth, and the Body in Early Modern France*. University of Chicago Press.

Soufan, Ali. 2009. "Testimony of Ali Soufan." Available at http://fas.org/irp/congress/2009_hr/051309soufan.pdf.

Soufan, Ali H. 2011. *The Black Banners: The Inside Story of 9/11 and the War Against Al-Qaeda*. New York: W.W. Norton & Company.

Sullivan, Andrew. 2007. "Verschärfte Vernehmung." *The Atlantic*, May 29. Available at http://www.theatlantic.com/daily-dish/archive/2007/05/-versch-auml-rfte-vernehmung/228158/.

Suskind, Ron. 2006. *The One Percent Doctrine*. New York: Simon & Schuster.

Sussman, David. 2005. "What's Wrong with Torture?" *Philosophy & Public Affairs* 33(1):1–33.

Tenet, George and Bill Harlow. 2007. *At the Center of the Storm: My Years at the CIA*. New York: HarperCollins Publishers.

Thiessen, Marc A. 2010. *Courting Disaster: How the CIA Kept America Safe and How Barack Obama Is Inviting the Next Attack*. Washington D.C.: Regnery Publishing.

United States Senate. 2006. "Report of the Select Committee on Intelligence on Postwar Findings about Iraq's WMD Programs and Links to Terrorism and How They Compare with Prewar Assessments together with Additional Views." Washington D.C.: United States Senate. Available at http://www.gpo.gov/fdsys/pkg/CRPT-109srpt331/pdf/CRPT-109srpt331.pdf.

United States Senate. 2014*a*. "Select Committee on Intelligence Study of the Central Intelligence Agency's Detention and Interrogation Program, Findings and Conclusions, Executive Summary." Washington D.C.: United States Senate. Approved December 13, 2012, Updated for Release April 3, 2014, Deciassification Revisions December 3, 2014. Available at http://fas.org/irp/congress/2014_rpt/ssci-rdi.pdf.

United States Senate. 2014*b*. "Select Committee on Intelligence Study of the Central Intelligence Agency's Detention and Interrogation Program, Minority Views, Additional Minority Views." Washington D.C.: United States Senate. Approved December 13, 2012, Updated for Release April 3, 2014, Declassification Revisions December 3, 2014. Available at http://fas.org/irp/congress/2014_rpt/ssci-rdi-min.pdf.

Wallach, E. 2006. "Drop by Drop: Forgetting the History of Water Torture in US Courts." *Columbus Journal of Transnational Law* 45:468.

Weiser, Benjamin. 2014. "Some Captured Terrorists Talk Willingly and Proudly, Investigators Say." *New York Times*, October 13. Available at http://www.nytimes.com/2014/10/14/nyregion/some-captured-terrorists-talk-willingly-and-proudly-investigators-say.html?module=Search&mabReward=relbias%3Ar.

Wisnewski, J. Jeremy and R. Dillon Emerick. 2009. *The Ethics of Torture*. New York: Continuum International Publishing Group.

INDEX

Figures and tables are indicated by "f" and "t" following page numbers.

CPSIA information can be obtained
at www.ICGtesting.com
Printed in the USA
BVHW030336090119
537369BV00004B/20/P